LF

*Enterprise and the State*

*in Korea and Taiwan*

A volume in the series

*Cornell Studies in Political Economy*

EDITED BY PETER J. KATZENSTEIN

A full list of titles in the series appears at the end of the book.

# Enterprise and the State in Korea and Taiwan

## Karl J. Fields

Cornell University Press

*Ithaca and London*

First published 1995 by Cornell University Press.


Printed in the United States of America

☉ The paper in this book meets the minimum requirements
of the American National Standard for Information Sciences—
Permanence of Paper for Printed Library Materials, ANSI Z39.48-1984.


Library of Congress Cataloging-in-Publication Data

Fields, Karl J.
    Enterprise and the state in Korea and Taiwan / Karl J. Fields.
        p.   cm. — (Cornell studies in political economy)
    Includes bibliographical references and index.
    ISBN 0-8014-3009-7 cloth
        1. Industrial organization—Korea (South)   2. Industrial organization—
Taiwan.   3. Conglomerate corporations—Korea (South)   4. Conglomerate
corporations—Taiwan.   5. Industrial policy—Korea (South)   6. Industrial
policy—Taiwan.   I. Title.   II. Series.
HD70.K6F54   1995
338.95124'9—dc20
                                                                        94-46142

*to Melanie*

# Contents

# Tables

# Preface

Contemporary economic theory is the study of how economic forces would interact if institutions did not exist; political economy is the study of how economic theory is actualized through institutions.

—Chalmers Johnson, 1988

Writing in 1791, Alexander Hamilton warned: "Capital is wayward and timid in lending itself to new undertakings, and the State ought to excite the confidence of capitalists, who are ever cautious and sagacious, by aiding them overcome the obstacles that lie in the way of all experiments." Hamilton thus acknowledges something recent generations of Western social scientists had nearly forgotten or chosen to ignore: institutions influence market outcomes.

All markets are embedded in an environment filled with a variety of institutions that compete for legitimacy and shape the incentive structure for all market participants. Although the caution and sagacity of Hamilton's capitalists may (or may not) be rational, the dominant neoclassical paradigm, with its atomistic and utilitarian biases, sheds only partial light on their actions. Entrepreneurs and their enterprises do not, and cannot, avoid the political, cultural, and communal institutions structuring their market transactions. This was just as true for Adam Smith's pinmaker as it is today for a German investment banker or a Hong Kong dress designer.

This book offers a timely and particularly appropriate test of the validity of this claim of "embedded enterprise." It examines developmental capitalism in the two most successful political economies to emerge in the postwar era: the Republic of Korea (Korea) and the Republic of China on Taiwan (Taiwan). More specifically, it analyzes the patterns of enterprise organization and the role of state and sociocultural institutions in shaping the most significant private economic organization in these two political economies: the private business group.

A handful of gargantuan business conglomerates dominates the Korean economy and has provided the engine for Korea's postwar development. Taiwan, too, can claim private business groups, but they are organizationally very different from their Korean counterparts, much smaller in both relative and absolute terms, and in many ways much less consequential to Taiwan's developmental success.

At first blush, the distinction seems highly counterintuitive. How can Korea and Taiwan, sharing stunning development successes, differ so widely in terms of enterprise organization, the fundamental driving force behind their development? Contrary to elegant theories that attribute market outcomes to some fundamental human disposition or overarching social structure, this book contends that the difference, like the devil, lies in the details.

Drawing on the recent renaissance of theoretical interest in institutionalism within the social sciences, I employ an institutional theory of "embedded enterprise" to explain why business groups are so different in Korea and Taiwan and to analyze the factors behind the groups' formation and development. Unsettling as it may be to the champions of monocausality, one must examine both the "nature" and the "nurture" of these two dynamic political economies to explain this key difference in industrial organization. Such "messy" explanations—assessing the impact of dynamic histories and ongoing social and political relations on economic actors (both public and private) and analyzing the institutions that shape their preference structures and constrain their actions—may not attract World Bank funds; they are nonetheless heuristically useful and empirically more accurate than monocausal theories.

This institutional framework allows us to analyze and explain the relative isomorphism of business groups within each country, as well as the striking variations between the two cases. These differences are examined in terms of the groups' organizational structure and relationship to the state (Chapters Two and Three), capitalization and sources of finance (Chapters Four and Five), and trading networks (Chapters Six and Seven). Chapter One acquaints the reader with South Korea and Taiwan, highlights the significant similarities of these two "miracle mini-dragons," and notes their substantial variance in enterprise organization. It then traces the theoretical roots and validity of the "embedded enterprise" approach, justifying the need to incorporate both statist and sociocultural institutions. Chapter Eight returns to these issues, briefly discussing the future agenda for research on business groups, the developmental state, and comparative political economy.

This book analyzes the most important patterns of business organization in two of the most successful high-growth political economies in the world. Not coincidentally, the most successful case of high-growth, developmental capitalism, Japan, is also dominated by business groups, and provides a frequent template of comparison for the cases of Korea and Taiwan. But beyond its obvious empirical significance, this framework of state-informed, institutional embeddedness sheds light on the formation and development of a wide variety of "economic" organizations and helps us understand the structure of virtually any political economy where state institutions and actors intervene in the market.

State intervention is particularly prevalent within those "late-industrial-izing" economies where state formation has preceded industrialization. However, states of all ideological stripes and at varying stages of development intervene in their economies to restructure, not just regulate, economic organizations and market behavior. Any attempt to explain these organizations and this behavior must examine the institutional environment in which the market is embedded and the political and sociocultural factors creating and sustaining these institutions.

The individuals who have assisted me are too numerous to acknowledge adequately here. To several, however, the debt is too great to go unmentioned. The idea for this project first took shape in conversations with Chalmers Johnson across the desk of his seventh floor Barrows Hall office at the University of California, over the summer of 1986. His contribution to my intellectual development, however, began well before that summer and still continues. The fruits of his lectures and writings, as well as his comments, suggestions, and encouragement during the writing of this book are thoroughly embedded in the pages that follow. Robert Scalapino provided introductions and opened doors for me in Korea, Taiwan, and Japan. More important, his insights and wisdom opened my mind to the wonders and challenges of Asia. Tom Gold's patience with my theoretical shortcomings and his willingness to offer detailed comments and suggestions on chapter drafts have been invaluable. His intimate knowledge of Taiwan, I fear, is not adequately reflected in this book.

I was supported during my field research in Taiwan and Korea by grants from Taiwan's Pacific Cultural Foundation and the C. K. Cho Fund, administered by U.C. Berkeley's Center for Korean Studies. In Taiwan, I must single out Wu Yu-shan, Wei Wou, Jimmy Chang, and Yu Tzong-shian; in Korea, Chang Dal-Joong and Kim Duk-Choong. Tamio Hattori and his colleagues at the Institute for Developmental Studies in Tokyo were very helpful. And special thanks go to Ichiro Numazaki, who was also doing research in Taiwan on business groups and gave me many valuable insights.

For help during the writing stage, I thank the members of our Berkeley political economy study group, including Leslie Armijo, Danny Unger, Jim Mahon, Andrew Green, Liz Norville, Mark Tilton, and Wes Young.

## Preface

Michael Gerlach provided valuable comments and suggestions on my writing. I also acknowledge my great debt to the work and continued guidance of Gary Hamilton and those who worked with him in the Research Program in East Asian Business and Development at the University of California, Davis.

Since I moved to the Northwest, my Berkeley network has expanded, much to my delight and gratitude. As I have revised the manuscript, I have received valuable guidance and essential encouragement from Rick Doner, Stephan Haggard, Ben Schneider, and Alasdair Bowie. The University of Puget Sound has provided a supportive climate, both intellectually and financially, in which to prepare this manuscript for publication. The university has awarded me several research grants, and now a research sabbatical, without which this project would never have reached fruition. My department chair, Don Share; my colleagues in the Politics and Government Department; and economics professor Michael Veseth also deserve special mention. I am grateful for the trenchant and detailed suggestions of Cornell's anonymous external reader and the consistent support and optimism of Cornell editor Roger Haydon.

My biggest debt of all, however, is owed to Melanie. My first and last thanks are to her: my wife, editor, and dearest friend. It is to her that I dedicate this book.

KARL J. FIELDS

*Tacoma, Washington*

*Enterprise and the State*
*in Korea and Taiwan*

# CHAPTER ONE

# Institutional Embeddedness and the State

The primary problem of employing the comparative method in social science research is, in Arend Lijphart's words, one of "many variables, small number of cases."[1] To minimize this problem, Lijphart advises the comparative theorist to "focus the comparative analysis on 'comparable' cases," where "comparable" refers to cases that are "similar in a large number of important characteristics (variables) which one wants to treat as constants, but dissimilar as far as those variables are concerned which one wants to relate to each other."[2]

This chapter first establishes that Korea and Taiwan are "comparable cases" on each count, by highlighting significant similarities and the important variations to be accounted for in the following chapters. I then present the hybrid "embedded enterprise" framework employed to explain this difference and trace its heritage in the "new institutionalism" of economics, sociology, and political science. True to its institutionalist lineage, this embedded enterprise thesis rejects reductionist accounts of social processes. It is part of a developing "new comparative political economy" in which history and ongoing social and political processes and institutional arrangements matter.

## SIMILARITIES

The development experiences of Korea and Taiwan are indeed similar, sharing a large number of both superficial and more fundamental com-

[1]Lijphart, p. 683.
[2]Lijphart, p. 687.

monalities (see Table 1-1). Any discussion of these similarities must begin with an introduction to the developmental "miracles" in Korea and Taiwan.

One can scarcely scan a newspaper or business magazine without coming across an article lauding the successes of one (or more typically both) of these capitalist developmental dragons. The banner headlines—as well as the recent inroads of Hyundai automobiles, Leading Edge computers, and Samsung VCRs and microchips, and the ubiquitous "Made in Taiwan," stamped on everything from ten-speed bicycles and tennis rackets to machine tools and oil tankers—dim our recollection of the remarkable changes that have occurred in these two East Asian nations since the 1950s.

Left as flotsam in the wake of World War II and the Korean War, Taiwan and Korea were as unlikely candidates for spectacular growth and economic transformation as one was likely to find. In 1949, Taiwan had a per capita income of U.S.$224 coupled with an inflation rate of over 3,000 percent. Most of its Japanese-built industry and infrastructure had been destroyed by American bombing raids or siphoned off to the Chinese mainland by private carpetbaggers and Nationalist Chinese government agencies.[3] Generalissimo Chiang Kai-shek's ruling Nationalist regime, reeling from its defeat at the hands of the Chinese Communists, was infamous for its corruption and ineptitude.

Over the next three decades, however, this situation was reversed beyond anyone's hopes or expectations. By the 1960s, Taiwan's inflation rate had dropped from 3,000 percent to 1.9 percent, and by 1992 official per capita income had passed the U.S.$10,000 mark. (If the huge infor-

*Table 1-1.* 1991 comparison of basic economic data, Korea and Taiwan

| Category | Korea | Taiwan | Ratio[a] |
|---|---|---|---|
| Area (1,000 sq. km.) | 99.22 | 36.00 | 2.76 |
| Population (million) | 43.27 | 20.60 | 2.10 |
| Density (persons/sq. km.) | 436.1 | 572.2 | 0.76 |
| GNP (U.S.$ billion) | 280.9 | 180.1 | 1.55 |
| Per capita GNP (U.S.$) | 6,498. | 8,742. | 0.74 |
| Exports (U.S.$ billion) | 71.8 | 76.2 | 0.94 |
| Real GNP growth rate (1985 constant prices) | 8.4 | 7.3 | 1.15 |
| Real economic growth rate (1982–1991 avg.) | 9.89 | 7.99 | 1.23 |

SOURCE: KOTRA, 1992.

[a]Korea: Taiwan.

[3]Gold, 1986, p. 50.

2

mal sector were included, this figure would be much higher.) Perhaps more significant in terms of development, these economic gains have been matched by positive indicators of equitable income distribution and other indicators of improved living standards. Nearly 80 percent of the families in Taiwan own their own homes in a country with a population density of nearly 600 people per square kilometer (second in the world only to Bangladesh). As of 1991, there were 98 color television sets for every 100 homes, 98 refrigerators, and 166 telephones. (More significant for any who have braved the streets or sidewalks of Taipei, there are some 166 motorcycles for every 100 families.) Unemployment hovers at around 1.5 percent, and inflation has been insignificant.[4]

The destruction of Taiwan during and after World War II, however, pales in comparison with the devastation visited upon South Korea during the early 1950s. The newly divided country had just emerged from a physically and psychologically devastating civil war that claimed hundreds of thousands of South Korean soldiers. In addition, one out of every nineteen South Korean civilians died during the war, virtually the same civilian mortality rate as that of the Soviet Union during World War II.[5] Most of Korea's industrial plant lay above the 38th parallel and was lost to the Communist North. Of what remained, most was destroyed during the war along with much of the economic infrastructure and housing. In the wake of the war, Korea's inflation rates rivaled those of early postwar Taiwan, and its per capita income, at U.S.$145 in 1953, was much smaller.[6]

In fact, by 1963, Korea's per capita income was still less than Taiwan's some ten years earlier, and the country was plagued by increasing social unrest and political instability. But as in Taiwan, recent decades have witnessed a phenomenal turnaround in the Korean economy. GNP exceeded $280 billion in 1991, up from only $3 billion in 1965, and per capita GNP stood at $6,500. And as in Taiwan, there is increasing evidence that material wealth is being shared: virtually every household has a television set (most of them color), over 70 percent have refrigerators, and about half have telephones. In 1970, very few Korean homes had any of these items. Life expectancy is seventy-four years for a child born in Taiwan in 1990 and seventy years for her or his counterpart in Korea. Virtually all children in these countries go to elementary school, and 45 percent of Taiwan's students and 37 percent of Korea's obtain at least some higher education (compared with 22 percent of British students).[7]

Demonstrating their strength, Taiwan and Korea have established

[4]*Free China Journal,* various issues.
[5]Green.
[6]Unless otherwise indicated, figures for Korea are from KOTRA, various years.
[7]*Economist,* 7/14/90.

themselves as important players in the international economic system in their own right. Annual growth rates in these two countries since the mid-1960s have averaged over 8 percent, and well over 10 percent for peak years. With a little over 1 percent of the world's population between them, Korea and Taiwan each produces more manufactured exports than all of Latin America combined, and with Hong Kong and Singapore produce over half of all developing country manufactured exports.[8] Because of this rapid, export-led growth and industrialization, Taiwan and Korea are now both among the top thirteen trading nations in the world. The financial magazine *Euromoney* ranked Taiwan first in the world in 1988 in terms of macroeconomic market value and rate of return on investments. In the same study, South Korea and Taiwan were ranked second and third in the world behind Japan in terms of projected economic performance.[9]

While the rate and extent of this developmental success are understandably surprising, the fact that both Taiwan and Korea rank so high is perhaps less so, given the numerous similarities between them. At a certain level of generality, they are indeed comparable. In terms of enterprise organization, however, they are strikingly divergent. In order to highlight this difference, we first note some of the more significant commonalities.

The first is geographical proximity. Taiwan and South Korea are located near each other and share Japan and China as their closest neighbors. While perhaps by itself not that significant, this proximity has led to two other important similarities. Nearness to the Chinese mainland gave Korea and Taiwan a shared Sinitic Confucian heritage. Taiwan, a former province of China, is largely populated by Han Chinese, and Korea, a former tributary of China, preserved a Confucian orthodoxy unprecedented in the rest of Asia. Second, proximity to Japan fated Taiwan and Korea to be the first victims (or benefactors) of Japan's imperialist designs and hosts to its lengthiest and most successful colonial ventures.

Another similarity, noted above, is the tremendous destruction and upheaval both countries experienced as a result of war. Likewise, each country remained in a state of (now softening) siege with its closest Leninist neighbor: North Korea, adjoining South Korea, and Taiwan, separated from China by the 100-mile-wide Taiwan Strait. This situation has led to a similar emphasis on military preparedness and unusually high defense expenditures.

Both Taiwan and Korea, largely as a result of their precarious location vis-à-vis their Communist neighbors, were recipients of huge amounts of U.S. military and economic aid and technical assistance. Between 1945

[8]Wade, 1990, p. 34.
[9]*Euromoney*, 12/88.

*4*

and 1979, South Korea received some $13 billion in American military and economic aid, and Taiwan some $5.6 billion. In comparison, all of Africa received a total of less than $7 billion, and all of Latin America less than $15 billion, during the same period.[10] Taiwan and Korea, lacking virtually all natural resources, both have a severe shortage of arable land, small geographical size, and staggering population density.

These shared situational imperatives and historical legacies inspired the respective governments to adopt broadly similar economic policies, commencing with sweeping land reform programs and import-substituting industrialization. Both countries shifted relatively quickly to export-led industrialization, entering the global economy under the aegis of the American-sponsored liberal trade regime. Finally, Taiwan and Korea's postwar economic development has been orchestrated by a developmental state—a bureaucratic apparatus characterized by developmentally oriented technocrats enjoying relatively high degrees of political autonomy and economic policy-making and -implementing capacity.

In spite of these broad similarities and the many contingent similarities these variables have spawned, there remains a very significant difference in these two countries' political economies. In Korea, huge, horizontally and vertically integrated business conglomerates (*chaebol*) have emerged and flourished. In Taiwan, on the other hand, while private business groups or "related enterprises" (*guanxiqiye*) contribute significantly to the local economy, they are much smaller and very different from their Korean counterparts in terms of capital, scale, control of their own trade, and government connections. This book is concerned with explaining this variation.

A business group is an organized network of independent firms.[11] Labeling and organizing them variously as business groups, enterprise groups, economic groups, combines, networks, or conglomerates, a growing number of students and scholars of both developed and developing economies have focused on them as distinct units of analysis.[12] Such groups are the most important form of business organization in East Asia

---

[10]Cumings, p. 67.

[11]Hamilton, Zeile, and Kim. Granovetter (1994) offers a similar definition—"a collection of firms bound together in some formal and/or informal ways"—but clarifies the "level of binding" as "intermediate," excluding "on the one hand, a set of firms bound merely by short-term strategic alliances, and on the other, a set of firms legally consolidated into a single one" (p. 4).

[12]Bibliographies of this growing body of multidisciplinary literature are still largely area-specific, but they are increasingly comparative within regions. For a broad but brief general survey of the literature, see Granovetter, 1994. For studies of European business groups, see Stokman et al.; for Japanese business groups, see Gerlach, 1992; for Latin America, the Near East and South Asia, see Leff, 1978, 1986; for East and Southeast Asia, see Hamilton and Biggart, 1988, 1991; and Hamilton, Zeile, and Kim. For a comparison of groups in East Asia and Latin America, see Gereffi.

and hold dominant positions in the high-growth political economies of Korea and even Taiwan, as well as Japan and much of the rest of East and Southeast Asia. The prominence of these groups in the local economies, combined with the international economic success of these two nations, has drawn increasing scholarly attention to Taiwan's and particularly Korea's versions of the business group.[13]

Business groups in Korea and Taiwan are relatively stable, in sharp contrast with their American counterparts. American conglomerates are typically short-term "combinations of convenience," as witnessed by the flurry of sell-offs, buy-outs, and takeovers characteristic of the American corporate scene.[14] Also unlike American conglomerates, which have legally recognized ties among their constituent firms, Taiwan and Korean business groups are typically not recognized as single juridical entities. Often sharing economic or financial ties, the group firms typically have no overarching accounting or management systems that coordinate their activities. Rather, a group is usually connected through the ownership or control of all the firms by an individual or small circle of individuals linked by family ties or other personal relationships.[15]

Patterns of business group organization are quite isomorphic within Korea and within Taiwan. However, the scale and relative significance of the groups vary dramatically between the two countries. Table 1-2 highlights this variance.

As indicated in Table 1-2, Korea's five largest groups alone had total

Table 1-2. Comparison of scale and centrality of Korean and Taiwan business groups, 1983

|  | Korean top 50 | Korean top 5 | Taiwan top 5 | Taiwan top 96 |
|---|---|---|---|---|
| Total sales | 54,663 bil. won | 34,228 bil. won | 203.3 bil. NT$ | 663.7 bil. NT$ |
| Equivalent U.S.$ (billion) | 68.32 | 43.98 | 5.28 | 16.48 |
| Percent of GNP | 93.8 | 52.4 | 10.3 | 31.7 |
| Number of workers | — | 446,906 | 126,279 | 330,000 |
| Number of firms | 552 | 124 | 117 | 745 |
| Firms/business group | 11.04 | 24.80 | 23.40 | 4.76 |
| Workers/firm | 1,500 | 3,604 | 1,079 | 444 |

SOURCE: Adapted from Hamilton et al., 1987.

[13]English-language studies for Korea include E. M. Kim (forthcoming); Amsden, 1989; Steers et al.; Jones and Sakong; and L. Jones. For Taiwan, see Numazaki, 1986; and Hamilton and Kao. Comparative studies of business groups in Japan, Korea and Taiwan include G. Hamilton, 1989; Orru et al.; Hamilton, Zeile, and Kim; Hamilton, Orru, and Biggart; and Whitley, 1992.

[14]Pfeffer and Salancik as cited by Orru et al., p. 14.

[15]Hamilton, Zeile, and Kim.

sales of U.S.$44 billion and employed nearly half a million workers in 1983. Taiwan's five largest groups, on the other hand, had roughly one tenth the sales of Korea's top five and employed less than one-third the number of employees. In fact, Taiwan's top ninety-six groups had sales equal to somewhat more than one-third of Korea's top five and employed only three-fourths as many workers. The relative significance of the groups is even clearer when measured in terms of centrality to their respective economies. Sales of Taiwan's top five business groups accounted for only 10 percent of Taiwan's total GNP for 1983, while the figure for Korea's top five groups was over 50 percent. Sales of the top ninety-six groups accounted for nearly a third of Taiwan's GNP, whereas Korea's top fifty accounted for nearly 94 percent of Korea's 1983 GNP.

Taiwan's top five groups have grown substantially since 1983, with combined annual revenues of over U.S.$22.2 billion in 1992, more than four times the 1983 figure.[16] Taiwan's national economy, however, has grown so that revenues still represent just over 10 percent of total GNP. Korea's top five lost ground slightly, but still had sales worth U.S.$116.6 billion in 1991, accounting for just under 50 percent of Korea's 1991 GNP.[17] In comparison, *Fortune*'s 1992 "Global 500" listing indicates that in 1991, the top five business enterprises in both France and Germany had sales equal to 12 percent of GNP, more than Taiwan but less than one-fourth the concentration of Korea. The same figure for the United States was 7 percent, roughly one-seventh the Korean total. Korea's Samsung Group alone had sales worth 15 percent of Korea's 1991 GNP; the American equivalent (in terms of sales weight) would combine sales of the top twenty American firms (GM, Exxon, Ford, IBM, GE, and fifteen others).[18]

## EXPLAINING THE DIFFERENCE: INSTITUTIONAL EMBEDDEDNESS

Accounting for Korea's and Taiwan's individual economic success has become a growth industry in a variety of social sciences with little consensus or even commensurability among competing explanations.[19] Though fewer studies have attempted to explain these two nations' different paths to comparable success, consensus has been just as elusive and conclusions are even more tentative.[20] Efforts to explain the structure and functioning

---

[16] *Juoyue*, 9/93.

[17] Sales figures for top five Korean groups are taken from *Economist*, 6/8/91.

[18] *Fortune*, 7/92. GNP figures from KOTRA, 1992.

[19] For recent reviews and extensive bibliographies of these accounts, see Islam; Wade, 1992.

[20] For a neoclassical account of the differences, see Scitovsky. For a statist (or "regimist") comparison, see T. J. Cheng, 1990. For a world systems/product cycle approach to the difference, see Cumings.

of economic organizations in mature and developing capitalist economies traditionally have been largely the domain of economists, and in specific settings, of sociologists and anthropologists. Traditional theories derived from these disciplines that could be applied to the Korean and Taiwan cases, however, are at best inadequate and at worst counterfactual. As James March and Johan Olsen have declared, "what we observe in the world is inconsistent with the ways in which contemporary theories ask us to talk."[21] The remainder of this chapter demonstrates that reductionist class-based or behavioral theories, of either the rational or the cultural variety, are particularly handicapped as explanations for the enterprise organization because of their typically rigid and static categorization. In response to these rigidities, social scientists from a wide variety of disciplines have rediscovered the empirical reality and heuristic utility of economic, sociocultural and political *institutions*.

This resurgence of "new institutionalism" and its theoretical fruits are giving shape to a "new comparative political economy" and provide the springboard for the embedded enterprise framework employed in this book. Before turning to this framework, I must define the concept "institution," identify its utility as a critique of alternative approaches, and demonstrate its applicability to the analysis of enterprise organization in Korea and Taiwan.

In his study of Thorstein Veblen, David Seckler claims there is "hardly any word in the English language more ambiguous and yet more indispensable" than "institution."[22] He defines institutions as "patterns of interaction between individuals" that provide an analytical bridge between "primitive individualism" and "mystical collectivism."[23] Michael Gerlach similarly defines institutions as "specific systems which create order in social life, both in the organization of tangible exchanges and in the processes of defining that order and assigning meaning to it." With Seckler, he places institutions at an analytical level between the individual and society and at an interpretive level between cultural explanations emphasizing unchanging characteristics of society and economic rational choice explanations. Both explanations, he argues, tend to "overlook history and

---

[21]March and Olsen, p. 747.

[22]For evidence of this, Seckler cites Walter Hamilton's definition from the *Encyclopedia of the Social Sciences*: "Institution is a verbal symbol which for want of a better describes a cluster of social usages. It connotes a way of thought or action of some prevalence and permanence, which is embedded in the habits of a group or the customs of a people. In ordinary speech it is another word for procedure, convention or arrangement; in the language of books it is the singular of which mores or folkways are the plural. Arrangements as diverse as the money economy, classical education, the chain store, fundamentalism and democracy are institutions" (Seckler, p. 87).

[23]Seckler, p. 88.

universalize behavior under assumptions of one-best-way forms of organization."[24]

Simply put, institutions are social constructs ordering human interactions.[25] They may be formal or informal, temporary or regularized. Once constructed, they persist in time and constrain or otherwise modify the behavior and actions of groups and the individuals associated with those groups. Economic activity, like all forms of human interaction, is embedded in these ongoing and evolving structures of social relations. An institutional embeddedness approach, therefore, provides an interpretive and analytical middle ground between utilitarian and cultural explanations for economic behavior and enterprise organization.

In fact, this "new institutionalism" emerged as a response and reaction to these alternative explanations for human behavior, particularly economic action. The word "new" signals not so much a departure from an "old institutionalism" as it acknowledges the debt contemporary students of institutions owe to their predecessors, particularly late nineteenth-century cultural anthropologists and institutional economists. Though the new and the old are not identical, March and Olsen concede that "cycles in ideas have brought us back to considerations that typified earlier forms of theory."[26] In fact, the nature and structure of state and sociocultural institutions and their effect on market processes have been of interest to social scientists from Adam Smith onward. Like most other questions of social theory, however, shared interest over time has hardly produced consensus.

The dominant paradigm for explaining economic action, in both its classical and neoclassical forms, has been the utilitarian tradition, viewing economic activity ideal—typically as atomized, arms-length transactions motivated by rational self-interest. In this paradigm, social relations and state interventions are viewed as frictional drags on otherwise competitive markets. As Adam Smith cautioned: "People of the same trade seldom meet together, even for merriment and diversion, but the conversation ends in a conspiracy against the public, or in some contrivance to raise prices."[27] And while Smith's state may have had a role in maintaining order, establishing infrastructure, and curbing the envy of the poor, it certainly had no business involving itself with business.

The normative and analytical preoccupation of classical and neoclassi-

[24]Gerlach, 1987, p. 3.
[25]Nabli and Nugent offer three characteristics basic to the concept of a social institution: (1) rules and constraints that are (2) able to govern relations among individuals and groups and are (3) relatively predictable and stable (p. 1335). See also Myhrman; North; and Doner.
[26]March and Olsen, p. 738.
[27]Smith, vol. 1, p. 117.

cal economists with an idealized, disembedded market has maintained its intellectual and political dominance in large part because self-regulating, "free" markets have proved politically attractive. Utilitarian assumptions remove the issue of order and the proper role of the state from the political agenda and elegantly exclude the analytically troublesome impact of history and social relations.[28]

Certain anthropologists joined economists in endorsing this conception of market participants as rational, atomized utility-maximizers, arguing that even in premarket societies, social relations were largely inconsequential to economic life.[29] This rationalist position came to be known as "formalism," which posited the universal applicability of neoclassical economic analysis.[30] As with all ideal types, this formalism entails real trade-offs, often forgotten (or ignored) over time, and is subject to reification. Most consequentially, this approach sacrifices historical influence and social context on the altar of elegance. Clifford Geertz points out that the principles said to govern the organization of commercial life are "less derivative from [profit-maximizing] truisms . . . than one might imagine from reading standard economic textbooks, where the passage from axioms to actualities tends to be rather nonchalantly traversed."[31]

Veblen, an "old institutionalist," offers a particularly derisive lampoon of utilitarianism's formalistic caricature of empirical reality:

> The hedonistic conception of man is that of a lightning calculator of pleasures and pains, who oscillates like a homogenous globule of desire of happiness under the impulse of stimuli that shift him about the area, but leave him intact. He has neither antecedent nor consequent. He is an isolated, definitive human datum, in stable equilibrium except for the buffets of the impinging forces that displace him in one direction or another. Self-imposed in elemental space, he spins symmetrically about his own spiritual axis until the parallelogram of forces bears down upon him, whereupon he follows the line of the resultant. When the force of the impact is spent, he comes to rest, a self-contained globule of desire as before.[32]

More sophisticated versions of this marginalist perspective are certainly less rigid. Individuals can "satisfice," not necessarily maximize, economic utility under conditions of "bounded rationality."[33] Preference structures

[28]Rueschmeyer and Evans; Granovetter, 1985.
[29]Peters distinguishes between anthropologists endorsing a "thin" sense of rationality—consistency between an individual's intentions and actions—and a less sustainable "broad" version—substantive rationality of an individual's intentions or beliefs (p. 1063).
[30]Granovetter, 1985.
[31]Geertz, p. 29.
[32]Thorstein Veblen, "Why Economics Is Not an Evolutionary Science," *Quarterly Journal of Economics* (July 1898), as cited by Seckler, p. 52.
[33]Simon.

at least theoretically need not exclude noneconomic motivations such as security, acceptance, and the like, as long as individuals are rational in the sense of choosing consistently.[34] Game theoretic formulations of rational choice theory allow for a "softer" analysis of dynamic interactions and the alteration of preferences over extended or iterated games.[35] But even if *Homo economicus* is discarded, there is growing consensus that atomistic and ahistorical neoclassical analysis still requires "heroic assumptions" about complete information, static equilibrium, and stable and exogenous preferences.[36] More fundamentally, it preempts the study of values, structures, ideas, habits, and so on; in short, it preempts the analysis of institutions.

Initial critics of these assumptions of rational economic man based their attack on the nineteenth-century discovery of cultural relativism. A group of "substantivists" emerged, over and against the dominant neoclassical paradigm of disembedded markets, arguing that economic behavior in traditional, premarket societies was heavily embedded in social relations. Economic transactions in these societies, the substantivists contend, are penetrated by and embedded in social structures that alter not only access to information but motivations as well. The extent of embeddedness—this meshing of the social and economic spheres in primitive society—they argued, became less over time, as the societies modernized.[37] This substantivist school has come to be associated with Karl Polanyi, who argued that the period since the "great transformation" to modern capitalism is unique, because never before had the "formal" rationalistic definition of economy matched the "substantive" one.[38] Polanyi and those who followed, including the "moral economy" scholars in history and political science, argued that the assumptions of neoclassical economics could not be applied to traditional, embedded economies.[39]

New institutionalism, as employed in this book, provides a middle-ground challenge, offering correctives to both the cultural and the utilitarian explanations for economic behavior. It contends that the extent to which economic activity is embedded in the social structure is generally lower in traditional, nonmarket societies than substantivists and modernization theorists assume and has changed less through the process of modernization than their paradigm assumes. On the other hand, new

[34]Bates, 1993; Zukin and DiMaggio.
[35]Bates, 1988.
[36]Stein and Wilson, p. 1049; Nabli and Nugent.
[37]Seckler; Granovetter, 1985; Gerlach, 1992.
[38]Polanyi; Gerlach, 1992.
[39]The term "moral economy" comes from E. P. Thompson, "The Moral Economy of the English Crowd in the Eighteenth Century," *Past and Present* 50 (February 1971):76–136. See also Scott.

institutionalism holds that the degree of embeddedness has always been greater than has been assumed by formalists and rational-man theorists.[40]

This embeddedness critique, best articulated by Mark Granovetter, criticizes both the undersocialized formalists and the oversocialized substantivists for falling victim to the same misconception. Both view behavior as the result of transhistorical decisions or actions by atomized actors. "In the undersocialized account, atomization results from narrow utilitarian pursuit of self-interest; in the oversocialized one, from the fact that behavioral patterns have been internalized and ongoing social relations thus have only peripheral effects on behavior. . . . Under- and oversocialized resolutions of the problem of order thus merge in their atomization of actors from immediate social context."[41] In contrast, the new institutionalism attempts to simplify complex systems and behavior within them by positing social constructs that are "relatively invariant in the face of turnover of individuals and relatively resilient to the idiosyncratic preferences and expectations of individuals."[42] From this perspective, actions are the fulfillment of duties and obligations deemed socially or politically appropriate, rather than the fulfillment of choice based on individual values, interests, and expectations.

Not all new institutionalists would endorse this embeddedness critique. In fact, rather than a consensual research program or a distinct paradigm, this new institutionalism thus far has taken the form of a "collection of challenges to contemporary theoretical thinking" in a number of social science disciplines.[43] These include branches of economics ("new institutional economics"), history ("new economic history"), sociology ("new economic sociology" and "organizational sociology") and political science ("positive theory of institutions," "international regime theory," and "political institutionalism" or "statist theory").[44] Walter Powell and Paul DiMaggio note that these "new institutionalisms" are as numerous "as there are social science disciplines . . . united by little but a common skepticism toward atomistic accounts of social processes and a common conviction that institutional arrangements and social processes matter."[45]

Despite divergent interests, assumptions, and conclusions, work within each of these strains of new institutionalism has advanced our use of institutional analysis as a mans of understanding economic action in general

[40]Granovetter, 1985; Gerlach, 1992.
[41]Granovetter, 1985, p. 485.
[42]March and Olsen, p. 741.
[43]March and Olsen.
[44]The fields of positive theory of institutions informed by public choice literature and international regimes theory are less relevant to this study and, unlike the others mentioned, will not be discussed further. For reviews and bibliographies of these literatures, see Powell and DiMaggio, pp. 5–7.
[45]Powell and DiMaggio, pp. 1–3.

and enterprise organization and business groups in particular. The following sections introduce these approaches and discuss their respective contributions to the embedded enterprise framework used to explain the development, organization, and behavior of business groups in Korea and Taiwan.

## NEW INSTITUTIONAL ECONOMICS

The new institutional economics (NIE) represents the most dominant strain of new institutionalism and the least radical departure from neoclassical economics. Drawing on the analytic heritage of Ronald Coase's work on property rights,[46] institutional economists, economic historians, game theorists, and public choice theorists have argued that rational individuals do attempt to maximize their preferences in social, economic, and political transactions.[47] Such maximization, however, occurs under conditions of cognitive constraints, imperfect information, and difficulties in monitoring and enforcing compliance, and hence entails transaction costs.[48] In contrast to ideal arms-length market exchange, institutions arise to reduce uncertainty and economize transaction costs under imperfect market conditions.

Oliver Williamson, the most influential of these new institutional economists, terms his version of institutional analysis "transaction cost economics." In this approach, the organizational form (market, hierarchical firm, relational contracting) present in a given situation is that which most efficiently reduces the costs of economic transaction. Contracts and corporations are institutional arrangements designed to overcome the uncertainty of transactions stemming from conditions of economic actors' bounded rationality and opportunism.[49] For Williamson, multiple-unit corporations or enterprise groups are formed when the parties concerned perceive that internally conducted transactions will cost less than open market transactions.[50] Transaction costs are the basic determinants of institutions and provide the framework within which economic activity occurs. They are determined by the market structure, which in turn is the result of how property rights are apportioned and enforced.[51]

[46]Coase.
[47]Nabli and Nugent divide the NIE literature into two components: (1) the transaction and information costs approach, which includes the work of Williamson on transaction costs, Coase's property rights analysis, and other works on asymmetries of information and principal-agent problems; and (2) literature on collective action and free rider dilemmas, and the rent-seeking literature.
[48]Powell and DiMaggio; see also Nabli and Nugent; Myhrman.
[49]Williamson, 1975, 1985.
[50]Hamilton and Biggart, 1988.
[51]North, 1984.

Of direct relevance to our concern with East Asian industrial organization, several scholars have usefully applied the approach to the organization and operation of firms in areas where Western legal-rational contracts and legal ties among separate firms are less common. Nathaniel Leff argues that the economic success of business groups in less developed countries is typically based on communal, ethnic, or tribal trust. This trust lowers the transaction costs of monitoring performance and providing sanctions, and enhances efficiency under imperfect market conditions.[52] Similarly, in her study of economic transactions within Chinese marketing middlemen groups in Southeast Asia, Janet Landa concludes that these groups formed a "moral community" joined by kinship, ethnicity, and a shared code of Confucian ethics. These institutional arrangements serve as "an alternative to contract law and the vertically integrated firm, which emerged to economize on contract-enforcement and information costs in an environment where the legal infrastructure was not well developed."[53] Yoram Ben-Porath discusses the specific role of families in establishing trust through the "specialization of identity" with efficiency consequences for the organization of firms in imperfect markets.[54]

The transaction cost approach of NIE has also been employed to analyze the organization of firms in Korea and Taiwan. Sea Jim Chang and Unghwan Choi conclude that Korean chaebol chose an integrated and "relational" structure in a successful effort to reduce transaction costs and achieve superior economic performance under imperfect market conditions.[55] Chung H. Lee argues that the Korean government and chaebol comprise a "quasi-internal organization" with an internal capital market that has reduced communications costs, uncertainty, and opportunism, and has allowed the government to efficiently implement developmental policies.[56]

Brian Levy compares industrial organization in Korea and Taiwan and the strategic orientations of firms in several sectors. Cross-national differences in firm size are attributed to "rational, organizationally-efficient" choices in the face of different levels of industrial development at the outset of postwar industrialization and associated higher transaction costs in less-developed Korea.[57] Ashoka Mody, too, works from an NIE-inspired framework, arguing that high financial and technological entry costs into internationally competitive industries give Korean groups an institutional

[52]Leff, 1986.
[53]Landa, p. 350.
[54]Ben-Porath.
[55]Chang and Choi.
[56]C. H. Lee.
[57]Levy, 1988, 1991; Levy and Kuo, 1991.

advantage over smaller firms in Taiwan.[58] Tyler Biggs and Levy explain Taiwan's firms' preference for market over hierarchy in terms of declining transaction costs stemming from the positive externalities associated with multiple participants,[59] and attribute the efficiency of Taiwan's dual financial system to its ability to push transactions involving risky smaller firms to personal levels governed by norms of reputation and personal relationships.[60]

These NIE analyses move beyond pure utilitarian formalism, acknowledging the presence and influence of institutions as responses to imperfect markets. For the most part, however, those working in this framework view these institutional arrangements as efficient solutions rationally supplied to resolve particular economic problems. This "optimistic functionalism" reduces institutions to the instrumental means and ends of rational individuals and precludes the interpretation of social, cultural, and political dynamics of groups over time.[61] As such, the analysis is tautological, moves little beyond the neoclassical approach it purports to supersede, and falls short of the kind of framework necessary for analyzing business groups in Korea and Taiwan on at least two counts.

First, the institutional economists, like their neoclassical predecessors, typically disregard or downplay the role of the state in the creation, maintenance, and transformation of these institutions.[62] Although Williamson acknowledges the significance of authority structures in establishing contracts and ordering economic transactions, he maintains that "the governance of contractual relations is primarily effected through the institutions of private ordering rather than through legal centralism."[63] If state influence beyond mere regulatory passiveness is acknowledged, it is often handled in ad hoc fashion as dysfunctional, irrational, or corrupt.[64]

Government, for Chang and Choi, is simply one of several environmental factors surrounding the Korean chaebol, not an independent variable affecting profit. They conclude their elegant transactions cost analysis of

[58]Mody, 1990.

[59]Biggs and Levy, 1991.

[60]Biggs, 1991.

[61]"Optimistic functionalism" is Kuran's term as quoted by Powell and DiMaggio, p. 4. For institutionalist critiques of NIE and rational choice theory, see also Granovetter, 1985, 1990, 1992; Bates, 1988, 1993; Peters; and Stein and Wilson.

[62]For a significant exception, see North, 1984. Also, Seckler notes that nineteenth-century institutional economists, influenced by the German historical school of economics (*Historismus*), held that "the state is of paramount importance in the actual conduct of industrial life; it thus deserves a place in economic analysis as a basic factor of production" (E. J. James, "The State as an Economic Factor," in Henry C. Adams et al., *Science Economic Discussion* [New York: Science Company, 1889], p. 24, as cited by Seckler, p. 16).

[63]Williamson, 1985, p. xii.

[64]See, for example, Leff's analyses of business groups (1978; 1986) and his study of corruption and development (1965).

the chaebol by confessing they "cannot, of course, rule out the possibility that factors not accounted for in this study might be exerting some influence over profit, such as political or personal connections between large business groups and the makers of government policy." Their justification for this oversight (whose magnitude will be made very clear in the remainder of this book): "at the time there is no scientific method to accommodate the murkier factors into the analysis."[65]

Second, this transaction cost approach discounts culture. Williamson admits his "conception of human nature is stark and rather jaundiced. Those who would emphasize more affirmative aspects of the human condition and wish to plumb features of economic organization that go beyond economizing will understandably chafe over such a choice of behavioral assumptions."[66] In Granovetter's terms, the analysis is undersocialized, not allowing for the influence of concrete (and murky) personal relations beyond the institutions themselves. Even when institutional economists acknowledge the role of trust or other social norms, these norms—as the product of optimizing agents—become merely optimizing agents themselves, lacking social content.[67] Even culturally specific norms are portrayed as generalized and automatic maximizing responses, "even though moral action in economic life is empirically hardly automatic or universal."[68]

Having offered this critique, it should be noted that the best of these NIE studies are acknowledging these shortcomings and moving to overcome them. Douglass North has acknowledged and addressed the importance of both the state and ideology in maintaining institutions through the specification and enforcement of property rights.[69] C. H. Lee, in his study noted above of the Korean chaebol and the state, gives full credit to the state as partner to the chaebol in a quasi-internal hierarchy and posits Korea's Confucian ethos as an ideology reducing the costs of monitoring in this principal-agent relationship.[70] Levy and Biggs, too, acknowledge the role of the state in Korea and Taiwan, with Levy acknowledging at one point that his discussion of the government in shaping firm size "begins to blur the distinction between political and economic determinants."[71]

Addressing the cultural jaundice of NIE, George Akerlof contends that social customs disadvantageous to the individual may in fact persist if

[65]Chang and Choi, p. 155.
[66]Williamson, 1985, pp. xii–xiii.
[67]Peters, p. 1069.
[68]Granovetter, 1985, p. 488.
[69]North, 1981, 1984.
[70]C. H. Lee.
[71]Levy, 1991, p. 167. See also Biggs, 1991; and Biggs and Levy, 1991.

disobedience of these customs leads to the loss of reputation in the community. Challenging the utilitarian thesis, he concludes that "nonindividualistic-maximizing behavior may result in equilibria that are qualitatively different from those obtained from individualistic-maximizing behavior."[72] North, too, laments NIE's lack of social content, acknowledging that "the economic models we employ have little room for such behavioral complexity. Trust, ethical standards of conduct, and moral precepts do influence the costs of contracting and the performance of economies, as also do ideologies." He (accurately) concludes: "A major challenge to the social scientist is to develop political-economic models that both are institutionally rich and can take into account more complex behavior than has been done heretofore."[73] That, precisely, is the objective of this book.

## NEW ECONOMIC SOCIOLOGY

NIE approaches acknowledge the limits of utilitarian theory and the empty formalism of atomistic impersonal markets, but generally exclude a priori noneconomic motives or factors.[74] Although Williamson's work may be revisionist, his transactional approach tends to "deflect the analysis of institutions from sociological, historical and legal argumentation and show instead that they arise as the efficient solution to economic problems."[75]

While economic rationality is obviously a dominant influence in the economic behavior of entrepreneurs in Korea and Taiwan and the organization of their firms, they are motivated by other goals, obligations, and constraints not entirely explicable in terms of individual rationality, economic or otherwise. These include the dynamics of familial and peer approval, community status, political power, and implicit and explicit coercion. In order to analyze these factors, one must move from an approach that takes transaction costs as its independent variable to one that focuses on the broader institutional environment.

The new economic sociology (NES) assumes that the ongoing social relationships in which economic action is embedded shape the structure and organization of this action and "establish the very criteria by which people discover their preferences."[76] Here the explanation of economic action shifts from choice based on individual preferences and expecta-

[72]Akerlof, p. 752.
[73]North, 1989, pp. 113–14.
[74]Peters.
[75]Granovetter, 1985, p. 505.
[76]Powell and DiMaggio, p. 11.

tions to the fulfillment of duties and obligations imposed by the environment.[77] Economic behavior can be viewed as rule-driven, or at least rule-constrained. Economic organizations develop and adapt not solely in pursuit of technical efficiency or "fit" with a narrowly construed task environment, but also to secure cultural legitimacy, peer respect, and political tolerance.[78]

These two institutional approaches to the organization of economic behavior approach the issue of institutions from opposite directions. Institutional economics examines the effects of contracts and other microlevel transactions on macrostructures such as vertical integration, and "presents the possibility of infinite universe of institutional forms, each most efficient in its own idiosyncratic context."[79] Economic sociology, on the other hand, examines the effects of sociocultural macrostructures on economic microstructures, and emphasizes how historical and structural factors in fact narrow the range of institutional forms that actually emerge in a given society.[80]

The NES approach promises great utility for the analysis and comparison of industrial organization across geographical and cultural boundaries, and has been fruitfully applied in the East Asian setting in recent years by a number of sociologists, organizational behavioralists, and anthropologists. Gary Hamilton and those working with him (initially through the Research Program in East Asian Business and Development at the University of California, Davis) have made the most comprehensive effort to apply this new economic or institutional sociology (termed "authority approach" in their early writings) to comparative studies of industrial organization in East Asia.[81] Their path-breaking studies are often cited and provide an important foundation for this book. Representative of this work, Marco Orru, Nicole Biggart, and Hamilton argue that while technical environments influence economic organization, the institutional or "socially-constructed normative worlds in which organizations exist" also shape and distinguish the organizational and interorganizational structures of firms in Japan, Korea, and Taiwan.[82] Richard Whitley, too, in his comparative studies of business systems in these three countries (and Hong Kong) concludes that the systems vary because of the socially constructed nature of their imperfect markets and significant differences in their institutional environments.[83]

[77]March and Olsen, p. 741.
[78]Lincoln, p. 12. For the distinction between technical and institutional environments, see Meyer et al.
[79]Gerlach, 1987, p. 10.
[80]Gerlach, 1992.
[81]Hamilton; Hamilton, ed.; Hamilton and Biggart, 1988, 1991; Hamilton and Kao; Hamilton and Orru; Hamilton, Orru, and Biggart; Hamilton, Zeile, and Kim; Orru et al.
[82]Orru et al.
[83]Whitley, 1992. See also Whitley 1991, 1990.

Similarly, Gerlach contends that the "alliance capitalism" of Japan's business groups is a consequence not just of the strategic interests of member firms but also of the constraints and opportunities imposed by social institutions in which the groups are embedded.[84] Ichiro Numazaki also employs an embeddedness framework in analyzing the networks within and among Taiwan's business groups,[85] as does Susan Greenhalgh in her study of the "microlevel institutions" of families and networks in Taiwan's economic development.[86] Jay Kim and Chan Hahn, and E. M. Kim, also adopt institutional versions of social organizational theory in their studies of the Korean chaebol.[87]

These studies agree that firm organization within each East Asian country is relatively "isomorphic,"[88] reflecting the business groups' respective institutional embeddedness while varying widely across the cases. This does not mean economic motives or resource dependencies have not also shaped industrial organization in these countries. But "as institutional environments vary across time, industry, and nationality, so too do the normative institutional forms, apart from considerations of transactional or technical efficiency."[89]

James Lincoln warns that societies differ in the extent to which constraints on a given organization are more those of "competitive technical efficiency as opposed to legitimacy and other cultural and political resources." He nonetheless concludes: "With its explicit attention to the role of cultural, legal, and political influences in shaping the strategies and designs of organizations, institutional theory would appear to be uniquely tailored to the task of accounting for societal contrasts in organizing styles."[90]

Speaking broadly of the theoretical utility of institutional approaches, Lincoln hits upon an important shortcoming of much of the NES literature as it is applied in practice. Though he mentions specifically the influence of legal and political institutions, economic sociologists often tend to downplay or neglect the role of politics and the state in structuring institutional environments. Gerlach, in his book-length study of Japan's enterprise groups, says virtually nothing about politics and excludes the Japanese state from his conceptual framework.[91] Granovetter, in an essay on business groups, notes numerous examples of government in-

[84]Gerlach, 1992. See also Lincoln.
[85]Numazaki, 1986, 1991.
[86]Greenhalgh.
[87]Kim and Hahn; E. M. Kim, 1991.
[88]DiMaggio and Powell.
[89]Gerlach, 1987, p. 10.
[90]Lincoln, pp. 13–14.
[91]Gerlach, 1992.

fluence on enterprise groups in various countries, but argues "there is no theoretical reason why business groups might not evolve largely independent of state influence."[92] Elsewhere Granovetter calls for a "sophisticated economic sociology" that will "seek to understand how modern economics can be integrated with a social constructionist account of economic institutions, and what the division of labor must therefore be between sociology and economics."[93] Such a division of labor threatens to exclude the state as an analytical category altogether.

In fairness, a number of these studies in the new economic sociology do acknowledge the role of the state. Defining embeddedness as the "contingent nature of economic action," Sharon Zukin and Paul DiMaggio identify four types of institutional embeddedness: cognitive, cultural, structural (or social), and political. The latter category concerns the way in which economic institutions and decisions are "shaped by a struggle for power that involves economic actors and nonmarket institutions, particularly the state and social classes."[94] In the East Asian literature, Hamilton and his coauthors and Whitley give some causal weight to the state, particularly in Korea.[95] But even in these studies, the state remains "at best one of several actors embedded in a greater social system."[96]

The states in Korea and Taiwan beg for and deserve more attention and causal weight in the formation and development of the business groups than is afforded by mainstream economic sociology or certainly by economic analysis of either the institutional or neoclassical variety. Sociology's embeddedness approach to institutional analysis provides the springboard for analyzing industrial organization in Korea and Taiwan, but any such analysis must give full consideration to the role of the state. Only by understanding the social and political institutions in which the business groups are embedded and how this environment has evolved over time can one account for the variation in enterprise structure between the two nations.

## New Political Economy and the Developmental State

A new political economy or statist approach to economic development has been advanced primarily by political scientists and sociologists, partic-

[92]Granovetter, 1993, p. 41. I am indebted to Ben Schneider for bringing these examples to my attention.
[93]Granovetter, 1992, p. 5.
[94]Zukin and DiMaggio, p. 17.
[95]For Hamilton and his coauthors, see note 81; for Whitley, see note 83. See also E. M. Kim, 1991.
[96]Schneider, p. 39.

ularly those working on East Asia and Latin America.[97] This new political economy provides the essential third institutional leg for analyzing the embedded enterprise groups of Korea and Taiwan. Such a state-informed embedded enterprise approach has utility in analyzing any political economy. But in late-developing countries, the dominant "role played by the state in capital accumulation and enterprise formation in the early stages of industrialization can permanently shape the internal structure of business enterprises and the institutions of the economy as a whole."[98]

Because state formation (first colonial, then republican) preceded industrialization in both Korea and Taiwan, and because of the particular ways in which these "strong" states were historically constituted and have evolved over time, these states have left indelible, though very different, imprints on their respective business groups. This dominant role of the state in their economies requires that any conceptual framework analyzing the private business networks in Korea and Taiwan must be capable of giving full attention to the causal weight of political factors.

Revisionist assessments of the role of the state in the original industrial revolution and recent conclusions that "effective state intervention is now assumed to be an integral part of successful capitalist development" aside,[99] Western scholarship has been hesitant to acknowledge the role of the state in the formation and transformation of the economic institutions of capitalism. This resistance to viewing the state as an autonomous and potentially positive or "developmental" influence on the market and its participants has its roots in the Anglo-Saxon tradition of laissez-faire economics and government by association. This is the outgrowth of the industrial and democratic revolutions of Western Europe in the eighteenth and nineteenth centuries, in which largely unfettered private capital and private interests paved the way. Theda Skocpol notes that "these founding theorists quite understandably perceived the locus of societal dynamics—and of the social good—not in outmoded, superseded monarchical and aristocratic states, but in civil society."[100] For Smith, this meant the market; for Emile Durkheim and Herbert Spencer, the industrial division of labor; for Karl Marx, class relations.

Drawing on this tradition, twentieth-century scholars advanced two conceptions of the state and its role in explaining the causes and consequences of economic development. In the liberal model, the state is portrayed as a forum for civil society with no interests of its own, allowing equal political, social, and economic access for all participants. In the

[97]For useful reviews of this "development state" literature, see Onis, 1991; Islam; Wade, 1992.
[98]Lincoln, p. 20.
[99]Rueschmeyer and Evans, p. 44.
[100]Skocpol, p. 6.

Marxist model, although the state is seen as an instrument of force, this instrument is entirely in the possession of the dominant social class, and is thus still a reflection of societal characteristics or preferences."[101]

Over and against these society-centered paradigms emerged a "statist" approach, drawing on an earlier Continental intellectual heritage. Focusing on the historical experiences of nineteenth-century continental Europe, such as mercantilism and authoritarian rule, theorists such as Max Weber and Otto Hintze refused to accept this Anglo-Saxon disregard of the state. However, this statist perspective of capitalist development was given little currency as long as Britain and the United States managed to maintain their positions as unchallengeable "lead societies." Under such conditions, "western social sciences could manage the feat of downplaying the explanatory centrality of states in their major theoretical paradigms."[102]

The dogged empirical failure of postcolonial late industrializers to live up to these Western theories forced development theorists to acknowledge and reexamine the state. Early calls from developmental economists for state-led industrialization to overcome market failure soon gave way, however, to a "neoclassical resurgence" that documented "the failures and disasters of regulatory, interventionist states."[103] This "neoutilitarian" account of the process of development incorporates a "public choice" model of the state that sees state officials as rational maximizers creating, capturing, and distributing "rents" through their intervention in the market.[104] In dialectic fashion, this neoutilitarian vision of the "predatory" state has been countered by a "statist counterrevolution" launched by scholars of East Asian development under the rubric of the "developmental state."[105]

Chalmers Johnson first formulated this concept of the "developmental state" in the context of Japan and subsequently applied it to Korea, Taiwan, and selected Southeast Asian states.[106] The coincidence of strong bureaucratic apparatuses and phenomenal economic success in these East Asian cases has "firmly entrenched" the concept in the developmental literature.[107] This notion of a developmental state has been re-

[101]Skocpol; Krasner.

[102]Skocpol, p. 6.

[103]Bardhan as cited by Islam, p. 70.

[104]Evans, 1989, 1992; Islam.

[105]For "predatory state" see Evans, 1989. The term "statist counterrevolution" is from Islam. Discussion of the term "developmental state" follows.

[106]For Japan, see Johnson, 1982. For Taiwan and Korea, see Johnson, 1987. For an argument of its applicability as a broader "Asian capitalist model," see Johnson, 1992.

[107]Islam, p. 76. Islam points out, however, that this same economic success among the East Asian newly industrializing economies was earlier taken, and still remains in some circles, as "vindication of the neo-classical view of development" (p. 70).

fined and reformulated by a number of authors writing on East Asia,[108] comparing East Asia with Southeast Asia and Latin America,[109] and developing more general heuristic categories of development.[110]

This developmental state literature is fundamentally institutional in its logic. These late industrializers, unlike their predecessors, required statist institutional arrangements (Gerschenkron's "compulsory machinery of the government"[111]) to accumulate capital, provide entrepreneurship, discipline and respond to private business, and insulate the state from societal interests. Johnson offers an institutional model of the developmental state that includes an elite bureaucracy led by a pilot planning agency and an authoritarian political system designed to insulate bureaucratic decision makers and close formal and informal linkages between the state and big business.[112]

Developmental state theorists are generally conscious of their association with the new institutionalism and convinced of its explanatory utility, particularly in East Asia. Stephan Haggard frequently uses the terms "statism" and "institutionalism" interchangeably,[113] Yun-han Chu speaks of disaggregating the institutional features of the developmental state,[114] and Alice Amsden argues that reciprocity between the state and big business is the key institution of successful late development.[115] Richard Applebaum and Jeffrey Henderson, while acknowledging that "the role of the state in Japan and the East Asian NICs must be contextualized both culturally and historically," nonetheless conclude that state institutions in the form of "state policy and influence should now be accepted as the single most important determinant of the East Asian economic miracle."[116]

This book argues that these state institutions are also the key determinants of enterprise organization in Korea and Taiwan. Such confidence in this "strong" version of statist institutionalism threatens, however, the same kind of monocausal exclusivity and reification for which this chapter has criticized the other institutional aspirants. The best of the East Asian statist literature has overcome this, acknowledging politics within the state,[117] networks between the state and business or the "embedded" au-

[108]See, for example, Wade, 1984, 1990, 1992; White; Amsden, 1989; Haggard, 1990; Deyo; Castells. For critical assessments of its application to Japan, see Samuels; Friedman. For Taiwan, see Arnold. For Korea, see Moon; Moon and Prasad.
[109]For Southeast Asia, see Islam; and Doner.
[110]See Evans, 1989.
[111]Gerschenkron, p. 20.
[112]Johnson, 1987. See summaries of this model in Islam; Wade, 1990; Castells.
[113]Haggard, 1990, 1994.
[114]Y. Chu, 1989.
[115]Amsden, 1989.
[116]Applebaum and Henderson, p. 23.
[117]Moon and Prasad; Moon, 1994; Noble; Haggard, forthcoming.

tonomy of the state,[118] and the key role of private social and economic institutions in shaping policies and accounting for the particular developmental paths and industrial organization of these political economies.[119]

These latter studies, like the more nuanced studies from the institutional economics and economic sociology literature, are forming the tentative foundations of an emerging comparative historical-institutional approach labeled by Peter Evans and John Stephens as a "new comparative political economy."[120] Although these studies neither meet the challenge of Occam's razor nor achieve the elegance of neoclassical formalism, they nonetheless begin to fulfill North's summons, noted above, to formulate institutionally rich political-economic models capable of handling complex behavior. The final chapter returns to the prospects of this new comparative political economy. The final section of this chapter introduces the embedded enterprise framework as one variant of such an approach, and intervening chapters apply the framework to the comparable cases of Korea and Taiwan.

## EMBEDDED ENTERPRISE: BUSINESS GROUPS AND THE STATE

Although the owners and managers of business groups in Korea and Taiwan—operating within domestic and international capitalist markets—have pursued rational economic goals, their efforts to do so have been significantly recast by the normative constraints of their respective institutional environments. These environments are simultaneously (and dynamically) structured by pervasive state policies, persistent cultural norms, and ongoing social and political relations. These institutions shape not just the economic actions but the preferences of the owners and operators of the groups.

This embedded enterprise approach provides a hybrid institutional framework for comparing business groups in Korea and Taiwan. In so doing, it follows in the best efforts of those working to meld the virtues of these various institutional approaches. Skocpol, in outlining the requirements of statist research, notes that "a complete analysis, in short, requires examination of the organization and interests of the state, specification of the organization and interests of socioeconomic groups, and inquiries into the complementary as well as conflicting relationships of state and societal actors."[121] Although Geertz laments that interdisciplinary interchange between economics and anthropology has typically been

---

[118]R. Shin; Y. Chu, 1989; Moon and Prasad; Evans, 1989.
[119]Doner; E. M. Kim, 1991; Y. Chu, 1989.
[120]Evans and Stephens.
[121]Skocpol, p. 20.

instances of each "skimming off the other's more generalized ideas and misapplying them," he applauds recent efforts to incorporate socio-cultural factors into the discussion of markets.[122] He acknowledges that the building block of much of this "genre-mixing" has been the institution.[123]

The chapters that follow utilize an embedded enterprise framework in order to account for the dominant institutional influences shaping the formation and development of business groups in Korea and Taiwan. Profit-maximizing responses to market opportunities are the stimuli behind individual and enterprise participation in the market. Market uncertainties, bounded rationality, and opportunism do indeed spur the establishment of contracts and prompt integration in order to reduce transaction costs, as the institutional economists have argued. But as the cases of Taiwan's and Korea's business groups reveal, it is also necessary to examine dominant social and political institutions in which these market transactions and economic organizations are embedded.

Economic activities are constrained, aided, or otherwise affected by ongoing social relations and cultural norms that vary over time and across national boundaries. In the cases of Korea and Taiwan, the role of the state as an environmental factor has been even more important in shaping, manipulating, and even creating economic organizations. Comparing enterprise organization in Japan, Korea, and Taiwan, Orru et al. argue that each society has created "a context of fiscal, political, as well as social institutions that limit and direct the development of fit organization forms . . . [and] the important role of the state in economic affairs leads us to believe that institutional and normative factors are particularly important to organizational viability in those nations."[124] In order to analyze these state influences on industrial organization, it is necessary to examine the ideologies and goals of policymakers, and the strategies and policies they formulate and implement in order to achieve these goals.

However, just because state policymakers have a desire to influence economic actors and the organizations such as business groups through which they function, the success of their efforts is far from guaranteed, even in the "strong" states of Korea and Taiwan. In addition to the constraints of international pressures, state policies often must overcome the persistence of sociocultural institutions "embedded in emotion and the style of life." Dietrich Rueschmeyer and Peter Evans note that these "deeply ingrained and firmly institutionalized expressive behavior patterns may resist attempts at state-sponsored change even with an extremely unfavorable distribution of power resources."[125]

---

[122]Geertz, p. 28.
[123]As cited by Gerlach, 1987, p. 3.
[124]Orru et al., p. 41.
[125]Rueschmeyer and Evans, p. 70.

Therefore, in addition to state policies and programs, an explanation of the business groups must account for dominant social institutions structuring the environment in which the groups are embedded and analyze the degree to which these societal structures and cultural norms are in harmony or conflict with state institutions. To the extent that state policies comply with existing legitimate or otherwise dominant social norms and institutions, the policies may succeed as long as they are perceived as economically rational by the affected private entrepreneurs. Rueschmeyer and Evans warn: "This is not to deny that rational behavior must not be underestimated in any context and that scarcity and intense interest are spurs that move people toward rational action even against such obstacles as custom, ignorance, and norms defining which options are reasonable and which are 'unthinkable.' However, rational behavior is impeded by such obstacles."[126]

When state economic policies challenge sociocultural norms and entail economic risks, the successful implementation hinges on the state's willingness and ability to influence the preferences, behavior, and norms of the economic actors. This in turn will depend on the state's internal coherence and autonomy, its ideological constraints and developmental strategies, the institutional "compliance mechanisms"[127] at its disposal, and its institutional relationship with the key private economic actors. The subsequent comparative chapters demonstrate fundamental and causally significant differences in the institutions structuring the environments in which the business groups of Korea and Taiwan are embedded.

For a crucial period of time beginning in the early 1960s, the Korean state was composed of a tightly organized, like-minded group of military and civilian political leaders and technocrats oriented toward the well-defined national goal of rapid economic growth. For much of this period, the state overcame sociocultural obstacles to its policies and ensured the compliance of "private" economic actors by offering massive subsidies and other incentives to a handful of rapidly expanding industrial combines and ruthlessly disregarding the thousands of small and medium-sized firms. The chosen chaebol thrived in this favorable environment, developing as junior partners of the state and typically yielding to government pressure when traditional corporate culture clashed with regime goals. Although this state policy achieved the desired objective of unprecedented rapid economic growth, the social and political costs of this strategy forced the state to revise its industrial policy at the expense of an

---

[126]Rueschmeyer and Evans, p. 71.

[127]Concerning these compliance mechanisms, Mason et al. note that "behavior may be modified by the use of incentives and disincentives or by command. The former expands an individual's opportunity set, leaving him free to alter his behavior or not, while the latter constricts it" (p. 264).

increasingly powerful and autonomous big business sector. This has significantly altered the nature of state-business group relations and the environment in which the groups will develop.

In Taiwan, on the other hand, state ideology, historical experience, and political necessity converged, prompting the transplanted minority Nationalist regime to adopt an industrial policy and create an institutional framework designed, above all, to maintain price stability and prevent the concentration of private financial power. This policy has greatly restricted the scale, concentration, and influence of Taiwan's business groups. Nonetheless, this less aggressive policy created an environment in which traditional sociocultural norms and institutions have been much more influential in shaping the development and organization of the business groups, checked only when these cultural proclivities or economic aspirations challenged the regime goals of stability and relatively equitable income distribution. As the economic limitations of this conservative policy have become more apparent and the political and social roots of the state's strength have declined, conflicts over appropriate policy both within the state and between the state and the business groups have undercut the internal coherence and autonomy of the state and its capacity and will to curtail the growth of the business groups.

The case studies of Taiwan's and Korea's business groups explored in the chapters that follow demonstrate the utility of this embedded enterprise framework for understanding the complex interplay of rational economic behavior and social and political structures in two specific environments. It allows us to understand why enterprise organization can vary so widely in two cases that are in other ways remarkably similar.

The value and heuristic utility of this version of a comparative political economy approach, however, go well beyond illuminating these specific cases. Markets do not and cannot exist apart from a nation's institutions and historical setting. These institutions have interests irreducible to individuals and individual behavior. This framework explains economic outcomes through the intervening variable of institutions, both formal and informal, temporary and regularized. While it is particularly useful in analyzing the developmental states of Korea and Taiwan, its utility extends to all settings in which the state intervenes in the economy and society.

CHAPTER TWO

# Chaebol and the State in Korea

Once heresy, it is now generally acknowledged that state intervention is, and always has been, very much a part of capitalist economic development.[1] This is particularly the case for late-developing nations, where state formation has typically preceded industrialization. In their efforts to overcome relative "backwardness,"[2] the regimes in these political economies have to varying degrees assumed the responsibilities of guarding the gate to and from the international political economy, accumulating capital, and even taking on the entrepreneurial roles of deciding what, when, and how much to produce. In fact, the successful developmental experiences of some of these most recent industrializers have bridged the once-gaping theoretical (and ideological) abyss between market capitalism and state socialism.[3]

Only recently has scholarship begun to keep pace with this reality. Claiming a middle ground between the market-rational, regulatory economies of the West and the plan-ideological systems of state socialism, Chalmers Johnson has introduced the concept of developmental capital-

[1]This does not mean, however, the realization was new. Scholars from Friedrich List, Otto Hintze, and Max Weber to Karl Polanyi and Alexander Gerschenkron have challenged the description, and often prescription, of capitalist development void of state intervention. For contemporary discussions see Evans, 1992; Rueschmeyer and Evans; Amsden, 1989; and Wade, 1990.

[2]Gerschenkron.

[3]Note, for example, Hamilton's apology for applying "a method developed for a centrally planned economy to a capitalist development process such as that of South Korea, where the foundation of growth has indisputably been the accumulation of private capital operating in the comparatively anarchic environment of the free market, albeit with state involvement in many areas" (C. Hamilton, p. 52). For other valuable polytheoretical analyses see Y. S. Wu; Wade, 1990.

ism and applied it to the capitalist developmental states of East Asia.[4] Alice Amsden applies the notion more specifically to Korea, contending that developmental regimes in Korea and elsewhere have "augmented the market" and deliberately gotten relative prices "wrong" in order to overcome the disadvantages of backwardness.[5]

Unfortunately, old theories, regardless of how badly misused or misplaced, die hard. A Western economist, referring to Korea and Taiwan, wrote: "While others were planning big pushes, widening bottlenecks, and filling various gaps, these economies seemed to be 'getting the prices right': heeding the wisdom of neoclassicists, and doing quite well by it."[6] More boldly (blindly), a Korean economist wrote in 1986: "Although Korea did follow a policy of promoting specific industries for a brief period during the 1970s and some marginal industry specific incentives remain, it would be incorrect and unfair to characterize Korea's development as having been based on industrial targeting."[7]

Despite the hopes of the apologists of neoclassical economics both outside and inside Korea, the overwhelming presence of the state in the Korean economy since the 1960s cannot be denied. Acknowledging this reality, another Korean economist admitted (also in 1986): "The governmental intervention in the private sector became ubiquitous, and with the exception of private ownership of firms, Korean firms were not capitalistic in the true sense of the word. The concentration of economic power that occurred, therefore, was not necessarily the product of the market system."[8]

This chapter examines the emergence, development, and current status of Korea's large, diversified business groups or chaebol. This analysis begins with the assumption that any explanation of Korea's developmental experience in general or discussion of its industrial organization in particular must give full consideration to the policies, institutions, and norms of the Korean state and the motives and ideology informing these interventions. Jang-jip Choi, writing in 1987, underscores the state's dominant and developmental role: "The Korean state, in relation to various private areas of civil society is comprehensive, penetrating, technocratic and repressive. It is virtually impossible to make a distinction between public and private domains. . . . The key element that makes Korea's economic growth extraordinary is just this effective capability of putting

[4]Johnson, 1982, 1987.
[5]Amsden, 1989.
[6]Stephen D. Younger, as cited by Alam, p. 233.
[7]B. Y. Koo, p. 2.
[8]K. U. Lee, p. 237.

plans into effect. It would otherwise merely be no more than an amusement for theoretical economists and bureaucratic planners."[9]

The state is not, however, the sole environmental influence or motivating factor in shaping the chaebol. Ironically (or perhaps predictably), the powerful presence of developmental states in Korea and its neighboring East Asian political economies has tempted observers into the analytic pitfalls of reification and monocausality that have trapped neoclassical economists. In fact, warning flags have already been posted. Praising the utility of the East Asian developmental model, Cal Clark and Steve Chan nonetheless caution that this model "might have created some stereotypes of its own and that closer attention must be paid to these societies if the new East Asian development model is not to follow its predecessors in reifying its own overly restrictive assumptions."[10]

Concerning South Korea, Clive Hamilton warns that accounts of its industrialization "attribute enormous impact to the policies of the state, almost as if industrialization occurred by fiat." He cautions that such isolated analysis is inadequate "without an understanding of the social foundations on which the state rests."[11] Eun Mee Kim also notes the shortcomings of the "strong state" perspective in explaining Korea's economic development, arguing it has been the "interaction of state actors and the powerful local conglomerates that provided the structural basis for the rapid industrialization of Korea."[12] Referring specifically to Korea's business groups, Ku-hyun Jung warns that emphasis on the dominant role of the state in the growth and development of the chaebol should not obscure the skill of the chaebol founders in seizing the opportunities at hand, skillfully manipulating market inefficiencies, and adapting to the changing institutional environment they faced.[13]

This institutional environment, in all its complexity, contains the shaping forces of Korean industrial organization. While theoretical abstraction may claim heuristic utility, it is empirically inaccurate and analytically misleading to focus exclusively on state or market or, for that matter, cultural, variables at the expense of other factors in accounting for the creation and development of Korea's large industrial combines.

Private chaebol owners' and managers' rational profit-maximizing responses to market opportunities and imperfections tell us much about the reasons for their participation in the market and their organizational strategies. It is also necessary, however, to examine the dominant normative institutions in which these market transactions are embedded. Time-

[9]J. J. Choi, pp. 316–17.
[10]Clark and Chan, p. 2. See also Doner; Moon and Prasad.
[11]C. Hamilton, p. 8.
[12]E. M. Kim, 1988, p. 106. See also E. M. Kim, 1992.
[13]K. H. Jung, 1988, pp. 78–79.

tested, legitimate sociocultural norms in Korea, such as familial loyalty and patriarchy, continue to exert tremendous influence on industrial organization and business management, despite the market's "invisible hand" of individual self-interest and the state's much less subtle wielding of carrots and sticks.

In Korea, this explicit state intervention has proven to be the most significant environmental factor in shaping, and in some instances literally creating, the business groups. Carter Eckert concludes that "the whole process of private capital accumulation in Korea since the colonial period has been filtered in one way or another through the state."[14] Although a handful of the Korean groups got their start under the adverse circumstances of the Japanese occupation and the Korean War, nearly all of today's successful chaebol owe their positions to specific policies of postwar regimes. Many of the groups thrived on the rent-seeking opportunities the Rhee regime offered them during the 1950s in exchange for filling the political and personal coffers of key politicians and bureaucrats. After the fall of the Rhee regime in the early 1960s, military leaders and civilian technocrats assumed power and promoted export-oriented, rapid industrialization with the chaebol as chosen agents of this strategy. This "sword-won alliance" of accumulation achieved its desired objective[15] but unleashed unintended economic and sociopolitical consequences. These consequences are now altering the relationship between the state and the chaebol and calling into question the foundations and raison d'être of the Korean developmental state.[16]

This chapter (1) describes the development and current status of the chaebol groups, noting their market expansion and entrepreneurial diversification; (2) examines their distinctive patrimonial organizational features; and (3) discusses their evolving relationship with the Korean state and the state's dominant role in the groups' developmental process. It is only through such an examination of the nexus of rational economic motives, legitimate sociocultural norms, and dominant state policies that a clear picture emerges of the developmental experience of the Korean chaebol.

## Chaebol and the Economy

From 1982 to 1991, the Korean economy grew at an annual rate of nearly 10 percent, one of the most rapid growth rates in the world. GNP

---

[14]Eckert, 1990–91, p. 122.

[15]The term "sword-won alliance" is from T. J. Cheng, 1990.

[16]For a discussion of how the developmental state, by virtue of its success, becomes its own "gravedigger," see E. M. Kim, 1992; and Evans, 1992.

grew from U.S.$8 billion in 1970 to over U.S.$280 billion in 1991, and total trade from U.S.$4 billion in 1972 to U.S.$154 billion in 1991.[17] There is little dispute either within Korea or abroad that the economic engines of this meteoric growth have been the chaebol.

Though not legally recognized as single entities, these Korean business groups are readily discernible within the Korean economy. The chaebol (a direct translation of the Japanese *zaibatsu*,[18] financial clique) may be defined as any group of two or more legally independent firms producing goods and/or services within various product sectors of the Korean economy.[19] In practice, however, most chaebol are considerably larger and share a number of common features. They typically are (1) owned and controlled by a single family and managed paternalistically; (2) completely independent from one another, with unambiguous firm membership; (3) diversified across products and industries; (4) (historically, at least) not in control of major financial institutions and thus dependent on external sources of funds; and (5) closely linked to the government.[20]

## Origin and Development

Although Korean industrialization began prior to 1945, Japanese concerns maintained a virtual monopoly of industrial capital during the colonial period.[21] From the outset, the Japanese colonial administration consciously restricted the development of indigenous capital, though competing against the established Japanese zaibatsu dominating the Korean market would have been virtually impossible even without administrative restrictions. After the 1919 anti-Japanese uprising, "a wafer-thin stratum of Korean capitalists was deliberately cultivated" as a means of furthering collaboration.[22] Although Korea developed during the 1930s and 1940s as the most industrialized country in Asia after Japan,[23] by 1940 there were still only fourteen agricultural and ten industrial Korean-owned companies with capital exceeding 500,000 yen.[24] Of those firms

[17]Korea Foreign Trade Association, 1992; China External Trade Development Council, 1992.
[18]The Korean word *chaebol* and the Japanese *zaibatsu* are written with the same Chinese ideographs, pronounced in Mandarin Chinese as *caifa*. This term is seldom used, however, in Chinese-speaking societies to refer to business groups (see Chapter Three).
[19]Mardon, p. 24.
[20]For discussions of these features see L. Jones; Steers et al.; J. S. Kim and Hahn; Yoo and Lee; von Glinow and Chung.
[21]Hamilton notes that even prior to Japanese colonization, business in Korea was foreign dominated (C. Hamilton, p. 13).
[22]Amsden, 1989, p. 33. See also McNamara, 1990; and Eckert, 1991.
[23]Eckert, 1990–91.
[24]McNamara, 1988, p. 174.

with capital of 1 million yen or more in 1940, Koreans invested only 6 percent of the total paid-in capital.[25]

From these unfavorable conditions, perhaps several thousand Korean businessmen "sprouted" as true capitalists and "assumed a position of influence after liberation and formed an important component of the new class of commercial and industrial capitalists which grew up in the 1950s."[26] In fact, many of the successful entrepreneurs of liberated Korea were a part of this group.[27] It is significant, however, that only three of the twenty largest chaebol as of 1986—Samsung, Daelim, and Kia—got their start prior to the end of Japanese colonization (see Table 2-1).

As Table 2-1 indicates, the majority of today's largest chaebol (as well as many other significant chaebol and nonchaebol enterprises) got their start during the late 1940s and 1950s, after liberation from Japanese rule and during the period of the Syngman Rhee regime (1948–60).[28] During this period, the nascent chaebol accumulated capital by using political

*Table 2-1.* 1986 top twenty chaebol and their year of founding

| Rank | Group | Colony | Rhee | Park |
|------|-------|--------|------|------|
| | | Year founded | | |
| 1 | Samsung | 1938 | | |
| 2 | Hyundai | | 1950 | |
| 3 | Lucky-Goldstar | | 1947 | |
| 4 | Daewoo | | | 1967 |
| 5 | Sunkyung | | 1953 | |
| 6 | Ssangyong | | 1954 | |
| 7 | Korea Explosive | | 1952 | |
| 8 | Hanjin | | 1945 | |
| 9 | Hyosung | | 1957 | |
| 10 | Daelim | 1939 | | |
| 11 | Dong-A | | 1945 | |
| 12 | Dae Han Kyo Bo | | 1958 | |
| 13 | Doosan | | 1952 | |
| 14 | Lotte | | | 1967 |
| 15 | Dongboo | | | 1964 |
| 16 | Kia | 1944 | | |
| 17 | Cho Yang | | | 1961 |
| 18 | Kolon | | 1957 | |
| 19 | Shin Dong-A | | 1946 | |
| 20 | Dongkuk Je Kang | | 1954 | |

SOURCE: Adapted from S. M. Lee, p. 183.

[25]H. C. Choi, p. 61.
[26]Eckert, 1990–91, p. 119; C. Hamilton, p. 19.
[27]These include the founders of Samsung, Hyundai and Lucky-Goldstar, three of Korea's four largest chaebol (Steers et al.).
[28]A survey of the top fifty chaebol in 1978 found that thirteen of them had been established by 1952, eighteen from 1953 to 1961, and nineteen from 1962 to 1978 (C. Hamilton, p. 33).

connections to gain favorable concessions from the government in exchange for political contributions.[29] Initially, this meant tapping the huge quantities of U.S. foreign aid. Amsden notes that "more energy was spent plundering the existing surplus than producing more, the surplus itself arriving in the alluring form of U.S. foreign aid for war reconstruction."[30]

The successful entrepreneurs emerging during this period were typically generalists utilizing the urgent needs of politicians for political funds and the corruption of ranking bureaucrats to gain preferential access to government-controlled resources and other government favors. These included the disbursement of foreign aid, government-controlled foreign exchange and low-interest loans, the divestment of state-owned properties expropriated from the Japanese, the awarding of government construction contracts and import monopolies, and the tolerance of large-scale tax evasion.[31] Capitalizing on the rent-seeking opportunities made possible by these favors under the protective conditions of import substitution, these budding chaebol reaped large windfall profits that they used to expand the business activities and create the capital base for these future industrial giants.[32]

Although many chaebol got their start prior to 1960, their real growth period came after the fall of the Rhee regime and the short-lived Second Republic, with the establishment of the military junta led by General Park Chong Hee. The chaebol expanded particularly rapid during the decade following 1965. By this time, Park had firmly established his regime, identified friendly and capable entrepreneurs, and begun to channel resources to them in fulfillment of the state's developmental goals. By 1975, the major groups had solidified their positions and were beginning to show they could survive on their own.[33] (See Table 2-2, which lists the top ten chaebol for 1965, 1975, 1985, and 1993.) While only three on the 1965 list were on the 1975 list, all but three on the 1975 list remained among the top ten in 1985 and all but two on the 1985 list were on the 1993 list.

Since becoming firmly established during the 1970s, the chaebol as a group—and particularly the largest among them—have continued to

[29]K. D. Kim, p. 469.
[30]Amsden, 1989, p. 40.
[31]K. H. Jung, 1988; K. D. Kim.
[32]Cheng notes import-substitution industrialization (ISI) degenerated into predatory rent-seeking in South Korea because of Rhee's need to maintain autocracy in a "democratic, albeit often abused framework." This he did by collecting political contributions from the highest bidders for monopoly favors (T. J. Cheng, 1990).
[33]Cho divides government-chaebol relations into four periods, reflecting major shifts in the political institutional environment surrounding the chaebol: 1945–60 (laissez-faire); 1961–72 (mercantilism); 1973–79 (paternalism); 1980–91 (constitutionalism) (D. S. Cho, 1992).

*Table* 2-2. Top ten chaebol in 1965, 1975, 1985, and 1993

| 1965 | 1975 | 1985 | 1993 |
|---|---|---|---|
| Samsung | Samsung | Lucky | Hyundai |
| Lucky | Lucky | Hyundai | Samsung |
| Kumsung (Ssangyong) | Hyundai | Samsung | Daewoo |
| Panbon | Hanjin | Sunkyung | Lucky |
| Samho | Hyosung | Daewoo | Sunkyung |
| Samyangsa | Ssangyong | Ssangyong | Hanjin |
| Tongyang | Daewoo | Hanjin | Ssangyong |
| Taehan | Doosan | Korea | Kia |
| Kaepoong | Dong-A-Construction | Daelim | Hanwa (Korea Explosives) |
| Hwashin | Shin Dong-A | Hyosung | Lotte |

SOURCES: K. H. Jung, 1983; *Business Korea*, 6/93.

expand and extend their dominance of the Korean economy. This has occurred despite at least nominal attempts by the Park regime, and—after Park's assassination in 1979—during the subsequent Chun, Roh, and now Kim governments, to curb the chaebol and various aspects of their concentration, diversification, ownership, speculation, and indebtedness. To understand the motivations of the state for curtailing chaebol expansion as well as the private chaebol owners' incentive and increasing ability to resist these limitations, it is necessary to examine the overwhelming extent of chaebol dominance and the economic and sociocultural motivations for private resistance.

## Current Dominance and Continued Expansion

The chaebol dominate the Korean domestic economy and have gained increasing international recognition as well. In 1983, the top fifty chaebol had sales equivalent to nearly 94 percent of GNP.[34] Among the fifty largest firms in Korea in 1986, thirty were owned by the ten largest chaebol. That same year, these top ten chaebol had total sales of over U.S.$65 billion, more than 65 percent of Korea's 1986 GNP. In 1991, the top five chaebol had revenues of U.S.$116 billion, equivalent to just under half of Korea's 1991 GNP.[35] Internationally, *Fortune*'s 1992 "Global 500" listing of the world's largest industrial corporations includes nine Korean chaebol (see Table 2-3).[36]

[34] Hamilton et al., 1988.
[35] S. M. Lee, p. 182; *Economist*, 6/8/91; KFTA, 1992.
[36] Hyundai Heavy Industries and Hyundai Motor, both members of the Hyundai chaebol, are listed separately in the "Global 500" rankings, giving the Koreans ten entries involving nine groups. If the state-owned enterprises Pohang Steel (ranked 190th) and Honam Oil Refinery (ranked 357th) are included, Korea's entries total twelve (*Fortune*, 7/26/93).
For the 1984 non-U.S. "Fortune 500" listing, Lee determined only twenty-seven were

*Table 2-3.* Chaebol in *Fortune*'s 1992 "Global 500" listing of largest corporations (in U.S.$ millions)

| Rank | Chaebol | Sales | Assets | Employees |
|------|---------|-------|--------|-----------|
| 18 | Samsung | $49,559 | $48,031 | 188,558 |
| 41 | Daewoo | 28,334 | 39,251 | 78,727 |
| 87 | Ssangyong | 14,610 | 12,234 | 24,000 |
| 90 | Sunkyong | 14,530 | 13,321 | 22,419 |
| 170 | Hyundai Motor | 8,606 | 7,523 | 44,474 |
| 232 | Hyundai Heavy Industries | 6,518 | 6,412 | 38,274 |
| 236 | Hyosung | 6,335 | 4,860 | 26,000 |
| 307 | Goldstar | 4,917 | 4,342 | 30,848 |
| 333 | Kia Motors | 4,385 | 5,263 | 23,549 |
| 390 | Doosan | 3,673 | 4,447 | 17,810 |

SOURCE: *Fortune*, 7/26/93.

The huge size of these business groups relative to the Korean economy has led to a high degree of concentration at all levels.[37] In addition to chaebol's dominating the whole economy, their affiliates not surprisingly control most of the specific industries in which they participate.[38] Noting these oligopolists' omnipresence, one critical observer of the chaebol's "expanding tentacles" cites the following feasible, if not factual, scenario:

A Samsung alarm clock wakes up Mr. Kim in the morning. He rolls out from under a Hanil Synthetic Fibre blanket, goes to the bathroom, where he uses Ssangyong toilet paper. The washstand is from Daelim. Kim busies himself with a Lucky-Goldstar toothbrush, Lucky-Goldstar dental cream, Daewoo shampoo, Lucky-Goldstar soap, a Lucky-Goldstar razor and Pacific Chemical after-shave lotion. When Kim sits down for breakfast, he sees a Hyundai table setting. His morning snack consists of Lotte milk, Samsung ham and bread from a near-*chaebol* bakery chain. In preparing the meal, Mrs. Kim was helped by a Daewoo refrigerator, Samsung microwave oven and Lucky-Goldstar toaster. Kim proceeds to dress himself for the day—a Samsung necktie, Dainong shirt and Samsung suit. Then the mid-ranging company manager, in his early forties, drives a Hyundai car away from his Hanyang-built apartment. Mrs. Kim turns to a Lucky-Goldstar washing machine, Daewoo TV and Samsung stereo for her late-morning routine. Junior Kim, who wears Kukje

---

private Third World firms. Of these, eight were Korean chaebol, comprising seven of the ten largest. But although the Korean chaebol are large in the aggregate even on an international scale, this is much less the case when individual firms are compared. Hyundai Motor, Korea's largest automobile manufacturer, was, in 1983, only one-twentieth and one-hundredth the size of Toyota and General Motors, respectively, in 1978, measured in terms of sales volume (Y. K. Lee, 1986, pp. 184–85).

[37]Jones and Sakong note that economic concentration has two dimensions: business concentration, the share of a given number of affiliated enterprises in all markets; and industrial concentration, the share of a given number of enterprises in a given market (p. 258).

[38]Hamilton et al., 1988.

shoes, likes Korea Explosives ice cream and Haitai candies and has recently joined the Doosan (OB Bears) pro baseball team's fan club, also leaves for school.[39]

This high level of diversification of the largest chaebol allows them to dominate the majority of Korea's various industries. In 1981, the chaebol produced 1,438 mining and manufacturing goods, 64 percent of all the industry products of the four-digit Korean Standard Industrial Classification denominations.[40] A partial list of the activities of the fifty-five affiliated firms of the Samsung group includes textiles, electronic assembly and equipment, semiconductors, fiber optics, ceramics, precision equipment, detergents, petrochemicals, military equipment, shipbuilding, wholesale trade, land development, construction, insurance, stock brokerage, a newspaper, broadcasting, a hospital, and a university. It hopes soon to add automobile manufacturing and set up a chain of clothing boutiques. Uncharacteristically, it recently shed its five-star hotel, a department store, and a paper products manufacturer.[41]

Moreover, the chaebol, both as a group and individually, are highly concentrated. Table 2-4 shows that the five leading groups have been consistently larger than the next five groups when measured in terms of combined group sales for the years 1974 to 1984. Likewise, each chaebol is dominated by three or four major affiliates. Young-ki Lee notes that the top four companies typically contribute more than 70 percent of the group's aggregate sales. For example, in 1983, four companies accounted for 71.5 percent of the Hyundai group's total sales, with the other thirty-one affiliates making up the remaining 28.5 percent.[42]

*Table 2-4.* Combined sales of top ten chaebol as percent of GNP, 1974–84

| Groups | 1974 | 1975 | 1976 | 1977 | 1978 | 1979 | 1980 | 1981 | 1982 | 1983 | 1984 |
|---|---|---|---|---|---|---|---|---|---|---|---|
| 1 | 4.9 | 4.3 | 4.7 | 7.9 | 6.9 | 8.3 | 8.3 | 10.5 | 10.4 | 11.8 | 12.0 |
| 2 | 7.2 | 7.5 | 8.1 | 12.5 | 12.9 | 12.8 | 16.3 | 19.1 | 19.0 | 21.2 | 24.0 |
| 3 | 9.0 | 9.8 | 11.3 | 16.0 | 16.9 | 17.6 | 23.9 | 27.6 | 27.4 | 30.5 | 35.8 |
| 4 | 10.3 | 11.4 | 12.9 | 18.2 | 20.7 | 22.1 | 30.1 | 35.2 | 35.6 | 38.7 | 44.3 |
| 5 | 11.6 | 12.8 | 14.5 | 19.8 | 22.9 | 24.6 | 35.0 | 41.3 | 42.2 | 46.7 | 52.4 |
| 6 | 12.7 | 14.1 | 16.1 | 21.3 | 24.7 | 26.6 | 38.2 | 44.9 | 46.0 | 51.0 | 56.2 |
| 7 | 13.5 | 15.3 | 17.5 | 22.8 | 26.4 | 28.5 | 41.0 | 48.0 | 49.2 | 54.2 | 59.4 |
| 8 | 14.3 | 16.2 | 18.4 | 24.0 | 27.7 | 30.3 | 43.6 | 50.9 | 52.2 | 57.1 | 62.1 |
| 9 | 14.7 | 16.7 | 19.3 | 25.2 | 28.9 | 31.6 | 46.0 | 53.3 | 55.1 | 59.8 | 64.8 |
| 10 | 15.1 | 17.1 | 19.8 | 26.0 | 30.1 | 32.8 | 48.1 | 55.7 | 57.6 | 62.4 | 67.4 |

SOURCE: Amsden, 1989, p. 116. Used by permission of the publisher, Oxford University Press.

[39] *Business Korea*, 7/84.
[40] *Business Korea*, 7/84.
[41] L. Jones, p. 11; *Business Korea*, 6/87, 6/93; *Far Eastern Economic Review*, 5/13/93.
[42] Y. K. Lee, 1986.

Table 2-4 also indicates the extent to which concentration has been increasing over time. The table measures the aggregate net sales of the largest ten groups. With each passing year, a significantly greater portion of economic clout has been held by a smaller number of groups. In 1974, the top ten accounted for 15 percent of Korea's national product. Ten years later, the three largest chaebol alone accounted for three times that figure. Both the government and society at large have noted this increasing concentration, but it persists despite state efforts to curb its progress. The final section of this chapter discusses the causes and consequences of this increasing concentration and the state's response. We first turn to the sociocultural environment in which these groups are embedded.

## CHAEBOL AND SOCIOCULTURAL NORMS AND INSTITUTIONS

The rapid transformation of the Korean economy since the mid-1960s has, not surprisingly, spawned changes in the traditional cultural norms and institutions and ongoing social relationships that both structure and give meaning and value to the economy. Equally predictable has been the resistance of traditional values to challenging new norms and principles. The resultant mix, with its competing influences, creates the milieu in which owners and managers make their decisions concerning the organization and activity of the chaebol.

Although various indigenous folk religions and customs, as well as the imported religion of Buddhism, have had significant influence on Korean culture, Confucianism, an earlier import, has had the greatest and most lasting effect on traditional Korean culture and society. Mahn-Kee Kim notes that although Confucianism originated in China and thus to the Chinese became "a skin that could not be rubbed off . . . , Korea became an honor student of Confucianism, more faithful to the tenets of Confucianism in some aspects than the Chinese people themselves."[43] In contrast with the metaphysics of Buddhism, the Confucianism that developed in Korea offered a very pragmatic system of hierarchical and reciprocal political, social, and familial relationships and norms of behavior for living in this world. Despite the effects of capitalist marketization and a highly interventionist developmental state, this Confucian influence is still evident and influential in Korean corporate culture.[44] At times, government and corporate leaders have called upon or manipulated these

---

[43]M. K. Kim, p. 117.

[44]Kim concludes that "today's [Korean] businessmen have both westernized attitudes as well as Confucian traits combined together" (D. K. Kim, p. 156).

traditional values to ease and facilitate Korea's industrial transition.[45] Still other traditions have fallen victim to the exigencies of state and market factors. At other times, however, cultural norms have conflicted with institutional alternatives and nonetheless persisted, even when rational economic logic and state strategies would have the chaebol act otherwise. This persistent, traditional Confucian influence will be examined as it affects chaebol organization, management, ownership, and succession.

Like their pre–World War II Japanese namesakes, the chaebol are a tightly knit, hierarchically organized group of legally independent firms. Unlike the prewar zaibatsu, however, there is relatively little separation between ownership and management of the chaebol firms.[46] All group firms are invariably under the control and ownership of a single family dominated by a single patriarchal figure who is almost without exception either the original founder or his chosen familial successor. In a 1982 study, Ung-Ki Lim found the average proportion of family stock ownership of listed Korean companies was 27.5 percent. This figure, however, is deceptively low.[47] Founder Chung Ju-yung and immediate family members are estimated to hold nearly 68 percent of Hyundai group firms' total shares.[48] A 1993 study conducted by Korea's Fair Trade Commission measured the concentration level of family ownership of the top thirty chaebol at 43 percent, down 3 percent from the previous year.[49]

From his position of president (*hoejang*), the family patriarch makes key decisions himself or delegates them among a close-knit group of sons, brothers, or relatives, or others with special relationships to him. A 1978

[45]One observer notes, for example: "As South Korea's Confucian society has moved through rapid modernization since 1962, old prejudices against entering commerce or industry—money making—rather than the highly esteemed state bureaucracy have been modified to view employment in the managerial staff of a big company as an extension of the bureaucracy. It additionally bestows the all-important identification with a group which small private business cannot offer" (*Far Eastern Economic Review*, 12/12/85). For a discussion of a similar state-manipulated transition in Confucian Japan, see Marshall.

[46]Hattori (1984) indicates that in the case of the Japanese zaibatsu, virtually all management decisions were made by professional managers, not familial stockholders.

[47]U. K. Lim acknowledges that many stockholders do not identify themselves by their real names in order to evade taxes. Moreover, listed firms represent only the tip of the Korean corporate iceberg and are obviously those firms in which familial ownership is most diluted. As of 1991, only 266 of a total of 915 chaebol affiliates sold shares to the public (*Far Eastern Economic Review*, 10/10/91).

[48]*Asian Wall Street Journal*, 11/25/91. Steers et al. note that in 1985, Chung, his family members, and other group firms jointly held at least 50 percent ownership in sixteen of Hyundai's twenty-four companies. The Chung family held roughly 50 percent of four of the remaining eight firms (Steers et al.). Strategies of family control, however, are not uniform. Samsung's Lee family maintains a high degree of stock ownership, but its participation in management is limited. In Lucky-Goldstar, the family tries to control the chaebol through management capability, not stockholding. Hyundai, the most traditional of the top-tier groups and still in the hands of its founder, has maintained family control over both stock and management (Hattori, 1989).

[49]*Business Korea*, 6/93.

study of the top 100 chaebol found 13.5 percent of top executives were related to the founder by blood or marriage and occupied 21 percent of all top managerial positions. One out of twenty top executives was either the son or brother of the founder.[50] Sangjin Yoo and Sang M. Lee found 31 percent of all executive officers of the top twenty chaebol in 1984 were members of the owners' families and that most core management positions were held by family members, including "new family ties through marriage."[51] A 1987 study of the 108 top chaebol found nearly 9 percent of top management positions were filled by close relatives of the owner.[52] In order to survive and thrive under the watchful eye of an authoritarian and sometimes arbitrarily interventionist state, the chaebol have had to rely on a variety of evasive tactics, form illicit ties, and engage in illicit transactions with member firms and even with the state. Important in all corporate settings, this threatening political environment places a premium on secrecy and loyalty among core executives. The family, bound by Confucian norms, has been an efficient source of such trust. But because the pool of family members is finite and the chaebol have expanded rapidly, affinity and trust based on a shared homeland or common school have become ascriptive substitutes for family ties.[53] Of the two, regional bonds are stronger than alumni ties in hiring decisions, and most chaebol are associated with a particular geographical region.[54] As in Japan, however, have attended the same high school or college can be an important ascriptive linkage, and particular chaebol have reputations for hiring preferences based on specific schools.[55] Although ascriptive ties

[50]Shin and Chin; Kim and Kim.

[51]Yoo and Lee, p. 99.

[52]H. C. Lee. For example, although family members make up only 7 percent of Hyundai's top managers, the family maintains exclusive possession of the highest-ranking posts. Founder Chung Ju-Yung has four younger brothers, one sister, seven sons, and one daughter. All but three of his brothers and his daughter's husband are in Hyundai management positions (Hattori, 1989). Chung Ju-Yung turned formal leadership of the Hyundai group over to his second younger brother, Chung Se-Yung, in 1986, though the elder Chung, age seventy-eight, is still very much in command. The three brothers all worked for the senior Chung at one time, and now all head their own businesses but maintain close sale and purchase agreements within the family (*Korea Business World*, 3/91).

[53]Shin and Chin; H. C. Lee.

[54]Seven out of the top ten chaebol are owned by families from southeastern Korea and continue to seek native sons in hiring executives. The "TK mafia," referring to the military, political, and corporate elites hailing from Taegu and the surrounding northern Kyongsang Province, has been a particularly cohesive and influential regional affiliation (C. S. Chang; Shin and Chin; *Far Eastern Economic Review*, 5/13/93).

[55]Samsung, for example, recruits largely from Seoul National University, Korea University, and Sungkyunkwan University, and Hyundai from Korea University (von Glinow and Chung, p. 37). Nine of Daewoo's top eleven executives graduated from Seoul's prestigious Kyunggi High School. These alumni ties have been particularly important in the case of Daewoo because its relatively youthful founder, Kim Woo-Choong, has not included family members as core executives. The "K-S" mark (having degrees from Kyunggi High School and Seoul National University, Korea's best) has been an important credential for aspiring

may be necessary criteria for selecting core executives, they are generally not sufficient. Chaebol leaders are increasingly able to recruit and promote top-rate professional managers from these ascriptive pools, including from their own families.

Despite the dominant position of the typical patriarch and the autocratic nature of his hierarchical rule, his entrepreneurial and managerial responsibilities are nonetheless limited by both state and market forces. During the chaebol's formative years, the state made many of the entrepreneurial decisions concerning what, when, and how much to produce. In addition, the huge scale and broad scope of today's chaebol and the technical complexity of their products and production processes have made it impossible for one man or one family to make all or even most relevant managerial decisions, despite the legendary efforts of some hoejang to do just that.[56]

Although the small or nonexistent general offices of the chaebol indicate that decisions at the top are made autocratically, not bureaucratically, most significant decisions are made by salaried managers—primarily trained as engineers.[57] A 1984 Korean Chamber of Commerce study confirms this, finding that founder-owners and their sons accounted for only 42 percent of the decision-making structure and professional management experts accounted for the remaining 58 percent.[58] Hoejang functions, Amsden contends, "have been limited to three areas: (1) making group-wide decisions about which government initiatives to follow and to what extent; (2) deciding how to apportion financing within the group; and (3) making key personnel decisions and inspiring the workforce to work harder."[59]

If familial dominance of management is prevalent but declining, familial ownership of the chaebol is still very much the rule. The entrenched nature of this traditional Confucian legacy is best seen in the continued resistance of the chaebol to listing their shares on the stock exchange and the various strategies they employ to ensure familial succession. The motivations (traditional and rational) and consequences of this persistent unwillingness to dilute ownership through the public selling of significant

top managers. In 1985, 62 percent of the top executives (excluding founders and successors) from the top seven chaebol graduated from Seoul National, with another 22 percent coming from Yonsei and Korea universities, the next two most prestigious (C. S. Chang).

[56]For example, Samsung founder Lee Byung-Chull sat in on every hiring interview for every new Samsung employee from 1957 until 1986, a total that must have exceeded 100,000 interviews. Hyundai founder Chung Ju-Yung and Daewoo's Kim Woo-Choong are famous for their year-round twelve-to-fourteen-hour workdays and their hands-on management styles (*Business Korea*, 1/86).

[57]Amsden, 1989.
[58]As cited by D. K. Kim, p. 143.
[59]Amsden, 1989, p. 167.

portions of shares in the group firms are examined in detail in Chapter Four. Here, it need only be pointed out how this familial domination takes place. In order to maintain their dominant ownership position, chaebol families typically adopt one of three stockholding patterns: (1) "chairman monopolization," where the chairman and his family retain a large proportion of shares of most or all group firms directly in their names; (2) "holding company control," where the chairman and his family own majority stock in a holding company that in turn controls the other group firms; or (3) "reciprocal stockholding," where group firms are linked through cross-shareholdings, with the chaebol family as dominant shareholders of key firms.[60]

Although the Korean government has gone to great lengths, with some recent success, to entice and sometimes force these chaebol to break with tradition and publicly list their firms (see Chapter Four), the greatest catalyst for diluting familial ownership and control of the chaebol may, ironically, be the traditional pattern of familial succession. In Korea, convention holds that the eldest son should take over the family business when the father steps down. Upon the patriarch's death, family wealth and property are distributed among all sons (but not daughters) according to a system of "diminishing shares," whereby the eldest son receives a disproportionately large inheritance. This differs from Taiwan's Chinese tradition of inheritance shared among all sons *and* daughters, in which the most responsible son, who has the duty to take care of the elderly parents, receives more shares, and the Japanese tradition, where the eldest son is the single heir to all properties.[61]

Moreover, in Korea (and Taiwan), succession is strictly patrilineal, based on blood kinship. Again, Japan differs on this count. In Japan, succession within the family firm (*ie*) was traditionally based on either blood or fictive kinship. In fact, the primary purpose of the ie was to maintain family wealth under the leadership of a capable person rather than being forced to bequeath the wealth to a possibly less capable blood relative.[62] In Korea, however, and in Taiwan, the division of property among family members threatens the continued existence of the chaebol as a responsibly managed single entity. Thus, Kim Suk Won, the youthful second-generation successor of the Ssangyong group noted, "No chaebol ownership is going to last three successive generations."[63]

Given the short history of the chaebol, this prediction has not yet been

[60]Hattori, 1984.
[61]I am grateful to Tun-jen Cheng for his clarification of these differences. See also Kim and Kim, p. 209.
[62]Hattori, 1989.
[63]*Far Eastern Economic Review,* 12/12/85. This "Buddenbrooks" effect is also an accepted truism in Taiwan business circles (see Chapter Three).

put to the test. As of 1989, only two of the top nine chaebol were still chaired by their founder and the other seven were headed by second-generation familial successors (see Table 2-5).

In anticipation of the centrifugal tendencies of property inheritance norms, the complexities of multiple-firm management and state policies designed to separate ownership and management, the chaebol have taken measures to assure familial succession and chaebol longevity. Many of the founders established foundations to which they turned over much of their personal assets. Ostensibly charitable organizations, these foundations have provided a convenient institutional method for circumventing cultural norms of succession and inheritance as well as means of "legalized tax evasion" for passing on assets outside the scrutiny of government policymakers and tax authorities.[64]

Hyundai's Asan Foundation is to receive some 90 percent of founder Chung Ju-yung's wealth. Chung passed the chairman's responsibilities to his younger brother Chung Se-yung in 1987, in an effort to create a period of transition while the elder Chung prepares his second son to become the long-term successor.[65] Although many predict that Daewoo's founder and chairman, Kim Woo-choong, will select his successor from among the ranks of Daewoo's professional managers, Kim has in the meantime given all his personal assets to the Daewoo Fund.[66] Samsung's founder, Lee Byung-chull, intent upon preventing the division of his chaebol, broke with Confucian tradition by passing over his two eldest sons and selecting his more able third son, Lee Kun-Hee, as his successor.[67] Tamio Hattori notes that "under the atmosphere of Korean fami-

*Table 2-5.* Years of founding, succession, and relationship of successors of 1989 top nine chaebol

| Group | Year of founding | Year of succession | Relationship of successor |
|---|---|---|---|
| Samsung | 1938 | 1987 | son |
| Hyundai | 1950 | 1987 | younger brother |
| Lucky-Goldstar | 1947 | 1970 | younger brother |
| Daewoo | 1967 | | |
| Sunkyung | 1953 | 1973 | younger brother |
| Ssangyong | 1954 | 1975 | sons |
| Hyosung | 1957 | 1970s | son |
| Hanjin | 1945 | | |
| Korea Explosives | 1952 | 1981 | son |

SOURCE: Compiled from various sources.

[64]Eckert, 1991, p. 143.
[65]*Far Eastern Economic Review,* 6/18/87; *Business Korea,* 6/93.
[66]Aguilar and Cho.
[67]*Korea Business World,* 2/86.

lism," making such a selection could lead to social friction. In order to minimize the friction, Lee transferred a large portion of family stock to two foundations, Samsung Foundation and Samsung Mutual Aid, during this period of succession uncertainty. This, Hattori argues, allowed the two institutions to play "the symbolic role of a united Samsung." After Lee determined his successor, "the function and hence, the stockholdings of these two institutions decreased accordingly."[68]

Familial dominance of ownership and top management positions, at least in the short run, is likely to persist. Breakup of these huge conglomerates is also not in the cards, at least not in the next generation. In addition to orchestrations by the chaebol owners to keep them intact, the synergistic advantages of integration and diversification have overcome divisive tendencies. Both the Hyundai and Kumho groups divided at one point because ownership in each case was shared by two brothers. But the economic costs of separateness prompted both chaebol to opt for reunification.[69] Fault lines are showing again in the Hyundai group and in Samsung as well, as the sons and founders jockey for position in taking control over the prize plums within Korea's two largest conglomerates.[70] But despite rumors of breakups, the institutional linkages among these firms will not easily disengage. Regarding Hyundai, one analyst noted that "the group's complex cross-holdings and financial guarantees, quite apart from political considerations, will stand in the way of the breakup of a machine whose turnover [in 1986] accounted for 11 percent of Korea's GNP."[71]

## CHAEBOL AND THE STATE

Having examined the role of market and sociocultural factors in the formation and development of the chaebol, I will, in this final section of the chapter, analyze the Korean state's institutional relationship with the chaebol as manifest in its policies toward the business groups. The dominant role of the state in fostering the development of the chaebol requires particular scrutiny. Before turning to the state's specific chaebol policies, we must first investigate the factors behind the government's capacity and inclination to take on this developmental role.

Specifically, this section first examines the autonomy and capacity of the Korean state that made possible its ability to intervene in the economy and impose (at least historically) its own strategy of enterprise organiza-

[68] Hattori, 1984, p. 139.
[69] Hattori, 1984.
[70] *Business Korea,* 6/93, 12/91.
[71] *Far Eastern Economic Review,* 6/18/87.

tion and development. Next, it analyzes the ideology and objectives of the Korean state as they relate to enterprise organization. That is, even if the state has been insulated from society and able to impose its will upon relevant economic actors, what motivated the state to choose developmental goals over alternative ones? And why did it opt to foster the private chaebol as its chosen instruments for achieving these developmental objectives? This section concludes with a discussion of the specific chaebol policy incentives and disincentives chosen by the state to bring about these goals and considers the consequences of these policies.

In short, the success of the Park and Chun regimes in creating a favorable environment for the rapid growth of the chaebol as junior partners in the Korean political economy has in turn altered this environment. Although the social, political, and even economic costs associated with the pro-chaebol policies under conditions of genuine democratization have increasingly tempered the state's willingness to continue its support of big business, the sheer size and dominance of the chaebol have undermined the state's ability to alter the institutional supports of this previous strategy. Ironically (and mistakenly), in this authoritarian state where free markets have been sacrificed on the altar of developmental policies, recent regimes have placed their hopes on foreign pressures for market liberalization to check the chaebol where state policy has failed.

### "Strong" State

Amsden argues that in all late industrializing countries, the state deliberately subsidizes domestic industry to distort relative prices in order to stimulate economic activity. The Korean state has differed from other late developers not in providing subsidies but in being able to impose performance standards on the private firms that receive these subsidies. This Korean capacity, she contends, and its absence elsewhere, "does not reflect differential abilities among policymakers. It reflects differences in state power."[72]

What are the sources of this state power? This state dominance of and autonomy from societal interests are often attributed to the personnel and policies of the Park military regime, and juxtaposed to the weakness of the Rhee regime preceding it. In fact, however, many of the traditional norms and institutional means for achieving a strong state authority where already in place when Rhee came to power in 1946. Much has been written about Asian cultural proclivities toward a strong, centralized, authoritarian state. Although some of this analysis is too general to be of

---

[72]Amsden, 1989, p. 145. Amsden argues Taiwan's state, too, has been capable of imposing these performance standards on industry.

much comparative utility (even if it is accurate),[73] Korea has had specific "situational motivations" making its society particularly conducive to an authoritarian political tradition. Gregory Henderson cites Korea's ethnic, cultural, and linguistic homogeneity, combined with territorial compactness, as factors leading to its strong state tradition.[74] Though Japan and Korea share each of these features, Korea has had no historical experience with feudalism, as did Japan, or with any other system of legitimate autonomous centers of authority. In fact, unlike in the West, only in this century has it been valid to speak at all of a state-society dichotomy in Korea, and then largely as a result of strong bureaucratic institutions of the Japanese colonial state, not an autonomous Korean society.

This precedent of a colonial interventionist state greatly facilitated the efforts of subsequent indigenous regimes.[75] Jang-jip Choi notes two forces pushing toward a strong Korean state by the end of World War II: the lingering influence of a traditional culture that made bureaucratic authoritarian rule easy and a contemporary political culture that intentionally reproduced this traditional culture. Further, the Korean War added ideological homogeneity to an already culturally homogeneous population galvanized in its hatred of the Communists to the north and the Japanese to the south.[76] The Korean War also greatly enhanced the strength and skills of the Korean state's instruments of power. By the end of the war, the Republic of Korea had a standing army of roughly 600,000 disciplined personnel, compared with 75,000 in 1950.[77]

The Rhee regime, however, was largely unable to capitalize on these potentialities for state power separate from particular societal interests. After the Japanese left in 1945, the traditional landed elite, in the words of Bruce Cumings, "succeeded in recapturing the state in 1945 and 1946, under American auspices, and used it in traditional fashion to protect social privilege rather than to foster growth. They prevented major land reform until the Korean War began, and showed no interest in developing the economy."[78] Even after the invading North Koreans, and following them, U.S. advisers, implemented thoroughgoing land reform, Rhee's government remained "penetrated by superannuated landlords who re-

[73]See, for example, Pye.
[74]Henderson.
[75]See E. M. Kim, 1988. In his comparison of colonial Korea and Taiwan, Cumings notes that the Japanese "emphasized not only military and police forms of control but also development under strong state auspices. This was particularly true after the Depression, when Japan used a 'mighty trio' of state organization, central banking and zaibatsu conglomerates to industrialize Korea and parts of Manchuria. Although strong in both colonies, the state in Korea bulked even larger in the economy than in Taiwan" (p. 53).
[76]J. J. Choi.
[77]Cumings.
[78]Cumings, p. 66.

tained political influence" and "incapable of the autonomy to direct growth."[79] Though certainly authoritarian in its draconian policies of social control, the regime became increasingly beholden to nascent capitalists who, as K. D. Kim noted, skillfully "played on the urgent need for political funds on the part of politicians and the prevalent corruption of high-ranking bureaucrats" to ensure the continuation of state policies guaranteeing their windfall monopoly profits.[80]

After seizing power in 1961, General Park Chong Hee quickly capitalized on these corrupt symbiotic ties between the Rhee government and private capital and the disorder that followed the toppling of Rhee's regime. Park sought quickly to assemble both a mandate and the means to assure an autonomous state capable of guiding economic development. Answerable only to the military, Park was not dependent on support from either the landed or the capitalist class, as his predecessor had been. Though Park never gained genuine popular support for his authoritarian rule, he had developed strong support from big business by the time he stood for civilian election.

After taking power, Park moved swiftly to institutionalize the state's autonomy and capacity to pursue economic development. One of his first acts was to create the Korean Central Intelligence Agency as an independent political support apparatus. Established in 1961 with 3,000 personnel, it was expanded by Park to some 370,000 employees in just three years.[81]

For directing the economy, Park concentrated virtually all state economic powers in a newly created superministry, the Economic Planning Board. Its director, given the rank of assistant prime minister (now deputy prime minister), became the highest-ranking economic policymaker answerable directly to the president. Park also formed the Council of Economic Ministers, composed of the prime minister, the deputy prime minister, and the ministers of finance, commerce and industry, agriculture and fisheries, transportation, communications, and foreign affairs. Any decisions that could not be agreed on at their twice-weekly meetings were referred directly to Park for arbitration.[82] These institutions together had exclusive budgeting authority and very broad jurisdiction to coordinate fiscal, monetary, trade, and industrial power.[83]

The Korean bureaucracy has been staffed with talented personnel bound in a Weberian sense by a shared confidence in their own skills and their national mission. Korea, like its sinicized neighbors, has a long

[79]Cumings, p. 67.
[80]K. D. Kim, p. 468.
[81]Johnson, 1987.
[82]Mardon.
[83]Y. H. Chu, 1989.

bureaucratic tradition based on relatively meritocratic civil service appointments. This legacy, Peter Evans notes, provides "legitimacy for state initiatives and non-material incentives for the 'best and brightest' to consider bureaucratic careers."[84] Though neither as elitist nor as prestigious as its Japanese counterpart, the bureaucracy selects its personnel from among the most talented graduates of the most prestigious universities. Only 2 percent of a growing pool of those sitting for the annual higher civil service exam are accepted.[85] With his bureaucratic general staff, Park nationalized the banks, confiscated ill-gotten private assets of big business, and gained control over virtually all resources vital to business. From this position of dominance and institutional capacity, the Park regime engineered Korea's export-oriented industrialization with the private chaebol as the chosen instruments to carry out this strategy. The chaebol quickly learned that to "go along with the state was to get along,"[86] and with state support thrived in strategic industrial sectors.

Predictably, the chaebol have grown into large and powerful economic and political interest groups increasingly capable of challenging this state strength. In the three regimes succeeding the Park government there was a gradual shift from state dominance over the chaebol to a relationship of symbiosis to, most recently, increasing friction and animosity.[87] Pacing the dynamics of this evolving relationship, the government's chaebol policy objectives have shifted and the degree of chaebol compliance with these policies has declined over time. Moreover, the Chun regime that followed Park's rule, and to a lesser extent the Roh and current Kim governments as well, have lacked legitimacy when coming to power while facing increasingly strident demands for political and economic liberalization. In addition to this erosion of Park's hard-won autonomy, the size and complexity of the economy and its chaebol engines have limited the Korean state's capacity to dictate the chaebol's developmental path. These changes have called into serious question the "sword-won" alliance first forged by Park and the underpinnings of the developmental state.[88]

## Economic Ideology and Objectives

Given the dominant position of the Korean state during much of the period of the chaebol's rapid growth and development, there is substantial evidence that the state is largely responsible for this particular devel-

[84]Evans, 1992.
[85]Evans, 1992.
[86]Mason et al., p. 265.
[87]For a discussion of this shift from state "dominance" to "symbiosis," see E. M. Kim, 1988.
[88]T. J. Cheng, 1990.

opmental path. Why, then, did the state choose development as its primary goal and the chaebol as the instrument to achieve it? Clearly, without such a strategy, the chaebol would not have grown and prospered as they did. Although the Nationalist regime in Taiwan was even more autonomous and nearly as capable, its ideology and historical experience gave the state different priorities and constrained it from taking steps similar to Korea's in fostering large-scale industry. Both regimes have been interventionist by nature and developmental in motivation, but they have adopted different strategies of development with specific consequences for the embedded enterprises.

It is necessary to examine the ideology and objectives of the Korean state and its key political leaders in order to understand these economic outcomes. As Jang-jip Choi notes, "During the Park and Chun periods, the dominant role of the President at the apex of power has made the personality of the ruler extremely important to policymaking."[89] This was no less true during the Rhee regime. Although the Rhee regime had relatively less autonomy and capacity than its successors, Rhee's motives and goals still proved consequential.

> There was then, no dearth of plans and planning activity before 1961. The reason this activity had so little effect on policy was, essentially, that President Rhee was interested in other things than in economic development. As in so many of the new states, the leader who fought for independence proved not to be a man capable of effective administration. . . . He seemed to be unable to understand the relation of economic growth to the attainment of his own goals. Thus his anti-Japanese measures retarded the resumption of trade with a natural and traditional partner, and his yearning for reunification was carried to the extreme that there was an unwillingness to build up the South as an independent and integrated economy.[90]

This was certainly not the case with President Park.[91] Writing of Park's rule, Bun Woong Kim observed that "presidential political leadership and a significant portion of the bureaucratic elites have given their top prior-

[89]J. J. Choi, p. 318.
[90]Mason et al., p. 253.
[91]This is true in terms of attitudes toward both Japan and economic development. Unlike Rhee, Park had great respect for Japan and explicitly adopted the developmental model of Japan's Meiji era for Korea. Although Park received one year's training in the United States as a South Korean military officer, most of his education and military training was at the hands of the Japanese; he graduated from both the Manchukuo and Japanese military academies. Park served in the Kwantung army as Lieutenant Okamoto Minoru (C. Hamilton). C. S. Lee notes that Park was "not able or did not wish to adopt American patterns of behavior." This affinity for Japan and resentment of the United States were reinforced by an incident in 1963. The United States withheld PL480 foodstuffs from Korea during a serious food crisis because of Park's harsh military rule. Park then turned to Japan's Mitsui business group, which sold him 100,000 metric tons of flour on credit (C. S. Lee, p. 62).

ity to economic development. Government economic intervention was too severely advocated to argue against its necessity. The intervention mechanism was solidified by an exceptional commitment of the late President Park Chung Hee toward economic development."[92]

Obsessed with the task of ushering Korea into the ranks of the developed nations, Park "pursued his goal relentlessly and achieved considerable results."[93] For Park, growth took precedence over other claims, including democratization or social equality. In 1962, he wrote: "In human life, economics precedes politics or culture. . . . The gem without luster called democracy is meaningless to people suffering from starvation and despair." Concerning income distribution, he wrote: "The economic, social, and political goals we set after the revolution are: promotion of the public welfare, freedom from exploitation, and the fair distribution of an income among the people. It is obvious that these goals cannot be reached overnight. . . . We must take a great leap forward toward economic growth."[94]

Having been trained under the Japanese, Park consciously patterned his developmental strategies after those of Meiji Japan, including an emphasis on the role of large-scale private enterprise. Concerning the role of big business, he wrote: "One of the essential characteristics of a modern economy is its strong tendency towards centralization. Mammoth enterprise—considered indispensable, at the moment, to our country—plays not only a decisive role in the economic development and elevation of living standards, but further, brings about changes in the structure of society and the economy. . . . Therefore, the key problems facing a free economic policy are coordination and supervisory guidance, by the state, of mammoth economic strength."[95]

Park explicitly chose economic growth as his regime's highest objective both as an end in itself and as a means to maintain external sovereignty and achieve internal legitimacy. Park and his technocrats saw creating jobs and increasing exports as the critical factors in economic growth and fostered the chaebol and channeled their profit-making activities to obtain these ends. Over the course of Park's rule, legitimacy became inextricably tied to the fate of the economy, and the fate of the economy increasingly depended on the burgeoning chaebol.

Coming to power literally over Park's dead body, General Chun Doo-Hwan, too, had legitimacy problems. However, early promises of taming the chaebol, promoting economic stability, and developing a welfare state

---

[92]B. W. Kim, pp. 149–50.
[93]Bunge, p. 38.
[94]Park, p. 224.
[95]Park, pp. 228–29.

quickly gave way to a similar pro-growth strategy and reliance on the chae-bol as the engines of that growth when economic slowdown threatened the Korean economy with fewer jobs and shrinking exports. Despite their democratic mandates and rhetoric to the contrary, Roh Tae Woo and even Kim Young Sam also have had to renege on pledges to curb the growth of the chaebol for fear of the sociopolitical costs of an economic downturn in the chaebol-dominated economy.[96]

## Institutional Relationship with the Chaebol

Amsden contends that all late-industrializing countries intervene in their economies through the use of subsidies. The difference in the case of Korea, she holds, is that "by building a meritocratic element into its system of awarding subsidies, the state extracted from the chaebol—an institution of possibly unprecedented power—a growth rate of output and productivity that may also have been unprecedented."[97] This ac-countability was vigorously sought and enforced through the use of both carrots (e.g., preferential loans, access to foreign exchange, tax conces-sions, import rights) and sticks (e.g., tax penalties, revoked import li-censes, calling in of loans).[98] In fact, the very success of these policies in achieving their intended goal has jeopardized the state's ability to con-tinue to significantly shape the development of its former protégés.

This evolving institutional relationship between the Korean develop-mental state and the private business groups is best illustrated by examin-ing the government's major policy initiatives toward the chaebol and the chaebol responses to these measures.[99] Two of these policy areas—finance and trade—will be the specific subjects of Chapters Four and Six, and are included here only in the broadest terms. This section examines several policies specifically designed to shape the course of chaebol develop-ment.[100]

### Illicit Wealth Accumulation Law (1961)

Private economic interests succeeded in completely penetrating and dominating the Rhee government during the 1950s.[101] By the early

[96] *Far Eastern Economic Review*, 3/1/90, 10/10/91, 4/8/93.

[97] Amsden, 1989, p. 152.

[98] There are numerous accounts of these "compliance mechanisms" of Korean industrial policy (see, for example, Jones and Sakong; Mason et al.; Y. I. Lim; and Amsden, 1989). Although Taiwan also utilized incentives and disincentives to shape industrial organization, Scitovsky notes that "there is a great difference in the number and nature of inducements used and in the forcefulness with which they are applied" (p. 152).

[99] For a useful periodization of the historical evolution of state-chaebol relations, see D. S. Cho, 1992.

[100] I am particularly indebted to E. M. Kim's valuable study (1988) for the analysis of this section. See also K. T. Lee; and Moon, 1994.

[101] The following paragraphs draw on K. H. Jung, 1983; E. M. Kim, 1988; and K. D. Kim.

1960s, the Korean populace was frustrated with this political corruption and the economic stagnation resulting from big businesses' rent-seeking activities. The well-connected recipients of these windfall profits became fitting (and wealthy) targets for those seeking to replace Rhee. In August 1960, the short-lived Chang Myon regime announced a policy to clean up the "illegal and unfair profiting" of these chaebol entrepreneurs. The policy was not implemented, however, until May of the following year, less than two weeks after Park took power.

After enacting the Illicit Wealth Accumulation Law, Park immediately arrested prominent chaebol leaders and other company heads (thirty in all) and ordered them to return all profits gained through unfair and illicit activities since the signing of the Korean War truce in 1953.[102] Genuinely cowed, many of the accused agreed to pay the fines in cash or by turning over their assets to the government. Because of this submission, and also because the government quickly realized that these entrepreneurs were the only viable agents for developing the country, the Park junta backed down. In August, Park reduced the total fines by 90 percent, then cut that amount in half again in January 1962. Further, instead of being required to pay these reduced fines, some of those charged were allowed to build strategic factories (with government financing) and then donate them to the state.

In implementing this measure, Park sought to achieve several objectives. First and foremost, it was an effort to gain popular support for a regime that had come to power through military coup, not by popular mandate. Park moved swiftly to make a clean break with the corrupt and unpopular Rhee regime and its chaebol accomplices. Second, it gave Park a means to firmly establish the state in a superior position and assure the chaebol's subservience to the government and its developmental plans. Finally, it gave the Park regime control of a large amount of valuable and productive assets.

It should be noted, however, that even at this time of seeming state dominance, the chaebol hardly surrendered. These entrepreneurs exploited factionalism and disagreements within the ruling elite and utilized the proven methods of bribes and kickbacks to assure political favors. Also at this time these businessmen organized "a self-defense interest and lobbying organization" for the chaebol that would eventually be-

---

[102]Those activities designated as constituting illicit and unfair wealth included tax evasion, illegal contribution to political funds, illicit purchase of national vested properties, extraordinarily preferential monopoly of contracts for construction and supply activities, unusually large and monopolistic allocation of foreign capital, misallocation of foreign funds, and other capital illegally taken out of the country (K. D. Kim). Kim notes that the entrepreneurs arrested were primarily those who had accumulated monopoly profits dealing in the lucrative "three powders": flour, sugar, cement (E. M. Kim, 1988).

come the powerful Federation of Korean Industries, Korea's equivalent of the Japanese Keidanren.[103]

By the mid-1960s, the Park regime was firmly in place and had probably reached its "apex of unilateralism" vis-à-vis the chaebol.[104] By this time, the government had firm control over capital and other resources, had identified friendly and effective entrepreneurs, and had developed the institutional means to channel these resources to them. These state institutional means for aiding the rapid capital accumulation and growth of the chaebol are the focus of Chapters Four and Six. By far the most important subsidies came in the form of preferential interest rates on commercial bank loans and chaebol access to scarce foreign exchange and the government's own substantial development funds. The highly leveraged chaebol reaped the benefits of this risk socialization when they complied, but also experienced the costs of noncompliance in terms of called-in loans and in some cases even receivership.

### Emergency Decree for Economic Stability and Growth (1972)

By the early 1970s, the government began to show concern about the rapid expansion of the chaebol relative to the rest of the economy. At the same time, however, the Park regime launched a strategy of industrial deepening and import substitution in heavy and chemical industries (HCI), once again upon the backs of the business groups.[105] Moreover, as opposition to Park's rule increased in the latter half of the 1970s, the regime used rapid economic growth to obscure its political shortcomings. As Ku-hyun Jung concludes, the regime was "really not in a position to regulate the business groups who were the workhorses in the achievement of its economic goals."[106]

As a result, while the government's HCI promotion goals were achieved (at great cost), concurrent measures designed to correct the imbalances of overconcentration and other chaebol excesses during this period had little effect on their professed targets. The first of these measures was the President's Emergency Decree for Economic Stability and Growth announced in August 1972. The primary purpose of this decree was to improve the highly leveraged financial situation of Korean businesses by freezing loans on the informal or curb market and turning them into bank loans with considerably more favorable (state-subsidized) terms. Al-

[103]K. H. Jung, 1988, p. 77. Cheng notes the capacity that the FKI developed over and against the state to protect its interests and resolve collective action problems (T. J. Cheng, 1990).

[104]Amsden, 1989, p. 81.

[105]The best discussions of the political causes and consequences of this vertically integrated, import substitution industrialization drive is T. J. Cheng, 1990.

[106]K. H. Jung, 1988, p. 72.

though the decree was intended to assist firms of all sizes, in fact the chaebol, as the dominant borrowers, received the bulk of the benefits. In addition, some chaebol were privy to the plan and were able to take out huge amounts of curb market loans just prior to the decree and then reap windfall profits as a result. The consequence was a further concentration of the economy and a solidifying of ties between the state and the chaebol.[107]

### Legislation of 1974

A second policy package, the Special Presidential Directives of May 29, 1974, was designed to induce the tightly held chaebol and other family firms to go public in order to separate ownership and management and to limit the concentration of business assets in the hands of a few individuals or family groups. Despite an impressive package of carrots and sticks, the chaebol resisted these efforts to make them give up family ownership and control (See Chapter Four). However, the additional Measure on Bank Credit and Business Concentration, issued by the Ministry of Finance (MOF) in conjunction with the Special Presidential Directives, proved to be an effective institutional means of state control. As part of the measure, the MOF introduced a bank credit control system known as the prime bank system, in which one bank was assigned to each overindebted chaebol. This streamlined the government's ability to call in the loans of noncompliant groups, a "stick" that proved fatal for at least one chaebol, the Kukje Group. The events surrounding its toppling by the Chun regime in 1985 are recounted in Chapter Four.

Another policy implemented in 1974, in the wake of the first oil crisis, was the Act Concerning Price Stabilization and Fair Trade. Its purpose was to control prices and assure fair trade through the prevention of monopoly practices. However, of 100 cases of alleged unfair trade investigated between 1976 and 1979, not one firm was charged with undue restriction of competition. In fact, the law was used to legalize a cement cartel on four separate occasions.[108] Thus, a measure ostensibly designed to ensure free competition in fact endorsed chaebol collusion, revealing the government's pro-chaebol bias.

### Reorganization of HCI (1979)

Like the Park government it succeeded, the Chun regime suffered from a lack of legitimacy. Also like its predecessor, this regime attempted to distance itself from old policies and programs in order to overcome

[107]E. M. Kim, 1988. Eckert contends that the initiative for the decree came, in fact, not from the state but from the FKI (1991–92).
[108]K. U. Lee et al., 1986.

the legitimacy gap. For Chun, this meant promises of economic stability, increased social programs, a reduction of state intervention in the economy, and an end to preferential treatment of the chaebol. But, as with the Park government, the sociopolitical consequences of economic downturn and the temptation to use interventionist institutions already in place proved too great to lessen either the government's developmental role or the chaebol's economic dominance. The Chun regime "pursued the same agenda and tactics as the old one and forced *chaebol* in sectors characterized by overexpansion and 'excessive competition' to amalgamate, to specialize, or to exit."[109]

Although the agenda and tactics may have been the same, the balance of power had decidedly shifted to one of greater equality between the state and the chaebol. This is evident in the reorganization of the HCI announced by the Park regime in May 1979. Among other reorganization measures, this plan called for the rationalization of the electric generator industry. The Hyundai group was to take over Hyundai International Company to form one firm, and Daewoo and Samsung were ordered to merge and form the second company.

Resistance by the chaebol parties concerned, however, led to the scrapping of the plan when Chun came to power. After a summer of intense negotiations with the chaebol "deeply involved in the decision-making process," Chun announced a compromise in which Daewoo was to take over electric generator production, automobiles were to go to Hyundai, and Kia Motors was to specialize in buses and trucks.[110] However, plans to meet Daewoo's request for state financing of its rationalization efforts were ultimately canceled under pressure from the other chaebol, which saw this as unfair favoritism toward Daewoo. In a move uncharacteristic of the Korean state (though commonly employed in Taiwan), the government chose to establish a state-owned electrical generator enterprise rather than stand accused of preferential treatment. Eun Mee Kim labels this move "an especially meek compromise," given the government's preference for private enterprise and its track record of firm-level interventionism.[111]

### September 27 Action (1980)

Like its predecessor, the Chun regime fretted about the hyperleveraged financial position of the chaebol. In a move with objectives similar to Park's Presidential Directives of 1974, Chun announced measures in 1980 calling on the largest chaebol to divest a number of their subsidiar-

---

[109]Amsden, 1989, p. 108.
[110]E. M. Kim, 1988, p. 117.
[111]E. M. Kim, 1988, p. 119.

ies, limit the future expansion of new business lines, and sell nonproductive real estate, and use the proceeds to improve their capital structure. The government also abolished some trade associations suspected of collusive action, tightened supervision and restriction of bank credits provided to excessively leveraged business group firms, and strengthened and broadened the enforcement of external auditing.

Although these measures were strictly enforced during the first year of their implementation and chaebol compliance was relatively high,[112] government vigilance declined in the following years. Predictably, so did the groups' compliance. By 1985, the chaebol had sold off a total of 166 firms but had acquired 120 new ones. They auctioned off some nonproductive real estate but purchased new properties worth twenty times as much as the land sold.[113] As was the case in 1974, the effect of the presidential action was limited because of "insufficient follow-ups and supporting measures."[114] And even more so than during the 1970s, the Korean economy had grown so dependent on the chaebol that it was becoming almost impossible to curb their activities without doing irreparable harm to the economy.

### Monopoly Regulation and Fair Trade Act (1981)

Stepped-up domestic and foreign demands to liberalize the Korean political economy seemed to give the Chun government a convenient and politically popular alternative to state intervention for regulating the increasingly unpopular and incorrigible giant conglomerates. In adopting the Monopoly Regulation and Fair Trade Act (MRFTA) in September 1981, the Chun regime hoped to gain popular support and chaebol respect by disciplining the business groups as Park had in 1960, though using market competition, rather than explicit state intervention, as the means for achieving this end.[115]

Like American antitrust legislation, MRFTA makes illegal the abuse of a market-dominating position, restricts vertical and horizontal integration, prohibits collusive activities, forbids unfair trade practices, and even limits the establishment of new firms. Unlike its U.S. counterpart, however, MRFTA preserved gaping loopholes. Although it restricted horizontal and vertical integration, the act did not cover conglomeratization (mergers between firms in unrelated business lines), the typical Korean method

---

[112]Lee notes, however, that of the ninety-five firms disposed of by February 1982, thirty-two had been jettisoned prior to the policy announcement, and another twenty-six were reclassified as nonsubsidiaries but not shed (K. T. Lee).

[113]Moon, 1994.

[114]K. H. Jung, 1983, p. 73.

[115]For discussions of MRFTA, see Y. K. Lee, 1986; K. U. Lee et al., 1986; E. M. Kim, 1988; and Amsden, 1989.

of concentrating economic power. Therefore, while perhaps limiting market concentration, it did nothing to restrict the overall concentration of the Korean economy. In addition, even vertical and horizontal mergers are permitted for purposes of strengthening international competitiveness.

Given these loopholes, the chaebol remained virtually unfettered. In a 1983 study of 487 cases of new businesses founded since MRFTA, 258 (53 percent) were the result of large chaebol horizontal integration into areas in which they had no previous experience.[116] A later study of cases handled under MRFTA from 1981 through 1985 revealed similar findings. Although the number of firms designated by the government as market dominating more than doubled, from 105 to 216, during this period, only ten were actually accused of having abused their position. Of 1,172 requests for vertical or horizontal integration during this period, 1,170 were approved.[117]

In fact, these and other liberalization efforts the Chun government initiated actually opened the way for the chaebol to increase their economic clout and financial autonomy. Freeing the market has not leveled the playing field. "Liberalization," Amsden concludes, "therefore, contributed to a rise, not to a decline, in economic concentration. Nor should this have been unexpected. It is difficult to achieve equity through market forces in the presence of large agglomerations of economic power."[118]

The growing economic power of the chaebol during the 1980s should not, however, be overestimated. Bureaucratic dominance held through much of the 1980s, but dependence was, nonetheless, mutual. Like its predecessor, the Chun regime relied on the chaebol to implement industrial transformation, the basis of the regime's legitimacy. Policymaking in "Korea, Inc." was characterized by "close consultation between the highest ranking state officials and top business leaders through both interpersonal links and formalized channels and by consultation between responsible state agencies and state sponsored industrial associations."[119] These channels included Japanese-style deliberation councils and discussion groups, extensive informal administrative guidance, and descents from bureaucratic heaven into the chaebol corporate boardrooms.[120]

[116]As cited by E. M. Kim, 1988, p. 116.
[117]As cited by Lee et al., 1986, pp. 17–18.
[118]Amsden, 1989, p. 136. See also Moon, 1994.
[119]Y. H. Chu, 1989, p. 654.
[120]This "special recruitment" (*tuk chae*) of high-ranking military officers and civil servants, like its Japanese (*amakudari*) and French (*pantouflage*) counterparts, provides an important source of executives (Kim and Kim; C. S. Chang). A 1984 study of the top twenty chaebol found 31 percent of executive officers were family members, 29 percent were professional managers promoted from within, and 40 percent were recruited from the outside. A "large portion" of this latter category were former high-ranking officials or retired gener-

Chung H. Lee calls this "intimate" relationship a "quasi-internal organization" that allowed a more direct exchange of information than was possible through market channels.[121] Dense and mutualist in nature, these institutions and intermediate organizations functioned not so much as mechanisms of interest representation as the bureaucracy's "liaison" to the private sector and as "transmission belts" for implementing state policies.[122]

Moreover, the government still had the means and, on occasion, the will to humble even the biggest chaebol. In 1985, the Chun government brought down and dismantled the Kukje group, then the country's sixth largest. This and other rationalization measures—most prominently in shipping and construction—demonstrated that the Chun regime was far from willing to abdicate its developmental role. But decisions counter to the interests of the chaebol became increasingly difficult to make stick, despite the developmental predilections and institutional means of economic policymakers. As one observer noted in 1985, "the largest business groups are now so big that, though the government still has the power to pull the financial rug out from under their feet, it dare not risk doing so. However, on an intellectual level, given the centralized, top-down system of authority traditional to South Korea, accepting such a change in thinking at the top will be a long time coming."[123]

### Democratization and State-Chaebol Relations

The democratically elected Roh and Kim governments have had to deal with an additional challenge to the state's former dominance. In addition to chaebol interests, the Sixth and Seventh Republics have been compelled to take into consideration the wishes of a vocal and increasingly powerful popular constituency. This has undercut both state autonomy and capacity and has therefore shaped motivation. Though proud of the chaebol's international stature and prowess, the Korean populace has grown more and more dissatisfied with these "economic monsters." Press exposés since 1983, National Assembly debates since 1985, and sensational trials since 1987 have revealed oppressive labor and subcontracting relations, speculative real estate and financial activities, and corrupt linkages between the chaebol and the state. But even as these governments have felt increasing pressure to rein in the chaebol, the economy has grown ever more dependent on their continued success.

---

als, hired not for their managerial skills but for their personal and political influence (Yoo and Lee). According to one estimate, some 20 percent of the Daewoo group's senior management was recruited from the military (R. Shin).

[121]C. H. Lee, p. 189.

[122]Y. H. Chu, 1989, p. 654.

[123]*Far Eastern Economic Review,* 12/12/85.

Faced with these opposing demands, the Roh government entered into the same cycle of chaebol bashing and boosting that marked the two prior regimes. Roh attempted to reform the chaebol by ending preferential credits for exporting financing, reducing access to cheap funds for capital investment, strengthening the MRFTA, forcing the repayment of excessive bank borrowings, and restricting cross-shareholdings and investments in subsidiaries. Although the Roh government achieved some success in limiting cross-holdings among group affiliates,[124] it had more difficulty gaining the compliance of the chaebol in other areas. Two measures exemplify this ambiguous relationship and shifting balance of power.

In May 1990, the Roh government announced measures requiring forty-nine separate chaebol to sell by year's end huge holdings of real estate that the government claimed were being held for speculative purposes, or face punitive tax penalties and a severance of new loans. The government hoped proceeds from these sales would be plowed into the tumbling stock market or invested in research and development. Ten chaebol, including the five largest, pledged to comply with the order. By September, however, noncompliance forced the government to reissue the warning with new threats of punitive measures. Indicative of the government's declining clout was the extension of the deadline to March 1991 and substantial reduction of the tax penalties. In May, the government announced new loans would be halted to the twenty-two chaebol still not complying if they did not follow the government's order to sell off their nonproductive real estate holdings. The deadline came and went with eight of these groups still not complying despite the government's extensive cajoling.[125]

That same spring, the government issued a policy calling on each of the thirty largest chaebol to select three core areas in which it would like to specialize. Using a combination of both carrots and sticks, the Roh regime announced that borrowing constraints imposed earlier on the top fifty chaebol would now apply only to the top thirty groups. Further, these top thirty groups would have borrowing limits only on ventures outside of the three core areas in which they were to specialize. These core companies would be free to borrow as much as lending institutions were willing to lend.

Although it was designed to rein in the broadly diversified groups and enhance their global competitiveness in key sectors, this specialization policy has been used by the chaebol to channel funds into the most heavily leveraged firms and those unable to find credit elsewhere. Twelve of the top thirty groups have selected petrochemicals as one of their core

---

[124]*Far Eastern Economic Review,* 6/13/91, 10/10/91.
[125]*Asian Wall Street Journal,* 5/14/90, 5/6/91; *Far Eastern Economic Review,* 5/16/91.

areas because of its capital-intensive nature, raising government concerns of excess capacity. As with earlier policies, the chaebol have been reluctant to comply fully. While willingly snatching the carrot of unconstrained borrowing in the three core units, few of the groups have shown a willingness to shed companies outside the designated areas of specialization. The Samsung group sold its department store, a hotel, and paper company (all to family members), but then acquired a brokerage firm and a detergent manufacturer, and is planning to set up a chain of clothing boutiques.[126] In a more promising response, Hyundai announced in June 1993 that it would comply with the Kim government's policy of "reducing the equity ownership of a business group by a family" by separating its insurance company and two other subsidiaries from the group. Again, most observers see Hyundai founder Chung Ju-yung's move not as dutiful compliance with the original policy but as either an attempt to restructure the group in preparation for a post-Chung succession or a gesture of reconciliation by Chung toward the new Kim administration in the wake of Chung's failed bid for the presidency.[127]

Chung's foray into politics, his fierce attack on the government and his bitter denunciation of Kim Young Sam provide a "dramatic illustration of the deteriorating relationship between the corporate sector and the state."[128] In late 1991, the Office of National Tax Administration (ONTA) charged Hyundai with a record U.S.$172 million in back inheritance taxes and penalties.[129] Rather than pay the fees or negotiate a compromise, Chung defied the ONTA directive and went on the counteroffensive, forming his own maverick party (Unification National Party) in 1992. After modest success in National Assembly elections that spring, Chung finished a distant third in the December presidential election.

Throughout the campaign, the government never relented. Numerous Hyundai executives (including one of Chung's sons) were arrested and jailed on charges ranging from tax evasion and embezzlement to the violation of pollution laws. After his defeat, Chung retired from politics and negotiated a settlement with the new administration. But in November 1993, a Korean court sentenced him to three years in prison for illegally diverting over U.S.$60 million from the Hyundai group to his election campaign. At this writing, Chung was preparing to appeal the decision to

[126]*Asian Wall Street Journal*, 5/6/91, 5/27/91, 11/11/91; *Far Eastern Economic Review*, 5/16/91, 6/13/91, 10/10/91, 5/13/93.

[127]*Business Korea*, 6/93.

[128]Moon, 1994.

[129]Park established ONTA in 1966 and gave it the authority to subject firms guilty of tax evasion (virtually all Korean companies) to the payment of additional taxes and penalties, as well as criminal prosecution. Termed by one observer "the ultimate control agency of the government," it has been used by each successive regime as a highly effective means of humbling the chaebol (Eckert, 1990–91, p. 123).

Korea's Supreme Court.[130] As Chung-in Moon concludes, this episode, however it is ultimately resolved, signals, more than any other single event, the changing nature of relations between the chaebol and the state.[131]

Like his predecessors, Kim Young Sam was elected with a mandate to curtail the expanding tentacles of big business. But with an economy overwhelmingly dependent on the chaebol for both output and employment, and a conservative political coalition still reliant on big business for political support, even the Kim regime will find it difficult to turn either its back or an iron fist toward the chaebol.

The growing economic and political power of the chaebol, combined with the democratization of Korean society, has had a profound impact on the developmental coalition initially forged by Park. The hegemonic pact between state and business that created these industrial combines has unleashed new social forces that have in turn created a new environment filled with labor unions, opposition parties, and other distributional coalitions.[132]

But institutional arrangements, once in place, do not easily or quickly pass. Despite the chaebol's Frankenstein's monster image, government and popular ambivalence toward them will undoubtedly continue as long as the Korean economy remains dependent on the groups and economic success remains important to Korean nationalists. Moreover, neither economic nor political liberalization will curb the economic dominance of the chaebol in the near future. Democratization, however, will irrevocably change the institutional environment in which the chaebol are embedded. As Eckert concludes, "the great steel headquarters of corporate Korea" now rest on a growing "seismic fault of social disaffection."[133]

Although historical and political factors have made this evolving relationship from "dominance to symbiosis,"[134] and now to increasing antagonism between the state and the business groups in Korea, unique, it is not without parallel. Writing of an earlier "late developer" in which banks played the developmental role assumed by the state in Korea, Alexander Gerschenkron observed that "the specific features engendered by a process of industrialization in conditions of backwardness were to remain, and so was the close relation between banks and industry, even

---

[130]*Far Eastern Economic Review*, 11/28/91, 1/30/92, 4/9/92, 4/23/92, 5/27/92, 12/17/92, 1/14/93; *Business Korea*, 2/92, 5/92, 6/93; *New York Times*, 11/2/93.

[131]Moon, 1994.

[132]For discussions of the impact of democratization on the chaebol and the Korean developmental state, see Hamilton and Kim; and Cheng and Kim, 1994.

[133]Eckert, 1990–91, p. 148.

[134]See E. M. Kim, 1988.

though the master-servant relation gave way to cooperation among equals and sometimes was even reversed."[135] Neoclassical apologists seeking in Korea confirmation of their laissez-faire tenets would do well to take heed of these "conditions of backwardness" and their consequences for Korean capitalist development. Chapter Three will demonstrate, in fact, that although the political actors were similar in Taiwan, situational motivations were substantially different. These differences led to a very different relationship between the state and business groups in Taiwan and a very different developmental path for Taiwan's groups.

[135]Gerschenkron, p. 21.

CHAPTER THREE

# Guanxiqiye and the State in Taiwan

This chapter examines the emergence and development of Taiwan's "related enterprise groups" or *guanxiqiye* (gwon-shee-chee-yeh) in order to account for their variance from the Korean chaebol. Amending previous studies of Taiwan's enterprise organization that have focused primarily on market or cultural factors,[1] in this chapter I give full causal weight to the role of the state. Taiwan's Nationalist state—though more constrained in its economic intervention than its Korean counterpart—has exerted substantial and causally significant influence on the formation and development of Taiwan's embedded enterprises.

In Taiwan, regime ideology, particular historical legacies, and the political necessities of a transplanted minority regime led the Nationalist state to adopt a developmental strategy and create political and economic institutions markedly different from those of Korea. These state policies and institutions have had a profound impact on private capital, greatly restricting the scale, concentration, and influence (both economic and political) of the guanxiqiye. Amsden asserts that the relatively small size of Taiwan's diversified business groups "seems to have less to do with the natural functionings of the market mechanism than with government intervention that prevented them from growing larger."[2] This (and subsequent) chapters confirm her assertion.

Taiwan's developmental state has been at least as autonomous and nearly as capable as Korea's. Ironically, the same ideological predispositions and situational imperatives inspiring the regime to limit private capital have made it less willing to exert its will on the private business sector.

[1] See, for example, Galenson; Silin; and Redding.
[2] See Amsden, 1992, p. 81. See also Amsden, 1991.

This less aggressive policy has created an environment in which rational market incentives and traditional sociocultural norms and institutions have exerted great influence in shaping the development and organization of the guanxiqiye. The government has not hesitated to intervene, however, when cultural proclivities or economic aspirations challenged the regime goals of political control, economic stability, and relatively equitable income distribution.

Compared with the chaebol, Taiwan's guanxiqiye bear less the imprint of the state and more that of cultural and market forces. The economic limitations of this more conservative developmental policy have led to conflicts over appropriate policy both within the state and between the state and the business groups. The democratic and demographic changes now sweeping Taiwan have heightened these conflicts, undercut the internal coherence and autonomy of the state, and further weakened the state's capacity and will to curtail the natural market growth of the business groups.

The guanxiqiye are not as central to Taiwan's domestic economy as the chaebol are to Korea's. It is misleading, however, to characterize Taiwan as an atomized, penny-ante capitalist economy. Taiwan's export-oriented economy depends on its small and medium-sized commercial and industrial firms. Enterprises employing fewer than 300 workers accounted for 70 percent of the work force and 60 percent of the nation's exports in 1990.[3] This dynamic downstream sector is, however, utterly dependent on large-scale upstream suppliers of raw and intermediate materials, and in many cases, of technology and finance.[4] Although state-owned enterprises and transnational corporations loom large in this upstream sector, Taiwan's medium-sized private business groups are nonetheless important players in the domestic and international marketplace.[5]

As of 1988, sales of the top 100 guanxiqiye accounted for 34 percent of Taiwan's total GNP.[6] In 1991, Taiwan's top ten groups had combined annual revenues of nearly U.S.$31 billion, representing just over 10 percent of GNP (see Table 3-1).

Of Taiwan's fifty largest private enterprises in 1981, forty were affiliated with guanxiqiye. Seventeen of these largest firms were related to seven groups, while the other twenty-three were each controlled by a separate

---

[3] *Economic News*, 12/24/90.

[4] Wade, 1990; Amsden, 1991.

[5] It is misleading, for instance, to compare, as Gereffi (1990) does, the Korean chaebol with individual firms from Taiwan. Measured as business groups, Taiwan's top four private guanxiqiye (see Table 3-1) would all have made *Fortune* magazine's 1992 "Global 500" (along with state-owned China Petroleum and twelve Korean groups/firms) (*Fortune*, 7/27/92).

[6] CCIS, 1991. Although this figure of 34 percent represents little increase over the past decade (see Table 3-2), the informal nature of linkages among many guanxiqiye firms, their dispersed investment strategy, and their extensive gray market operations tend to understate both their size and their influence on the economy (Chou; Leff, 1978; Numazaki, 1986).

*Table 3-1.* Taiwan's top ten guanxiqiye in 1991
(U.S.$ millions)

| Guanxiqiye | Sales | Assets | Employees |
|---|---|---|---|
| Formosa Plastics | $6,687 | $9,529 | $45,548 |
| China Trust | 3,228 | 12,191 | 14,008 |
| Linden International | 5,638 | 12,109 | 33,015 |
| Shin Kong | 3,511 | 7,263 | 30,950 |
| Far Eastern | 2,475 | 5,890 | 15,884 |
| Hualon | 2,458 | 3,913 | 17,459 |
| Evergreen | 1,849 | 3,638 | 7,053 |
| Yue Loong Motor | 2,580 | 1,946 | 10,693 |
| Yuen Foong Yu | 1,464 | 6,170 | 5,781 |
| Overseas Trust | 818 | 11,395 | 1,613 |
| Total | $30,708 | $74,044 | $182,004 |
| Percent of GNP | 17% | 41% | |
| Percent of total work force | | | 12.6% |

SOURCE: *Juoyue* [Excellence], 9/92.

business group. Of the ten nonaffiliated firms in the top fifty, six were joint ventures with foreign firms, leaving only four of Taiwan's fifty largest private firms independent.[7] In 1992, Taiwan's 1,000 biggest private firms accounted for 25 percent of aggregate capital and 6.5 percent of the total work force. The top ten firms accounted for nearly 40 percent of earnings in their respective sectors.[8]

The regime controls much of the commanding heights of the economy, however; and if its looming state- and party-owned enterprise networks are included, Taiwan's level of industrial concentration is substantial indeed. In fact, from the 1950s to the 1970s, the share of value added by firms employing more than 500 workers was greater in Taiwan than in Korea.[9] Despite recent privatization, sixty state-owned enterprises accounted for 15 percent of aggregate capital in 1992 and the Nationalist Party controlled enterprises with an estimated value in 1993 of U.S.$4.5 billion.[10] A 1992 survey ranked the Nationalist Party enterprise system as Taiwan's sixth largest "private" guanxiqiye.[11]

---

[7]Chou. Some large enterprises in Taiwan, however, remain single-unit operations with no connections to the guanxiqiye. Hamilton and Kao note that of the 500 largest manufacturing firms in Taiwan, only about 40 percent are formally affiliated with groups (p. 22). However, this figure, as explained in note 6, is likely understated.

[8]*Free China Journal*, 6/8/93.

[9]Amsden, 1991.

[10]The figures for the state-owned enterprises are from *Free China Journal*, 6/8/93, and for the party-owned enterprises, from *Time*, 8/23/93. Some estimates are even higher. A 1990 study produced by scholars sympathetic to the opposition Democratic Progressive Party valued state-owned assets at eight times that of the top 500 firms in 1988 and estimated the combined revenues of state- and party-owned enterprises that year at nearly U.S.$80 billion, fully 30 percent of GNP (*Economic News*, 5/21/90).

[11]*Juoyue*, 9/92.

In this chapter I will (1) describe the development and current status of the guanxiqiye, noting their entrepreneurial responses to the particular economic environment they face; (2) examine their distinctive familial organizational features; and (3) discuss their relationship with the Nationalist state on Taiwan and the influence of the state on the groups' development. As was the case in our examination of the chaebol in Chapter Two, it is only through such a comprehensive study of the nexus of rational market responses, persistent sociocultural norms, and state industrial policies that a clear picture emerges of the developmental experience of Taiwan's embedded enterprise groups.

## GUANXIQIYE AND THE ECONOMY

The Chinese term used most commonly to refer to business groups in Taiwan is neither the Chinese pronunciation of the ideographs for chaebol or zaibatsu (rendered as *caifa* in Chinese), nor the literal translation of "business group" used to refer to contemporary groups in Japan (*kigyoshudan*, rendered as *qiyejituan* in Chinese). Rather, the expression most often adopted by the groups and those studying them in Taiwan is "related enterprise," *guanxiqiye*. This term, in common usage in Chinese societies since the nineteenth century, was applied originally to the traditional "chain" (*lianhao*) markets of northern China.[12] *Guanxi* is an important Chinese word and concept referring to particularistic connections between persons that are based on some common or shared identification.[13] Ichiro Numazaki defines the guanxiqiye as a "cluster of enterprises owned and controlled by a group of persons tied by a network of various guanxi."[14]

Because Taiwan's business groups—like their Korean counterparts—have no legal status, they have no legal definition. Although there has been heated debate in Taiwan's legal and scholarly circles over exactly what comprises a "related enterprise" or business group and how it should be defined, the definition used by the China Credit Information Service (CCIS), which publishes a biennial survey of the 100 largest groups, has been adopted as the standard by most recent studies. The business groups encompassed within their definition and survey are generally the focus of this and subsequent chapters.[15]

---

[12]Liu et al.

[13]Numazaki, 1991.

[14]Numazaki, 1991.

[15]For discussions of this debate and its legal and economic consequences, see Z. Chu; and *Economic News*, 9/4/77. For a dissenting opinion on the acceptance of the CCIS definition, see Numazaki, 1987; 1991.

In its survey titled *Business Groups in Taiwan,* CCIS defines a business group (qiyejituan) as a cluster of three or more firms meeting the following requirements: (1) total assets and total sales must each exceed N.T.$400 million (approximately U.S.$16 million) or must combine for a total of N.T.$1 billion (approximately U.S.$40 million); (2) one person, a group of persons, or one of the firms must control or significantly influence the other firms in the group; and (3) all firms must acknowledge their common membership in the group.[16]

The CCIS survey distinguishes three different patterns of interlocking relationships among intragroup firms. Not surprisingly, given the familial nature of Taiwan's industrial organization, the authors of the survey use kinship expressions to identify these three basic models: (1) sibling model, where key investors or partners jointly form a number of companies that are operated cooperatively because of the investors' or family members' personal or "sibling" relationships; (2) parent-child model, where key investors establish a company that invests in a new company or companies in a core-subsidiary relationship; and (3) marriage model, where key investors jointly or singly found a number of companies and choose to cross-invest in the companies because of close personal relations.[17]

Although some vertical and horizontal integration does occur, conglomerate diversification into unrelated markets is the rule for the guanxiqiye. Though the chaebol also are highly diversified, this conglomeration is particularly remarkable in Taiwan because of the smaller size and number of firms in the groups. Even though the top 100 guanxiqiye averaged only 7.76 firms in 1983 (8.32 firms in 1988, compared with an average of over 20 firms per chaebol in 1992), Gary Hamilton, Marco Orru, and Nicole Biggart note that these few firms were spread across an average of four different industrial sectors. Rather than "vertically-integrated, tightly-controlled sets of firms," the guanxiqiye are "agglomerations of different-sized firms, mostly small, in different economic sectors."[18] To understand the reasons behind this organizational form and other differences between the guanxiqiye and the chaebol, we turn to the economic, sociocultural, and political factors shaping the development of the guanxiqiye.

## ORIGIN AND DEVELOPMENT

Like Korea, Taiwan was introduced to modern capitalism and capitalist development by imperial Japan, which acquired Taiwan as war booty in

[16]CCIS, 1991, p. 29.
[17]CCIS, 1983, p. 5.
[18]Hamilton et al., 1987, p. 97.

67

its victory over China in the Sino-Japanese War of 1894–95. Taiwan was Japan's first, and arguably its most, successful colonial venture. The Meji government's motives in colonizing Taiwan were to show the West that Japan deserved to be considered an equal and to support its overriding political goal of *fukoku kyoohei* (rich country, strong arm). But although the Japanese developed Taiwan as a means to other ends, they nonetheless undertook a variety of projects to build the physical, institutional, and human infrastructure on the island, laying a solid foundation for Taiwan's subsequent development.

Even more than the Confucian culture that Korea and Taiwan shared, Japan's "administrative and coercive colonialism" tended to homogenize these two nations, according to Bruce Cumings, taking "two quite different societies and political economies and molding them into look-alikes."[19] One should, however, beware such overgeneralization. The absence in Taiwan of a powerful landed gentry comparable with the Korean *yangban* and Japan's fostering of a class of indigenous progressive and entrepreneurial smallholders (*xiaozuhu*) in Taiwan had significant consequences for the economic and sociopolitical development of Taiwan during both Japanese and Nationalist Chinese rule. Cumings admits that what "could be done with economic incentives in Taiwan required coercion in Korea."[20]

Despite these nascent entrepreneurial impulses and some commercial opportunities, the Japanese prevented all but a few Taiwanese collaborators from participating in the modern industrial and financial sectors. Both legal restrictions and the sheer dominance of Japan's zaibatsu served as formidable obstacles to all but a handful of local entrepreneurs, with Japanese nationals holding 91 percent of industrial capital in 1929.[21] As in Korea, collaboration was the only avenue open to aspiring native entrepreneurs. Thomas Gold identifies five major Taiwanese family lines that benefited from varying degrees of collaboration with the Japanese.[22] Relying primarily on their traditional sources of capital and expertise, these few families were able to penetrate a number of modern industrial sectors, including mining, manufacturing, and banking. As Japan shifted to a war footing during the 1930s, however, the colonizers "forcibly merged most of the industrial concerns owned by Taiwanese into Japanese-owned enterprises"; they held approximately 95 percent of industrial capital by 1941. By the time of Japan's defeat in 1945, the "former Taiwanese bourgeoisie was devoid of industrial assets."[23]

[19]Cumings, p. 54.
[20]Cumings, p. 54.
[21]Grajdanzev.
[22]Gold, 1986, p. 66.
[23]The statistic is from Grajdanzev. The quotations are from Gold, 1981, p. 76.

Numazaki identifies three types of private entrepreneurs who emerged in Taiwan after its retrocession to Nationalist-controlled China.[24] The first group included those "refugee capitalists" who followed the Nationalists to Taiwan and brought with them their capital equipment and industrial experience, primarily in textiles and food processing. These entrepreneurs benefited substantially from their natural affinities and concrete "connections" with the transplanted Nationalist regime charged with administering U.S. AID funds and material. A second group included a small number of Taiwanese former landowners who had accumulated shares in the former Japanese enterprises privatized by the Nationalists. As part of the "land to the tiller" program of land reform, landholders were compelled to sell holdings in excess of seven acres to the government in exchange for a combination of land bonds in kind (rice for paddy land, sweet potatoes for dry land) and stocks in former Japanese enterprises. Not surprisingly, the biggest beneficiaries in this category were the Japanese-era collaborators who were also the largest landowners.[25] A final group consisted of "Taiwanese traders, petty bourgeoisie and peasants" able to acquire Nationalist or U.S. AID assistance or to rely on Japanese or overseas Chinese linkages for financing and expertise.[26]

From these three groups emerged the dynamic entrepreneurs who established and expanded Taiwan's guanxiqiye. Though handicapped initially by their lack of access to the Nationalist regime and persistent Nationalist suspicions of their political aspirations, ethnic Taiwanese have increasingly come to dominate the private big-business sector (as well as the overwhelming majority of small and medium-sized firms). Table 3-2 shows that six of the seven largest business groups and seven of the top ten groups in 1988 were in Taiwanese hands.[27]

At a time of unprecedented free trade and global economic expansion, these groups grew upward and outward, keeping pace with Taiwan's export led-development and industrial expansion during the 1960s and 1970s. In tracing the historical evolution of the guanxiqiye, we may divide their developmental course into four stages.[28]

[24]Numazaki, 1986. The public sector bureaucrat-entrepreneurs who came with the Nationalist regime to Taiwan in the late 1940s were a fourth group.

[25]Gold, 1988.

[26]Numazaki, 1986, p. 491.

[27]Although Table 3-2 appears to indicate little stability over time in the top ten guanxiqiye, the significant linkages among a number of the groups make these nominal changes over time somewhat misleading. For example, the Hualon group (1975) was closely linked to the Pacific Companies (1981) (see Chapter Seven). China Trust group (1985) is chaired by Jeffrey Koo, but the dominant figure is his uncle, C. F. Koo, patriarch of the Taiwan Cement group. In contrast with Korea, these intergroup linkages, both familial and nonfamilial, are quite common in Taiwan (Numazaki, 1987).

[28]For a comparable division, see Z. Chu, 1982.

Table 3-2. Top ten guanxiqiye in various years and their subethnic identification (measured in assets)

| 1975 | 1981 | 1985 | 1988 |
|---|---|---|---|
| Formosa Plastics (T) | Formosa Plastics (T) | Formosa Plastics (T) | Formosa Plastics (T) |
| Hualon (T/M) | Cathay Trust (T) | China Trust (T) | Linden International (T) |
| Far Eastern (M) | Far Eastern (M) | Linden International (T) | Shin Kong (T) |
| Xiao Brothers | Tainan Spinning (T) | Shin Kong (T) | China Trust (T) |
| Yue Loong Motor (M) | Tatung (T) | Far Eastern (M) | Far Eastern (M) |
| Tatung (T) | Shin Kong (T) | Tainan Spinning (T) | Hualon (T/M) |
| Rong Shing | Yue Loong Motor (M) | Tatung (T) | Tatung (T) |
| Tainan Spinning (T) | Linden International (T) | Yue Loong Motor (M) | Yue Loong Motor (M) |
| Shin Kong (T) | Taiwan Cement (T) | Overseas Trust (F) | Tuntex (T) |
| Chao Ting Chen (M) | Pacific Companies (M) | Chung Hsing (M) | Chung Hsing (M) |

SOURCES: *Commercial Times*, 4/1/85; CCIS, 1991.
KEY: T = Taiwanese, M = Mainlander, F = Chinese Filipino.

*Formative stage (1951–60).* During this period, Taiwan's economy was centered on agriculture and, with the exception of government enterprises, industrial and commercial firms were small in scale. The predominant industries during this period were import-substitution ventures in textiles, building materials, and chemicals. Most of Taiwan's big entrepreneurs got their start at this time, often with U.S. AID or other government assistance, and began to found "related enterprises" through horizontal mergers or cross-investment.[29]

*Growth Stage (1961–73).* With the shift from import-substitution to export-led industrialization, Taiwan's domestic economy prospered and private local industrial and commercial firms grew rapidly. The predominant industries during this period were textiles, building materials, food products, hardware, and plastic processing. During this period, virtually all successful industrialists adopted strategies of diversification and Taiwan's guanxiqiye flourished. By the 1970s, a cohort of Taiwanese and Mainlander groups began to emerge that continues to dominate Taiwan's private industrial sector (see Table 3-2). The Nationalist government restricted the growth of the groups during this period by limiting the amount of capital one company could invest in another and retaining state ownership of all commercial banks and other formal financial insti-

[29]Mark, 1982.

tutions. In addition, state- and Nationalist Party-owned enterprises continued to control the commanding heights of most industrial sectors.

*Retrenchment Stage (1974–81).* Following the shocks of oil price hikes, domestic inflation, and world recession, Taiwan's domestic industrial growth slowed to a standstill during the late 1970s. In order to enhance domestic firms' stability and international competitiveness, the government began to encourage mergers, increase the permissible amount of cross-investment, and allow private firms to establish insurance and trust companies as alternative sources of finance. Most sectors were sluggish during this period, though certain guanxiqiye in the plastics and construction industries fared well. The groups strengthened their structure during this period through retrenchment, initiating mergers among some of their member companies, and dissolving others. Other enterprises re-formed themselves as new guanxiqiye. Table 3-3 shows that during this period the guanxiqiye barely kept pace with Taiwan's overall growth, in stark contrast to the Korean experience of increasing chaebol growth and dominance.

*Internationalization Stage (1982–).* The international and domestic economic recovery of the 1980s, coupled with the Nationalist regime's liberalization of financial and trade policies, has given the guanxiqiye unprecedented opportunities for expansion. The government has encouraged joint ventures with foreign firms, attempted to engineer the merger of domestic firms, and sponsored the development of private trading companies (see Chapter Seven). Nevertheless, the guanxiqiye have grown at a snail's pace compared with their Korean counterparts during this period and more slowly than natural market growth would predict.[30] To understand why this has been the case, we must examine the institutions in which the guanxiqiye are embedded.

*Table 3-3.* Assets, net worth, and sales of top 100 guanxiqiye as percentage of GNP, 1975–88 (%)

| Year | Assets | Net worth | Sales |
| --- | --- | --- | --- |
| 1975 | 44.2 | 14.3 | 29.5 |
| 1977 | 36.4 | 12.3 | 29.1 |
| 1979 | 35.6 | 12.1 | 32.8 |
| 1981 | 35.3 | 11.2 | 30.0 |
| 1983 | 39.5 | 11.2 | 31.7 |
| 1986 | 33.4 | 10.9 | 30.3 |
| 1988 | 39.0 | 15.5 | 34.0 |

SOURCE: Compiled from CCIS, 1991.

NOTE: For the years 1983 and 1986, percentages are calculated on the average of 100 groups, although the CCIS study is based on ninety-six and ninety-seven groups, respectively, for those years.

[30]Chou, 1986.

## GUANXIQIYE AND SOCIOCULTURAL NORMS AND INSTITUTIONS

Just as the goals of Taiwan's developmental state are more complex than simply economic development, so the motivations of Taiwan's familial business groups are more complex than simply turning a profit or insuring continued growth. Given the state incentive structure, much seemingly irrational corporate activity is in fact economically rational. Onerous and progressive business taxes inspire a variety of creative tax evasions. Strict limits on formal sources of capital often make seeking funds at higher rates and higher risk on the informal market the only alternative. Nonetheless, some corporate activity is at odds not only with state regulations but with profit maximization as well. To seek an explanation for this behavior, it is necessary to examine the sociocultural norms and institutions structuring the environment in which the groups are embedded.

As in Korea, though with somewhat different consequences, in Taiwan the most important normative institution influencing the organization and activities of the guanxiqiye is the family. In his study of large-scale enterprise in Taiwan, Robert Silin argues that kinship, or the family relationship, is the only coherent set of organizing principles for governing interpersonal relations within the Confucian conceptual system.[31] This framework is still largely operational in Taiwan, and family or kin relationships offer the basic model on which society is organized and profoundly influence the organization of Taiwan's businesses.[32]

These kinship ties provide an "institutional medium" for trust and reciprocity among family members engaged in business.[33] Kwang-kuo Hwang points out that although economic and social exchange between strangers in a Chinese society is typically arms-length, instrumental, and maximizing, this is seldom the case in "expressive" or kinship relations. Hwang also notes a third or "mixed" tie governing exchange that combines instrumental and affective features, thus providing a means of extending trust and reciprocity beyond immediate family ties.[34] These connections of kinship and other shared attributes allow the creation of "guanxi networks" that become the building blocks of the guanxiqiye.[35]

In creating these "guanxi networks," family ties of blood and marriage are by far the most important. The dominance of this familial norm leads entrepreneurs often to distrust, or to use Silin's word, "non-trust," extrafamilial collectivities and to question the prospects for the success of ac-

[31] Silin.
[32] Greenhalgh.
[33] Hamilton, 1991.
[34] K. K. Hwang.
[35] Numazaki, 1991.

tion requiring sustained cooperative behavior beyond the circle of the family and a few close friends. The guanxiqiye are therefore typically formed around highly cohesive cliques of family members to ensure trust and facilitate cooperation.[36] But beyond kinship, shared ascriptive attributes such as the same native place (*tongxiang*), same surname (*tongzong*), and even same birth year (*tongnian*) can substitute for kinship not just in the provision of trusted managers, as in Korea, but also in sources of capital and the creation of business networks.[37]

The further one moves away from the immediate family, however, the more tenuous and temporary are the connections. Silin argues that these suprafamilial "cooperative groups" are "understood primarily as temporary coalitions rather than permanent alliances."[38] However tentative it may be, this horizontal "web of partnerships" that extends beyond and in fact overlaps the formal boundaries of the guanxiqiye clearly distinguishes the Taiwan groups from the chaebol with their more distinct boundaries and more institutionalized command structures.[39]

Because authority structures are less formal, the Confucian patriarchs who preside over the guanxiqiye feel compelled personally to oversee as much of the day-to-day decision making as possible. In order to maintain their superior status, they are hesitant to delegate any authority (especially beyond the family) and typically make all major and many minor decisions involving firms in the group. As the scale of the enterprise expands, "increasingly larger portions of the leader's time are spent in the routine administrative work that in other societies might be delegated to subordinates."[40] Unlike the chaebol owners, these Chinese bosses are hesitant to delegate even routine decision-making responsibility, thus limiting both the efficient operation of the guanxiqiye and incentive for further expansion.

To the extent that they are delegated, management control and ownership of the guanxiqiye are generally shared by a common directorship linked by personal, generally familial networks. In his study of thirty-seven Taiwanese business groups based on 1972 data, Numazaki identified four types of personal relationships that formed the basis of the groups: immediate family, descendants, marriage alliances, and native-place alliances.[41] The first three have obvious family relations, and there is evidence in that

[36]Silin.
[37]Numazaki, 1991; Hamilton, 1991. An even broader network of ethnic affinity among overseas Chinese has provided an important source of noncontractual trust and impetus for group formation in Southeast Asia and elsewhere. See Landa; Granovetter, 1994.
[38]Silin, p. 128.
[39]Numazaki, 1991.
[40]Silin, p. 131. See also Mark, 1972.
[41]Numazaki, 1986, pp. 501–4.

the Chinese setting, even the native-place alliance can be considered a familial tie.[42]

Using 1983 data, Gary Hamilton and Kao Cheng-shu found that a single individual or two or more close relatives owned sixty-three of the top ninety-six business groups. Of the remaining thirty-three, thirty-one were owned by "two or more individuals who in a Western legal sense would be considered partners, but . . . are included in what the participants regard as family relationships."[43] Because most guanxiqiye are owned and controlled by members of a single, albeit often extended, family, the patriarch in most cases is the top decision maker. The latter, or those within his inner circle,[44] holds virtually all significant management positions, with the family patriarch serving as chairman (*dongshizhang*) of all or most of the member companies.[45]

This family dominance of management and ownership is apparent even in Taiwan's largest and one of its most progressive guanxiqiye, the Formosa Plastics group (FPG), founded by the Taiwanese tycoon Wang Yongqing.[46] Although FPG is famous in Taiwan for its modern management techniques and its merit system of hiring and promotion, the "main artery" of group management is still the family, and "the figure entrusted with the final decision-making authority within the group is without a doubt its founder."[47] Wang or his brother Wang Yongzai was either president or general manager of all but six minor firms within the group's stable of sixteen firms in 1986. They held both positions in FPG's three premier firms, which are also the three largest private firms in Taiwan.[48] The Wang brothers have a combined total of seventeen children, and all of the sons and either the daughters or their husbands are either in significant management positions within the group or still in school (typically in Japan, the United States, or Europe), preparing for such positions.

Only four group firms are listed on Taiwan's stock exchange, and the majority of all stock in group firms is under Wang family control. Takao

[42]Wong. Hamilton (1991) cites Fei Xiaotong, who contends that forging alliances based on regional origins is in fact an extension of kinship ties.

[43]Hamilton and Kao, p. 12.

[44]This "inner circle," according to Hamilton and Kao, "consists of those few key people with whom the owner feels the greatest degree of trust and confidence"—ordinarily the owners, a few close family members, and possibly long-time business associates or even a mistress (p. 18). See also Silin.

[45]CCIS, 1983.

[46]The next two paragraphs draw on Taniura.

[47]Taniura, p. 80.

[48]In fact, these three firms—Nan Ya Plastics, Formosa Plastics, and Formosa Chemical and Fiber—were the only three private firms among the list of Taiwan's ten largest firms in 1987.

Taniura concludes that "group ownership has not progressed very far from the stage of direct control by the founder and his brother," and predicts that this capital ownership situation will not change in the near future.[49] Although founder Wang announced in 1981 that his successor would not necessarily be one of his children, both his and his brother's eldest sons have been groomed as the potential heir through education and rotating management positions within the group. Perhaps even more than in the Korean chaebol, this trend of professionalization of younger-generation family managers appears just as important as any trend toward the hiring of nonfamily professional managers.

The institutional "stickiness" of these familial norms is a particularly relevant issue because many of Taiwan's guanxiqiye are now faced with the death of their aging founders. Table 3-4 shows that six of the top ten guanxiqiye in 1988 were still in the hands of original founders, who had an average age of seventy-two that year. Of those groups that had experienced succession, all passed the mantle of authority on to a single, immediate family member, either the wife or a son. The remaining groups have formally or informally designated a likely successor, either a son or a nephew of the founder.

Concurring that the family is "the essence of Chinese economic organization," Wong Siu-lun develops an evolutionary model of the Chinese family firm that traces the consequences of familial management and inheritance.[50] Wong contends that despite Chinese "common wisdom" and

*Table 3-4.* Birth year of founder, year of succession, and relationship of successors or likely successor of top ten guanxiqiye, 1988

| Group | Birth year of founder | Year of succession | Relationship of successor (or likely successor) |
|---|---|---|---|
| Formosa Plastics | 1917 | | (son or nephew) |
| Linden International | 1924 | | (son) |
| Shin Kong | 1919 | 1986 | son |
| China Trust | 1917 | | (nephew) |
| Far Eastern | 1911 | | (son) |
| Hualon | | 1977 | son |
| Tatung | 1919 | | (son) |
| Yue Loong Motor | | 1976 | wife |
| Tuntex | 1911 | 1987 | son |
| Chung Hsing | 1912 | 1989 | wife |

SOURCE: CCIS, 1985, 1991.

[49]Taniura, p. 74.
[50]Wong, p. 58. Unless otherwise noted, the following paragraphs draw on Wong.

75

scholarly assertions that the practice of partible inheritance (*fenjia*) limits both the scale and life span of the Chinese family firm,[51] enterprises may in fact be "large or small, vigorous or enervated, depending on the point in their developmental cycle at which we make our observation.[52]

In its first or "emergent" phase, Wong argues, the Chinese firm is generally formed by a "partnership in which resources are pooled by persons largely unrelated by ties of descent or marriage." The firm is typically small and undercapitalized, and the partnership is notably unstable. It is only in the second, or "centralized," stage, when one shareholder and his *jia* (family) are able to attain majority ownership of the company, that this "father-entrepreneur" and his extended family begin to dominate the firm. As the undisputed boss, this father-entrepreneur has a maximum degree of flexibility of action, the freedom to transfer funds from one line of business to another for lateral expansion, and a strong cultural incentive to reinvest profits to ensure that he, as trustee, has valuable assets to support him in his old age and to pass on to future generations.

With the passing of the patriarch, the firm enters the third, or "segmented," phase of its cycle. Although the practice of relatively equal inheritance makes the division of *jia* properties a possibility at this point, the functional integration and synergy associated with business capital make this kind of fragmentation unlikely. Rather, the business remains intact while profits are divided. The division of management responsibilities, however, is more ambiguous, leading to the emergence of "distinct spheres of influence" for the male heirs and the "proliferation of departments, factory plants, or subsidiary companies within the family concern."[53] Herein lies one of the primary motives for diversification or "new building" of firms within the guanxiqiye.[54]

The new chief executive, usually the eldest or most responsible son, typically has less authority, less capital, and less entrepreneurial freedom than the founder and gradually resigns himself to the role caretaker rather than innovator. At this stage, if this son, or one of his brothers, in the segmented family firm can regain a majority stake in the enterprise, the firm could reenter the centralized stage. If this does not occur, and the managerial mantle passes to a third generation, the proliferation of heirs and the subdivision of shares cause the family firm to pass into the stage of "disintegration." At this point, Wong argues, family members as

[51]This "Buddenbrooks effect," or the intergenerational dilution of family wealth, common as well in Korean family firms, as discussed in Chapter Two, is captured in a traditional Chinese aphorism, *fu buguo sandai* (wealth cannot be passed down beyond three generations). For an analysis of its applicability to Taiwan, see Chinan Chen; Cai.

[52]Wong, p. 62.

[53]Wong, p. 66.

[54]Chou, 1986.

shareholders are "more concerned with immediate, tangible benefits than long-term business prospects," and the extended-family firm ceases to exist.[55] Few of Taiwan's guanxiqiye have reached this critical third-generation stage, but in some cases division had already occurred at the second generation.[56] In other cases, however, strategic alliances within and even among the guanxiqiye are forming that may preclude this cultural entropy. A potential focal point for these alliances, the newly formed private banks, is discussed in Chapter Five.

The dominant position of the family in the ownership and control of Taiwan's firms and its unwillingness to delegate authority to nonfamilial managers lessen these managers' commitment to the firm and often lead them to "spin off" from the firm and start their own independent businesses.[57] This independence is often short-lived, however, since these newly formed businesses will often serve as subcontractors to and receive financial assistance from the parent firm. This is frequently part of an effort by the boss to reintegrate the new firm into the orbit of the parent business. Silin notes the comments of one executive: "[The boss] despises most of the people who work for him. When someone wants to leave, the boss may say behind his back that he is not capable and will fail. Then I discovered that, when people leave, he has them come into his office to congratulate them. Then he asks them if they have enough capital. Most do not. So he offers to invest a bit and if he does not end up owning them, he owns at least a third of the operation."[58]

Silin discusses a final element of this business culture that has relevance for understanding the organization of the guanxiqiye. Although capital requirements for expansion and the absence of state subsidies comparable with those given the chaebol generally force even the owners of large firms to seek financial assistance outside the family, the owners fear lest any investor acquire too much stock. Thus, it is very common for large entrepreneurs in Taiwan—sometimes even competitors—to invest jointly in a new firm. Or, more commonly, they will cross-invest in each others' firms as silent partners, with only the major stockholder of each firm actually participating in the firm's operations.[59]

Silin cites several motives that "can induce even large investors to ac-

[55] Wong, p. 68.

[56] See, for example, the discussion of the Cathay group in Chapter Five.

[57] This lack of opportunities to advance within the company provides an important "push" motive to spin off. Equally important, however, in comparison with Korea are the "pull" or enabling factors in Taiwan. These include state macroeconomic incentives offered to all comers, not just the largest firms, and informal financial markets and an export regime very conducive to small, flexible, start-up firms. See Doner et al. For a useful discussion of the motives behind and consequences of these "spin-offs," see Shieh.

[58] Silin, p. 78.

[59] Numazaki, 1991.

cept noninvolved minority stock ownership in both public and private firms."[60] In addition to the rational economic motives of making money at preferential rates of interest and gaining otherwise closely held information about the firm's operations, a third motive was the desire to maintain "positive relations" or guanxi with others. By investing in a friend or colleague's business venture, an entrepreneur maintains rapport with the colleague and gives him "face" (*mianzi*) by expressing confidence in his venture. Silin quotes from an interview: "Even wealthy people, when they start a business, usually need capital so they come around and ask their friends to participate. They invest and we invest a bit. We are embarrassed not to invest so we have a share in many companies."[61]

Therefore, although control may rest in the hands of a single family and its patriarch, it is rarely the case that a single family completely owns all firms in a guanxiqiye, especially when the business group is large. More typically, as Wong's model would predict, several partnerships, often involving more than one family, will cooperate in establishing a guanxiqiye because "no single family usually has sufficient funds to expand their enterprises by themselves."[62] As will be demonstrated in Chapter Five, the guanxiqiye, lacking the massive government subsidies of their chaebol counterparts, are compelled to accept investments that, in Numazaki's words, create "significant human capital relationships" among families and between the guanxiqiye. Although a guanxiqiye may appear to be controlled by a single family, "it is not an isolated kingdom like the South Korean chaebol."[63]

This familial organization of business has shaped the guanxiqiye owner-managers' motivations and strategies for expansion and their methods for obtaining the funds necessary for this expansion. Above all, it has meant a willingness to sacrifice corporate interests and profits for family interests and profits. This varies significantly from Japanese tradition, in which the corporation is viewed as the family (ie) and from Korea, where the family is essentially the corporation.[64] Thus, while the capital require-

[60]Silin, p. 28.
[61]Silin, p. 28. See also Hwang.
[62]Lee et al., 1987, p. 18.
[63]Numazaki, 1987, pp. 18–19. In the final quote, Numazaki refers specifically to the Formosa Plastics group, though elsewhere he concludes that the intergroup investments are very common among the guanxiqiye (Numazaki, 1986, 1991).
[64]Regarding traditional Japan, Hirschmeier and Yui note: "In the merchants' community the House (*ie*) meant both the family and the business enterprise. . . . Looking at both the family as composed of parents and children, and the business enterprise, the latter weighed heavier in the thinking of the merchants. The living family was subservient to the continuous economic entity called the House" (p. 38). Clark notes that at least on the ideological level, this metaphor of the corporation as a fictitious family persists in contemporary Japan.
On the other hand, Hamilton et al. speak of the South Korean chaebol as organizations of "corporate patriarchy," where a family patriarch, as founder, majority shareholder, and

ments for the operation and expansion of even large firms in Taiwan require them to seek outside financial assistance, the owners are afraid to do so in ways that may harm the interests of the family.

This issue is particularly acute for many of Taiwan's groups as they face the deaths of their founders as well as efforts by the state to separate ownership and control of these private, predominantly Taiwanese empires. In order to understand the methods and motives for this state action, in the concluding section of this chapter I will examine the ambivalent relationship between the state and the guanxiqiye.

## GUANXIQIYE AND THE STATE

There is consensus in the literature regarding both the role of the Nationalist state in shaping the macrolevel policies and parameters of Taiwan's economic success and the strength of this developmental state measured in terms of autonomy and capacity.[65] There is also, however, increasing evidence that Taiwan's state has at times consciously chosen or failed to choose policies that have ultimately taken its political economy in a decidedly nondevelopmental direction.[66] In order to understand the government's role in shaping Taiwan's embedded enterprises, it is necessary to look beyond the strength of the state to examine the particular policy goals of the regime, the ideological and historical factors that have shaped its ambivalent attitude toward private capital, and the intraregime politics that have resulted from this ambivalence. Only then can we discuss how these state motivations have affected the state's relations with the guanxiqiye.

### *"Strong" State*

Taiwan's Nationalist state has been remarkably autonomous from Taiwanese society. There are several reasons for this. First, the organization of the Nationalist Party and state along Leninist lines gave the party direct control over the state. This organizational structure, combined with the Nationalists' extensive network of military and security agencies bent on

---

undisputed boss, often controls the entire group of enterprises with the assistance of a few family members in key positions and a group of professional managers (1987, p. 90; see also Hamilton and Kao, p. 12). As discussed in Chapter Two, unlike Japan, where the system of primogeniture prevailed and the eldest son, either fictive or real, inherited all power and property, in Korea division of property among all true (blood) sons (and in Chinese societies, daughters as well) of the following generation is the general rule (Hattori, 1984).

[65] See, for example, Amsden, 1979; Gold, 1981, 1986; Wade, 1984, 1990; Cumings; Johnson, 1987; Pang.

[66] See, for example, Arnold; Noble; Lam.

rooting out any corruption, collusion, or communism, ensured that the state organs remained autonomous from societal influences while formulating policies.[67] Gold notes nine separate "overt and covert quasi-military security agencies that have functioned or continued to function in Taiwan."[68] Moreover, this party-state organization, as a result of its direct control of a state- and party-owned economic base independent of the private sector, was largely financially independent. This financial autonomy prevented the top party leadership and their bureaucratic minions from becoming the captives of potential private capitalist clients.[69] It has also allowed the state to sponsor and control corporatist industrial associations.[70]

Second, unlike Korea, there was, from the outset, no strong local class—either landed or urban—to compete with Nationalist rule. Japan's conscious policies of land reform and the suppression of a Taiwanese bourgeoisie, and the Nationalists' decimation of the local intelligentsia during the "2-28 Incident" of 1947,[71] left Taiwanese society "leaderless, atomized, quiescent and apolitical."[72] The Nationalist-administered land reform virtually eliminated what was left of Taiwan's former landed class.

Third, there was a de facto division of labor between the newly arrived Mainlanders and the local Taiwanese. Virtually all the refugees arriving from the Mainland were military personnel or civil servants with no local property or familial connections. For these, and other political reasons discussed below, the Mainlanders filled all responsible political and government positions, leaving the bulk of the economic sector to the local Taiwanese.[73] Linguistic and cultural differences were (and remain) significant, compounding this subethnic division and giving the Nationalist state a high degree of autonomy from Taiwanese society.

The strength of the Nationalist state was also enhanced by a relatively high degree of capacity to formulate and implement its developmental policies. This is true in terms of both qualified personnel and effective

[67]T. J. Cheng, 1989.
[68]Gold, 1986, p. 62.
[69]Johnson, 1987.
[70]Y. H. Chu, 1994.
[71]The "2-28 Incident" refers to the series of events triggered by the beating of a Taiwanese black-market cigarette peddler at the hands of Mainlander Monopoly Bureau agents on February 27, 1947, in Taipei. In the fracas that followed, the agents also shot a protesting bystander. Local Taiwanese retaliated that evening by attacking a police station. The following day, and in ensuing weeks, greater numbers of Taiwanese violently protested corrupt mainlander rule in many localities throughout the island. In May of that year, Nationalist troops arrived from the mainland and systematically liquidated anyone suspected of being critical of Nationalist rule. Estimates of total Taiwanese victims range from 10,000 to 20,000 (Gold, 1986, p. 51; see also Kerr).
[72]Gold, 1986, p. 52.
[73]Cole. See also Pang.

institutions responsible for administering policy. The vacuum resulting from the departure of the Japanese colonial administrators was largely filled by the "disproportionate number of experts, technicians, and well-educated professionals" who followed Chiang to Taiwan from the Mainland.[74] According to Gold, those who came with Chiang "to an uncertain future on Taiwan were for the most part loyal and willing to make sacrifices, whereas the most egregiously corrupt and harmful persons by and large did not go to Taiwan at all."[75]

From 1950 to 1952, the Nationalists initiated a reform program, expelling those of doubtful allegiance and recruiting new talent into the party. American advisers and experts supplemented this domestic capacity at crucial junctures. These included U.S. AID personnel and the staff technicians of various contracted consulting firms.[76] Although the economic bureaucracy has traditionally succeeded in drawing its employees from among Taiwan's best and brightest, the proportion of students with Ph.D. and master's degrees entering the bureaucracy has declined substantially in recent years as public-sector salaries have failed to keep pace with those in the private sector.[77]

A complex of effective institutions greatly facilitated the tasks of these state administrators. The Nationalists inherited much of this from the Japanese colonial administration, including the revenue, banking, and state-owned enterprise systems. In addition, the Nationalist regime established a series of pilot agencies for administering its economic policies. These agencies developed a "little understood but apparently vigorous policy network" that Yun-han Chu characterizes as "fairly elaborate and resourceful."[78] These administrative organs were much more decentralized and had neither the autonomy from political leaders nor the longevity of their Korean counterparts. The reason for this was neither societal penetration of the state nor a lack of skilled personnel, but political conflicts over regime priorities within the governing structure. Before turning to these priorities, it is worthwhile to trace the tortuous path of these planning agencies.[79]

When Chiang Kai-shek came to Taiwan, he first vested economic authority in Chen Cheng, a trusted general serving concurrently as provincial governor of Taiwan and nominal head of the Taiwan Production

[74]Cumings, p. 65.
[75]Gold, 1986, p. 59.
[76]These consultants have included J. G. White Engineering Corporation (financed by U.S. funds), Stanford Research Institute, and Arthur D. Little, Inc.
[77]Wade, 1990.
[78]Y. H. Chu, 1989, p. 666; Wade, 1990.
[79]This discussion of Taiwan's planning agencies draws on Pang; Gold, 1981, 1986; Johnson, 1987; Tann; Kingjing.

Board (TPB), which Chen established in the spring of 1949. K. Y. Yin, vice chairman of the Board, handled actual direction of the TPB. The TPB had no power to execute economic policy, but it had very substantial responsibilities in formulating policies. In 1951, Finance Minister C. K. Yen formed and, with the provincial governor, chaired an ad hoc Finance-Economy Committee. This committee called for the creation of the Economic Stabilization Board (ESB), which absorbed the TSB upon its establishment in 1953.

Chaired first by the governor, and then by the premier when it was moved from provincial to national status, the ESB functioned for five years as the chief agency for economic planning, despite the coexistence of ministries with overlapping responsibilities. A primary reason for this functional redundancy was the significant advisory position of the Council on United States Aid (CUSA) within the ESB. Established in 1948 as an interministerial council, chaired by the premier, to supervise American assistance to the Nationalists, CUSA was not affiliated with any particular ministry and was semiautonomous in its funding and financial decisions. Moreover, CUSA staff members received substantially higher salaries than their ministerial counterparts, a policy intended to reduce the temptation of corruption. This gave CUSA a degree of efficiency and effectiveness not shared by the rest of the bureaucracy.

In 1958, the ESB was dissolved (partly because of ministerial jealousy) and its policy-making authority was shifted to CUSA, which was also made the chief organ for overall economic development. When the United States announced in 1963 that its assistance to Taiwan would end in 1965, CUSA was reorganized into the Council for International Economic Cooperation and Development (CIECD). This was done in anticipation of the discontinuation of U.S. aid and in recognition of the value of a centralized planning agency. CIECD had full responsibility for designing, coordinating, and evaluating the implementation of all economic policies.

In 1968, Chiang Kai-shek appointed his son, Chiang Ching-kuo, as vice premier and chair of CIECD. Chiang narrowed the CIECD's responsibilities and created his own Financial, Economic and Monetary Council as the new policy-coordinating body that included top officials from the Ministry of Finance, Ministry of Economic Affairs, Central Bank of China, and CIECD. Chiang presided over this council as well. In 1973, one year after assuming the premiership, Chiang Ching-kuo dissolved the CIECD and replaced it with the even weaker Economic Planning Council (EPC); real policy-making authority was centralized in the newly formed Finance and Economic Group, successor to the Financial, Economic and Monetary Council. This five-man group, reporting directly to Premier Chiang, was chaired by the governor of the Central Bank of China and included the ministers of finance and economic affairs, the secretary-general of the Executive Yuan, and the director-general of budget, accounting, and statistics.

Impressed by the streamlined efficiency of Park Chong Hee's EPB, the Nationalist regime sent a research team to Korea in 1977. At the EPB's suggestion it merged the EPC and the Finance and Economic Group to form the Council of Economic Planning and Development (CEPD). This extraministerial organ has proved to be an effective body for economic policy-making, although, like its predecessors, its autonomy and influence have varied, depending on the relationship between the CEPD's leadership and the political elite. For example, in 1990, Premier Hao Bocun established the Economic and Financial Consultative Council, which eclipsed the role of the CEPD as pilot agency, in order to assert his control over the policy-making process.[80]

Unlike Korea, whose central bank is dominated by the EPB and Ministry of Finance, in Taiwan the Central Bank of China exerts a strong and ultraconservative influence on the economic bureaucracy. Hands-on implementation of industrial policy and the gathering of information from the private industrial sector are carried out in large part by the Ministry of Economic Affairs' Industrial Development Bureau,[81] though Chu contends that the IDB "enjoys little clout in the overall economic bureaucracy, and has limited influence over fiscal and credit policy."[82]

## Economic Ideology and Objectives

The remarkable autonomy and relative capacity of Taiwan's political leaders and technocratic elite have given their vision of development and the economic policies implemented to achieve that vision considerable influence on the nature of Taiwan's development and on the structure and activities of the guanxiqiye. This state "strength" does not mean conflict over policy has not occurred. It does mean, however, these policy conflicts have occurred largely within the state apparatus.[83] This is key to understanding the effect of state policy on the guanxiqiye.

In order to understand the regime's attitude toward economic development—and more specifically, its ambivalence toward private capital—it is necessary to examine the ideological and historical factors shaping the goals of the regime. Despite a divergence between the fundamental political and economic objectives of Taiwan's developmental state, an elective affinity between the regime's political needs, economic goals, and ideo-

[80]*Economic News*, 9/3/90.
[81]Wade, 1990.
[82]Y. H. Chu, 1989, p. 656.
[83]Arnold; Noble.

logical underpinnings has nonetheless emerged. This has allowed the state to clothe its political objectives in moral wrappings and limit the concentration of private economic power by enforcing its multitude of regulations only when private business threatens state political control or the nation's economic and financial stability.

The Nationalist state has a distinct penchant for strict economic control and is concerned about the concentration of the private industrial, financial, and commercial sectors. There are several ideological foundations for these inclinations. Perhaps most fundamental is the Confucian disdain for the pursuit of personal profit or material advantage (li) and the injunction to avoid inequality (jun).[84] China's nineteenth-century tradition of bureaucratic capitalism, in which government officials contended that government control of modern industry would be both more efficient and more beneficial to society than private ownership, reinforced this formal aversion to private profit at the expense of public welfare.[85]

This legacy also influenced Sun Yat-sen, who emerged during this era as China's most significant revolutionary. Sun also drew—albeit selectively—from contemporary socialist thinkers such as Henry George and Edward Bellamy in forming his ideological program for economic development and social welfare under the rubric "Principle of People's Livelihood" (minsheng zhuyi).[86] Gold describes "People's Livelihood" as "a vague concept akin to socialism in advocating the regulation of capital and equalization of land tenure, but without class struggle and allowing a significant role for free enterprise."[87]

Fearing the consequences of the private concentration of capital, Sun formed a developmental vision for China that called for a mixed economy in which the state would own and operate those enterprises of a monopolistic nature, those beyond the financial or technological means of private investors, and those with low returns or other risks discouraging private investors. When Sun died in 1925, Chiang Kai-shek and the Nationalists deified him and canonized his economic and political doctrines, making them official dogma of the Nationalist Party and state.

Although the Nationalists were unable or unwilling to implement most aspects of "People's Livelihood" while still on the Mainland, the concept gained real significance for their policymakers on Taiwan, both to legitimate state policies and to assign parameters for appropriate private eco-

[84]Metzger.

[85]Balazs.

[86]See Gregor. He notes that this concept of "the People's Livelihood" (minjian yangsheng) was common among traditional Chinese intellectuals and appeared regularly in Confucian and neo-Confucian texts (p. 6). See also S. H. Chang and Gordon.

[87]Gold, 1986, p. 48.

nomic activities. Though Sun's eclectic attitude toward socialism and capitalism produced a vague and amorphous ideology, it was also comprehensive and extremely flexible, giving the Nationalists a wide range of legitimate options.[88] K. T. Li, one of several preeminent Nationalist technocrats, spoke of Sun's "People's Livelihood" as the "highest guiding principle" for Taiwan's economic development. He further noted that "in order to avoid such pitfalls likely to occur in the course of economic development and to put into practice the principle of equitable distribution of income and wealth according to the Principle of the People's Livelihood, our government has taken various fiscal and economic measures to prevent the excessive concentration of wealth in the hands of the few."[89]

These ideological supports for the control of capital through direct government ownership and the strict regulation of private capital have been reinforced in the minds of Taiwan's political leaders and policymakers by shared historical events. The bête noire in this historical saga has been the specter of inflation, whose historical role and consequent impact on financial policy is examined in detail in Chapter Five. Here it need only be stressed that inflation has been religiously controlled, not primarily for economic reasons but because of its potentially disastrous social and political consequences. In the minds of Nationalist policymakers, it breeds instability, stunts economic growth, and shakes investors' and savers' confidence, thereby providing enemies of the state, domestic and foreign, with opportunities to exploit the turmoil and to challenge the very survival of the Nationalist state.

Given this predisposition, the overriding goal of the Nationalist regime on Taiwan has been, in the words of its own maxims, "growth with stability" and "growth with equity."[90] This has given government officials a strong bent toward conservative control and an unwillingness to reduce intervention in the economy for fear a "reduction of controls could wreck hard-won price stability and bring back inflation." Gold states that "many officials still disliked businessmen, and [liberalization] policies would further the state's retrenchment from the economy and grant ever greater rein to private capital. This would entail concentration of capital, something Sun Yat-sen opposed."[91]

These ideological and historical concerns dovetailed with a final imperative of Nationalist policy: the need to retain political power while facing a rapidly expanding private sector dominated by ethnic Taiwanese. In-

[88]Pang.
[89]K. T. Li, 1976, pp. 486–87.
[90]K. H. Yu, p. 3.
[91]Gold, 1986, p. 77.

fluential Taiwanese families own and operate the majority of the nation's largest guanxiqiye, and these families are very much interested in influencing public policy on behalf of their private interests. This dominance is a result not only of the fact that ethnic Taiwanese comprise over 80 percent of the island's population but also of the regime's consciously engineered division of labor that placed virtually all political power in the hands of the minority Mainlanders and left the private sector open to the local Taiwanese. Although this mitigated Taiwanese opposition to political subjugation by providing economic outlets, it also raised concerns among political leaders that this economic power could be translated into political power.[92]

The minority Mainlander regime's ideological and cultural biases against concentrated economic power and autonomous centers of private power were further strengthened by this specific subethnic imbalance and its potential political consequences for Nationalist rule. The regime's early brutal treatment of the Taiwanese exacerbated this division and animosity. This gulf also created a dynamic of government-big business relations very different from that of the Korean political economy. In Taiwan, local capitalists and government officials have coexisted in a relationship of commensalism, that is, living together but with largely independent roles, as opposed to a relationship of symbiosis, or living together and acting as an integral unit, which more accurately describes the hegemonic pact between Korean bureaucrats and industrialists.[93]

*Institutional Relationship with the Guanxiqiye*

The stunted growth of large, private capital in Taiwan and the relatively distant ties between it and the state are a direct consequence of the regime's stance toward private capital. This anti-big business bias is manifest both in the government's informal "administrative guidance" of the guanxiqiye and in its formal policies and legislation. Unlike Korean political culture, which has tolerated and—at least under Park—institutionalized close government-business relations, the Nationalist regime has suspected such intimate interaction as collusion.

Although these suspicions are not without merit,[94] many developmental

[92]Gold, 1986.

[93]Fields, 1993. See also Pang. Barrett attributes this divergence of state and bourgeoisie interests in Taiwan in the first instance to the ethnic division and then to subsequent variances in class outlook, self-definition, and mobility strategies (Richard Barrett, "State and Economy on Taiwan, 1960–1980," unpublished manuscript [1983], cited in Pang, pp. 75–76).

[94]For valuable, though dated, discussions of the extensive corruption involving local government officials and entrepreneurs and other private interests in Taiwan, see Cole; Lerman.

initiatives and opportunities have been thwarted by the overly suspicious political elite. Chu notes that Taiwan's technocrats have approached any contact with private businessmen with caution, aware that such an association is subject to surveillance by both party and state security organs.[95] Taiwan's two most important developmentally oriented policymakers, K. Y. Yin and K. T. Li, were censured at different times by Taiwan's Control Yuan and Legislative Yuan for suspected corruption in their efforts to foster new enterprises.[96] Both were subsequently cleared of all charges. A former minister of finance noted efforts by President Chiang Ching-kuo to institute "ten commandments" regarding government officials' relations with private businessmen. Among these was the requirement that any government official who attended a social event at which private businessmen were present was to report this attendance to the government's Bureau of Personnel.

Chu contends that this absence of an "extensive web of channels" between the Nationalist state and private Taiwanese capital is the result of "the latter's potential threat to the former's political domination at the national level."[97] Peter Evans notes the striking "extent to which the Taiwanese private sector has been absent from policy networks," calling historical linkages between the state and private capital "sufficiently distant" to threaten the ability of the state to secure information and implement its policies. He nonetheless concludes that the "lack of embeddedness should not be exaggerated," and that while informal linkages are less dense than in Korea, "they are clearly essential to Taiwan's industrial policy."[98]

Despite the formal and substantive constraints it imposes, the Nationalist regime has frequently guided and communicated with the private business groups both informally and formally, though certainly not to the extent of the Korean government. In spite of the bureaucratic norm of distance to preserve autonomy, informal linkages between the public and private sectors do exist. Several of Taiwan's largest guanxiqiye are in fact owned and operated by families of Mainland, not Taiwanese, descent and have received government favors because of the privileged access this subethnic affinity provided. The state has also developed a "complex web of clientalistic relationships" with a number of prominent Taiwanese capitalists, co-opting them through oligopolistic rent-seeking opportunities and political access.[99] Similarly, just as the chaebol recruited retired military officers, so most Taiwanese conglomerates have hired token Main-

[95]Y. H. Chu, 1994.
[96]A. Liu; Evans, 1992.
[97]Y. H. Chu, 1989, p. 656.
[98]Evans, 1992.
[99]Y. H. Chu, 1994.

landers whose primary responsibility is to provide communication channels with the state.[100]

Numazaki argues that the same kind of affect-laden guanxi networks that are so important within Taiwan's business community link businessmen and bureaucrats as well. He cites a particular group of business, bureaucratic, and political elite who shared the same lunar calendar birth year and, on that basis, met and dined together once a month for nearly two decades. This twelve-member group, which spanned the Mainlander-Taiwanese gulf, included several financial bureaucrats and some of Taiwan's wealthiest and well-known businessmen.[101] Early on, the Nationalists seated several of Taiwan's largest native industrialists on their ruling Central Committee, thus providing them with direct access to the president and significant input (and even influence) on the policy-making process.

More formally, Industrial Development Bureau officials and other bureaucrats spend much of their time in the industrial trenches, working closely with the guanxiqiye and other private enterprises, monitoring policies, collecting information, and learning from the private sector.[102] The state also monitors and constrains private capital through informal and less easily documented institutions of administrative guidance. These allegedly include the brokering of new business licenses to politically correct clients and demands on especially prosperous Taiwanese firms for political "donations" to the Nationalist Party for particular projects.

One high-ranking government official noted that "In the past, any time a business wanted to begin a new project or enter a new industry, it had to get advice from the government." It is general knowledge that Wang Yongqing, founder of the Formosa Plastics group, had originally wanted to invest in many projects but could receive approval only for plastics. In subsequent years his plans to move into the newspaper industry (until recently monopolized by the government) and the cement industry also were thwarted.[103]

For the most part, however, natural and market constraints and studious government macroeconomic policies to restrict private capital in general obviated the need to curb expansion of the guanxiqiye through either informal administrative guidance or formal legislation. In fact, in the wake of the 1973–74 global oil crisis, the government began to fear the international vulnerability of its economy, dominated by small and medium-sized enterprises, and took measures to selectively build up its

[100]Gold, 1981.
[101]Numazaki, 1991.
[102]Wade, 1990.
[103]Taniura.

heavy and capital-intensive industries. Although this offered a potential opportunity for the guanxiqiye to expand (like the chaebol during Korea's HCI boost in the same period), the fears of key policymakers prompted the regime to parcel out many of these capital-intensive projects to state-owned enterprises.[104] Incentives offered to private capital were generally insufficient, and the restrictions attached were too onerous to make the projects attractive to potential investors.[105]

Nonetheless, during the 1970s the state eased some restrictions on the cross-investment of capital and encouraged—in some cases even sponsored—mergers between private firms. The most successful state-sponsored effort (conspicuous by its exceptional status) was the 1977 merger of five of Taiwan's major man-made fiber producers into the Hualon Corporation (formerly of the E-Hsin group and now flagship of the Hualon group). Gold's appraisal of this merger is worth quoting in full:

> Rumors about a merger began in May, 1977 and speculation centered not only on who would win control, but also how the government would act concretely, beyond moral encouragement. The answer came after completion of the merger when the government announced that it would convert NT$750 million debt owed to its banks into shares of stock. It also had representatives on the Board. This was a controversial move as some people felt it showed favoritism to its friends while others would go under; some mentioned the fact that Leu's [the new chairman] wife is the sister of Chiang Wei-kuo (Ching-kuo's brother)'s wife. Others stated that it revived a dangerous precedent of government helping large ailing firms and ending up taking them over. To others, it represented a contradiction: on the one hand, the government opposes overly large firms and concentration of capital, yet here it actively supported such a venture.[106]

Only two years later, the growing financial and economic power of the guanxiqiye prompted the Ministry of Economic Affairs to begin drafting

[104]In fact, in many ways Taiwan's huge state-owned and party-owned sectors are the more fitting equivalent of the "quasi-internal organization" of Korea's state-chaebol relationship discussed in Chapter Two (C. H. Lee, 1992). Evans (1992) notes the "vigorous policy network which links the central economic bureaus" with Taiwan's public enterprises and public banks. It is these public and quasi-public enterprises that have "taken all the major initiatives in building up the capital intensive sector" (Y. H. Chu, 1989, p. 656) and have served as the "point men" in many of the state's policy initiatives (either by design or by default).

[105]The Nationalist state did attempt to recruit a number of the guanxiqiye as junior partners for many of these second-stage import-substitution projects, just as the Korean state was doing at the same time. But when individual groups were singled out as likely partners, the government was assailed for favoritism. Other attempts to engage several groups in a single joint venture foundered on mutual distrust among the proposed partners and an unwillingness to cooperate. See, for example, Arnold. For a valuable comparison of state-capital relations in Korea and Taiwan on the eve of this HCI period, see T. J. Cheng, 1990.

[106]Gold, 1981, pp. 122–23.

the Fair Trade Law. This was the first legislative effort to deal directly with the burgeoning business groups. The MOEA patterned the draft after the Japanese, American, and West German fair trade laws, addressing in it such issues as monopoly, antitrust, counterfeiting, cartels, mergers, acquisitions, and the status of a Fair Trade Commission. Like its Korean counterpart, however, the proposed Fair Trade Law was to ban monopolies, mergers, and acquisitions only when they brought about an unreasonable restraint of trade or an exclusion of competition. The path-breaking nature of this draft, the breadth of its coverage, and the strong feelings of both proponents and opponents doomed it to a long legislative battle.[107]

In an effort to answer one of the sticking points of the debate, the CEPD in 1979 commissioned a year-long study to establish the definition of a guanxiqiye.[108] In lieu of a Fair Trade Law, the study called for the MOEA to revise the existing Company Law, Banking Law, and other relevant statutes to regulate the groups. Others spoke of the need for a specific Related Enterprise Law (*guanxiqiye fa*). Ironically, one of the biggest obstacles to progress was the government and Nationalist Party's unwillingness to consider including state and party-owned enterprises under the legislation's jurisdiction, citing Sun's "People's Livelihood" as justification. Critics pointed out that state-owned enterprises accounted for more than 66 percent of the local monopoly market.[109] This legislative battle was made even more significant by the strengthened hand of a democratizing legislature representing a variety of special interests; the guanxiqiye constituted one of the most influential of these interest groups. The government remained firm, however, in its unwillingness to loosen its control over the expansion of the guanxiqiye. The result was a thirteen-year battle to enact the Fair Trade Law, which was not promulgated until 1991 and finally implemented in 1992.

Among its forty-nine articles, the law calls for the close monitoring of potential monopoly enterprises or unfair trusts. Firms to be monitored include all private enterprises with over U.S.$40 million in annual sales (this included just under 500 firms in 1992, most affiliated with guanxiqiye), as well as any single business possessing a 50 percent market share, three companies with two-thirds of a product's sales, or five firms with three-fourths of a particular market.[110] Those business groups favored by the state with oligopolistic positions in certain markets—such as the Taiwan Cement group and the Yue Loong Motor group—were sent scrambling for legal counsel. Consistent with the regime's policy to maintain a

---

[107]*Economic News*, 2/29/88.
[108]This study was later published as Liu et al.
[109]*Economic News*, 2/29/88.
[110]*Free China Journal*, 2/14/92.

monopoly over the commanding heights of the economy, all state-owned enterprises were given a five-year grace period, and it was planned to place those government enterprises deemed "crucial to key economic policies" entirely beyond the purview of the legislation.[111] After one year, the Fair Trade Commission had targeted 101 companies and found that 40 of these had the capacity to dominate markets in 33 different fields. None, however, were charged with unfair trade practices.[112]

The Fair Trade Law, lauded by Premier Hao Bocun as a law that "institutionalizes the time-honored virtue of honesty for Chinese merchants," was branded by business leaders as yet another form of state harassment of large private capital without just cause.[113] Wang Youzheng, honorary chair of Taiwan's Chamber of Commerce and chairman of the China Rebar group (and also a member of the Nationalist Party's central standing committee), condemned the Fair Trade Act as "a wicked law that disdains the interests of businessmen" that was destined to "hurt the island's economic competitiveness."[114] Although there is certainly posturing on both sides, the fact that the regime automatically suspects any enterprise with sales exceeding U.S.$40 million in an economy with an annual GNP of over U.S.$200 billion dramatizes the state's penchant for control and bias against the concentration of private capital.

Evans juxtaposes state-business relations in Korea and Taiwan, describing Korea as "pushing at the limit to which embeddedness can be concentrated in a few ties without degenerating into particularistic predation." Taiwan, he says, demonstrates the opposite concern, "in which the relative absence of links to private capital might seem to threaten the ability of the autonomous state to secure full information and count on the private sector for effective implementation."[115]

Two different processes are eroding this state autonomy and its distance from private capital in ways that portend significant consequences for the guanxiqiye. First, an increasing proportion of key Nationalist Party politicians and technocratic policymakers are of Taiwanese descent, now including the party chairman and president (Lee Denghui) and much of his cabinet. The ethnic, linguistic, and regional affinities between this new public-sector elite and the predominantly Taiwanese private-sector elite have weakened the autonomy of the state and expanded business group leaders' access to political influence.

[111]*Free China Journal,* 2/11/92.
[112]*Free China Journal,* 2/9/93. During the first year, sixty-nine companies were punished under the law, mostly for false advertising.
[113]*Free China Journal,* 3/13/92.
[114]*Free China Journal,* 2/11/92.
[115]Evans, 1992.

The second related process is that of democratization, wherein the interests of the Taiwanese majority, and particularly the interests of the capitalist class, are finding greater voice. The institutional changes associated with democratization have created "strategic openings" the guanxiqiye have been able to exploit. Because great sums of money are a necessary if not a sufficient requirement for electoral success in Taiwan's political campaigns, the guanxiqiye have become sought-after patrons.[116] The groups and their executives finance campaigns, fund political foundations and policy institutes, and purchase legislative seats.[117] In the 1989 legislative elections, 38 of the 101 popularly elected legislators had publicly known ties with at least one guanxiqiye.[118]

The gradual "Taiwanization" of the Nationalist Party and the democratization of Taiwan's political system promise a resolution to subethnic tensions, but as in Korea, they will also further undermine the capacity of the developmental state to shape the destiny of the private business groups. Chu concludes that democratization is gradually transforming the Nationalist Party "from a political pact between the dominant mainlander state elite and subordinate native politicians, to a more broadly based conservative alliance linking the state elite, local party factions and big business."[119] As in Korea, though from more humble beginnings, the diversified business groups, in the hands of native Taiwanese, are increasingly becoming the most important economic and political actors in this new pluralist environment.

These evolving environments are examined specifically in chapters on Korea and Taiwan that analyze the financing of the business groups and state efforts to promote group-affiliated trading companies. Although market factors and cultural differences have influenced the very different natures of the chaebol and guanxiqiye, the key factor has been the Korean state's proactive chaebol policies and in Taiwan, the lack of comparable promotion efforts and the presence of specific constraints. I will turn first to the financial systems.

[116]Y. H. Chu, 1994.
[117]*Economic News*, 6/24/91.
[118]Y. H. Chu, 1994, p. 17.
[119]Y. H. Chu, 1994, p. 30.

CHAPTER FOUR

# Financing of the Chaebol

Financial capital is the lifeblood of any business enterprise, determining its ability to fund both current operations and future expansion. Korea and Taiwan's embedded enterprises are certainly no exception. Nonetheless, despite the similarities in Taiwan's and Korea's political economies, these groups have been shown to be vastly different in terms of organizational structure, scale, dominance of their respective economies, relations with the state, and—consequently—their developmental paths. Because financial capital is arguably the most important environmental factor for any capitalist enterprise, an investigation of the financing of Korea's and Taiwan's business groups provides an essential window for understanding this variance.

The following two chapters examine the financial environments in which the chaebol and guanxiqiye are embedded. What are the various sources of finance? By what methods are these liquid assets obtained? What factors determine how much and what kind of capital these groups receive? The answers to these questions further support the general argument of this book that state and sociocultural institutions have structured the business groups' environments in ways that have fostered very different patterns of enterprise organization in Korea and Taiwan.

Because they understand the key role of finance, both Korea's and Taiwan's developmental regimes have dominated their respective financial systems with the explicit intention of lending clout to industrial policies and influencing industrial organization in order to achieve regime goals.[1] In addition to this state influence, the Korean and Chinese business cul-

[1]See, for example, Wade, 1985, 1990; Woo; Johnson, 1987; Gold, 1986; Jones and Sakong.

tures have shaped the methods and nature of the groups' financing, and hence their scope, scale, and organization. State intervention, however, has been decisive. Financial institutions and markets (both formal and informal) are in many ways quite similar in Korea and Taiwan. The differences lie in how the respective governments have manipulated these institutions to achieve regime priorities and how the private entrepreneurs exploit these same institutions and policy incentive structures to achieve their private goals. Although these financial institutions provide a nexus between public policymakers and private business group leaders, the objectives of each sector in relation to these institutions have by no means always converged. Because of this, I seek an explanation beyond the confines of atomistic rational choice and explore the broader sociopolitical environments that shape the groups' financial activities.

In order to analyze the financing of the chaebol, in this chapter I (1) examine the financial goals and strategies of Korea's public policymakers and private business group leaders, and discuss the reasons for the relative convergence (at least historically) of their objectives; (2) introduce the Korean financial system, its supervisory agencies, and the formal and informal institutions that have supplied the massive amounts of capital that nurtured the chaebol; and (3) recount the government-orchestrated demise of the Kukje business group as further illustration of the embeddedness thesis of this study. It should also be noted at the outset that while the chaebol have served as the means to the regime's developmental ends, these once compliant creations of the government are increasingly willing and able to express and act on "private" interests. Although public and private interests converged for much of the postwar era, this has not always been, and increasingly will not be, the case. Financial capital is both the lifeline of this relationship and the battlefield of this struggle.

## GOALS AND STRATEGIES

### Public Control

While the motives and means of government domination of the Korean financial sector will require some explanation, the fact of this dominance can be quickly established. From 1961, when the private commercial banks were nationalized, until 1980, the government had complete control over Korea's bank-dominated, formal financial system. As owner-manager, the Korean state hired personnel and determined salaries, budgets, and credit ceilings for all commercial banks. Even since the privatization measures of the 1980s, the government still sets interest rates, rations policy loans, allocates operating funds, and chooses the banks' top personnel.[2] As a result, the Korean financial sector has been described as "heavily protected and regulated," "operating largely outside market forces," and "run like a military unit."[3] A decade after privatization, Jungen Woo could still write, "The Korean banking system exhibits the most extreme case of dependence upon the state."[4] An observer in 1993 concluded that it is "unclear when banks will ever become totally independent of the government.[5]

This public financial control had a precedent. The Japanese colonial administration established, owned, and operated Korea's first modern commercial banks, its central bank, and its unified currency system. Not surprisingly, large-scale Japanese enterprises monopolized funds generated by the system. David Cole and Yung Chul Park note that the system "was used to channel savings initially into Japanese industrial and commercial expansion and finally into the Japanese war effort. Koreans did have some access to the modern financial institutions, particularly the financial associations, but by and large they relied on their traditional institutions both as depositories for their savings and sources for their borrowings."[6]

The departure of the Japanese in 1945 and the chaos of the subsequent years created a dearth of skilled personnel capable of controlling South Korea's "shell of a modern financial system."[7] Only after the Korean War ended in 1953 was the Rhee regime able to turn its concern to rebuilding the financial system. At the same time it was strengthening the regulatory structure, the laissez-faire ideology of the Rhee regime and its U.S. advisers prompted plans to transfer the former Japanese commercial banks "as rapidly as possible from government to private ownership." By 1957, the government had sold all of its shareholdings in the banks to a small number of wealthy businessmen—primarily chaebol owners—who had already profited from access to monopoly import licenses.[8]

After seizing power in 1961, the Park regime accused chaebol entrepreneurs of illegal and unfair profiting and repossessed their commercial bank shares as illegally hoarded property. By fiat, all commercial banks became state property under the direct control of the Ministry of Finance (MOF).[9] Over the course of the next year, the Park regime reorganized

---

[2]Woo; Wade, 1985; *Asian Wall Street Journal*, 12/10/87; *Far Eastern Economic Review*, 6/10/93.

[3]*Asian Wall Street Journal*, 6/9/82; *Far Eastern Economic Review*, 4/25/85.

[4]Woo, p. 11.

[5]*Far Eastern Economic Review*, 6/10/93.

[6]Cole and Park, p. 46.

[7]Cole and Park, p. 48.

[8]Cole and Park, pp. 51–53.

[9]Mardon.

the banking structure, reformed fiscal policy, and restructured interest rates. In addition to rationalizing the financial system, these moves established the Korean capitalist developmental state's dominance over the chaebol, providing the regime with the means for assuring chaebol compliance with state goals.[10] In Gerschenkronian fashion, the Korean state "substituted" for group-affiliated banks that have been so important to business groups in Japan, Germany, and elsewhere. Woo notes that the state "mediates the flow of capital (domestic and foreign) to the *chaebol* and supervises its operations through a designated bank."[11] As one observer noted, "*Chaebol* act as sometimes rebellious offspring who must in the end follow the government's will. The government's main tool of control is credit: the *chaebol* grew and thrived on low-interest bank loans extended at government direction, and they have not lost their appetite. Credit is a leash that can be tightened to impose control with quick results."[12]

Despite a gradual shift in the balance of power between the state and chaebol and significant financial liberalization measures during subsequent regimes, Park's successors retained control over the major financial institutions and the allocation and channeling of investment funds. A 1985 study estimated that approximately 60 percent of bank credit was still being lent for government-designated purposes.[13] In 1990, subsidized "policy loans" were "still growing as a proportion of total assets and comprised 48 percent of the total rise in domestic credit" that year.[14] Although elected to office on a reform and liberalization platform, even Kim Young Sam and his "reform-minded advisors are loath to lose control of credit levers or private banks."[15] Public control of financial institutions and the discretionary allocation of their credit has been the primary mechanism the state has used for implementing its industrial policies, and has been the single most important environmental factor in the development of the chaebol.

What are these policies, and how has the state used them to shape the chaebol and attain its overall economic objectives? General Park Chong Hee's obsession—and an overriding goal of subsequent regimes—was economic growth, both as an end in itself and as a means to attain domestic legitimacy and bring Korea into the ranks of the developed nations.

---

[10]Amsden contends this state control of credit, and the state's resultant ability to exact compliance or "performance standards" from private firms, is precisely what has distinguished Japan, Korea, and Taiwan from all other late-industrializing countries (1989, p. 8).

[11]Woo, p. 150.

[12]*Far Eastern Economic Review,* 12/12/85.

[13]Skully and Viksnins.

[14]*Far Eastern Economic Review,* 6/13/91.

[15]*Far Eastern Economic Review,* 6/10/93.

In order to achieve this growth, the Korean state has been more willing than Taiwan to foster big business, often at the sacrifice of price stability and social equity. As one critic noted, this "growth-first development strategy" allowed the chaebol to grow "faster and bigger as tycoons showed unquestionable loyalty to government plans, which at times outweighed economic principles. In return, an indebted government lavished everything from restrictions on imports to subsidized bank lending and export financing on the tycoons."[16]

By far the government's most important financial incentives to the chaebol for achieving these goals have been its low interest rate policy—an intentional discrepancy between official rates and the real cost of credit—and its guarantee of a stable flow of bank loans regardless of short-term performance.[17] Ku-hyun Jung contends that during the period between 1960 and 1980, government control of commercial bank credit was "the single most important source both of the government's influence over the private sector and the *chaebol*'s capital accumulation."[18] The government controlled both the price and the quantity of domestic credit and foreign loans, and thus could ration scarce, cheap credit to compliant borrowers, typically the chaebol. One study estimated that chaebol profit-taking as a result of money market distortions during these two decades totaled more than U.S.$5 billion, over half the total net value of the top fifty chaebol in 1980.[19]

This was particularly true during the period of HCI second-stage import substitution. This "big push" into (ultimately) export-oriented heavy and chemical industries came in two thrusts (1968–76 and 1977–79) and was initiated and sustained by huge state investments in and subsidies to the chaebol participants. Even the largest business groups were reluctant to assume the risks entailed in these projects, and participated only when the state provided "a combination of guarantees, equity participation, and increasingly distorted incentives in the form of tax concessions and preferential low-interest credit."[20] Although the production and export goals of this period were met and in many cases vastly surpassed, these gains came at the expense of spiraling inflation and a climbing foreign debt. Praising the accomplishments of this period, Alice Amsden nonetheless acknowledges that "the pursuit of fast growth was not restrained in the interest of price stability."[21] The 1979 oil crisis and the political turmoil surrounding Park's assassination dealt further blows to the economy.

[16] *Business Korea*, 12/84.
[17] Y. J. Cho.
[18] K. H. Jung, 1988, p. 76.
[19] As cited in K. H. Jung, 1988, p. 77.
[20] Cole and Park, p. 277. See also T. J. Cheng, 1990.
[21] Amsden, 1989, p. 100.

After coming to power in 1980, Chun had little choice but to endorse a program of economic austerity, tight anti-inflationary policies, and financial liberalization. The regime began privatizing the state-owned commercial banks and instituted a policy of high interest rates.[22] It phased out concessional rates for export loans in 1982 and in 1983 directed banks to hold the 1984 and 1985 borrowings of the thirty largest chaebol to 1983 levels. In 1984, the state instructed foreign banks to freeze their loans to the five largest groups.[23] That same year, the government attempted to further deter chaebol borrowing by limiting cross-lending between member firms of the same group and pressuring the groups to trim unproductive or minor subsidiaries and to offer shares of remaining group firms to the public.[24]

With these measures, the Chun regime hoped to lower inflation, curb foreign debt, remove structural advantages accruing to the chaebol, weaken their economic dominance, and improve their highly leveraged position.[25] Although the inflation rate did drop,[26] this came at the expense of flagging investment, stagnating exports, and numerous company failures. During the mid-1980s, the Chun regime forcibly merged, liquidated, or sold more than eighty ailing private companies, most prominently the entire Kukje chaebol.[27] The measures had other consequences as well, including the proliferation of nonbank financial institutions, discussed below.

But before the other regime goals of lessening chaebol economic dominance and indebtedness could be fully addressed, the countervailing needs to maintain employment and investment at home and a favorable image abroad began to outweigh the desire to trim chaebol debt. These concerns, combined with strong pressure from the business groups through the Federation of Korean Industries and proponents in the media,[28] led the government in 1986 to ease credit and relax other restrictions placed on the chaebol. The potentially harmful consequences of these reflationary measures were eased considerably by the onset later that same year of the "three lows": falling oil prices, declining international interest rates, and the fall of the U.S. dollar against the Japanese yen.

[22]Scitovsky.

[23]*Business Korea,* 8/84.

[24]*Business Korea,* 12/84; *New York Times,* 1/4/85.

[25]*Business Korea,* 12/84; *Far Eastern Economic Review,* 12/12/85.

[26]The Consumer Price Index dropped from 28.7 percent in 1980 to 21.3 percent in 1981, 7.3 percent in 1982, 3.4 percent in 1983, and remained below 3 percent through 1988. CETDC, 1989.

[27]*Financial Times,* 8/4/93.

[28]*Far Eastern Economic Review* (5/16/85) notes a *Dong-Ah Ilbo* editorial calling for the resignation of policymakers associated with the tight money policy.

Like his two predecessors, Roh Tae Woo took office in 1988 vowing to rein in the chaebol by cutting off their financial favors and curtailing their speculative financial practices. Riding a wave of popular sentiment, Roh ended preferential credits for export financing, reduced access to cheap funds for capital investment, forced the repayment of excessive bank borrowings, and restricted cross-shareholdings and investments in subsidiaries. However, efforts to force the largest groups to sell huge holdings of real estate and to limit lending to "core areas" of specialization met with great resistance and only partial success.[29]

Amsden and Yoon-Dae Euh argue that it is misleading to characterize these financial liberalization reforms of the 1980s as a move toward freer markets. Korea's financial system, they contend, is embedded in the state's industrial policy. Rather than relying on the price mechanism, Chun and Roh achieved their financial reform objectives through the creation of new institutions that retained a prominent role for financial bureaucrats and their formal and informal guidance of the financial system.[30] The Kim government, elected in 1993, has pledged sweeping financial reforms, but the slow pace of actual change has led observers to remain skeptical.[31] Moreover, to the extent that liberalization does succeed in removing the state from the financial sector, it lessens the state's ability to limit or otherwise influence growing chaebol dominance of the financial arena. When state and *chaebol* interests have converged, this matters little. But public measures taken in the past decade to rein in the chaebol have met with increasing private resistance and acrimony. To better understand this evolving dynamic and the linchpin role of finance, we must turn to the financial goals and strategies of Korea's private business groups.

## Private Compliance

As discussed in Chapter Two, for most of the period since the Korean War, the chaebol have had every reason to comply with the state's industrial policies and to avoid the sure and swift disincentives for noncompliance. Either as full partners in the corrupt practices of Rhee's predatory regime or as the chosen engines of growth in the developmental regimes since Park,[32] the chaebol have been the major benefactors of the state's

---

[29] *Far Eastern Economic Review,* 6/13/91, 10/10/91; *Asian Wall Street Journal,* 11/11/91.

[30] Amsden and Euh. They note that the government's power to broker access to preferential credit and its informal "window guidance" of banks and other financial institutions remain intact.

[31] *Far Eastern Economic Review,* 6/10/93. The *Financial Times* (11/11/93) notes the longstanding practice of the Finance Ministry to herald reforms and then delay or simply cancel them.

[32] For the distinction between predatory and developmental regimes, see Evans, 1989, 1992.

lucrative financial incentives. But these subsidies, at least for most recipients during most of this period, were contingent upon relatively consistent adherence to "performance standards" in line with state objectives.[33] In the oft-quoted words of Edward Mason et al., "A firm that does not respond as expected to particular incentives may find that its tax returns are subject to careful examination, or that its application for bank credit is studiously ignored, or that its outstanding bank loans are not renewed. If incentive procedures do not work, government agencies show no hesitation in resorting to command backed by compulsion. In general, it does not take a Korean firm long to learn that it will 'get along' best by 'going along.' "[34]

Because of the highly leveraged position of the chaebol and state control of the formal financial institutions, financial carrots and sticks have been by far the most effective means of assuring private compliance with public policy. Mason et al. conclude that the "most potent instruments for implementing economic policy have undoubtedly been control of bank credit and access to foreign borrowers."[35]

The relative convergence of the objectives of both the state and big business for much of this period greatly facilitated the latter's compliance with state directives. Given Park's growth-first policy and his selection of the chaebol as the engines of this growth, the groups were more than willing to "go along" with policies designed to achieve this end. Moreover, private entrepreneurs in Korea are accustomed to an interventionist state. After nearly thirty years of developmental state intervention, businessmen have adjusted their market activities to accommodate and utilize the state's role. As one observer noted in 1987, "bankers and businessmen have come to rely on government intrusion. When the owner of Dong-A Motor Co., a jeep and truck maker wanted to sell his financially troubled enterprise this year, he asked the trade ministry to find him a buyer. A deputy minister telephoned Ssangyong's Mr. Kim, who bought Dong-A. 'That's the way deals are struck here,' says Mr. Kim."[36]

But public policy and chaebol objectives have certainly not been identical, even in "Korea Inc." Interests have diverged for both economic and sociocultural reasons. Publicly determined "performance standards," even when sweetened with generous incentives, are not necessarily economically rational for individual firms. Because of this, the chaebol, like their counterparts in Taiwan, have devised numerous means for subverting this process in pursuit of private gain. Moreover, the prevalence of

[33] Amsden, 1989.
[34] Mason et al., p. 265.
[35] Mason et al., p. 267.
[36] *Asian Wall Street Journal*, 12/10/87.

"continuous consultation between firms and public officials" has made
the financial system highly susceptible to corruption.[37] This symbiotic relationship has bred rampant scandals involving payoffs of public officials
for private favors. Although Mason et al. argue that "there is very little
evidence that such corruption as it exists interferes in any serious way
with production processes,"[38] revelations during the Roh and Kim admin-
istrations indicate that previously publicized scandals of the Rhee and
Park regimes are but a tip of the iceberg.[39] Although regime goals have
typically been met, there have often been predatory private gains at great
public expense.

Moreover, the interests of the chaebol family owners are not always in
the best interest of the business group as an economic enterprise.
Though corporate responsibility is generally more important to chaebol
owners than to their counterpart in Taiwan, the preservation of familial
ownership and control of the business group often takes precedent over
market opportunities and even lucrative government incentives and strident cajolery. In 1984, the Korean finance minister revealed that the government had unsuccessfully "urged" the Hyundai group's flagship,
Hyundai Engineering and Construction, to publicly list shares on twenty-
eight separate occasions.[40] At other times, public and private interests
have diverged because of opportunities for personal or familial economic
gain. Chaebol owners often "find private uses for loans which were supposed to go into the business; they are quite happy to let the business
become insolvent when things go wrong, while their own personal interests remain intact."[41]

A final divergence in this otherwise compliant relationship has resulted
when the regime has chosen policies specifically or indirectly designed to
limit the activities of the chaebol. Because of the popular perception of
chaebol corruption and the legitimacy needs of successive Korean regimes (as well as government concern over the growing power of the
chaebol), the government has periodically resorted to attacks on the business groups. Although often no more than rhetoric or smoke screen
shielding de facto chaebol support, some of this "chaebol-bashing" has
found its professed target.[42] A dramatic case of this was the government's
manhandling of the Kukje group (discussed in the final section of this

[37]Mason et al., p. 265.
[38]Mason et al., p. 265.
[39]For a discussion of government-business scandals during the Rhee regime, see K. D.
Kim. For parliamentary revelations of the extent of corruption during the Park and Chun
regimes, see *Business Korea*, 11/89.
[40]*Business Korea*, 7/84.
[41]*Far Eastern Economic Review*, 2/28/75.
[42]One observer refers to this "*chaebol*-bashing" as a "periodic South Korean pastime"
(*Far Eastern Economic Review*, 3/1/90).

chapter). Less drastic measures, such as tight credit policies and fair trade legislation, have met with stiff and continued resistance from the chaebol. Ironically, many government policies designed to liberalize the economy and level the playing field have in fact enhanced the growing financial power of the chaebol. The privatization of formal financial institutions allowed the chaebol to gain increasing control of these institutions, despite government efforts to limit the concentration of ownership. Through a system of interlocking directorates in financial institutions, the chaebol control most short-term finance companies, insurance companies, and securities firms, and have major stakes in the commercial banks as well. With the exception of the commercial banks, most domestic financial institutions are essentially subsidiaries of the chaebol.[43] The huge (though shrinking) informal credit market has also proved to be a valuable source of chaebol funds that is largely beyond the control of the state.

Finally, although the groups have chafed at government pressure to retire portions of their enormous debt, the success of this pressure has actually enhanced the chaebol's autonomy from their lenders. The declining debt ratios have increased the groups' retained earnings and improved their credit standing abroad, further lessening their dependence on the state. As will become apparent in the following two sections, however, the groups are still very dependent on the state for credit, and for the most part are very responsive to state-proffered incentives. But increasingly, the relationship is one not of dependence, as it once was, or independence, as it has approached in Taiwan, but one of interdependence or symbiosis.[44]

Financial capital lies at the heart of this relationship. As one Korean official noted, "the largest groups are now so big that, though the government still has the power to pull the financial rug from under their feet, it dare not risk doing so."[45] Although the Korean system of debt-based financing may in fact have given the state unprecedented leverage over private business,[46] the stakes have become so great that this leverage has nearly been reversed. Citing Theodore Lowi, Woo refers to this situation as a perennial " 'state of permanent receivership,' whereby any institution large enough to be a significant factor in the community shall have its stability underwritten (the system promotes bankruptcy, but the state cannot let big firms go bankrupt)."[47] During the heyday of development, the strategy of the private chaebol often was to expand to the point that

[43] *Korea Business World,* 3/91; Skully and Viksnins.
[44] E. M. Kim, 1988.
[45] *Far Eastern Economic Review,* 12/12/85.
[46] Wade, 1985.
[47] Woo, p. 13.

bankruptcy became socially unacceptable. As one Korean scholar observed when comparing the Korean situation between the chaebol and the state with that of Latin American countries and U.S. banks, "If you owe the bank a thousand dollars, it's your problem; but if you owe the bank a million dollars, it becomes the problem of the bank."

## FINANCIAL SYSTEM

### *Supervisory Agencies*

Throughout modern Korean history, the formal financial system has been highly centralized and regulated, with stringent restrictions on the entry and activities of financial institutions and the pricing and exchange of financial instruments. For most of this period, financial policy has been administered through a central bank firmly under the control of the top political leadership.

During the colonial period, the functions of a central bank were handled first by the Japanese Daiichi Ginkoo (1905–09) and then were turned over to the Bank of Korea in 1909, which was renamed the Bank of Chosen in 1911. This bank, under Japanese colonial administration, retained central bank authority until the departure of the Japanese in 1945. As part of the 1950 financial reform program, this bank was renamed the Bank of Korea (BOK) in the hope of transforming it into a strong, autonomous central bank responsible for managing monetary policy and supervising commercial banks. The BOK did little, however, until after the Korean War, and even then, it remained scarcely more than a funding source for the dominant Ministry of Finance.[48]

As part of his sweeping reforms to centralize management of the economy, Park amended the BOK charter in 1962, placing the central bank under the Monetary board chaired by the minister of finance. This gave the MOF direct control of the BOK. Any measures proposed by the finance minister but rejected by the Monetary Board reverted to Park for final decision, effectively placing financial supervision directly under the president.[49] With heavy influence from the MOF, the Monetary Board determines required reserve ratios and maximum deposit and loan rates for all banking institutions, the rates of discount and interest on BOK loans, and the volume of securities the BOK sells or buys in the open market. The Board can also set a ceiling on the total volume of a bank's outstanding loans and investments (even to specific industries) and re-

[48]Cole and Park.
[49]Mardon.

quire that all loans in excess of the specified ceiling be submitted the BOK for prior approval.[50]

Unlike their Western counterparts, Korean monetary authorities have relied primarily on direct controls for implementing monetary policies. By far the most essential of these direct controls has been the government's ability and willingness to set interest rates at artificially low levels for selected borrowers and/or projects, effectively reducing or eliminating the risks involved in targeted industrial or exporting ventures. Table 4-1 indicates the wide variety of rates and the extent to which specific policy loans were subsidized.

Table 4-1 reveals the extent to which the government has subsidized the interest rates charged to corporate borrowers. By both design and default, the primary beneficiaries of these concessional rates have been the chaebol. At times charging as little as half the ordinary bank rate, the inflation rate, and one-fourth the rate of curb market loans, the government was able to assure chaebol participation in government-promoted

*Table 4-1.* Loan rates and inflation rates in Korea (percent)

| Year | General loan | Policy loans (lending rates) | | | Curb market rate | GNP deflator |
|---|---|---|---|---|---|---|
| | | Export | Machinery Promotion Fund | National Investment Fund | | |
| 1962–70 | 21.5 | 8.3 | — | — | 55.75 | — |
| 1971 | 22.0 | 6.0 | n.a. | n.a. | 46.4 | 12.9 |
| 1972 | 15.5 | 6.0 | — | — | 37.0 | 16.3 |
| 1973 | 15.5 | 7.0 | 10.0 | — | 33.4 | 12.1 |
| 1974 | 15.5 | 9.0 | 12.0 | 12.0 | 40.6 | 30.4 |
| 1975 | 15.5 | 9.0 | 12.0 | 12.0 | 41.3 | 24.6 |
| 1976 | 18.0 | 8.0 | 13.0 | 14.0 | 40.5 | 21.2 |
| 1977 | 16.0 | 8.0 | 13.0 | 14.0 | 38.1 | 16.6 |
| 1978 | 19.0 | 9.0 | 15.0 | 16.0 | 39.3 | 22.8 |
| 1979 | 19.0 | 9.0 | 15.0 | 16.0 | 42.4 | 19.6 |
| 1980 | 20.0 | 15.0 | 20.0 | 22.0 | 44.9 | 24.0 |
| 1981 | 17.0 | 15.0 | 11.0 | 16.5–17.5 | 35.3 | 16.4 |
| 1982 | 10.0 | 10.0 | 10.0 | 10.0 | 32.8 | 7.1 |
| 1983 | 10.0 | 10.0 | 10.0 | 10.0 | 25.8 | 5.0 |
| 1984 | 10.0–11.5 | 10.0 | 10.0–11.5 | 10.0–11.5 | 24.8 | 3.9 |
| 1985 | 10.0–11.5 | 10.0 | 10.0–11.5 | 10.0–11.5 | 24.0 | 4.2 |
| 1986 | 10.0–11.5 | 10.0 | 10.0–11.5 | 10.0–11.5 | 23.1 | 2.8 |
| 1987 | 10.0–11.5 | 10.0 | 10.0–11.5 | 10.0–11.5 | 22.9 | 3.5 |
| 1988 | 10.0–13.0 | 10.0 | 10.0–11.5 | 10.0–11.5 | 22.7 | 5.9 |
| 1989 | 10.0–12.5 | 10.0 | 10.0–11.5 | 10.0–11.5 | 23.7 | 5.2 |
| 1990 | 10.0–12.5 | 10.0 | 10.0–11.5 | 10.0–11.5 | 20.6 | 10.6 |
| 1991 | 10.0–12.5 | 10.5 | 10.0–11.5 | 10.0–11.5 | 21.4 | 10.9 |

SOURCES: World Bank, vol. 2, p. 112; Sakong, p. 244.

[50]Nam and Park.

ventures in exchange for continued receipt of these lucrative policy loans. During the 1960s and 1970s, this difference between the general lending rates and preferential export rates averaged eight to fifteen points in Korea, compared with a spread of only five to seven points for Taiwan during the same period.[51] Since 1983, when the Chun regime began to phase out policy loans, bank rates have remained roughly half of curb rates, indicating a continued scarcity of funds and a brokering position for the state. This policy of artificially low rates has not come without costs. It has hampered the growth of savings and weakened the central bank's ability to use more subtle, open market operations to control the economy. In order to understand why the government has been willing to accept this trade-off and how it has affected the development and organization of the chaebol, we must turn to the business groups' specific sources of funds.

## Sources of Funds: Institutions, Markets, and Instruments

In order to understand the financial risks and opportunities the Korean financial environment imposes upon the chaebol, it is necessary to analyze the groups' funding sources. These are the instruments, markets, and institutions that make up Korea's financial system. A financial instrument is created when an economic unit—household, firm, government—produces more than it consumes or internally invests and then makes this surplus available to another economic unit in exchange for some kind of financial claim. Those units wanting to loan or borrow surplus funds exchange these instruments in financial markets. With the exception of arms-length transactions between individual savers and borrowers, these transfers occur through specialized formal or informal financial intermediaries or institutions.

Table 4-2 lists the major sources of chaebol debt and equity financing. These financial markets and institutions vary in their degree of sophistication, government control, and relative value to the groups. In order to understand the relative importance of these various sources to the chaebol, I will first explain the logic and motivations behind Korean businesses' debt-based capital structure. This is followed by a specific analysis of the formal, informal, and internal institutions and markets comprising the groups' sources of funds.

## Relative Importance of Various Sources of Funds

A breakdown of Korean firms' sources of funds reveals interesting trends. Although specific information on the chaebol is unavailable,

---

[51]Y. J. Cho.

Table 4-2. Major sources of chaebol finance

| Category | Markets and institutions |
|----------|--------------------------|
| Formal | domestic commercial banks |
| | investment and finance companies |
| | insurance companies |
| | bond market |
| | stock market |
| | foreign loan market |
| Informal | curb market |
| Internal | cross-lending and mutual guarantee |
| | cross-holding and joint investment |

Table 4-3 shows the general sources of funds for the corporate sector for various years. Table 4-3 indicates that during the early 1960s, Korean firms relied on internal sources (depreciation plus retained earnings) for nearly half of their financing, while the other half came from a roughly equal mixture of bank loans, nonbank loans (including curb loans), foreign loans, and securities. In 1963, in anticipation of normalizing relations with Japan, the Park regime introduced a system of bank guarantees for foreign loans. The government established these guarantees in order to facilitate the inflow of investment (debt) capital while allowing the

Table 4-3. Sources of funds for the corporate sector (percent)

| | 1963–65 | 1966–71 | 1972–76 | 1977–81 | 1982–86 | 1987–91 |
|---|---|---|---|---|---|---|
| Internal funds | 47.7 | 25.4 | 32.9 | 23.3 | 33.5 | 26.4 |
| External funds | 52.3 | 74.6 | 67.1 | 76.7 | 66.5 | 73.6 |
| Total | 100.0 | 100.0 | 100.0 | 100.0 | 100.0 | 100.0 |
| External funds | 100.0 | 100.0 | 100.0 | 100.0 | 100.0 | 100.0 |
| Borrowings from | | | | | | |
| Monetary | | | | | | |
| institutions | 48.4 | 41.8 | 51.1 | 53.7 | 41.8 | 36.0 |
| Banks | 33.5 | 32.8 | 34.3 | 32.6 | 22.6 | 17.0 |
| Nonbanks | 15.0 | 9.0 | 16.8 | 21.1 | 19.2 | 19.0 |
| Securities (direct | | | | | | |
| finance) | 27.6 | 14.3 | 21.8 | 24.8 | 27.5 | 37.4 |
| Debts | 1.2 | 0.7 | 2.5 | 4.2 | 11.0 | 14.5 |
| Stocks | 21.4 | 11.8 | 18.1 | 14.4 | 16.5[a] | 22.9[a] |
| Capital paid in | 5.0 | 2.7 | 1.3 | 1.9 | — | — |
| Corporate bills | — | — | 1.8 | 5.5 | 3.9 | 3.3 |
| Government and | | | | | | |
| curb market loans | 8.5 | 7.8 | −0.3 | 0.8 | 24.9[b] | 20.2[b] |
| Borrowing from abroad | 15.4 | 36.2 | 26.6 | 15.2 | 1.9 | 3.1 |

SOURCE: Amsden and Euh, p. 381. Copyright 1993. Reprinted with kind permission from Elsevier Science Ltd, The Boulevard, Langford Lane, Kidlington OX5 1GB, U.K.

[a]Stocks and capital paid in.

[b]Others included.

government to continue restrictions on Japanese equity investments. This was done out of fear of Japanese ownership and control of Korean business.[52]

These measures, coupled with interest rate reforms in 1965 that greatly increased the volume of loanable funds, made bank and foreign loans the dominant source of corporate funding. For the period of 1966–71, internally generated funds comprised barely one-fourth of the total. During the 1970s, Korea's corporate sector continued to rely heavily on indirect (bank and nonbank) external financing, which peaked in 1980 at 83 percent of total capital.[53] Over the course of the 1980s, there was a shift from foreign to domestic finance, from commercial bank to nonbank finance, and from indirect finance to direct finance (corporate securities).[54] Short-term renewable loans from investment finance companies (in addition to the curb market) and securities in the form of corporate bonds have been particularly popular, especially for the chaebol.

This reliance on borrowed funds or debt as a source of finance rather than owner equity (stock and retained earnings) is much greater among Korean firms than their counterparts in Taiwan. As Table 4-4 indicates, for the period 1980–84, Korean corporations were significantly more dependent on external funds than their Taiwanese counterparts, and nearly twice as dependent on loans for that external portion than were firms in Taiwan.

A comparison of debt/equity ratios for manufacturing firms in Korea and several other countries also reflects this difference. Since 1980, debt ratios in Korea have been greater than those in Japan, more than twice those of Taiwan's firms, and more than triple those of U.S. firms. (See

*Table 4-4.* Comparison of corporate finance, 1980–84 (percent)

| | Korea | Japan | Taiwan |
|---|---|---|---|
| Internal finance | 27.6 | 46.4 | 39.7 |
| External finance | 72.4 | 53.6 | 60.3 |
| Total | 100.0 | 100.0 | 100.0 |
| | | | |
| External finance | 100.0 | 100.0 | 100.0 |
| Indirect finance | 41.8 | 52.5 | 23.8 |
| (Stock capital paid in) | (17.9) | (5.4) | (34.3) |
| Borrowings from abroad | 5.0 | — | 8.6 |

SOURCE: J. S. Shin, 1988. Reproduced from *Monthly Review* by permission of Korea Exchange Bank.

[52]Cole and Park.
[53]J. S. Shin.
[54]Amsden and Euh; C. H. Roh, 1990.

Table 4-5.)[55] Despite government efforts to improve the capital structure since 1980, the debt/equity ratio of listed manufacturing firms was 350.9 percent in 1986, 340.1 percent in 1987, and 296 percent in 1988.[56]

Korea has relied more extensively than Taiwan on foreign borrowing as opposed to domestic savings to finance corporate debt. The forced nature of Korea's industrial investment drive, combined with considerably less domestic savings to draw upon, compelled the government to seek investment funds abroad.[57] As in Taiwan, much of Korea's early domestic capital formation (DCF) came from foreign savings in the form of American aid.[58] Nearly 80 percent of all domestic investment in 1960 was financed by foreign aid. For the period 1962–66, still more than half of DCF derived from foreign savings. With domestic savings still at only 8 percent of GNP, the remainder was funded by foreign borrowings (and

Table 4-5. Debt/equity ratio of manufacturing firms in selected countries, 1972–85 (percent)

| Year | Korea | U.S. | Japan | Taiwan |
|---|---|---|---|---|
| 1972 | 313.4 | — | 424.0 | — |
| 1973 | 272.7 | — | 449.0 | — |
| 1974 | 316.0 | 193.2 | 459.0 | 91.5 |
| 1975 | 339.5 | 60.6 | 488.0 | 99.3 |
| 1976 | 364.6 | 158.8 | 488.0 | 100.4 |
| 1977 | 367.2 | 172.0 | 475.0 | 97.4 |
| 1978 | 366.8 | 160.3 | 446.0 | 92.8 |
| 1979 | 377.1 | 160.5 | 418.0 | 85.3 |
| 1980 | 487.9 | 177.0 | 385.0 | 82.5 |
| 1981 | 451.5 | 175.9 | 378.0 | 78.6 |
| 1982 | 385.8 | 166.4 | 342.0 | 78.1 |
| 1983 | 360.3 | 158.5 | 324.0 | 84.8 |
| 1984 | 342.7 | 134.5 | 310.1 | 110.1 |
| 1985 | 348.4 | — | 289.1 | 121.2 |

SOURCE: Leipziger, 1988, p. 128. Reproduced from *World Development* by permission of the publisher, Pergamon Press, Inc.

[55]E. H. Kim argues that firms in Korea are much more highly leveraged than a dyadic comparison with Japan reveals because substantial portions of Japanese corporate assets have not been revalued since World War II, while well-performing Korean corporate assets are frequently revalued. Using market-value-based measures rather than book-value-based measures, Kim shows that equity ratios in Korea for the period 1977–86 averaged around 16 percent, compared with averages between 40 to 50 percent for Japanese and American corporations.
[56]C. H. Roh, 1990, p. 6.
[57]For a detailed discussion of the differences in savings rates between Korea and Taiwan, the reasons behind these differences, and their economic consequences, see Scitovsky, pp. 168–84.
[58]Cumings notes that for the period 1946–78, Korea received a total of nearly U.S.$6 billion in U.S. economic grants and loans, compared with a total of $6.89 billion for all of Africa and $14.8 billion for all of Latin America. "Only India, with a population seventeen times that of Korea, received more" (p. 67).

inflation). For the period 1965–80, 70 percent of investment came from domestic savings, with the remainder funded by inflation and foreign debt.[59]

This conscious government choice to rely extensively on foreign loans while restricting foreign investment has had distinct trade-offs. Korea's debt burden and debt-servicing costs—though now declining—have been much greater than Taiwan's, and once rivaled those of Latin America.[60] And although borrowing from abroad may offer a country more autonomy than allowing foreign equity ownership, Koreans are very much aware of the vulnerability inherent in excessive debt: the Japanese used unpaid debts as an excuse to annex Korea in 1910. These dangers notwithstanding, the Korean government has been able to use these foreign funds to finance its long-term investments and sustain its rapid growth. Not surprisingly, the primary recipients of these, and virtually all other, funds have been the chaebol.[61] The government, as broker of foreign funds, and in firm control of most domestic financial institutions, has made huge amounts of capital available to the groups.

As the main beneficiaries, the chaebol reflect the best and the worst of this skewed financial system. Their scale, diversity, and international competitiveness are in large part a consequence of their access to cheap, and often risk-free, financing. Given these benefits, it is not surprising that the chaebol dominate the financial system and are the most indebted of all Korean enterprises. In 1983, the top thirty business groups had capital loans and other payment guarantees equal to 48 percent of the nation's total bank credits. In Taiwan, by comparison, the 100 largest firms had an 11.6 percent share of total domestic credit and the top 333 had only 18 percent. The top three chaebol—Hyundai, Daewoo, and Samsung—alone received nearly 10 percent of all institutional loans that year.[62] In 1988, the top thirty chaebol held U.S.$55 billion in bank credit and another U.S.$10 billion in loans from nonbank financial institutions, equivalent to nearly 40 percent of GNP. Samsung along held nearly 6 percent of all bank loans and guarantees that year.[63]

In 1985, it was estimated that the chaebol as a group had an average debt/equity ratio of 450 percent, compared with 350 percent for the whole manufacturing sector, a situation making the chaebol "among the worst financially structured bodies in the world."[64] Another 1985 study

[59]Nam and Park; Mardon; Wade, 1985.
[60]Woo.
[61]In the period 1972–79, 79 percent of the asset growth of the top ten chaebol was financed by debt, compared with an average of 60 percent for all Korean corporations (Koo and Kim).
[62]*Business Korea*, 7/84; Woo.
[63]Bello and Rosenfeld.
[64]*Far Eastern Economic Review*, 12/12/85.

discovered that more than half of the top thirty groups had debt/equity ratios exceeding 500 percent,[65] and yet a third study that same year estimated an average debt/equity ratio for all the chaebol of 700 percent.[66] Seven of the top fifty chaebol had ratios of over 1,000 percent, with the worst at an astounding 47,699 percent.[67] Even by the end of the 1980s, despite continued state pressures for them to reduce their indebtedness, virtually all of the prominent chaebol still had major companies with astronomical debt burdens.[68] Although increased direct and indirect chaebol ownership of private financial institutions has decreased the groups' dependence on the state, it has had little effect on their indebtedness.

This situation prompts one final issue that must be addressed before examining specific financial institutions. Why have the state and its chaebol partners opted for this highly leveraged system of corporate finance? What has been the government's motivation for promoting the conditions and providing the incentives for this system to develop? If a government wants to promote rapid growth and development but cannot afford to wait for the slow growth of private firms' own profits or for the development of a fully functioning equities market, then it must encourage firms to borrow heavily. At the same time, the government must socialize the risks inherent in taking on these debts by placing the state in control of loanable funds.[69] This financial control gives the state a powerful incentive to continue a debt-based system. Chalmers Johnson notes, among other incentives, the "governmental ability to ration capital by manipulating its cost," the "utter dependence of private managers on their banks in order to operate at all," and "the power, combined with low political visibility it gives to Ministry of Finance bureaucrats."[70] The rationale behind this government control of debt-based industrial financing was "both economic and political: the credit instruments could be used to mobilize businessmen for major economic programs . . . , while on the political side [it] served to maintain control over, and cooperation from, the business community."[71]

If the system has been logical from the government's perspective, pri-

[65] *Far Eastern Economic Review,* 12/12/85.
[66] *Far Eastern Economic Review,* 8/22/85.
[67] Woo.
[68] *Business Korea* (9/87) provides a table of the thirty listed firms with the highest debt/equity ratios. The firm topping the list had a debt ratio of 6,396 percent. Samsung Construction was ninth at 853.1 percent. Samsung Semiconductor and Telecommunications was thirteenth at 819.3 percent. Korean Air, Lucky Development, Hyundai Engineering & Construction, Lucky-Goldstar, Intl., Daewoo Electronics, Samsung Aerospace, Doosan Glass, Daelim Industrial, and Sunkyong, Ltd., were among the top thirty. Samsung's debt ratio in 1990 was 675 percent; Daewoo's was 735 percent (*Business Korea,* 3/92).
[69] Wade, 1985.
[70] Johnson, 1987, pp. 148–49.
[71] Mason et al., p. 337.

vate motivations are even more obvious. The chaebol responded rationally to the financial environment in which they operated. This environment included chronic inflation, subsidized interest rates on formal loans, costly internal funds, meager corporate depreciation, high income tax on the retained earnings of privately held companies, and tax deductions for interest payments on loans.[72] As one small business owner bitterly complained: "People who do business with their own money are blockheads. A smart businessman should run into debt ten or fifteen times as high as his own net worth. Who would then dare to let this debt VIP go bankrupt?"[73]

Who indeed? As will be shown in the final section of this chapter, the most noteworthy exception to this policy of public protection fell because it failed to comply, both economically and politically. First, however, we turn to a brief description of the formal, informal, and internal financial institutions and markets supplying the chaebol.

## Formal Sources

### Domestic Commercial Banks

Korea's domestic commercial banks include the nationwide "city" banks as well as the provincial or local banks. Unlike the local banks, which have always been privately owned,[74] the city banks have had a much more intimate—though changing—relationship with the state. The strong uniformity among these banks in their organization and management is a result of extensive government intervention and their similar historical backgrounds. The three major commercial banks were Japanese owned, and like the financial system as a whole, they still reflect Japanese influence. With the departure of the Japanese in 1945, shares of these banks were transferred first to the U.S. military and then to the South Korean government. In 1954, under U.S. pressure, the government divested itself of its shareholdings in these banks. A small group of well-connected businessmen purchased the bulk of these shares. A fourth commercial bank, the Cho Heung Bank, had been largely Korean owned and did not go through this process.[75]

In 1961, Park repossessed all shares of the commercial banks held by large, private stockholders on the grounds they were illegally appro-

---

[72] E. H. Kim.

[73] *Business Korea*, 7/84.

[74] The local banks, first introduced in 1967 in an effort to promote regional development and balance the dispersion of the expanding commercial banking business, are now largely under the control of the chaebol. Their major clients are regional enterprises and public entities (Nam and Park).

[75] Cole and Park.

priated and hoarded. Through 1981, the government held roughly 30 percent of the shares of four of the five nationwide city banks,[76] which, as a group, dominated Korea's financial system, accounted for 85 percent of all bank loans and discounts in 1980.[77] After he came to power, Chun called for the privatization of these banks in 1981 as part of his liberalization campaign. His government authorized the establishment of two new private city banks: the Shinhan Bank in 1982, capitalized primarily by Koreans living in Japan, and the Koram Bank in 1983, a Bank of America joint venture with seventeen Korean companies.[78] Although the government had divested its shares of the city banks by 1983 and revised banking regulations to give the banks a freer hand in operations, the state still intervenes extensively in the banks' operations. Through the MOF, the government continues to appoint bank officers above the level of deputy head (often from the MOF's own ranks) and to approve all bank budgets and real estate purchases.[79]

Because of this continued state involvement, bank managers have very little to do with the management of their assets and, unlike their counterparts in Taiwan, have felt little accountability for the performance of their state-directed loans. Although the banks, in principle, require collateral for all loans except discounts on bills, government endorsement and guarantee of Korea's highly leveraged corporate expansion has lessened the significance of these collateral guarantees. Collateral pledged from the ten largest chaebol borrowers in 1983 covered only 86 percent of their combined bank debts.[80] This differs significantly from Taiwan's case, with obvious consequences for the growth and activities of the respective business groups.

The banks offer both long-term and short-term financing and payment guarantees to corporate borrowers. Short-term operations have traditionally dominated the market, with much of the demand for long-term funds being met through "rollovers" of short-term loans.[81] Much of the long-term bank credit comes not from deposits but through funds supplied by agencies of the federal government, such as the National Investment Fund (NIF). Administered by the BOK, NIF loans were first offered in 1973 to finance Korea's heavy and chemical industry (HCI) projects in the 1970s. The NIF mobilized public employee pension funds, the proceeds of national investment bonds (subscribed by financial industries), transfers from various government budgetary accounts, contributions

[76]The government privatized the Commercial Bank of Korea in 1972 (Nam and Park).
[77]Nam and Park.
[78]Skully and Viksnins.
[79]Amsden and Euh; *International Herald Tribune*, 5/25/87.
[80]*Business Korea*, 7/84.
[81]Kwack and Chung.

from other banks, and substantial private savings, and then channeled them through the commercial banks to HCI projects at heavily subsidized and often negative rates (see Table 4-1).[82]

Not surprisingly, the chaebol have been the dominant borrowers and beneficiaries of these commercial bank loans and payment guarantees. As of September 1983, the ten heaviest-borrowing chaebol had a combined total bank debt of nearly U.S.$10 billion, or 32 percent of all outstanding city bank loans.[83] In addition, 1983's 100 heaviest-borrowing companies—the majority of which are affiliated with chaebol—accounted for 46 percent of the banks' payment guarantees.[84]

Although Korea's banking laws limit the amount a bank can lend to one borrower to 25 percent of the bank's net worth, and the amount of payment guarantees to 50 percent, these limits have been violated frequently.[85] In fact, many of the largest chaebol debtors are major shareholders in the banks from which they borrow, a situation raising criticism that the chaebol have borrowed from the banks in order to purchase control of them. Many of the largest groups have extensive loans from banks in which they have significant equity positions.[86] Table 4-6 indicates the extent of these chaebol shareholdings.

Moreover, Korean law restricts single shareholders of the nationwide commercial banks (except for the two joint-venture banks) to 8 percent of total ownership. Like Park's earlier nationalization of the banks, this legislation was designed to prevent the banks from falling under the excessive influence of a few large (chaebol) shareholders.[87] However, as Table 4-6 reveals, "a number of the conglomerates exercise effective control by holding bank stock through a variety of associated companies."[88] This is only one of several ways (to be discussed below) in which the chaebol have utilized their multiple units to enhance their financial ca-

[82]Kwack and Chung.
[83]In announcing these figures, the MOF broke a long-standing tradition of silence regarding the extent of chaebol debt. Observers speculated that the ten heaviest-borrowing chaebol were Hyundai, Samsung, Lucky-Goldstar, Kukje, Ssangyong, Hyosung, Sunkyong, Daelim, Daewoo, and Hanjin (*Business Korea*, 7/84).
[84]*Business Korea*, 7/84.
[85]In 1983, there were thirty-one reported cases in which bank loans went beyond the 25 percent limit and twenty-one cases in which payment guarantees exceeded the 50 percent limit (*Business Korea*, 7/84).
[86]As of 1983, Ssangyong Cement (of the Ssangyong group) owed 43.9 billion won to Cho Heung Bank, in which it had equity interest (see Table 4-6). Daewoo Corporation (Daewoo) owed 54.9 billion won, and Inchon Iron and Steel (Hyundai) 19.3 billion won, to Korea First Bank. Samsung owed 37.4 billion won to the Commercial Bank of Korea. Daelim Industrial owed 35 billion won, and Lucky, Ltd. (Lucky-Goldstar), owed 18.4 billion won, to Hanil Bank. Dongkuk Steel Mill owed 26 billion won to the Bank of Seoul and Trust (*Business Korea*, 7/84).
[87]C. K. Lee.
[88]Skully and Viksnins, p. 113.

Table 4-6. Chaebol shareholdings in banks

| Group | Cho Heung | Korea First | Hanil | Bank of Seoul | Commercial bank |
|---|---|---|---|---|---|
| Hyundai | 2.14 | 9.35 | 7.27 | 11.83[a] | — |
| Daewoo | 1.23 | 23.82[a] | 2.22 | 5.29 | 4.48 |
| Samsung | 8.34 | 5.69 | 9.72 | — | 15.97[b] |
| Lucky-Goldstar | 1.71 | 5.30[a] | 5.87[a] | — | — |
| Hanjin | — | — | 8.47[b] | — | — |
| Taekwang | 3.77 | — | — | 4.56 | — |
| Ssangyong | 5.57 | — | — | — | — |
| Daelim | — | — | 9.29[b] | — | — |
| Shindongah | 7.98 | 7.24 | — | 9.90 | — |
| Dong Ah | — | — | 10.03 | — | — |
| Korea Explosives | — | — | 3.16 | — | — |
| Dongkuk | — | — | — | 4.59 | — |
| Hanil-Kukje | 4.05 | 2.18 | 3.69[b] | — | 1.91 |
| Hanyang | — | — | — | — | 1.40 |

SOURCES: Compiled from *Business Korea*, 7/84; World Bank, vol. 1, p. 92.
[a]Quasi-lead bank.
[b]Lead bank.

NOTE: Although shareholding data is from October 1993, Table 4-6 reflects Daewoo's 1984 acquisition of Sambo Securities and the 1985 merger of the Hanil Synthetic Fiber and Kukje groups.

pacities. In 1991, the government approved the transformation of three investment and finance to enhance their financial capacities. In 1991, the government approved the transformation of three investment and finance companies backed by major chaebol into two new commercial banks. Korean Investment formed one, and two other investment and finance companies—Hanyang and Lucky-Goldstar—merged to form the other.[89] Contrary to the objectives of the state, liberalization has increased the financial autonomy of the chaebol and "contributed to a rise, not to a decline in economic concentration."[90]

Investment and Finance Companies

Although Korea's nonbank financial firms include a variety of institutions, only the investment and finance companies and insurance companies have been important sources of finance for the chaebol. Barred from direct ownership of the commercial banks and suffering from insufficient funds generated by the government-controlled banks, during the 1970s and 1980s the chaebol began to rely increasingly on group-owned investment and insurance companies as "financial arms to mobilize and distrib-

[89]*Far Eastern Economic Review*, 6/13/91.
[90]Amsden, 1989, p. 136.

ute financial resources among the business firms they owned or controlled."[91] Both of these institutions will be examined.

Korea's investment and finance companies (IFCs) were launched in 1972 and in an effort to absorb curb market funds and meet the corporate sector's growing need for short-term funds. The government first authorized the establishment of sixteen private IFCs, then doubled this number in 1982 in a second assault on the curb market. The IFCs act primarily as brokers and dealers in short-term credit instruments, issuing their own paper as well as discounting, selling, accepting, and guaranteeing commercial paper issued by other firms. Although their interest rates are supposedly market-determined, their maximum rate ceilings are in fact set by the MOF; they average roughly 1 percent per annum higher than bank rates and three to five points cheaper than curb rates.[92] Customers are willing to pay more for IFC financing because these funds are easier to obtain than bank loans and require no collateral. The IFCs have been lax in evaluating firms' credit standings, assuming the government will bail out debtors rather than allow them to go bankrupt. Prior to the collapse of Kukje in 1985, this was a safe assumption; since then, the risks have been much greater.[93]

As a convenient source of short-term funds for the chaebol, the IFCs grew spectacularly during the 1970s but slackened during the early years of the Chun regime as a result of slowed corporate growth and government rate intervention. Chun's freeze on bank loans to the most highly leveraged chaebol firms in 1984 once again spurred the growth of the IFCs as the chaebol turned to them to cope with their cash-flow problems. By the end of the 1980s the thirty-two IFCs provided over half as many loans and received over half as much in deposits as the much larger commercial banks.[94] It is estimated that through interlocking directorates and shareholdings the chaebol control more than three-fourths of the IFC. Given this control, it is not surprising that the chaebol are the IFCs' largest customers. In 1983, the ten largest borrowers among chaebol accounted for more than 30 percent of the IFCs' outstanding loans.[95]

Insurance Companies

The first insurance firms were established in 1962, and Korea's domestic insurance market is now the twelfth largest in the world. The opera-

[91]Cole and Park.

[92]*Asian Wall Street Journal*, 3/11/87.

[93]The MOF accused the IFC of prompting the collapse of several construction and shipping firms (which relied heavily on their short-term, high-interest financing) by calling in the loans at the first sign of trouble. The IFC countered that while the banks, holding collateral, can afford to forgive loans and not foreclose, they (IFC) have to try to collect their loans before the faltering companies collapse (*Asian Wall Street Journal*, 3/11/87).

[94]C. H. Roh, 1990.

[95]*Business Korea*, 7/84; *Asian Wall Street Journal*, 3/11/87.

tions of the insurance companies are strictly regulated by the MOF, and until the mid-1980s, the market was essentially closed to foreign firms. Despite some liberalization measures, the fact that each chaebol relies on its group's insurance company has effectively kept the outsiders excluded. Of Korea's twenty-six life and nonlife insurance companies, eleven are under the ownership of a single chaebol and most of the rest are jointly invested by several of the groups.[96] In 1990, the top ten chaebol controlled nearly 40 percent of all insurance company assets and used these captive firms "to cater to the needs of their respective business groups."[97]

Most of the insurance companies' assets are channeled back into the business groups, which rely on the companies for some equity investments but primarily for large, direct loans. In 1985, life insurance companies' equity holdings accounted for only 5 percent of total assets, with more than two-thirds of assets in the form of direct loans, most of them to member firms.[98] One observer noted that price competition and profits are secondary to the companies because of the "business groups' habits of using the insurance companies as sources of ready cash."[99]

### Capital Markets

The capital or securities market is the market for bonds (long-term debt instruments) and stocks (long-term equity instruments). Until the 1970s, the formal capital market played virtually no role in raising funds for the chaebol (or other private Korean firms). There were compelling reasons on both sides. For investors, the curb market offered much higher rates, and profits could be pocketed untaxed. For those seeking funds, the underdevelopment of the capital market and the financial system's bias toward bank loans limited that market's growth.

Since the late 1960s, the Korean government has gone to great lengths to enhance the role of the securities market as a source of corporate finance, providing unprecedented carrots and sticks designed to bring both investors and companies to the market. These have included punitive taxes on real estate investments, forced conversion of curb loans to capital subscriptions, preferential dividends and tax exemptions for stock and bond holdings, tax benefits and depreciation allowances for listed firms, and tax penalties and curtailed access to bank credits for targeted firms refusing to list on the exchange.[100]

---

[96]Bello and Rosenfeld.

[97]*Economist*, 10/17/92; *Far Eastern Economic Review*, 10/3/85.

[98]Rowley; H. N. Kim.

[99]*Far Eastern Economic Review*, 10/3/85. In 1990, Samsung Life supplied U.S.$800 million in loans to its sister companies (*Korea Business World*, 3/91).

[100]For a discussion of the compliance mechanisms employed to enhance the capital market, see Nam and Park.

Despite these government efforts, Korea's capital market has been slow to develop and deepen, with a few notable exceptions. Familial business groups in Korea, like their counterparts in Taiwan, have been very reluctant to sell shares publicly, fearing a loss of familial control, a dilution of familial ownership, an increase in dividend payments, and the leakage of secret information to rival companies. Although these attitudes are gradually changing as the capital market grows in sophistication and the chaebol continue their rapid expansion, the most popular long-term capital instruments are still bonds, which require no dilution of ownership or control.

Korea's negligible bond market jumped to life in 1971 with the downward adjustment of bank deposit rates and the introduction of a corporate bond guarantee system. These steps made it possible for chaebol firms with good credit ratings to issue bonds at competitive rates. Since that time, the corporate bond market has grown steadily, and in the early 1980s it dwarfed the stock market in size and significance. By 1985, bonds accounted for 91.5 percent of total corporate financing through the capital market.[101] Interest in corporate bonds waned in the latter half of the 1980s as the government stepped up incentives for selling and buying equity issues. Bond trading is dominated by chaebol-affiliated institutional investors including insurance companies, securities companies, and security investment trust companies. Only securities firms can underwrite bond and stock issues, and nine of the top ten chaebol own such firms. Owning these "tame" securities firms enables the chaebol family to move funds secretly among member firms and to hold more shares in affiliated companies than is permitted by law.[102]

The relative popularity of the bond market can be attributed to government incentives and the debt status of bond instruments. Corporate issuers see the bonds as simply another form of debt; buyers prefer bonds because they are seen as a more stable investment than highly speculative stocks. This gap between debt and equity has been bridged since the issuance of Korea's first convertible bonds in 1985. All these bonds have been issued on foreign capital markets by listed, chaebol-affiliated companies. Acting initially without government approval or guidelines, the companies claimed that the issues provided them with a new method of improving their financial structure and enhancing their international experience and recognition. Despite its professed desire to bring greater sophistication and openness to Korea's capital markets, only since 1991 has the government shown any intention of allowing the conversion of the bonds to equity to proceed.[103]

[101] *Far Eastern Economic Review*, 4/25/85.
[102] *Economist*, 10/17/92.
[103] *Asian Wall Street Journal*, 11/12/87; *Far Eastern Economic Review*, 6/13/91.

The Korean Stock Exchange (KSE) opened in 1956 as a market for trading government bonds issued during the Korean War. During the 1960s, the only available shares were those of state-owned manufacturing enterprises and banks. As of 1969, there were only forty-two companies listed on the exchange. The pace of growth quickened, however, after the 1972 enactment of the Public Corporation Inducement Law, which offered numerous incentives to individual and institutional investors, as well as to listing companies. The number of listed companies jumped to 356 by 1978, but following the speculative "boom and bust" atmosphere of the late 1970s, the market stagnated until the mid-1980s. Although the capitalization had doubled since 1978, the number of listed companies had declined to 342 by 1985. Strict government caps on bank loans to the heavily indebted chaebol since 1987, and additional incentives to raise funds through public equity issues, boosted the stock market again.[104] Despite periodic booms and busts, the significance of the market has steadily climbed since then. The number of listed companies jumped from 389 in 1987 to 502 in 1988 and stood at 686 in 1991.[105]

In comparative terms, however, the KSE remains, in the words of one analyst, "a midget." As of 1985, it was only one-fifth the size of Hong Kongs's exchange, half the size of Malaysia's, and considerably smaller than the Taiwan Stock Exchange. In that year, the capitalization of the stock market equaled less than 9 percent of GNP, whereas foreign debt represented over 56 percent of GNP.[106] Although individual investors dominate the KSE (comprising well over half of total share ownership),[107] Korea's stock-trading population in 1983 numbered only 630,000, less than the total number of shareholders that year in the U.S. corporation AT&T.[108] The market is further constrained by the extensive, stable cross-holdings among chaebol firms that limit the total amount of shares available for trading. If one adds the holdings of the investment trust companies and security houses, the supply of floating stock is probably around 20 percent of the total listed. Because of this, the market is highly speculative and vulnerable to booms and busts. Like its counterpart in Taiwan, the exchange is driven more by hearsay and rumors than by sound investment fundamentals.[109]

[104]I. H. Kim.
[105]KFTA, 1992.
[106]Rowley, p. 65.
[107]In 1985, the breakdown of share ownership was as follows: individuals, 52.49 percent; other juridical persons, 25.76 percent; securities companies, 7.35 percent; banking institutions, 7.10 percent; insurance companies, 4.25 percent; foreigners, 2.63 percent; government and state-owned enterprises, 0.4 percent (Rowley, p. 83).
[108]*Business Korea*, 7/84.
[109]Rowley notes that every brokerage house has "rumor" men who circulate among the brokers and dealers, collecting this information. Lucky Securities, of the Lucky-Goldstar group, has a "rumor room" for collecting this information (p. 83).

Despite a renewed interest in the stock market among investors, most chaebol firms continue to resist listing their shares on the exchange even in the face of increasing government pressure to step up their public equity financing. In addition to the familial resistance noted above, firms cite other disincentives including tax deductions allowable for interest payments on borrowed capital but not for dividends on equity shares and Korean investors' expectations of unrealistically high dividends.

Ironically, although the Kim government has professed a desire to separate chaebol ownership from management through public stock issues, it has called for the removal of the chaebol's greatest incentive to list firms. In August 1993, Kim announced the end of Korea's long-standing policy of allowing financial transactions under false or borrowed names. This procedure allowed the chaebol (and all other participants) to evade taxes, manipulate stock prices, and bypass stock ownership regulations. Most important, it allowed chaebol families to maintain familial ownership of group firms even as they reaped the incentives of public listings. The Chun and Roh governments had attempted to enact this "real name transaction policy," but failed because of stiff resistance from both private and public beneficiaries (government officials found the old system a convenient way to hide corporate bribes and payoffs). Kim will meet similar resistance, but he has a democratic mandate and a level of popular support never enjoyed by his predecessors.[110]

The state retains significant power to force a private company to offer its stock publicly. In the most celebrated case, the Hyundai group finally agreed to publicly sell shares in its flagship company, Hyundai Engineering and Construction, in November 1984, after twenty-eight official requests from the MOF and "a hue and cry in the National Assembly." Even then, however, only 30 percent of the company's shares were offered, leaving control and ownership of the company (and the group) virtually unchanged.[111] In addition to these pressures on private firms, the government uses its 68 percent ownership of the KSE to closely regulate its operations. Anthony Rowley notes the MOF's "window guidance," whereby the "presidents or senior executives of Korea's 25 or so leading securities companies (who dominate trading) regularly get telephone calls from the MOF 'advising' them on whether to adopt a buying or selling posture in order to stabilize market movements. They rarely disobey."[112]

Corrupt activities are typically handled in a similar manner. Although the Korean Securities and Exchange Commission (SEC) has the power to arrest suspected wrongdoers, regulation is in fact done primarily through

[110]*Financial Times*, 11/11/93; *Korea Business World*, 8/90.
[111]*New York Times*, 1/4/85.
[112]Rowley, p. 81.

"administrative custom." As an SEC official explains, "in regulating the market we generally use persuasion or moral suasion rather than legal powers."[113] It remains to be seen whether the state will be willing or able, in a more liberal and democratic setting, to use either this administrative guidance or more formal institutional means to achieve its goals of separating the chaebol's ownership and management and promoting the stock market as a viable source of corporate finance.

### Foreign Loan Market

All foreign loans to the chaebol are either administered through state-controlled financial institutions or are subject to government approval. Because of the crucial role of foreign currency loans in financing Korea's economic development in general and the chaebol specifically, a brief explanation of how these loans have been attracted, regulated, and channeled is necessary.

Prior to 1967, Korea's foreign borrowings were minimal. Since then, however, the growing demands of export industrialization, the low domestic savings rate, and, most acutely, the end to American AID funds, inspired the Park regime to seek greater sums abroad. At first the loans were handled exclusively by the BOK, but soon the state authorized the commercial and development banks to receive these loans as well. Officially, enterprises wishing a foreign loan must first obtain approval from the Economic Planning Board (EPB). Once it is approved, the BOK or Korean Exchange Bank issues a guarantee to the foreign lender, and the Korean Development Bank (KDB) or a commercial bank issues a guarantee to the BOK. In practice, however, the banks involved play no critical role; once government approval is obtained, the arrangements are made directly between borrower and lender.[114]

The government's commitment to industrial expansion and its willingness to assume the risks associated with this funding from abroad gave both borrowers and lenders ample incentive to participate in the transactions. In an effort to assure capital inflow in the form of loans rather than direct investment, the Korean government offered interest income benefits to foreign lenders. More important, in the event the borrowing bank or company defaulted on the loan, the KDB and BOK offered guarantees to the foreign lenders that the loans would be repaid.[115]

In addition to benefiting from this virtually risk-free environment, the chaebol were eager to borrow from abroad because the cost of the gov-

[113]Rowley, p. 74.
[114]Nam and Park, pp. 162–63; S. Y. Kwack, p. 125.
[115]Cole and Park. This corporate safety net has frayed considerably in the 1990s. See, for example, *Far Eastern Economic Review,* 4/2/92.

ernment-subsidized foreign loans was much less than the cost of domestic funds. For much of the 1960s and 1970s, the real cost of borrowing abroad was negative. Moreover, these loans provided one of the few sources for scarce and badly needed foreign exchange. As explained in Chapter Six, exporting became the sine qua non for receipt of these subsidized loans; and the chaebol with their huge general trading companies, attracted the lion's share of these funds.

The government profited from these foreign transactions as well. As broker of these cheap, limited foreign funds, it was able to discriminate in favor of particular industries and firms, to its strategic, political, and even personal advantage. The government achieved its developmental goal of export expansion by linking loan access to exports. In addition, its brokerage role allowed it to exact monopoly rents from the loan recipients in the form of under-the-table compensation. Joungwon Kim explains that "since private loans required government approval and repayment guarantees, the Korean party receiving foreign loans was required to pay a percentage (popularly believed to be 10–15 percent and sometimes as much as 20 percent) of the loan amount in payoffs to obtain the necessary government guarantees." For 1966 and 1967 alone, Kim estimates a total of "political fund resources" of over U.S.$25 million from this source.[116]

A final, and consciously sought, advantage of this "borrow-abroad" policy was a certain degree of national autonomy from would-be foreign investors.[117] This autonomy—not shared to the same extent by Taiwan, which has much more readily welcomed direct foreign investment—is not without costs. Korea's development has proceeded under a huge and threatening foreign debt with an, at times, nearly unmanageable debt service burden. In very recent years, however, Korea has been able to significantly reduce this debt and its servicing costs, and to refinance many of its loans under more favorable terms.

To the minds of Korea's developmental technocrats, this debt reduction vindicates the nation's growth-at-all-costs strategy and has given the Korean government new confidence in its international financial dealings. Following the 1987 failures of several chaebol-affiliated shipping and construction firms, the government did not make good on their foreign loans, requiring the foreign banks to "stand in line with local banks to get paid off."[118] In the case of Kukje, just two years earlier, the government formally assured foreign creditors they would be paid back within days of Kukje's collapse.

---

[116]Joungwon Alexander Kim as cited in Johnson, 1987, pp. 157–58. See also Woo.
[117]This contrasts with the Latin American cases during the same period. See E. M. Kim, 1989–90.
[118]*Far Eastern Economic Review*, 6/4/87; *Asian Wall Street Journal*, 11/19/87.

*Informal Sources*

In addition to formal institutions and markets, informal and intragroup financial sources have been very important to the Korean chaebol. Although government control over the allocation of scarce credit has afforded the Korean and Taiwanese developmental states wide discretion over the scope and scale of industrial development, the resultant hunger for financing in nontargeted sectors has led to the development of alternative sources of finance outside the state's direct control. Recognizing that their modern, internationally oriented industrial economies require more flexibility than the formal, highly regulated financial systems have permitted, governments in both Korea and Taiwan have tolerated, to a greater or lesser extent, the functioning of these alternative markets.[119]

Unlike Taiwan, where the dominant borrowers of informal market funds (in terms of both numbers and value) have been the multitude of small and medium-sized enterprises, Korea's informal financial market is dominated by the chaebol. A 1976 study found Korea's private market to be "larger than most of its Asian neighbors and unique because it is used by relatively large businesses rather than petty traders."[120] Despite the transaction costs associated with this imperfect market, the excess demand for bank loans, lack of collateral, processing delays and other red tape associated with the regulated market, as well as illicit or speculative intentions, draw Korean firms to the informal market. Although accurate appraisals of its size are impossible, a 1964 estimate set the value of curb market assets and liabilities at twice that of commercial bank loans.[121] By 1972, the informal market was estimated at half the size of the much-expanded commercial bank system, with a credit volume of well over 354 billion won.[122]

Even though the Korean government channeled massive funds to the chaebol, its officials have been much more persistent than their counterparts in Taiwan in their efforts to "dry up" the curb market and bring these funds under state regulation. These efforts have included Park's sweeping emergency decrees in 1961 and 1972, the formalization of numerous private markets, and the creation of new instruments and institutions. Although the 1972 emergency decree disrupted the market temporarily, it grew in size and importance throughout the 1970s. However, it steadily declined in the 1980s as a result of the government's institutional reforms and liberalization policies.[123]

---

[119]In Taiwan, for example, central bank publications and Nationalist Party-owned newspapers post the "illegal" curb market rates on a daily and monthly basis.

[120]Nam and Park, p. 158. Y. I. Lim, however, contends that Korean manufacturing corporations drew, on average, less than 5 percent of funds from the curb market.

[121]Cole and Park, p. 126.

[122]Nam and Park, p. 159.

[123]Lee and Han.

Korea's informal or unregulated financial institutions are as varied as the types of borrowers. Cole and Park divide the unregulated market into five subcategories: (1) rudimentary private credit market; (2) *kye* market; (3) informal bill market; (4) curb market; and (5) private financial companies.[124] The first involves primarily arms-length consumer loans; and the last, private financial companies (*mujin*), have been legalized and brought into the formal financial system. The remaining three have been of direct value to the chaebol and will be the focus of this section.

Korea's kye, or rotating credit clubs, are a form of credit association found throughout East and Southeast Asia. Their history in Korea goes back at least several hundred years. Traditionally a peasant-based, mutual assistance organization, the kye have evolved into efficient installment-funded financial institutions typically involving a handful of friends or acquaintances—most often housewives. A 1971 survey estimated that fully 65 percent of all Korean households participated in the kye market, contributing up to 32 percent of the household's monthly income. This same survey found that much of these funds, commonly thought to be used for consumption financing, are in fact channeled to the big business sector via credit brokers in the curb market.[125]

A second source of informal funds is the private bill or commercial paper market. Although numerous instruments fall loosely into this category, one of the most relevant to the chaebol is the *wanmae*. Described as a "complex repurchase agreement arranged by security houses and secondary financial institutions,"[126] these short-term debt instruments were never officially recognized by the government as a legal transaction. Because their interest rates were unregulated (averaging approximately 15 percent per annum in the early 1980s), the government tolerated wanmae trading and even considered legalizing the wanmae as a way of liberalizing the capital market.

During the early 1980s the wanmae reached the height of their popularity as an alternative source of capital for chaebol suffering from the loan ceilings imposed by the Chun regime as a means of improving the groups' financial position. From 1981 to 1984, wanmae trading grew to a total of roughly U.S.$1.79 billion. Finally, in November 1984, the government banned the wanmae, charging that the high yield on these short-term instruments was diverting money away from savings accounts. This ban dealt a harsh blow to chaebol that were depending on the wanmae to ride out acute cash-flow problems. In the case of the Kukje group, the blow proved fatal.

[124]Cole and Park, p. 112.
[125]Kwack and Chung; *Far Eastern Economic Review,* 8/6/87; Cole and Park.
[126]*Far Eastern Economic Review,* 4/25/85.

The final, and largest, subsector of the informal market is the curb market, a term often used interchangeably with the unregulated market as a whole. In essence, it refers to the informal loan market that serves primarily large business firms, which use the loans for both working capital and, under certain circumstances, fixed investments. As in Taiwan, professional brokers or moneylenders and relatives or friends of the business owners are the primary lenders. Because the lenders have either a relationship of trust with the borrowers or an intimate knowledge of the firm, they typically require no collateral. This, and their efficient transaction, make the loans attractive, despite interest rates averaging 2.5 to 5 percent per month (see Table 4-1).[127]

In 1972, the curb market had an estimated value of 355 billion won, approximately 80 percent of the money supply.[128] Despite dogged efforts by the state to suppress the market, a 1984 study placed the total at 1.5 trillion won or U.S.$2.2 billion, and a 1985 estimate placed it at from one-fourth to one-third of all loans issued.[129] Significantly, the 1972 survey following Park's forced disclosure of all curb loans revealed that almost 30 percent of the total were actually loans made by chaebol equity holders or other executives who had access to the groups' government and commercial bank loans. By relending these subsidized funds at curb market rates, the chaebol reaped significant profits.[130]

*Internal Sources*

Even more than on informal sources, the chaebol have been able to draw on intragroup financial resources and institutional arrangements to secure both debt and equity funding. The most significant sources have been cross-lending and cross-guaranteeing of loans and the cross-holdings of equity among member firms.

Both cross-lending and intragroup guarantees are considered standard practice for Korea's highly indebted chaebol. The diversification of the groups allows ailing firms in some industries to weather cash-flow problems associated with business cycle downturns by taking short-term loans from other group firms not in recession. As noted above, major equity holders and executives within the group will often lend money informally

---

[127]However, rates vary significantly, reflecting great sensitivity to the risk differentials among borrowers, changing supply of and demand for funds in the formal market, and inflation rates. A 1984 government arrest of fifty-four curb dealers revealed that some of the operators were charging as much as 210 percent interest annually (17.5 percent per month) for some loans (*Far Eastern Economic Review*, 3/1/84; Nam and Park).

[128]Kwack and Chung.

[129]Skully and Viksnins, p. 108; *Far Eastern Economic Review*, 8/6/87.

[130]Koo and Kim; Cole and Park.

to their own firms at curb market rates in order to reap profits from the high interest rates. Core firms within the group are able to increase their working capital by squeezing the subcontractors associated with the chaebol, often with predatory designs. One observer explains that the "typical fate for a small subcontractor for a big group is to be paid with a nine-month promissory note for his supply, or to be gobbled up by the giant if he could not endure the financial pinch." In this way, the chaebol are able to keep the small and medium-sized contractors under their thumbs, pass recessionary shocks on to them, or even merge with them if it suits their plans. This has continued despite government regulations stipulating a mandatory sixty-day payment period.[131]

More common than intercorporate loans is the mutual guarantee of loans between group firms. Although one firm cannot legally own more than 10 percent of another company, there are no limits on the amount of bank loans one company can guarantee for another. Because the chaebol, like their Taiwanese counterparts, are not legally recognized as single units, there are no consolidated company accounts. This allows a highly indebted company unable to obtain bank loans on its own to continue to receive financing by relying on an affiliate with an apparently healthy balance sheet as guarantor of the loans. At the end of 1988, the top thirty chaebol had an estimated U.S.$66 billion in cross-payment guarantees.[132] The guarantees of thirteen core companies of the five largest chaebol totaled nearly U.S.$30 billion in 1991.[133] These arrangements, while advantageous to the struggling firms, can have dangerous ripple effects when a highly leveraged firm (or group) is pushed to the wall.

This borrowing practice has not gone unnoticed. One accountant explained that while Korea's local accounting system and personnel are quite good, "they concentrate on individual companies and don't have the capability to see whether they are related."[134] Bank officials are aware of the cross-guarantees, but in order to safeguard their own positions, they remain very secretive lest they tip off other creditors or investors about the actual debt situation of the company and group.

These institutional arrangements have benefited the groups in their foreign borrowings. When subsidiaries within a chaebol borrow money on foreign capital markets, the banks typically apply the credit ratings of the parent company, which gives these chaebol-affiliated firms a distinct advantage over comparable independent firms.[135] In fact, since 1978, Samsung companies have borrowed abroad without formal guarantees

---

[131]*Far Eastern Economic Review,* 12/12/85.
[132]*Business Korea,* 11/89.
[133]*Business Korea,* 3/92.
[134]Rowley, p. 85.
[135]*Asian Wall Street Journal,* 11/23/87.

from the government or local banks, relying instead on guarantees from other member firms. (The government's swift backing of other groups, however, surely affected foreign lenders' confidence in lending to Samsung, for that backing gave Samsung a tacit government guarantee.)[136]

Although the chaebol firms have generated valuable working capital through intragroup borrowing and guarantees, group expansion has often come through various forms of cross-investment and equity-sharing arrangements among member firms of the same chaebol. In fact, the primary motivation for cross-investment within the chaebol is to finance new ventures through "Ping-Pong equity investments." The simplest version of this method is for two member firms to "Ping-Pong" equity investments in each other, nominally building up the capital in both firms at little or no cost. Alternatively, member firms can jointly invest in a new firm without making any fresh capital outlay, which likewise results in a nominal increase in group capital.[137] A second motive for these cross-investments is to allow the familial owners of the chaebol to maintain control of group firms with relatively small personal holdings of equity. In 1983, the principal family owners of the top eight chaebol held only 9 percent of group shares, but cross-investments among group firms accounted for another 51 percent of equity, "locking up" a total of 60 percent of shareholdings.[138]

A 1983 survey of 128 company-to-company investments revealed that over three-fourths of the transactions involved member firms of the same groups. In that same year, one business group raised the net combined capital of its four member firms 350 percent, from 4 billion to 14 billion won. Another study estimated that the top eleven chaebol arranged for sixty-nine of their member firms to expand their capital through these zero-sum schemes by 41 billion won.[139] The nominal capital increases that result from these cross-investments allow the chaebol or their member firms to borrow more money from the banks. One survey found that up to 40 percent of capitalization in a newly acquired company typically comes from other firms within the group, while the rest is funded by newly available bank loans.[140]

The government has stepped up efforts to curb these practices, charging that this overvaluation of assets further weakens the already highly leveraged financial structure of the chaebol. In a move to strengthen the Monopoly Regulation and Fair Trade Law, the Roh regime called for the elimination of all cross-investments between affiliated companies and the

[136]*Far Eastern Economic Review,* 11/8/84.
[137]*Business Korea,* 7/84.
[138]Chang and Choi.
[139]*Business Korea,* 7/84.
[140]*Far Eastern Economic Review,* 12/12/85.

reduction of cross-holdings within the groups to no more than 40 percent of net assets. Although cross-investments among the top chaebol declined significantly following the proposal, they remained substantial in 1989, calling into question the chaebol's willingness to comply with the state's ability to persuade them to do so.[141]

## THE COSTS OF NONCOMPLIANCE: THE FALL OF KUKJE

Within a two-week period during February 1985, Korea's sixth-largest chaebol and Taiwan's second-largest guanxiqiye collapsed, sending shock waves through the economies of both countries that rippled throughout Asia. A *Wall Street Journal* editorial placed blame for their collapse on the familial nature of enterprises in Asia and the "crucial vulnerability" of their methods of finance. It noted that even successful family firms in Asia are unable or unwilling to expand equity interest in the companies in proportion to their growth; thus these two groups became too highly leveraged and succumbed to drops in inflation during the mid-1980s.[142]

While this assessment is not wholly incorrect, it is sorely inadequate. Although the editorial admirably includes both cultural and economic factors, it neglects the most important cause of the fall of these two giant business concerns. As will be demonstrated here and in the following chapter, these business groups fell because regimes in Korea and Taiwan chose that they fall. These developmental states used control of their respective financial systems to shut down these groups for political, not just economic, reasons. These cases offer resounding evidence that no analysis of the environment in which the business groups of Korea and Taiwan are embedded can be complete without thorough, if not primary, consideration of the role of the state.

In the words of one observer, the demise of the Kukje business group in February 1985 revealed "the best and worst of Korea, Inc."[143] In addition to exposing the intimate though often stormy nexus of public officials and private entrepreneurs, the rise and fall of Kukje involved many of the sources of business group finance—formal, informal, and internal—discussed above. Thus, it provides a fitting summary of this chapter.

### The Group

Beginning with a small Pusan shoe factory that he established in 1947, Kukje's chairman, Yang Chung-Mo, built his business empire into Korea's

---

[141]*Business Korea,* 11/89.
[142]*Wall Street Journal,* 8/22/86.
[143]*Far Eastern Economic Review,* 8/22/85.

sixth-largest business group by 1985. In 1984, Kukje's general trading company (GTC) merged with ICC General Construction to become Kukje-ICC, the flagship around which the remainder of the group's twenty-two member firms conglomerated. That year, the group had combined assets of nearly U.S.$1.7 billion, and Kukje-ICC accounted for 3.6 percent of the nation's exports.[144]

Although considered a "second-tier" chaebol in terms of scope and scale (compared with the four "first-tier" groups—Samsung, Hyundai, Lucky-Goldstar, Daewoo), Kukje was typical of these premier groups in its participation in a broad range of fields, including most prominently footwear (Korea's largest producer), textiles, and steel products. It was also very typical in its familial pattern of ownership and control: at the time of its collapse, Chairman Yang had seven sons-in-law in key management positions.

### Economic Problems

Like many of its chaebol competitors, Kukje's problems began with the 1983 slump in overseas construction, particularly in Saudi Arabia. By 1985, Saudi Arabian concerns owned Kukje over U.S.$120 million and Kukje-ICC had received no new construction contracts in the Middle East in more than two years. This prompted Kukje to launch diversification efforts into several new markets, including the construction of an aluminum smelter and power plants in Australia and the sale of shoe factories to China. During this same period, cash-flow problems plagued three of Kukje's domestic projects, including its towering new company headquarters in Seoul and hotels in Pusan and Cheju Island. The declining competitiveness of Kukje's labor-intensive textile and footwear industries, which had provided the bulk of its profits and exports for years, compounded this problem.

The Chun regime's freeze on new bank loans to the country's thirty most highly leveraged chaebol firms in early 1984 further exacerbated these financial problems. Chun tightened the freeze in September, forcing Kukje, like most of the other chaebol, to turn to the investment finance companies (IFCs) to borrow working capital. In addition to IFC funds, Kukje borrowed roughly U.S.$240,000 in wanmae (at the time still a quasi-legal financial instrument) from Korean securities companies. Less than two months later, however, the government banned the wanmae, contending that its high yield on the open market (under conditions of great credit scarcity) was drawing money from commercial bank savings accounts. Caught in this government-initiated credit squeeze,

---

[144]*Far Eastern Economic Review*, 2/28/85; *Business Korea*, 7/84.

Kukje was unable to repay U.S.$460 million in short-term debt (out of a total debt of U.S.$1.3 billion).[145] In response, and to no one's surprise, the MOF ordered Kukje's lead banks—Korea First, Commercial Bank, Cho Heung, and Bank of Seoul—to lend Kukje U.S.$165 million. As part of the loan package, the government demanded that Kukje cut its labor force by 30 percent and reshuffle its management. Although Kukje was able to cut its short-term debt in half between December 1984 and February 1985, it could not repay some U.S.$341 million in short-term debt that came due in February. At this point, in contrast to some three months earlier, the government refused to bail out the group and had the banks immediately call in their loans to Kukje, effectively putting the group into receivership. Yang was forced to hand over management of the group to the banks and sell off his personal assets, including his home in Seoul.

## Political Noncompliance

Why was the government willing to come to Kukje's assistance in December but not in February? More significantly, why was Kukje singled out, "rather than almost any of the other highly-leveraged, loosely managed *chaebol?*"[146] Kukje's financial problems (with a debt/equity ratio of over 900 percent), though monumental by Western standards, were not much worse than those of Hyundai or Daewoo or dozens of lesser groups. Whereas Kukje consumed roughly one-fourth of Korea First's total loans, Daewoo accounted for nearly half.[147] In order to understand why the Chun regime chose to topple this one, of several, tottering giants, it is necessary to examine the politics behind the financial decisions.

Unlike the four top-tier groups, Kukje had its roots in Pusan, and as such was a political outsider with few connections to the Chun regime. In fact, Yang was a known supporter of the opposition party, which won a seat for Pusan in National Assembly elections just days prior to Kukje's collapse. Moreover, in 1982, Chun established the Ilhae Foundation as a government-directed research entity, ostensibly in memory of government officials killed in the Rangoon bombing carried out by North Korea, that was chaired by Chun Doo Hwan and was to be funded by donations from the chaebol. The foundation's membership included government and industrial elite and was housed in a well-appointed compound on the

---

[145]Kukje borrowed some U.S.$57 million from over thirty foreign banks as well. This compared with a national average of ten foreign banks tapped by each chaebol (*Far Eastern Economic Review,* 8/22/85). These foreign banks were promptly repaid after Kukje's collapse.

[146]*Far Eastern Economic Review,* 2/28/85.

[147]*Financial Times,* 8/4/93.

outskirts of Seoul. The foundation was to be "the power base from which President Chun wished to exert political and economic influence following the end of his constitutionally mandated single, seven-year term as president."[148] It is no coincidence that Chun's pen name is Ilhae.

Chun charged Hyundai chairman Chung Ju-Yung with collecting some U.S.$40 million to fund the project from the business community. Although Hyundai, Samsung, and Posco dutifully kicked in approximately U.S.$6 million each, Yang refused to contribute.[149] Yang also had scrimped on his "quasi-tax" payments for another of Chun's pet political projects, the Saemaul Undong, or "New Village Movement," from which Chun's brother profited immensely. Yang donated only U.S.$400,000 when other chaebol were giving as much as U.S.$1 million annually.[150] To add insult to injury, Yang arrived late at a state dinner hosted by Chun in December 1984. Korea First Bank began refusing to pay Kukje's checks five days later.[151] Although Kukje's financial sins were many, they were typical. It was the political sin of noncompliance that was egregious, and ultimately fatal.

## Public Response

Over the course of the spring and summer of 1985, the Chun regime parceled out the twenty-odd member firms of the Kukje group to other chaebol through its proxies in the Korea First Bank and other lead banks. As one Korean executive noted, "When the banks come in to rearrange things, they take their orders from above, and that means the government."[152] In a subsequent lawsuit, Yang alleged that bank officials told him in February that "people would get hurt" if he opposed Kukje's liquidation.[153] Kukje's firms were sold to chaebol with close ties to the Chun regime, particularly those that had been major contributors to Chun's political projects. In order to make these highly leveraged firms more attractive, the recipient chaebol were given substantial tax and financial sweeteners.[154] Although Dong Suh Securities—Kukje's brokerage house and the plum of Yang's business empire—had several suitors, Korea First elected to retain it. Further to underscore the political nature of this case,

[148]Mardon, p. 26.
[149]Bello and Rosenfeld.
[150]Steers et al.
[151]*Far Eastern Economic Review,* 4/21/88.
[152]*Far Eastern Economic Review,* 8/22/85.
[153]*Far Eastern Economic Review,* 4/21/88.
[154]For a breakdown of which firms were sold to which groups, see *Far Eastern Economic Review,* 8/22/85.

a former ruling party politician was given the presidency of Dong Suh as a political fiefdom.[155]

At the time, the message to the other chaebol was clear: "Both above and below the table, the government was not to be disobeyed."[156] Times (and regimes), however, have changed. In 1988, Yang filed suit against the government, seeking return of U.S.$8.1 million in Kukje stock from Hanil Synthetics, claiming he was forced to sign over the stock for a fraction of its value. The Roh government did not act on the case, but an opposition Parliament member from Pusan, Kim Young Sam, backed Yang's claim.[157] In August 1993, less than a year after Kim assumed the presidency, a Korean constitutional court found in Yang's favor, overturning the forced dissolution of Kukje as an illegal infringement of property rights. Kim welcomed the ruling as an important step in promoting economic deregulation.[158] The chaebol must also be pleased; the ruling gives them both economic clout and constitutional safeguards to defend themselves against Kim's efforts to force the chaebol to deconcentrate.

As Leroy Jones and Il Sakong conclude in their landmark study of government-business relations in Korea: "Government control of the banks is thus the single most important economic factor explaining the distinctly subordinate position of the private sector."[159] As is convincingly demonstrated in the government's disposal of the Kukje group in 1985 (though it was ultimately for political, not developmental, motives), this financial control has taken a multitude of (typically less drastic) shapes and forms over the course of South Korea's postwar history.

The period since 1987 has witnessed both unprecedented financial liberalization and burgeoning chaebol power, which has shifted the relationship from one of chaebol subordinate compliance to one of symbiotic cooperation and increasingly divergent interests. But as the private dependence on public finance lessens, so will the developmental virtues and collusive vices of this relationship. The former junior partners of Korea, Inc., may soon be neither junior nor partners. As Danny Leipziger concludes, "The future relationship between business and the government on matters of industrial policy will depend on the financial organization that emerges."[160] The next decade will reveal the fate of this new relationship.

[155]*Far Eastern Economic Review,* 3/29/84, 5/31/84, 2/28/85, 4/25/85, 8/22/85; Mardon.
[156]Steers et al., p. 43.
[157]*Far Eastern Economic Review,* 4/21/88.
[158]*Financial Times,* 8/4/93.
[159]Jones and Sakong, p. 122.
[160]Leipziger, p. 132.

The following chapter reveals that the most significant factor in the differences in scope and scale of the Korean and Taiwanese groups is the cost of and access to sources of financial capital. Although the state controls the formal financial markets in both political economies, the Korean state intentionally channeled highly subsidized funds directly to the chaebol, whereas the Nationalist state on Taiwan constrained the flow of funds to the largest business concerns. Chapter Five examines how Taiwan's guanxiqiye have organized in order to assure adequate capital resources in the face of these constraints.

CHAPTER FIVE

# Financing of the Guanxiqiye

This chapter examines the financial environment in which Taiwan's business groups are embedded. Like Korea, Taiwan's state has dominated its financial system. Unlike its Korean counterpart, however, the Nationalist regime's motivation for creating and ruling over a repressive formal financial system has been, above all, to maintain price stability and prevent the concentration of private financial power. At the same time, the state has tolerated a flourishing informal or "curb" market and has given the private sector relatively wide latitude to pursue certain circumscribed legal financial activities and evade countless financial regulations. Private entrepreneurs have followed strategies designed to exploit this particular incentive structure within the parameters of an influential familial corporate culture.

These environmental influences have constrained the financial resources and instruments available to the guanxiqiye, thus limiting their willingness and ability to expand and develop along the lines of their Korean counterparts. Despite significant financial liberalization since 1987, many of the formal constraints remain in place. In order to analyze this environment and the financing of the guanxiqiye, in this chapter I will (1) examine the goals and strategies of Taiwan's financial policymakers and private business group leaders, explaining their divergence; (2) introduce the financial system with its relevant supervisory agencies and the formal and informal financial institutions comprising the guanxiqiye's sources of funds and the public-private interplay within this financial arena; and (3) relate the circumstances of the "Cathay scandal," in which the financial and political aspirations of Taiwan's second largest private business group provoked a public response with lasting consequences for

Taiwan's government-business group relations and business group finance.

## GOALS AND STRATEGIES: PUBLIC RESTRICTIONS, PRIVATE DISREGARD

Despite the government's 1991 approval of the chartering of fifteen new private banks, state domination of the formal financial system remains more extensive in Taiwan than in any other non-Communist East Asian country.[1] This state dominance has included an extensive system of pervasive financial regulations, ownership or control of virtually all commercial banks, and significant state or Nationalist Party interests in numerous other financial institutions. But despite this looming presence, the state-controlled financial system has not been the significant intermediary between savers and industrial borrowers it has been in other countries, such as Japan or even Korea.

The government and its financial regulations have unquestionably influenced corporate financial strategies. However, the nature of government-business relations in Taiwan has meant this influence has been neither as direct nor as predictable as one might expect. This is partly because the economic and financial goals of Taiwan's policymakers have been more complex than simply fostering the rapid growth of private industry, as explained in Chapter Three. Speaking of the state's reluctance to pass savings on to industry, one analyst traced this attitude back to the Nationalists' "odd style" of government: "This cannot be called repressive, or centralized, or interventionist—the truth is untidier than that. The KMT government is a compulsive busybody. It has not managed to shed its urge to meddle and to check since 1949. . . . Except in the matter of external security, where the state is extremely strict, many things in Taiwan take place in a murky half-light between freedom and state control."[2]

The priorities of the Nationalist state inspiring this untidy intervention diverge significantly from the goals and objectives of Taiwan's entrepreneurs. This is particularly true of the owner-managers of large-scale business groups, who, paradoxically, have been among the major benefactors of the current system and at the same time among those most chafing under its welter of financial regulations. This has created a unique dynamic of public restrictions and private disregard that is the focus of this chapter.

[1]Wade (1985) notes that Hofheinz and Calder (1982) are wrong to attribute this distinction to South Korea.
[2]*Economist*, 3/28/87.

Although the skirting or abuse of public financial regulations for private gain is not unique to Taiwan, entrepreneurs there have perfected the art of outwitting (or otherwise persuading) accountants, loan officers, auditors, and even finance officials. In seeming deference to these skills, the government has matched the pervasive scope of its financial regulations with an almost equally extensive disregard for their piecemeal violation. The result is a cat-and-mouse game in which minor infractions gradually multiply until the government either recognizes the de facto situation and de jure sanctions the previously banned activity or punishes the most flagrant offenders as a warning to the rest, in which case the process begins again.

This dynamic has its roots in the historical development of relations between the Nationalist Chinese government and the private business sector. Imperial Chinese precedent should not be ignored. Discussing the Confucian ambivalence toward active and passive state intervention in economic affairs in imperial China, Tom Metzger notes that "sometimes the power of merchants was asserted at first illegally and then was gradually legalized and institutionalized, as laws and institutions followed changes in custom."[3] The relations between private capital and the Nationalist state on the Chinese Mainland was one of mutual distrust. Private bankers and industrialists had much experience trying to avoid being "squeezed, threatened and oppressed by the corrupt Nationalist officials who had their own economic interests."[4]

An atmosphere of plunder, opportunism, and speculation followed the Nationalists to Taiwan, where it was exacerbated by the island's perceived status as a temporary haven with an uncertain future. Despite the successes of the Nationalists in cleansing government and party of corruption during the 1950s, a tendency toward quick turnover and profit-by-any-means prevailed in the private sector. Thomas Gold notes that "some say the business practices of today developed out of the experiences of those years once the honesty of the Japanese period was destroyed."[5] The Nationalists' early brutal treatment of the Taiwanese majority and the enforced exclusion of the Taiwanese from participation in the government intensified this division and animosity between the government and private sector.

This division has had a significant effect on the regime's willingness and ability to enforce its financial regulations and on the legitimacy of these regulations as perceived by those intended to obey them. Certainly, the financial activities of the guanxiqiye are greatly circumscribed and

[3]Metzger, p. 43.
[4]Gold, 1981, p. 81.
[5]Gold, 1981, p. 78.

channeled as a result of regime policy. But much goes on outside of this formally sanctioned financial arena, with varying shades of illegality.

## PUBLIC RESTRICTIONS

The state's penchant for enforcing pervasive restrictions with one eye closed is the result of an elective affinity between the regime's political needs, economic goals, and ideological underpinnings. As discussed in Chapter Three, the political imperative for the Nationalist state has been to maintain power and legitimacy as a minority Mainlander regime surrounded (and increasingly penetrated) by a Taiwanese majority more and more capable of translating economic wealth into political power. The regime's developmental goals have been to pursue stable economic growth under conditions of relative income equity. The ideological justification for these political and economic objectives has come primarily from Sun Yat-sen's concept of "People's Livelihood." This elective affinity has allowed the state to clothe its political-economic objectives in moral wraps. The ideological and historical factors shaping this affinity have been discussed in Chapter Three. Their specific effect on the financial system is examined here.

The Confucian disdain for personal profit has unquestionably left its impact on the modern financial system and its bureaucratic caretakers. Although he received his training at the Wharton School of Finance, K. P. Chen, founder of the Shanghai Commercial and Savings Bank (Republican China's largest), is typical of this heritage. Andrea McElderry notes that Chen "deemphasized profit for the sake of profit," instead linking profits to the welfare of the group, whether the family, the society or the nation. She quotes Chen: "The basic purpose of a bank is not to make a profit but to serve society. Banks are society's most pertinent institutions. If an area has a bank, it can take floating capital and develop industry and commerce making everyone better off."[6] Sun Yat-sen's quasi-socialist principle of "People's Livelihood" reinforced this bias against private gain at public expense. A high-ranking finance official invoked Sun's principle to justify the state's strict control over Taiwan's banks, arguing that the financial system should not be "privatized because it holds the public's money."

These ideological supports for the control of capital through direct ownership and strict regulation have been reinforced in the minds of Taiwan's political leaders and policymakers by specific shared historical events. These have given Nationalist leaders, in the words of one business-

[6]McElderry, pp. 403–7.

man, a "historical paranoia" regarding the consequences of financial mismanagement and private meddling in fiscal affairs. The greatest villain in
this historical saga has been inflation, which has been a primary cause of
dynastic downfall in China since the eleventh century, when paper money
was introduced. From that time forward, China's ruling groups frequently
abetted their own demise by expanding the money supply through issuing
notes to finance government expenditures. This trend persisted in the
twentieth century. Despite efforts by Shanghai bankers to check galloping
inflation in Republican China (1911–49), decades of war and repeated
government issues of currency to finance deficits pushed the nation up
its most disastrous "inflationary spiral."[7] By the late 1940s, financial chaos
hyperinflation, greatly exacerbated by hoarding, speculation, and capital
flight, had virtually doomed the Nationalists' hopes of defeating the Communists.

Despite last-ditch efforts by Chiang Kai-shek and the Nationalist government to arrest this inflation—including the dispatch of Chiang's son
Ching-kuo to Shanghai to stabilize China's financial center, the source of
much of this chaos—it was in fact the government's failure to deal effectively with these financial problems earlier that sealed its ultimate fate. A
Shanghai banker later noted:

> This leadership, failing to understand the nature of the economic forces
> with which it dealt, chose to ignore them. The government could find no
> alternative with which to finance itself. Inflation was to run its course, and
> the ultimate fate of the government was sealed. Economic instability finally
> led to a general loss of confidence in the Nationalist government, and total
> collapse of political and social morals followed. Into this chaos and political
> and moral vacuum almost any militant group promising a clean sweep could
> have moved without strong opposition; and the Communists were there to
> take full advantage of the situation.[8]

Although they were able to escape their Communist rivals by fleeing to
Taiwan, the Nationalists were less successful in evading inflation. When it
was retroceded to the Nationalists in 1945, Taiwan suffered from deficit
spending, corruption, and financial chaos as well as sudden capital in-
flows from the Mainland. Prices jumped 1,145 percent in 1948 and 3,000
percent in 1949.[9] There is no doubt whatsoever in the minds of Nationalist leaders who experienced these events that hyperinflation and financial
instability spawned by deficit spending and reckless speculation were the

[7]K. N. Chang.
[8]K. N. Chang, pp. 366–67.
[9]Gold, 1986.

primary factors leading to the Nationalists' defeat on the Mainland and the perilous struggles during their early years on Taiwan.[10]

Nationalist leaders have demonstrated through four decades of conservative financial policies that they learned well these "lessons of the 1940s."[11] Upon assuming chairmanship of the Bank of Taiwan in 1960, K. Y. Yin, the dominant figure in Taiwan's economic takeoff until his death in 1963, indicated the government's resolve: "The underlying principle of all measures of the Bank of Taiwan is to maintain the currency value and establish economic stability by avoiding or mitigating monetary inflation in coordination with government policies."[12] In a 1971 speech, K. T. Li echoed this concern: "Mindful of the fresh, painful lesson of a vicious unarrested inflation of the currency, our financial authorities have since made painstaking efforts to maintain a balanced budget in spite of all sorts of difficulties."[13]

Financial regulations, however, have gone far beyond maintaining a balanced budget, as the following section of this chapter attests. Noting that "history stands in the way" of reforming Taiwan's financial system, one observer concluded in 1987 that Taiwan's ruling Nationalist elders "have long memories—maybe too long. . . . They blame inflation and its effects for the fall of Chinese civilization as they knew it. Many fear loosening control over the island's financial system could lead to inflation and chaos. Instead of putting its faith in a free economy, the government is introducing new controls to fight problems caused by controls."[14]

These concerns and controls meshed with a final imperative of Nationalist policy: the need to retain political power while facing a rapidly expanding private sector dominated by ethnic Taiwanese. Taiwan's largest guanxiqiye are owned and operated by powerful Taiwanese families very much interested in influencing public policy. From the regime's perspective, there would seem to be reason for genuine concern about their growing economic and financial clout. In the late 1970s, Wang Yongqing, the Taiwanese founder of the Formosa Plastics group, Taiwan's largest, was involved in a dispute with the Ministry of Finance. When Wang threatened to remove all of Formosa Plastics' substantial holdings from the

---

[10]See for example K. H. Yu, p. 2; C. C. Chang, p. 3; and K. T. Li, 1976, p. 75. The 1989 conjunction of high inflation and political unrest in the People's Republic of China came as no surprise to Nationalist elders on Taiwan.

[11]Another "lesson" Taiwan's leaders learned from the 1940s was to avoid dependence on foreign borrowing. Top Nationalist political leaders reportedly have long been haunted by memories of those years when Taiwan's letters of credit were not accepted abroad (*Euromoney*, 5/87). As discussed in Chapter Four, this differs greatly from the South Korean strategy under Park and Chun.

[12]*Industry of Free China*, September 1961, p. 23.

[13]K. T. Li, 1976, p. 75.

[14]*Forbes*, 4/6/87.

banks—a sure precipitant of instability—the problem was swiftly resolved in Wang's favor.

An influential 1979 study of Taiwan's business groups, commissioned by the Council for Economic Planning and Development, discussed the deleterious economic, social, and political consequences of private control of financial institutions.

> First, the close relationship between the banks and large businesses causes the banks to have little desire to support small and new businesses because to do so would harm your original customers. Second, in making loans, banks definitely do not allocate capital according to ideal principles or utilize capital in the most optimal way. Third, banks often provide cheaper capital, more complete information and better service to their large, business group clients. . . .
>
> Because of the extensive financial power of a related enterprise group formed around a financial institution, it will inevitably have a profound influence on politics and society. If the people within these groups have an interest in politics or if they feel holding political influence would be advantageous to the operations of their enterprise, it is then very possible that they would utilize their financial power to develop political and social influence. . . . Today, if we actually want to complete Sun Yat-sen's nation-building ideals, we must protect against this phenomenon.[15]

The 1985 Cathay financial scandal, involving the Taiwanese Cathay business group (at the time, Taiwan's second largest), served to justify and reconfirm in the minds of Taiwan's Nationalist elders their ideological and experiential predispositions for financial rigidity and conservatism. When Cathay's illicit efforts to cultivate its own private sources of finance were exposed and runs occurred on several financial institutions, many financial authorities resolved anew their commitment to keep the public's money out of the hands of private speculators and industrial oligopolists, despite strong counterpressures to liberalize and privatize the financial system.

Thus, ideological commitments to social equality and bureaucratic control were justified by historical events demonstrating the problems of financial mismanagement and instability. A former minister of finance and governor of Taiwan's central bank spoke of this meshing:

> Deficit financing is something we have tried to avoid because it exerts upward pressures on prices, and price stability is one of the foremost concerns of the government. This concern stems primarily from two considerations: One is the adverse effect of inflation, once it gets out of control, on the

[15]Liu et al., pp. 13, 56.

livelihood of the masses, especially on people in the low income bracket. The other is our strong belief that economic growth cannot be sustained under inflationary conditions, and that continued economic progress and prosperity is our best insurance against Communist subversion and aggression.[16]

Inflation is the enemy, not primarily for economic reasons but because of its potential social and political consequences. Its appearance breeds instability, stunts economic growth, and shakes investor and saver confidence, thereby providing enemies of the state, domestic and foreign, with opportunities to exploit the situation and challenge the survival of the Nationalist state. Therefore, and ultimately for political reasons, Taiwan's policymakers have formulated and put in place repressive financial regulations designed to prevent inflation and financial instability and those activities that can breed it: deficit spending, speculation, consumer credit, and the private concentration of financial and industrial capital.

In order to achieve its developmental goal of growth with stability, and in contrast to its track record on the Mainland, the Nationalist regime on Taiwan instituted a wide range of effective fiscal and monetary policies. During the 1950s, the government generated revenue and redistributed income from the agricultural to the industrial sector through land reform, land taxes, compulsory rice sales at below market rates, and mandatory rice exchange for state-monopolized fertilizer. These measures leveled society, stabilized prices, eased budget crunches, lessened dependence on foreign borrowing, and freed capital for industrial investment.[17] Early monetary policies included drastic devaluation of the currency, "preferential interest rate deposits," and a closed foreign exchange system. These measures stabilized prices, encouraged domestic savings, and stemmed capital outflows.[18] Policies during the 1960s that were designed to liberalize the economy and financial system faced substantial resistance from government officials who feared that "reduction of controls could wreck hard-won price stability and bring back inflation . . . , further the state's retrenchment from the economy and grant ever greater rein to private capital. This would entail concentration of capital, something Sun Yat-sen opposed."[19]

These overriding concerns have assured that despite numerous liberalizing policy reforms in the 1970s and 1980s, the financial system has retained a unique "murky half-light" mixture of financial repression and restraint. This blend distinguishes Taiwan's financial system not only from

[16]C. C. Chang, p. 3.
[17]Sasamoto, p. 37.
[18]Kaufman-Winn, p. 8.
[19]Gold, 1986, p. 77.

the Anglo-American "free enterprise" economies and the Leninist command economies, but also from those of the more comparable developmental states in Korea and Japan.[20]

This variation entails distinct trade-offs. As in Korea, relative financial rigidity has benefited Taiwan's developmental efforts by (1) getting financial savings into the banks; (2) keeping real savings within the country for use by domestic investors; and (3) encouraging an active industrial policy by giving the government a powerful tool for influencing the private industrial sector.[21] Taiwan's state, however, has been much less vigorous than the Korean state in applying a number of financial controls, such as concessionary credit allocation and the use of tariffs and quotas as instruments of selective protection. Although exporters (who received a subsidized rate) and large enterprises (which could obtain bank loans) have in fact received favorable credit rates relative to other private sector borrowers, fears of inflation and of private concentration of capital and accusations of favoritism have made Taiwan policymakers much more reluctant than their Korean counterparts to use preferential financial treatment—whether concessionary loan rates or direct financial bailouts—to foster the development of the few at the expense of the many.[22] K. T. Li warned that "it would certainly be neither feasible nor desirable for the government . . . to accord preferential treatment to specific industries for unduly extended periods of time. . . . Development does not justify the dispensation of excessive incentives for investment. In the meantime, we will redouble our efforts for more equitable distribution of wealth and income lest the widening gap between the poor and the rich should create grave social problems and produce undesirable effects on growth."[23]

Through a consistent monetary policy of relatively high interest rates, Taiwan's financial authorities have maintained price stability and encouraged one of the highest private savings rates in the world, both crucial factors in Taiwan's rapid industrial growth. These achievements, however, have sometimes come at the expense of investment and industrial expansion. The goals and ideological biases of Taiwan's political leaders have created a financial system with an inevitable tension between the objectives of growth on the one hand and stability and equity on the other. This tension has had significant consequences for Taiwan's business groups in terms of costs of funds, ability to expand, and freedom to participate in financial activities.

[20]Johnson, 1987.
[21]Wade, 1985.
[22]In contrast with Korea, and despite the failure of many industrial companies, Taiwan banks largely refused to offer tangible financial support to ailing companies during their reorganization efforts in the recessionary early 1980s (Kaufman-Winn, p. 25).
[23]K. T. Li, 1974, pp. 15–16.

## Private Disregard

The familial nature of enterprise organization in Taiwan prompts guanxiqiye leaders to make business and financial decisions that often are contrary to both the rational dictates of sound business management and the desires of government planners. One observer estimated that roughly 80 percent of Taiwan's family firms that go public fail within three years because "the family feels little hesitation about 'borrowing' the money put in by non-family investors."[24]

The motives behind this behavior and the methods for seeking and obtaining financing for this expansion cannot be understood without taking the sociocultural environment in which the groups are embedded into account. This environment fosters a willingness to subvert financial policies of the state and even to sacrifice the interests of the corporation for the benefit of the family when these interests do not coincide.

## Financial System

### Supervisory Agencies

Ostensibly, the structure for financial policy and regulation in Taiwan is quite simple and straightforward. The Ministry of Finance (MOF) is constitutionally responsible for formulating all financial regulatory policies and licensing financial institutions. The Central Bank of China (CBC) is responsible for carrying out monetary and financial regulatory policies and serves as watchdog for all financial institutions.[25] As in Korea, however, real financial control remains in the hands of the top political leadership, in this case the ruling Nationalist Party. As discussed in Chapter Three, the most powerful policy-making organs have varied, depending on the specific policymakers associated with them and the agencies' relationship to the top political leadership.

Unlike Korea, where political leaders placed the central bank under MOF supervision, in Taiwan the Central Bank of China has had considerable influence over both the formulation and the administration of financial policy. It serves as banker and fiscal agent to the government, manager of foreign exchange holdings, lender of last resort to the commercial banks, and institution responsible for determining the banks' interest rates and reserve requirements. Through its wide-ranging fiscal and monetary controls, the CBC exerts a dominant influence over virtually all financial institutions comprising the guanxiqiye's sources of funds. It also

[24]*Economist,* 3/19/88.
[25]H. S. Cheng, pp. 147–48.

performs a substantial research function, advising political leaders and policymakers on a wide range of financial and economic matters. The MOF, located next to the CBC (in an older and smaller building), has typically played a secondary role in establishing financial policy. Most CBC governors have been former finance ministers, a situation that has strengthened the relationship between, and the CBC's position of dominance over, the two bodies.[26]

The CBC was founded in 1924 and began serving as the central bank for the Republic of China in 1928. For the next twenty years, it functioned both as the bankers' bank and as a commercial bank. The activities of the CBC, tainted by its association with the corrupt financial dealings of Chiang Kai-shek's brothers-in-law T. V. Soong and H. H. Kung, were suspended in 1949 and not reactivated until 1961. During the interim the Bank of Taiwan, established by the Japanese colonizers, took on many of the functions of a central bank. Since its reactivation, the CBC has been prohibited from engaging in commercial activities.[27]

The CBC's most effective tool for influencing financial policy, and thus the entire economy, has been its control of loan and deposit rates.[28] The CBC has exercised these controls largely in an effort to maintain price stability, often at the expense of other possible objectives, such as investment. Although subsidized loan rates were offered to exporters, these low-interest loans were not nearly as significant for firms in Taiwan as they were for the Korean chaebol. In Taiwan, the rates were not as heavily subsidized as in Korea, were offered to all comers, and never comprised nearly as large a portion of total borrowings or total capital needs as was the case in Korea. For the period 1971–86, these export loans averaged only 11 percent of total loans and discounts of domestic banks, with a high of 18.2 percent in 1972 and a low of 6.1 percent in 1985.[29] In stark contrast to Korea, "even the most favored businesses have had to pay positive real interest rates."[30]

Nonetheless, a tiered credit market did emerge, favoring not only exporters but also firms large enough to provide the necessary collateral to obtain bank loans at the lower secured rate. Table 5-1 indicates the wide

[26]Caldwell, p. 732; Pang, p. 62.
[27]Liang and Skully, p. 175; Emory, p. 2.
[28]Financial reforms since 1980 have limited the CBC's control over these rates, though state control has not been substantially weakened. The CBC's role as rate setter has been largely supplanted not by the market but by the Taipei Bankers' Association, a bureaucrat-dominated banking cartel.
[29]B. Wu. This export loan program began in 1957 and was designed to provide short-term funding for export manufacturing. The funds for this program derive from the government's postal savings system and are channeled through the central bank to the state-owned commercial banks.
[30]Little, p. 481.

*Table 5-1.* Loan rates and inflation rates in Taiwan, 1956–86 (percent)

| Year | Bank rates | | | Curb rate | Consumer price index |
|---|---|---|---|---|---|
| | One-year savings deposit | Unsecured loan | Export loan | Unsecured loan | |
| Average | | | | | |
| 1956–62 | 17.0 | 20.9 | 11.2 | 41.1 | 8.4 |
| 1963–73 | 10.1 | 14.1 | 7.7 | 25.4 | 3.4 |
| 1974 | 13.5 | 15.5 | 9.0 | 29.3 | 47.5 |
| 1975 | 12.0 | 14.0 | 7.0 | 26.4 | 5.2 |
| 1976 | 10.7 | 12.7 | 7.0 | 27.6 | 2.5 |
| 1977 | 9.5 | 11.5 | 6.5 | 25.6 | 7.0 |
| 1978 | 9.5 | 11.5 | 6.5 | 27.2 | 5.8 |
| 1979 | 12.5 | 15.2 | 10.5 | 30.1 | 9.8 |
| 1980 | 12.5 | 16.2 | 10.5 | 31.3 | 19.0 |
| 1981 | 13.0 | 15.2 | 11.0 | 30.1 | 16.3 |
| 1982 | 9.0 | 10.7 | 8.2 | 27.7 | 3.3 |
| 1983 | 8.5 | 10.2 | 8.0 | 26.8 | 1.8 |
| 1984 | 8.0 | 10.0 | 7.7 | 29.9 | 1.7 |
| 1985 | 7.0 | 9.5 | 6.25 | 27.4 | −0.2 |
| 1986 | 5.0 | 9.0 | 5.75 | 24.3 | 0.5 |

SOURCES: H. S. Cheng; Y. J. Cho.

variety of loan rates available to borrowers and the CBC's relative success in maintaining price stability. In order to understand this variance and its effects on the guanxiqiye's borrowing strategies and constraints on their growth, we must turn to the groups' specific sources of funds.

## Sources of Funds and their Relative Importance

As in Korea, the institutions, markets, and instruments listed in Table 5-2 vary in their degree of sophistication, government control, and relative

*Table 5-2.* Major sources of guanxiqiye finance

| Category | Markets, institutions and instruments |
|---|---|
| Formal | domestic banks |
| | credit cooperatives |
| | investment trust companies |
| | insurance companies |
| | organized money market |
| | bond market |
| | stock market |
| Informal | curb market |
| Internal | employee deposits |
| | cross-lending and mutual guarantee |
| | cross-holdings and joint investment |

importance to the business groups. After a preliminary discussion of the relative importance of these various sources, I will examine in turn the formal (official), informal ("curb"), and internal (intrafirm and intra-group) institutions, markets, and instruments of business group finance.

Before we turn to a description of specific institutions, the extreme difficulty of weighing the relative importance of the various sources of funds should be noted. Because the guanxiqiye are not legal entities and generally are closely held by familial owners who treat financial information with the utmost secrecy, efforts to determine the relative significance of various sources of funding are difficult and can, at best, only be estimated.

Although specific studies have analyzed the financing of private enterprises in general and the distribution of bank credit among large and small private enterprises,[31] no comprehensive study of guanxiqiye financial sources has been attempted. Nor can such a study be carried out as long as such financial information remains confidential. In fact, one of the motives for choosing the informal, "related enterprise" mode of organization has been to facilitate unmonitored financial flows to the groups and among group firms. Despite these limitations, we can nonetheless get some idea of the relative significance of the various sources listed in Table 5-2 by generalizing from available information regarding private enterprise. Not only do these estimates provide the setting for the description of the institutions that follows, they also demonstrate that the financial system has constrained the groups' ability and willingness to expand and develop along the lines of their Korean counterparts.

Although Taiwan's formal money and capital markets are relatively backward compared with those of more advanced countries, the financial system has deepened considerably since the 1950s.[32] In the immediate postwar period, private industry had virtually no access to capital except personal savings and funds brought from the Mainland in the form of private capital flight. The major Taiwanese capitalists of the colonial period lost most of their assets during the war.[33] Those government funds that were available were directed almost entirely to the dominant public enterprise sector. Meager private sources were gradually supplemented by foreign capital resources in the form of U.S. AID loans, overseas Chinese capital, and other foreign private capital.[34] Most important among these sources was U.S. AID funds. Although the Nationalist government had

[31] See, e.g., Qiu and Shen; Zhang.

[32] Measuring this deepening in terms of monetary assets as a percentage of GNP, Wade demonstrates that financial deepening has proceeded in Taiwan much faster than in Korea, the Philippines, or even Japan (1985, p. 111).

[33] Gold, 1988.

[34] Sasamoto.

relatively wide discretion over the disbursement of these funds, American advisers were influential in directing the loans toward private, as opposed to public, enterprises and small-scale, labor-intensive industries instead of large-scale showcase industries.[35]

Many of Taiwan's business groups were formed or revitalized during this period. Despite U.S. complaints of favoritism, many of the initial beneficiaries were Mainlander textile interests that became the core of such business groups as Far Eastern, Yueloong, and Chung Hsing. U.S. AID assistance was also instrumental in the founding of several native Taiwanese enterprises at this time, including Tatung and Formosa Plastics. Wang Yongqing established the latter, now the flagship of Taiwan's largest business group, in 1954 with U.S.$25,000 in local capital and U.S.$650,000 in soft loans from U.S. AID. Lindy Li Mark describes Formosa Plastics as Taiwan's "most successful enterprise initiated with United States technical and economic aid."[36]

As Taiwan's economy stabilized and took off in the 1960s and 1970s, loanable funds increased. Unlike Korea, however, which relied extensively on foreign borrowing and an inflationary expansion of the money supply to finance its high-speed growth, Taiwan financed its industrial investment almost entirely out of domestic savings. In the period 1965–80, Taiwan's domestic savings as a percentage of GNP averaged 28.7 percent and its gross domestic capital formation (DCF) was 28.4 percent of GNP. Although Taiwan has suffered sharp declines in DCF in recent years, for this period it was perhaps the highest in the world. Korea's DCF during this period, at 26.5 percent, was also high, but only 70 percent of investment came from domestic savings, the remainder being funded by inflation and foreign debt.[37] Despite the increase in loanable funds and virtually unequaled rates of domestic savings, private firms in Taiwan—both large and small—have until very recently continued to face chronically short supplies of credit. Like their Korean counterparts, Taiwan's familial business groups prefer nonnegotiable debt (loans) as the primary source of finance.

But although the structure of private firms in Taiwan is weighted toward borrowed funds as sources of financing, as opposed to owner equity (stock and retained earnings), Taiwan's firms in general, and the guanxiqiye in particular, are not nearly as indebted as the chaebol. Table 4-5 shows the estimated the debt ratio of Taiwan's manufacturing firms at less than half of those of Korean and Japanese firms and more compa-

[35]Su; Gold, 1981.
[36]Mark, 1972, p. 32.
[37]Wade, 1985; C. H. Liang.

rable with those of U.S. firms.[38] In 1967, manufacturing firms in Taiwan obtained an average of nearly 60 percent of their operating funds through debt financing; the remainder came from owner equity. Of this, contributed capital (stock) represented nearly 30 percent and retained earnings made up the other 11 percent.[39] Despite significant financial deepening since 1967 and the emergence of more sophisticated money and capital markets, the capital structure of Taiwan's private enterprises remains little changed. In a study based on a CBC survey of private enterprise capital sources, Jingbo Qiu and Ruifan Shen found a similar breakdown of financial sources for 1980. In that year, firms obtained approximately 57 percent of operating funds through debt and 43 percent from owner equity. Of the equity funds, stock represented 31 percent of operating funds and retained earnings 12 percent.[40] Table 5-3 shows a breakdown of sources of corporate funds.

Table 5-3 indicates that internal funds in the form of contributed capital or stock are an important source of corporate finance in Taiwan, certainly compared with the Korean corporate sector. This reflects both the small average size of Taiwan's firms (which therefore are fundable through family shareholdings) and the informal institution of "silent" or

*Table 5-3.* Source of corporate funds, 1967 and 1980 (percent)

| Source | 1967 | 1980 |
| --- | --- | --- |
| Internal | 40.5 | 43 |
| External | 59.5 | 57.0 |
| **Total** | **100.0** | **100.0** |
| Internal | 100.0 | 100.0 |
| Stock | 72.8 | 72.0 |
| Retained earnings | 27.2 | 28.0 |
| External | 100.0 | 100.0 |
| Bank loans | 64.7 | 51.0 |
| Shareholder and private credit loans | 27.5 | 22.1 |
| U.S. AID | 7.8 | — |
| Negotiable debt (bonds, bills) | — | 13.7 |
| Foreign loans | — | 13.2 |

SOURCES: K. S. Kuo; Qiu and Shen.

[38]Wade (1985) estimates the debt/equity ratio for Taiwan's private firms for the period 1971–80 at between 160 and 180 percent, compared with a ratio of 50 to 90 percent in Britain and the United States and 310 to 380 percent in Korea. Other estimates are higher: *Euromoney* (7/86) placed the average ratio for Taiwan's manufacturing enterprises at 200 percent in 1986. The *Economist* in 1985 noted that 250 percent is "acceptable" (8/24/85). Chuang, writing in 1986, complained that Taiwan's companies "have grossly overborrowed," contending that a 400 percent ratio, not including unrecorded private loans, is common (p. 235).
[39]K. S. Kuo.
[40]Qiu and Shen.

"guanxi" shareholders outside the family, and the extensive cross-share-holding networks within and even among the guanxiqiye. The table likely underrepresents, however, the role of curb or "private credit" loans, which are generally underreported.[41]

Taiwan's commercial banks favor larger enterprises as potential bor-rowers. A 1983 study notes that whereas the top 600 private enterprises received over 50 percent of bank funds made available to all manufactur-ers, an equitable distribution based on GNP share would have allocated these 600 firms less than 25 percent of the total.[42] But despite this bank bias toward larger firms, even large enterprises, whether or not they are affiliated with a guanxiqiye, still seek a significant portion of their financ-ing from informal sources. Although he acknowledges that large firms are somewhat less dependent than smaller ones, Wade estimates that for the years 1976–81 Taiwan's private corporate sector obtained up to 40 percent of its financing from the "unregulated, semi-legal credit mar-ket."[43] Taiwan's finance minister, speaking in 1983, also estimated that 40 percent of Taiwan's capital needs are being met by the curb market.[44]

Gary Hamilton et al. estimate that the guanxiqiye obtain more than 60 percent of their financing from family and close friends.[45] This figure agrees with the estimates here. Because most guanxiqiye affiliates are tightly held by the founding group of family and friends, nearly all equity investment (estimated above at 43 percent of total financing) derives from this source. If one-third of debt financing (estimated at 57 percent of total financing) is obtained through private loans and discounts from trusted others, this yields an approximate total of 60 percent financing from family and friends. The corporate capital structure that emerges from this is one much less heavily weighted toward debt than that of the chaebol, and shows a preference for bank and private loans rather than negotiable debt instruments. These institutions and markets are exam-ined below.

### Formal Sources of Funds

Domestic Banks

Like the Korean state, the Nationalist state has historically dominated the formal financial system through its outright ownership or control of

---

[41]State-owned banks conducted both of the surveys on which the studies were based; the subjects of the surveys were likely to be larger, more stable, and less risky than the average Taiwan firm. Not only would the subjects' reliance on private creditors be lower than aver-age, but their hesitance to report these quasi-illicit sources of capital to government officials would skew the results.

[42]Zhang.

[43]Wade, 1985, p. 112.

[44]Kaufman-Winn. Writing in 1975, Caldwell estimates that Taiwan's private firms raised an astounding 82 percent of their financing requirements "in the form of borrowings from individuals in the unorganized money market" (p. 736).

[45]Hamilton et al., 1988.

the domestic banks. Given the dominant position of the banks in the system, their limited number, and the importance of debt financing to the corporate sector, this dominance has proved effective. The 1991 decision to grant new bank licenses—the first in twenty years—to private investor groups, many of them representing guanxiqiye, promises far-reaching changes in the system if this liberalization move is allowed to take its course.

Prior to 1991 there was little diversification of the formal financial system. Deposit-taking institutions (banks, the postal savings system, and credit cooperatives) consistently accounted for well over 90 percent of total assets of all financial institutions, with the domestic banks forming the backbone of the system.[46] The limited number of banks further streamlined this control. Prior to 1991, there were only twenty-four domestic banks, and all but three of them were majority government-owned (at the national, provincial, or local level). Of these twenty-one state banks, the top seven accounted for almost 90 percent of total deposits in domestic banks in 1980. The three private banks accounted for just over 2 percent of total deposits.[47]

By far the most important commercial bank is the Bank of Taiwan (BOT), established by the Japanese during the colonial era. The BOT served as the de facto central bank between 1949 and 1961 and has retained a close relationship with the monetary authorities since then.[48] The BOT also functions as the fiscal agent for the Taiwan provincial government. The City Bank of Taipei does the same for the Taipei municipal government. The Chang Hwa, Hua Nan, and First Commercial Banks are partly owned by the provincial government, and thus provide extensive islandwide commercial banking facilities. Known as the "big three," these government banks controlled nearly 80 percent of Taiwan's banking market as recently as 1991.[49]

This public dominance of the commercial banking sector was substantially reduced in 1991 as part of a long-planned but grudgingly enacted financial liberalization program. The original bargain struck in the late 1980s between the government and guanxiqiye interests in the legislature was first to privatize the big three commercial banks and then to issue a limited number (five or six) of private bank charters, thereby creating new private banks whose stock would be widely dispersed among public shareholders. In the end, pressures by provincial politicians resisting privatization of the big three and by the guanxiqiye promoting the new banks proved much greater than anticipated. After putting privatization

[46]In 1980, the domestic banks' portion of total formal financial institution assets was nearly 52 percent (Liang and Skully, p. 177).
[47]H. S. Cheng; Wade, 1985.
[48]Caldwell.
[49]*Asian Wall Street Journal,* 7/1/91.

plans for the government banks on hold, financial authorities in 1991 issued private commercial banking licenses to fifteen of nineteen applicant investor groups.[50] In 1992, the government for the first time allowed a private investment trust company to convert to a private bank and issued one additional bank charter, for a total of seventeen new private banks.[51]

Expressing nervousness about how it would "prevent companies using the banks as fund raisers for their other businesses,"[52] the government imposed rigorous criteria on all successful applicants. These included start-up capital requirements of U.S.$400 million, fully automated services, and a 5 percent ceiling on individual ownership and a 15 percent ceiling on institutional ownership of bank shares. The new banks were restricted to opening five branches the first year (only in Taipei) and three additional branches in each subsequent year. The big three commercial banks, in contrast, have a combined total of over 700 branches throughout the island.

MOF officials reported that all the investor groups "violated in minor ways" these limits on capital concentration, but the government has thus far overlooked these violations.[53] Business groups backing the private banks further skirted the intent of these capital ceilings by assembling the requisite investors from among their related companies, thereby assuring in most cases virtual control of these financial institutions. Table 5-4 lists the private banks and their major investors.

Of these seventeen, only Hua Hsin is directly linked to the Nationalist state. The Nationalist Party holds nearly 15 percent of its shares through its Central Investment Holding Company and two other party-affiliated investment companies.[54] Unsuccessful applicants included an investor group described as members of the Gaoxiung Chamber of Commerce, Cathay Life Insurance, Collins (see Chapter Seven), and another investment group from Ilan County.

It is too soon to assess the full impact of these privatized banks. The immediate benefactors of this liberalization have been the heretofore neglected consumers. Y. H. Chu predicts the emergence of loose, *keiretsu* (Japanese postwar business group)-type alliances among several "compatible" guanxiqiye with the banks as strategic nodes of agglomeration. This, he argues, will be the unintended consequence of the government- im-

---

[50]*Far Eastern Economic Review,* 5/7/92.

[51]Prior to the 1991 granting of private bank charters, three small private banks operated in Taiwan. They have maintained low profiles and have been very responsive to government requests (*Far Eastern Economic Review,* 9/17/85, 2/12/87). Combined with the seventeen new banks, this means twenty of Taiwan's thirty-one banks are private.

[52]*Far Eastern Economic Review,* 4/4/91.

[53]*Far Eastern Economic Review,* 7/11/91.

[54]*Far Eastern Economic Review,* 7/11/91; *Asian Wall Street Journal,* 7/1/91.

*Table 5-4.* Taiwan's new private commercial banks and their major investors

| Banks | Major investors |
| --- | --- |
| Ta-An | Pacific Wire and Cable, USI Far East |
| Wan-Tai | Prince Motors, San Fu Motors |
| Far East | Far Eastern Textiles, Asia Cement |
| Ta Chung | Formosa Plastics |
| Asia-Pacific | Taichung city businesses, ADI Corp. |
| Chung Hsing | Hua Eng Copper & Iron |
| Grand Commercial | President Enterprises, Universal Cement |
| Yu Shan | Taiwan Match, Eagle Food |
| Union | Union Enterprise Construction |
| Hua Hsin | Central Investment Holding, Tuntex |
| Pao Tao | Yakult |
| Fu Pang | Foremost, Evergreen Marine Corp. |
| Chung Hua | China Rebar |
| Pan Asia | Chang Yi Group |
| Tai Hsin | Shing Kong Synthetic Fiber, Weichuan Food Corp., Teco |
| China Trust | China Trust Group, Taiwan Cement |
| An Tai | — |

SOURCE: *Far Eastern Economic Review,* 7/11/91, 9/24/92.

posed personal and corporate shareholding ceilings and the steep minimum capital investments, measures designed precisely to prevent group dominance of the banks.[55] Even if the state were to tolerate them, the evidence and analysis of Taiwan's corporate culture offered in Chapter Three cast doubt on the feasibility of such multigroup institutional alliances, at least in the short run. But like the Korean chaebol in the wake of the privatization of Korean commercial banks, the guanxiqiye's participation in the banks will surely increase their financial, economic, and ultimately political influence. It is such a potential situation that kept financial control in the hands of the state for so many years and will likely slow the pace of these and other liberalization efforts.

In establishing its monopoly of the banking system, the Nationalist state from the outset developed numerous restrictions designed to retain this monopoly and enforce its policies of price stability and the prevention of private economic concentration. The state intentionally limited the number of banks and kept them out of the hands of the private sector. This lack of competition led government-appointed management and staff to operate the banks as bureaucracies, seeking neither profitability nor development but safety and the avoidance of error. This conservatism is compounded by the fact that civil servant loan officers may be punished for, or even held personally responsible for the repayment of, bad loans.[56]

[55]Y. H. Chu, 1994.
[56]In a 1986 case, four officials of the First Commercial Bank's Singapore branch were held responsible for extending N.T.$350 million in loans to two affiliates of the Tainan

Also, loan procedures are complicated and cumbersome, typically requiring lengthy approval periods and a second guarantor. Until 1975, commercial banks could not lend for terms over six months, and three-fourths of all loans had to be fully collateralized. Since 1975, maximum loan maturity has been lengthened to one year with no set collateral requirements.[57] Lending officers have remained very conservative, however, demanding collateral for most loans—often real property or other fixed assets to insure that private lenders will not hear the banks to the collateral in case of insolvency.[58]

Often these onerous restrictions inspire private borrowers to be much more creative in their circumvention, thus reconfirming the conservative convictions of financial authorities. The guanxiqiye, with a multiplicity of difficult-to-trace linkages among member firms, have been ideally suited to exploit this system. In fact, facilitating finance is one of the primary motives for the groups' organization. Member corporations of the same group frequently fabricate or forge invoices of intragroup sales transactions or accounts receivable to be used as loan collateral.[59] In order to cover their tracks in these and other illicit financial transactions, it is common practice for business firms in Taiwan to maintain two or even three sets of books or account ledgers: one for bankers, one for auditors and public stockholders, and an authentic set for the family or inner circle of management.

Under these circumstances, banks are unable to make rational decisions about a firm's financial situation and thus continue to rely on substantial collateral for loans. Although this system has tended to favor large, stable firms over the multitude of traditional small- and medium-sized enterprises, even the large, well-established guanxiqiye have chafed under the multitude of lending restrictions and have devised numerous

Spinning group that subsequently defaulted. The two affiliates had total annual revenues of less than N.T.$10 million and debt/equity ratios of 5,000 and 9,000 in 1982 and 1983 (*Economic News*, 7/7/86).

[57]Despite this limit on maximum maturity, banks lend to their regular customers with little concern for the term of the loan. As in Korea, these short-term loans are typically rolled over indefinitely, so in many ways they are the functional equivalent of an equity investment. Known in Taiwan as "evergreen" financing, this practice has retarded the development of the securities market, and thus has provided Taiwan's private businesses with a cheaper alternative than equity capital without their giving up managerial autonomy. In essence, the banks bear the risk but have no participation in management decisions (Kaufman-Winn, p. 17).

[58]Kaufman-Winn.

[59]In a 1986 case, four executives from the China Man-made Fiber Corporation were arrested and charged with using forged sales invoices to obtain N.T.$1.1 billion in illegal bank loans. One press account noted that their arrest made the local business community nervous because "the use of this method to obtain financing is actually a widespread and longstanding practice" (*Economic News*, 7/7/86). The same company was involved in a 1989 insider trading scandal.

ways to utilize their institutional networks to subvert the system in order to maximize capital at minimal risk and cost.

### Credit Cooperatives

Credit cooperatives are privately owned institutions that include credit departments of farmers' and fishermen's associations in rural areas as well as urban credit cooperative associations. Although technically restricted to accepting deposits from and granting loans and other limited services to association members only, in the past these credit cooperatives provided illegal loans to directors and their business interests. The seventy-five credit unions, with more than 400 branches and nearly 16 percent of total financial assets as of 1984, have been a tempting source of funds for the guanxiqiye and have come under government scrutiny for their illegal business investments.[60] By far the most egregious violation has been the Tenth Credit Cooperative's involvement in the 1985 Cathay scandal, the subject of the final section of this chapter.[61]

### Investment and Trust Companies

The most controversial institutions in Taiwan's formal financial system have been the investment and trust companies (ITCs). It is no coincidence that they have also been the financial institutions most closely linked with the guanxiqiye and their expansion efforts. The ITCs were established in 1971 in response to the dearth of medium- and long-term corporate financing and persistent lobbying by overseas Chinese for permission to set up banks.[62] The government's original objective was to have these private sector firms engage in medium- and long-term (three to five years) corporate loans and security investments with long-term funds generated from time (one year or more) deposits.

Despite government intentions to limit their scope, private ambition and the lack of a clear public mandate led the ITCs to gradually take on functions more similar to merchant or investment banks in other countries. Their operations included direct and syndicated loans, securities underwriting and trading, commercial paper guarantees, and direct investments in securities, real estate, and productive enterprises. The major difference between the ITCs and the commercial banks is that short-term lending and checking account deposits were to be limited exclusively to the banks. In fact, the ITCs ultimately took on these activities as well.[63]

---

[60]Caldwell; H. S. Cheng.

[61]In the wake of the Cathay scandal, guidelines were proposed to prevent the business groups from using these credit unions as a source of funds. They included the specific proposal that major stockholders of guanxiqiye not be allowed to serve as credit cooperative directors (*Free China Journal*, 9/7/85).

[62]Claire Chen.

[63]Claire Chen; Liang and Skully.

In all, eight ITCs have been established since 1971. Of these, three—China Development Corporation, Taiwan Development and Trust Corporation, and China United Trust and Investment Corporation—are either partly or wholly owned by the state or Nationalist Party.[64] A fourth, Taiwan First Investment and Trust Company, is 40 percent owned by Citibank. Despite efforts by the MOF to exclude the guanxiqiye,[65] they established the remaining four—Cathay Investment and Trust Company, China Investment and Trust Company, Overseas Investment and Trust Company, and Asia Trust and Investment Corporation (see Table 5-5).

Prohibited from owning their own banks and in large part excluded from the formal financial sector, the groups utilized these trust companies much like private banks. By offering a rate of return slightly higher than commercial bank rates (legal), adding to this a 4 percent bonus above interest (illegal), and accepting demand deposits (also illegal), the ITCs were able to generate substantial funds. In 1980, their share of total financial assets stood at 4.3 percent, with 58 percent of these funds employed as loans to private enterprise, 27 percent in securities investment, and the remainder in direct investments in real estate and productive enterprises.[66] At the end of 1991, the eight ITCs had U.S.$21.6 billion in assets, or 6 percent of Taiwan's total financial assets.[67] The ITCs will likely decline in importance, however, in the wake of the government's 1992 decision to allow China Trust, the largest ITC, to convert to a bank. Five of the remaining seven ITCs have expressed interest in making the same transition.

Unlike commercial banks, however, the trust companies were not legally prohibited from making equity investments. During their heyday, the private ITCs combined deposited funds with their own capital to loan to and invest in other group firms, acquire new firms through takeovers,

Table 5-5. Investment and trust companies with guanxiqiye affiliation, 1983

| Trust company | Rank (assets) | % of total group assets | Group affiliation | Rank (assets) | Rank (sales) |
|---|---|---|---|---|---|
| Cathay | 1 | 72% (NT$51 bil) | Cathay Trust | 2 | 8 |
| China | 2 | 83% (NT$41 bil) | China Trust | 3 | 14 |
| Overseas | 5 | 51% (NT$10 bil) | Overseas Trust | 10 | 21 |
| Asia[a] | — | — | Asia Trust | — | — |

Source: CCIS, 1985.

[a]Figures unavailable.

[64]Economic News, 10/21/85.
[65]Chuang.
[66]H. S. Cheng; Economic News, 10/29/84; Liang and Skully.
[67]Free China Journal, 5/26/92.

and speculate in the real estate and stock markets. As these trust-based groups rapidly expanded, so did government concern about the consequences of their high-risk, speculative investments and growing financial power. The Cathay scandal best typifies this concern and the ultimate consequences.

### Insurance Companies

Until 1961, the insurance business was limited to government-owned companies and two private companies that followed the Nationalists to Taiwan. After the ban on new insurance companies was lifted, a handful of licenses was granted to private local companies, bringing the total number to nine life and fourteen fire and marine insurance companies.[68] Of the dozen or so private firms, four are key member firms of business groups. These groups have used the reserve funds generated from their insurance business to fund group expansion, extending loans and making equity and security investments both within and outside of their groups.

Very few provident or employee benefit plans in Taiwan are operated in such a manner as to build up substantial long-term assets.[69] Not surprisingly, the insurance sector's share of total financial assets has remained quite small—2.4 percent as of 1984.[70] Nonetheless, as Table 5-6 shows, at least four of these group insurance firms have contributed significantly to placing their respective guanxiqiye among Taiwan's largest.

### Organized Money Market

Although commercial bank lending—as a source of short-term debt financing—technically takes place within the realm of the money market, the latter term typically refers to the market in which short-term negotiable (tradable) debt instruments are bought and sold. The most popular such instrument in Taiwan is the postdated check, which, because of its quasi-legal status, will be taken up below. Here we will discuss the fledg-

*Table 5-6.* Life insurance companies with guanxiqiye affiliation, 1983

| Insurance company | Rank (assets) | % of total group assets | Group affiliation | Rank (assets) | Rank (sales) |
|---|---|---|---|---|---|
| Cathay Life | 1 | 70% (NT$34 bil) | Linden Intl. | 4 | 18 |
| Shin Kong Life | 2 | 44% (NT$17 bil) | Shin Kong | 5 | 6 |
| Kuo Hua Life | 3 | 16% (NT$3 bil) | E-Hsin | 12 | 12 |
| China Life | 5 | 2% (NT$1 bil) | China Trust | 3 | 14 |

SOURCE: CCIS, 1985.

[68]Liang and Skully.
[69]Caldwell.
[70]H. S. Cheng.

ling formal market for such instruments as commercial paper and bankers' acceptance, a growing source of short-term financing for Taiwan's guanxiqiye.

No formal money market existed prior to the 1970s. In 1975, Premier Chiang Ching-kuo ordered the establishment of a money market in hopes of increasing government control over the money supply and credit and of drying up the unregulated curb market.[71] The government authorized the establishment of three finance companies to deal in, underwrite, and broker commercial paper, bankers' acceptances, negotiable certificates of deposit, and treasury bills. Government banks financed all three of these companies; two are owned by the Nationalist Party, and one is controlled directly by the party's finance committee.[72] Judy Li notes that the "operations of the three local bills finance corporations can best be characterized as conservative."[73]

Despite the conservatism of these state-owned institutions, the formal money market grew rapidly in the wake of their creation and in response to government incentive measures, a signal of real interest in corporate financing options beyond the banks and curb market. In 1984, commercial paper held 52 percent of the money market, bankers' acceptances 36 percent, negotiable CDs 9 percent, and trade acceptances 3 percent. Government-issued treasury bills made up less than 0.5 percent of the total. The first two of these instruments—commercial bills and bankers' acceptances—the primary instruments of corporate finance, jumped from a value equal to 1 percent of total bank loans and discounts in 1976 to about 15 percent in 1984.[74]

Although much of the short-term financing needs of group firms are still met through informal intragroup transfers, these money market instruments have become an increasingly popular source of group finance. Issuing these bills has required a degree of financial sophistication that only the larger corporations, many of which are associated with business groups, have possessed. Formosa Chemical and Fiber Corporation, one of Formosa Plastics group's (and Taiwan's) largest corporations, was the first firm to issue commercial paper, in a deal orchestrated by the government in 1975.[75] The group-owned ITCs' ability to guarantee commercial paper issued by guanxiqiye affiliates has greatly enhanced the groups' ability to dominate this market. In the wake of the Cathay scandal, the three bills finance companies were left holding over U.S.$25 million in

[71] *Far Eastern Economic Review,* 3/14/75; *Economic News,* 9/16/85.
[72] *Asian Wall Street Journal,* 7/11/88.
[73] J. Li.
[74] H. S. Cheng.
[75] *Far Eastern Economic Review,* 3/14/75.

commercial paper issued by Cathay Trust firms and guaranteed by Cathay Trust.[76]

### Capital Markets

Although "money market" typically refers to the market for short-term funds and "capital market" to long-term funds, the two blend imperceptibly in Taiwan. There, "capital market" traditionally refers to the markets for bonds (long-term debt instruments) and stocks (long-term equity instruments). Corporate and state motives have joined to create a systemic bias toward privately held equity and bank-issued debt financing for both short-term and long-term needs. Because short-term bank loans to creditworthy corporate clients are regularly rolled over, even long-term financing (beyond three to five years) is often obtained through the banks. This bias has stunted the development of the securities market as a source of corporate finance in Taiwan.

The bond market, including government bonds, corporate bonds, and financial debentures, remains largely undeveloped in Taiwan. Total funds raised during the 1970s through the bond market averaged less than 3 percent of the amount obtained through loans by financial institutions. During the period 1973–77, government agencies and state-owned enterprises accounted for over 80 percent of these issues. Private enterprises raised an amount equivalent to less than 1 percent of their borrowing from financial institutions through the bond market during this same period.[77] By 1984, total bonds outstanding in Taiwan were valued at U.S.$2.2 billion, or 4 percent of GNP, while in Korea bonds were valued at over U.S.$12 billion, or 18 percent of GNP. More significantly, only a minuscule portion of these bonds were issued by private corporations. In 1984 only 15 percent of total bonds outstanding were issued by private firms, compared with 45 percent in Korea.[78]

Because corporate issues, unlike government bonds, are fully taxable, they have been unable to attract investors by offering the same rate of return. Moreover, the government has restricted the eligibility to issue bonds to large enterprises with substantial assets. Approval for bond issues must come from the SEC; such approval is not routinely given and requires the issuing firm to open its books to the authorities.[79] These large firms, because of their creditworthiness, are able to obtain loans from the banks at lower rates, and thus have had little incentive to borrow through the bond market at the rates necessary to compete for investors' money

[76]*Economic News*, 9/16/85.
[77]H. S. Cheng.
[78]*Economic News*, 4/22/85.
[79]*Economic News*, 4/22/85.

against tax-free government issues and tax-free, long-term savings accounts.[80] Thus, despite calls for the expansion of the private corporate bond market as a means of drying up the curb market, deepening the financial system, and more efficiently allocating funds for long-term investment,[81] government objectives of price stability and high savings have considerably hampered this process.

Although it dwarfs the bond market in terms of capitalization and trading volume, Taiwan's stock market has not been a major source of corporate finance. The formal securities market was established in the 1960s with the creation of the Securities and Exchange Commission (SEC) in 1960 and the formation of the Taiwan Stock Exchange (TSE) in 1961. The TSE was formed by forty-three party, government, and private agencies, banks, and enterprises.[82] Trading commenced in 1962 with eighteen listed companies.

The government has encouraged the development of the stock market in order to channel private savings into industrial investment and obtain economies of scale without the private concentration of wealth. Thus far, government incentives offered to both listed companies and investors have not been great enough to overcome private unwillingness to list. One MOF official recalled a meeting in 1982 at which some suggested that like Korea, Taiwan should force private companies to list. This idea was rejected, he noted, because "it was felt the decision of whether or not to list should be left to the firms, not the government."

By 1970, only 42 companies were listed; and by 1980, 102. As of 1981, only 0.06 percent of Taiwan's total registered corporations listed stocks on the TSE. A more telling statistic is that only 81 of the top 500 compa-

[80]H. S. Cheng. There have been exceptions to this rule. The Far Eastern Textile Group has raised substantial funds through the bond market for a number of years. Of total corporate bonds issued in 1986, 68 percent were issued by Taipower, a state-owned enterprise. Of the remaining 32 percent, Far Eastern Group firms accounted for 25 percent of the issues, with a total value of over U.S.$78 million (Securities and Exchange Commission). Nearly all of the remaining bonds (5 percent) were issued by three firms affiliated with the Zhao family business group, whose founder, Zhao Tingzhen, got his start as a partner of Formosa Plastics' Wang Yongqing, and, like the Far Eastern group's Xu family, came to Taiwan from Jiangsu Province on the mainland (CCIS, 1991). A second, more creative exception has been the Yuen Foong Yu Paper Company, which in 1987 issued Taiwan's first convertible bonds. Although Taiwan's antiquated laws prevent corporations from issuing true convertible bonds, Yuen Foong Yu skirted this restriction by allowing the holders to convert its bonds into shares of Chung Hwa Pulp Corporation, a separately listed concern affiliated with Yuen Foong Yu (Asian Wall Street Journal, 11/26/87; Shen).
[81]Ing; Claire Chen; J. Li.
[82]These included the Nationalist Party's Central Investment Holding Company, numerous state-owned banks and enterprises, and several of Taiwan's large private enterprise groups (Asian Wall Street Journal, 7/11/88). The 1986 Taiwan Stock Exchange Annual Report lists Wang Yongqing (Formosa Plastics group), Lin Tingsheng (Tatung group), He Shouchwan (Yong Feng Related Enterprise group), and Huang Keming (Wei-Chuan Foods group), all Taiwanese leaders of guanxiqiye, among the TSE's board of directors.

nies did so.[83] In 1987, there were 130 listed companies, compared with 330 listed companies in Korea and 169 in Hong Kong. In 1990, the total had climbed to only 185.[84] This situation of relatively few listed firms is made worse by the fact that only a small percentage of each firm's total shares is actually traded. It is estimated that fully 70 percent of the shares of the listed companies (only a small fraction of Taiwan's total number of firms) are controlled by the Nationalist Party, government enterprises, and familial business group cross-holdings, all of which are reluctant to sell.[85] Although all shares of a listed company are technically available for purchase, these companies are actually required to distribute only 10 percent of the shares to the public. As a further incentive to "list," this percentage has been reduced for large firms.[86] Moreover, private shareholders (most often family members) can buy back this small percentage, thereby gaining government incentives for listing without giving up control, and essentially reprivatizing many of these supposedly publicly traded companies.

TSE's meager number of tradable shares and small capitalization relative to the total numbers and capitalization of Taiwan's corporations has in no way discouraged the market's frenzied pace and volume of transactions.[87] By September 1988, daily transactions were averaging about U.S.$2 billion (2 percent of Taiwan's GNP), compared with U.S.$6 billion for the New York Stock Exchange (0.2 percent of U.S. GNP), making it the second busiest exchange in Asia after Tokyo. With this much money flooding the market, one might expect stocks to be a valuable, if untapped, source of corporate finance. Although a majority of listed firms are in fact affiliated with guanxiqiye, few of the groups have used the stock exchange as a source of capital funds. The groups usually list one member firm in order to appease government "go-public" teams and reap government incentives, and publicly trade only a small fraction of that firm's total shares.

[83]Chow.

[84]*Asian Finance*, 7/15/90.

[85]*Asian Wall Street Journal*, 10/8/87.

[86]As of 1987, the percentages were as follows: for firms with assets up to N.T.$2 billion, 10 percent; N.T.$2–5 billion, 5 percent; and over N.T.$5 billion, 2 percent. Therefore, the largest firms need give up only 2 percent equity ownership to public shareholders to receive the incentives reserved for "publicly held" enterprises.

[87]In 1985, the four most actively traded stocks—Hualon-Teijran, Chung Shing Textile, Yue Loong Motor, and Tatung—accounted for over 19 percent of the total value of transactions and over 21 percent of total volume. The top ten accounted for 34 percent of value and 35 percent of total volume (*Taiwan Stock Exchange*, 1985). Caldwell notes that as of 1973, the ratio of registered capital of listed companies to the registered capital of all incorporated enterprises stood at 8.5 percent. TSE's capitalization at the end of 1986 stood at U.S.$13.2 billion, or 22.3 percent of GDP, compared with Korea's U.S.$14 billion, or 16.5 percent of GDP (*Asian Wall Street Journal*, 3/19/87). By May 1987, capitalization of Taiwan stocks was U.S.$17 billion (*Euromoney*, 5/87).

Public restrictions, private economic rationale, and sociocultural imperatives have dampened the groups' interest in the stock market. Critics contend the government does not provide enough incentive for privately held companies to list shares on the market. Whereas Taiwan's listed companies are eligible for a 15 percent corporate tax reduction for the first three years of listing, the Korean government offers a 37.5 percent reduction with no time limit.[88] Large corporate investments in the stock market are discouraged. Net income from securities in excess of N.T.$30,000 is subject to a significantly higher tax rate, and a 0.3 percent transfer tax is levied on the sale of all securities. Despite calls for relaxing these requirements, one observer predicts continued resistance, noting that "the government's stonewalling is the result of fear of capital concentration in private hands, which would lead to further reduction of authority over economic growth."[89]

In a further effort to control the market, financial regulations require all margin transactions (purchase or sale of securities on credit) to be handled by the Fuh Hwa Securities Finance Company. Fu Hwa, established in 1980, is 49.5 percent owned by the Nationalist Party, with the Bank of Taiwan and Land Bank of Taiwan as other major stockholders.[90] Though established to reduce the volatility of the market and undercut illegal lenders, the company's low lending ceiling and cumbersome credit investigations have discouraged large investors and assured the private lenders plenty of business. Illegal investment houses flourished in the late 1980s, until the MOF cracked down on them in 1990.[91]

In addition to these government restrictions and the volatility and speculative nature of the stock market, Taiwan's guanxiqiye have other reasons for hesitating to list shares on the market as a means of raising capital. Listed companies are required to prepare and make public an annual report and corporate financial records.[92] Not only are these procedures costly and time-consuming, but accurate reports would reveal past tax evasion and make future tax dodges much more difficult (and thus offset financial incentives for listing).

Moreover, like their Korean counterparts, Taiwan's closely held familial groups are reticent to share ownership of their companies and managerial decisions with outsiders. In the words of one second-generation busi-

[88] *Economic News*, 8/2/82.
[89] *Far Eastern Economic Review*, 12/5/80.
[90] *Asian Wall Street Journal*, 7/11/88.
[91] *Economic News*, 11/23/90.
[92] Although only listed corporations must release their financial statements to the public, in fact all corporations, whether publicly or privately held, are required to file financial statements with the Ministry of Economic Affairs (MOEA) prior to annual shareholder meetings. However, few corporations comply with this ruling and the MOEA does not have the resources to enforce it (Chuang).

ness group leader, listing "would just be a lot of hassle." He added that growth is fast enough with currently available funds, and that shareholders would restrict decision making to the detriment of the business group. The guanxiqiye also are unwilling to share profits with outsiders. Often a business group will list shares from only one or two of its firms, holding the other firms privately. Profits from the listed firms are then channeled back to privately held affiliates or listed as retained earnings. Numerous listed firms consistently show strong annual profits but pay low yearly dividends, a source of much rancor among small investors.[93] Thus public restrictions and private reluctance have combined to limit the securities market as a significant source of corporate funds.

## Informal Sources of Funds: Curb Market

In addition to the formal institutions and markets, informal sources of financing have been very important to Taiwan's private corporate sector. As in Korea, these sources of funds remain popular because of the inability of the formal system to meet the financial needs of private firms. Or, when funds are available, entrepreneurs perceive their costs—measured in terms of expensive audits, time-consuming bureaucratic procedures, relinquished ownership or control, and disclosure of illicit activities—as outweighing the benefits of significantly lower interest rates. Although the informal market has been most important to the multitude of small and medium-sized enterprises that generally have had nowhere else to turn, even large enterprises and member firms of well-established business groups have sought funding through the informal or unorganized curb market.

Wade defines the curb market as an "unregulated, semi-legal credit market in which loan suppliers and lenders can transact freely at uncontrolled interest rates."[94] Despite the high risks, even higher interest rates have lured huge amounts of savings into the system, which lends them through a wide variety of creative forms and instruments. These include revolving credit associations (*biaohui*), private lenders (*qianzhuang*), private lottery clubs, pawnbrokers, currency swap markets, and employee deposit schemes. Small companies and individual consumers are the major customers of many of these institutions.[95] As sources of business

[93] *Economic News*, 10/3/83.
[94] Wade, 1985, p. 112.
[95] Perhaps the most studied of these informal markets are the rotating credit associations (*hui*), the Chinese equivalent of the Korean *kye*, which are ubiquitous in Chinese communities. A 1985 survey indicated that up to 85 percent of the public in Taiwan participates in *hui* (Kaufman-Winn, p. 19). Useful accounts of their functioning in Taiwan are in H. Jones; and Stites.

group finance, only employee deposits and private lenders are significant. Employee deposit schemes are also an internal source of finance and are discussed in the following section. Here we examine the private loan market and its most popular instrument, the postdated check.

Private lenders may include anyone from immediate family members, other relatives, friends, and business associates who may or may not have a direct interest in the business enterprise, to underground "bankers" or loan sharks with links to the criminal underworld. Estimates of the size of this market and its importance to corporate finance vary, with most studies placing the curb market's share of total private business loans between 35 and 40 percent.[96] This range is comparable with, if not somewhat larger than, the estimated contribution of the Korean curb market to total corporate loans, which has varied from 10 to 20 percent of total loans to a maximum of 40 percent.[97] The curb market is popular despite exorbitantly high interest rates—three times the already high bank rate during the 1950s and twice as high during the 1970s and 1980s (see Table 5-1). This is because "frequently the availability of credit is a more pressing problem to the borrower than its cost."[98]

Although some of these curb market loans are completely unsecured, the most common form of financing is through the use of the postdated check (PDC).[99] Typically a businessman, unable or unwilling to obtain credit through a bank or wait for credit approval, will write a PDC on his bank account to pay for goods or services. The check, postdated anywhere from ten days up to a year later (with thirty days, ten days, and ninety days the most common time periods), becomes in essence a form of commercial paper. The recipient has the option of holding the check to maturity or discounting it to a curb dealer, who can either hold it or sell it to private investors, company treasurers, or even banks.[100]

There are a number of reasons for the PDC's continued popularity. From the borrower's perspective, the major advantage is that it provides

[96]A 1985 study placed the curb market's share of the total capital market at 25 percent in 1961, 19 percent in 1971, and 12 percent in 1981. Despite this decline, the value of total transactions jumped from U.S.$245 million in 1961 to U.S.$4.8 billion in 1981 (see Kaufman-Winn). Using government figures for "loans made by enterprises and households" (which include supplier credits), H. S. Cheng estimates that curb market loans made up 29 percent of domestic financial assets in 1970, 30.9 percent in 1980, and 25.9 percent in 1983. As a percentage of total loans to private business, 1976 and 1981, an estimated 60 percent came from formal financial institutions, with most of the rest from the curb market (Wade, 1985, p. 113). Other estimates place the curb market share of corporate loans between 33 and 40 percent (*Far Eastern Economic Review*, 3/7/85; *Christian Science Monitor*, 9/9/85; Kaufman-Winn).

[97]Wade, 1985.

[98]Caldwell, p. 740.

[99]For a detailed explanation of the PDC's functioning in Taiwan, see Meeng. For a more recent useful account, see *Asian Wall Street Journal*, 8/26/91.

[100]H. S. Cheng; Chuang.

credit without collateral. Also, despite the much higher rate, the loans are accessible to anyone with a checking account and, again unlike bank loans, very quick to execute with a minimum of bother. From the creditor's perspective, the primary incentive is the rate of return, typically twice that of the organized money market during times of relative credit scarcity. In addition, the PDC, backed by government statute, has been a relatively safe instrument. In an effort to increase confidence in checks, in 1965 the government implemented the Law of Negotiable Instruments, which gave the holder of a PDC the rights to (1) invoke the sanction of criminal law if the debtor defaults (up to three years' imprisonment, though seldom enforced); (2) demand payment on sight, regardless of the date on the check; and (3) use ordinary banking channels for its collection. A final advantage for both the creditor and the borrower is that the PDC is virtually untraceable by tax authorities. Despite the dropping of criminal sanctions for writing a bad check in 1987 (another effort by the state to dry up the informal market), the long-standing popularity of the PDC is not likely to wane as long as state restrictions on formal institutions, and corporate demand based on the comparative advantages of the curb over the formal market, keep curb rates for loans higher than bank rates.[101]

Although the guanxiqiye arguably have greater access to both formal credit markets (by virtue of their creditworthiness) and internal markets (because of their linkages to other group firms), they have sought funding through various informal markets. Among other wrongdoings, Cai Zhenzhou, the central figure of the 1985 Cathay Group scandal, was convicted of bouncing 539 PDCs valued at U.S.$2.5 million.[102] Many of these checks were placed with close friends and business associates, an indication of how the guanxiqiye are ideally situated to exploit one of the key ingredients of curb market exchanges: trust. Most curb market activities, by virtue of their bilateral nature, function on the basis of "trust" (*xinyong*) between the lender and borrower.[103] Although this trust is invested in the individual and his reputation, it is often carried over to the founder or chairman's guanxiqiye.[104] We will see how this groupwide trust was used and abused in the Cathay case.

### Internal Sources of Funds

The final sources of guanxiqiye finance are internal. These include employee deposits—a financing method also common to group firms—as well as several sources unique to the guanxiqiye.

[101] Chuang; H. S. Cheng; Caldwell.
[102] *Economist*, 8/24/85.
[103] See Biggs, 1991.
[104] Chuang.

## Employee Deposits

Because of the formal financial system's inability to serve as an adequate intermediary between private savers and corporate borrowers, most large companies in Taiwan accept deposits from their employees (and other individuals) and extend loans much like a bank. Until the early 1980s, Taiwan's banking laws did not prohibit these employee deposit schemes, but since then the government has attempted to restrict them in order to separate commerce and banking. The practice is so common and such an important source of corporate finance, however, that the government has been unable or unwilling to terminate it.[105]

J. Alexander Caldwell cites an "observer" who estimated that up to 25 percent of all unorganized money market activity in the late 1960s involved private deposits with firms.[106] If firms receive 30 to 40 percent of their financing from the curb market, this suggests that firms participating in employee deposit schemes may obtain as much as 10 to 12 percent of their financing through them. This practice entails trade-offs for both the depositors and the companies. Depositors earn higher interest rates than those offered by formal institutions but have no legal protection. The companies secure convenient and unmonitored financing but risk the consequences of a run as a result of corporate or economywide problems.

Over the years, large guanxiqiye member firms reaped both the benefits and the costs of these employee deposit schemes. In the wake of the Cathay scandal, both the Cathay Group and the Tatung Group (then Taiwan's largest in terms of employees) and other major corporations suffered runs on company coffers as employees and other individuals sought to withdraw deposits and call in loans.[107] Tatung admitted it had relied on employee deposits since 1957 and that these borrowings had reached U.S.$275 million by 1985. Tatung was able to cover employee withdrawals through loans from foreign banks.[108] The recent granting of bank licenses to private business concerns will likely succeed in drying up this informal source of funds because these group-affiliated banks can legitimately solicit employee deposits.

## Intragroup Lending and Guarantee

Employee deposits may be considered primarily an intrafirm source of funds that is informal and technically illegal. Cross-lending and cross-

[105]Kaufman-Winn; *Far Eastern Economic Review,* 4/11/85. An indication of the real demand for this credit can be found in the interest rate offered to depositors compared with other rates in the organized and unorganized money markets. For example, market rates for deposits with firms in 1980 was 1.9 percent per month, compared with 1.04 percent per month for one-year savings deposits in state-owned banks (Liang and Skully; H. S. Cheng).

[106]Caldwell, p. 739.

[107]*Far Eastern Economic Review,* 3/7/85, 4/11/85.

[108]*Economic News,* 6/24/85.

investment, on the other hand, are intragroup. Though the guanxiqiye are ostensibly monitored by the state, their organizational features have made them uniquely qualified to reap both the formal and the informal, the legal and the illicit, synergies and other benefits of these sources.[109] Although intercorporate financing does occur quite regularly in Taiwan even among unrelated companies (based largely on the particularistic relationships between the owner-managers of the firms involved), these transactions become routinized and institutionalized among member firms of the same group.[110]

Financial transactions between member firms include not only lending and borrowing of funds but also intercorporate guarantee and endorsement of loans, exchange of PDCs, and coborrowing by two or more related firms. These transactions are a valuable source of financing for the firms involved and the business groups as a whole. Richard Chuang claims that "without this sort of financing, especially short-term loans, most of the corporations in Taiwan would not have sufficient working capital to run their businesses.[111] In their study, Shuishen Liu et al. determined that facilitating intercorporate finance ranked fourth among the fifteen most popular motives for forming business groups in Taiwan. They estimate that fully three-fourths of all member firms participate in group lending, borrowing, and/or guaranteeing activities.[112]

Perhaps the most common of these activities is the intercorporate guarantee. The collateral requirements necessary to obtain bank loans in Taiwan have meant that long-established, financially stable companies must serve as guarantors for most corporate loans. Parent or flagship companies of the guanxiqiye are able to perform this function for newer, smaller, or less financially sound firms within their groups. Moreover, because of limits on how much a bank or other financial institution can lend to any one company, the group as a whole is able to borrow much more than it could as a single entity.[113] A common method for subverting the collateral requirement is to fabricate dummy transactions between member firms. Banks will often accept invoices (accounts receivable) as security for loans. Therefore, companies often obtain a dummy invoice issued by another member firm and present this as collateral for a loan.

Because the guanxiqiye are able through creative accounting to obtain

[109]Although intragroup synergies exist in other areas of corporate activity, such as R&D, personnel, marketing and sales, and raw material provision, financial synergy is most easily achieved because financial capital is the most fundamental, and most fungible, of all factor inputs or activities.
[110]Numazaki, 1986; Chuang.
[111]Chuang, p. 189.
[112]Liu et al., pp. 7, 14.
[113]In fact, some groups establish dummy firms and take out loans in their name to subvert lending limits.

loans well beyond the value of the guarantor's or entire group's collateral, banks often require the founder or CEO of the group to furnish a personal guarantee for credit extended to member firms of his group. Formosa Plastics' founder Wang Yongqing is routinely requested to lend his personal stock to member firms as collateral to secure loans. Nonetheless, Chuang notes that even in Wang's case, by "the end of 1982, his group had some U.S.$958 million in debts. Although Wang is one of the richest men in Taiwan, his personal assets cannot be as great as the debts he guaranteed for his group of corporations."[114]

Alternatively, firms lend funds directly to other group firms or their controlling persons. These funds can originate from either bank loans or surplus profits. Because Taiwan's conglomerates are active in multiple sectors, member firms in profitable sectors can provide temporary or long-term relief to financially strapped affiliated companies in ailing sectors or sunrise industries. For example, three listed firms of the Far Eastern Textile group declared in their prospectuses a total of over U.S.$50 million in loans to other member firms within the Far Eastern Group for the period 1980–81. Na Ya Plastics of the Formosa Plastics group disclosed in 1982 that it provided nearly U.S.$7.4 million in loans to six of its related enterprises.[115]

Though technically in violation of Taiwan's Law Governing Company Organization, which prohibits a company from lending to shareholders (in these cases, other member firms) or other individuals, the government has not restricted these activities. Other, more egregious violations, however, have been prosecuted. For example, Yuan I Industrial Company, textile flagship of the Yuan I group, set up an affiliate, I Sun Textile Company, to supply Yuan I with raw materials at a price near cost. I Sun in turn purchased finished goods from Yuan I at considerable markup. Thus, while the parent company profited, the affiliate remained debt-ridden. But because Yuan I was able to show strong profits, it was able to borrow large sums of money from unsuspecting banks that it then used to keep I Sun afloat.[116] Even more widespread is the practice of borrowing

---

[114]Chuang, p. 264. Chuang also notes that Nan Ya Plastics Corporation, Formosa Group's largest member firm, borrowed some 36,699,400 Formosa Plastics shares, 9,185,000 Formosa Chemical Fibers Corporation shares, and 108,000 Sunrise Wood Products Corporation shares from its own "shareholders" to serve as collateral for securing Nan Ya bank loans in 1981 (Chuang, p. 178).

[115]Chuang.

[116]*Economic News*, 2/21/83. In addition to the Yuan I Group, financial authorities have investigated and implicated the following companies in 1980s intragroup loan scandals: Pao Lung Pulp and Paper Corporation, Great Wall Enterprise, and Lien Hwa Industrial Corporation (the firms technically were not part of the same group, but their executives belonged to the "Shandong Clique" (*shandong bang*), Chia Hsin Flour and Feeding Company and China Rebar Corporation (China Rebar group), Chia Hsin Cement Company (Chia Hsin group), Atlantic Beverage Corporation, and Li Chang Jung Chemical Company (*Economic News*, 8/22/83; *China News*, 3/1/87; Chuang).

short-term funds ostensibly for a specific project not requiring collateral or extensive documentation, then using the loan to invest in riskier ventures of affiliated firms.

The chairman and other top executives of Yuan I were found guilty of channeling loan and capital funds directly to their individual accounts. As noted in Chapter Three, major shareholders of many family-run businesses in Taiwan feel few qualms about borrowing corporate funds. One Western banker noted in the wake of this scandal that "the company is just like another pocket to them, and they consider the company a convenient place to deposit or take money out at will."[117]

Although these intercorporate financial ties can provide valuable sustenance for ailing member firms, massive overborrowing within the guanxiqiye can lead to groupwide collapse if the healthy firms become overextended or recession affects the entire economy. It was such an economic downturn in the early 1980s that struck down a number of highly leveraged groups and prompted financial authorities to expose a number of previously ignored violations, culminating in the 1985 Cathay investigation.

### Intragroup Cross-Holding and Joint Investment

The familial context of corporate culture in Taiwan, combined with the pervasive system of state financial restrictions, has created an environment in which the guanxiqiye owners have found it advantageous to turn to family and friends as a major source of financing. Unlike Japanese groups, which rely largely on group bank-based financing and institutional cross-holdings of shares, and Korean groups, which depend on state-controlled debt-based financing, Taiwan's related enterprises have turned to family and friends as a major source of financing.

When immediate family savings or retained earnings are insufficient to meet capital requirements for new or existing business operations, an entrepreneur will often ask extended family members or trusted friends sharing a common "connection" to participate as minority stockholders. Alternatively, several entrepreneurs (brothers, classmates, etc.) will jointly invest in each other's firms or set up a number of independent corporations with only the major stockholder of each firm participating in that firm's management. This practice of "joint investment and separate management" (*gongtong touzi, fenbie jingying*) is a common method of corporate finance in Taiwan and has been the impulse behind the original formation and subsequent expansion of many of Taiwan's guanxiqiye. These arrangements allow for the mutual provision of debt and equity

[117] *Wall Street Journal,* 4/22/84.

financing in an environment of relative trust and security, free from government intervention and monitoring.

Parent companies also preserve autonomy by providing majority investment in group subsidiaries. Until 1990, Taiwan's company law limited the extent of cross-investment among companies, stipulating that a corporation's investments in any one other corporation could not exceed 40 percent of its own paid-in capital. When the limit was lifted in 1990, one observer noted that the previous investment restriction had made it difficult for the guanxiqiye to grow and diversify, citing it as "a major reason why Taiwan has few corporations of world class dimensions."[118] Significantly, however, the law did not (and still does not) restrict the percentage of shares one corporation may hold in another. Because of this, many large corporations have established numerous smaller subsidiaries in which they own at least 51 percent of the shares. In its 1981 prospectus Far Eastern Textile listed nine companies in which it controlled more than 50 percent of the outstanding shares. In one case, it held 99.98 percent of outstanding shares.[119]

These subsidiaries are in a position to cross-invest (since 1990 with no limits) in the parent corporation or other group firms, thereby creating internal group finance. In fact, many of the guanxiqiye have established investment companies to function as holding companies that handle the flow of capital within the group. Profits or bank loans from the parent company and other group firms are channeled to these holding companies, which can then make equity investments in other group firms. An executive for the American Chinese Investment Corporation, an investment company of the Chinese-Filipino Asia Trust group, described this role: "Our purpose is to provide financial support directly to our associated companies and to diversify the scope of our business through the acquisition of stock in other firms. With equity investment from us, our affiliates don't need to borrow from outside; that saves a lot of interest, and the financial structure of those firms is significantly improved as a result."[120] During the first two years of operation (1979–81), this company invested some U.S.$20 million in twenty different firms.

As the number and activities of these group-affiliated investment companies expanded, so did government concerns about their operations. And not without justification, for they were increasingly seen as vehicles for tax evasion, stock and real estate speculation, and group expansion. For example, Pao Lung Pulp and Paper established the Pao Tung Investment Company and proceeded to channel extensive interest-free loans to

[118]*Economic News*, 10/29/90.
[119]Chuang.
[120]*Economic News*, 8/31/81.

the affiliate. Pao Tung, with the same business address as Pao Lung and no listed business activities beyond securities investment, reinvested nearly all of these funds in Pao Lung stock, driving up its price. Although Taiwan's company law prohibits a firm from repurchasing its own stock, this indirect cross-investment (similar to the chaebol's Ping-Pong cross-investments) technically bypassed the law. However, Pao Tung was found guilty of numerous other violations in a 1983 investigation of its activities.[121]

Government efforts to put legal limitations on these investment companies have been undermined by the fact that the largest local investment companies are owned and operated by the Nationalist Party. Kuang-Hwa Investment Holding Company has investments in four different enterprises and controls the Fuh Hwa Securities Finance Company. Central Investment Holding Company owns or has significant investments in some twenty-six different enterprises, including four of Taiwan's biggest plastics makers, two steel companies, a cement company, a tennis racket manufacturer, and the Taiwan Stock Exchange and China Development Corporation. These holding companies for the extensive Nationalist Party financial network have come under increasing public criticism, which makes calls for curtailment of their private counterparts more difficult.[122]

A final form of intercorporate investment should be mentioned because of its significance for group expansion. Mergers and acquisitions in the Western sense are very uncommon in Taiwan. Unlike Korea, which does have hostile takeovers, vertical and conglomerate expansion in Taiwan typically occurs through a process of "new-building."[123] Nonetheless, certain groups have expanded the scope and scale of their operations through conglomerate acquisitions, typically as the result of a creditor firm taking over an insolvent borrower. For most of their existence, the ITCs, unlike commercial banks, have been permitted to make equity investments in other enterprises. Thus, the guanxiqiye most active in these takeovers were the groups centered around ITCs. The most active of all was the Cathay Group. Gold cites one observer:

> Cathay Trust uses equity capital purchases to acquire firms. After taking 50 percent, the company is theirs. They buy shares as they lend money. Many of the firms involved are not on the market. In bad times, it is very easy to do this. They can offer help at a good rate, for instance, loaning a certain amount of money in exchange for temporary control of shares. When the firm can't repay, Cathay loans the rest and takes the shares. The government

[121] *Economic News*, 8/22/83.
[122] *Asian Wall Street Journal*, 7/11/89.
[123] Chou.

does not control such activities. Although it opposes the growth of conglomerates, it can't prevent the public purchase of shares.[124]

Although the government did not prevent Cathay Trust and the other ITCs from engaging in these activities, these actions did raise concerns within the government and among the public at large about these groups as "predatory Frankensteins."[125] By the late 1970s, the group most fitting of this description was the Cathay Trust Group.

## Cathay Scandal

The year 1985 was not a good one for the Taiwan government.[126] The coal mine that had taken 167 miners' lives in 1984 and had allegedly been shut down by government order claimed another 7 lives in June. Contaminated imported corn, which authorities had promised to use only in industrial starch, appeared that summer as an ingredient in government monopoly-produced liquor. In August, it was discovered that moon cakes and other food products were regularly made with cooking oil produced from recycled pig swill. Worst of all, Taiwan ended the year with an economic growth rate of only 5.1 percent, less than half the figure for both the prior and the following year. For a government whose legitimacy has been measured, more than most, in terms of GNP, this was a serious problem.

Intimately related to this last problem was the Cathay scandal,[127] described as "the most traumatic business drama in Taiwan's history." In February 1985, the state suspended operations at the Tenth Credit Cooperative Association of Taipei, Taiwan's largest credit cooperative and one of several financial institutions controlled by the Cai family's Cathay business empire. The initial reason given for the shutdown was that the cooperative's loans exceeded legal limits. News of Tenth Credit's problems

[124]Gold, 1981, p. 266.

[125]*Economic News*, 9/4/78.

[126]In piecing together this account of the Cathay scandal, I have collected information from multiple sources. Primary sources include interviews with several of the figures involved in the scandal, as well as bureaucrats, Nationalist Party officials, scholars, and journalists familiar with the events. In addition, I have drawn information from the following secondary sources: *Asian Wall Street Journal*, 5/6/87; *Business Week*, 4/1/85; CCIS; *China Post*, 2/26/87, 4/20/87; *Christian Science Monitor*, 9/9/85; Chuang; *Economic News*, 7/9/79, 10/29/84, 2/18/85, 3/4/85, 3/7/85, 3/11/85, 8/19/85, 10/21/85, 5/4/87; *Economist*, 8/24/85; *Euromoney*, 7/86; *Far Eastern Economic Review*, 9/6/74, 3/7/85, 3/28/85, 4/11/85, 9/12/85; *Free China Journal*, 8/18/85, 8/25/85, 4/10/89; Gold, 1981, pp. 265–66; *Hong Kong Standard*, 3/3/85, 5/31/85, 8/5/85, 7/22/86; *International Herald Tribune*, 10/7/85; Kaufman-Winn; *South China Morning Post*, 6/26/85; *Time*, 9/16/85.

[127]It has been estimated that Taiwan's economic growth rate dropped at least 0.5 percent as a result of the Cathay scandal and its fallout (*Far Eastern Economic Review*, 3/28/85).

quickly spread and prompted runs by customers not only on Tenth Credit but also on Cathay Investment and Trust Company (CITC), other ITCs, and numerous deposit-taking manufacturing corporations.

As the scandal unraveled during the Chinese New Year, it claimed as victims not only Cai family members, Cathay and Tenth Credit executives, and various banking officials but also the ministers of finance and economic affairs and the ruling Nationalist Party's secretary-general. The state assumed management of Tenth Credit, CITC, and a second, unrelated ITC (Overseas Trust), and many of the Cathay business group's related enterprises were threatened with collapse. The scandal prompted the launching of unprecedented reform efforts that are coming to fruition in the 1990s.

This drama is worth retelling because the event itself and the trauma it generated were closely connected with nearly all the channels of business group finance—formal and informal, legal and illicit—discussed above. Moreover, this scandal and its subsequent exposure illuminate the financial system's public-private interplay, revealing not only the methods and motives of private disregard of public restrictions but also the consequences when this disregard became too great.

Cathay Trust was not the first private ITC to have its operations taken over by the state because of financial problems, nor was it the last.[128] It was, however, the largest. More important, Cathay was the first private trust with the potential to become a genuine financial center of a business group. By 1984, the Cathay group had become powerful enough monetarily to challenge the government politically regarding economic policy. Although the state could (and did) tolerate extensive informal financial activity by Cathay and the remainder of the private sector, it could not allow this political rivalry and its consequences for Taiwan's financial stability. It was only when the Cai family tried to translate its economic power into political power that the state took measures to expose its long-standing economic corruption and assume control over much of its operations.

This chain of events reveals much about the state policymakers' attitudes toward the guanxiqiye and served further to galvanize their convictions about the ill consequences of concentrated economic and financial power in private hands. It also revealed the "inability of Taiwan's financial system to provide an efficient orderly flow of capital to the private sector" and the fundamental need for financial reform.[129]

---

[128]In 1983 the International Commercial Bank of China took over operations of the Asia Trust and Investment Corporation (Asia Trust Group) after savers withdrew N.T.$6.7 billion (U.S.$167 million) in three days. A run on the Overseas Trust Corporation in September 1985 led to its takeover by the United World Chinese Commercial Bank (Claire Chen).

[129]*Far Eastern Economic Review,* 4/11/85.

*Cathay Business Empire*

Cai Wanchun, founder of the Cathay (*Guotai*) business empire was the eldest son of a poor peasant family in southern Taiwan. At the age of sixteen, he came to Taipei and began working as a cosmetics salesman for a Japanese company during the occupation. With personal savings he bought a small department store in 1938 and then a soy sauce factory. After the war and retrocession, Cai capitalized on the vacuum created by the Japanese withdrawal, branching out into real estate, lumber, pottery, and private banking.

With his brothers he founded the Cathay business group in the early 1950s. Sensing opportunities in finance, Cai took over management of the Tenth Credit Cooperative Association of Taipei in the late 1950s. The group rapidly expanded and diversified in pace with Taiwan's shift to export-led development in the 1960s and 1970s. By the end of 1977, Cai and his brothers owned 24 firms with combined assets of nearly U.S.$1 billion (over 4 percent of Taiwan's GNP) and over 20,000 employees. By this time a household name, Cathay had become Taiwan's largest group measured in assets and included the largest private insurance company, the largest private investment and trust company, the largest equipment leasing firm, and the largest private construction firm. Cai received many government awards and honors for his business success and philanthropic activities.

After being paralyzed by a stroke in 1979, Cai divided the Cathay empire (*fenjia*) into five nominally independent branches that are allotted among his two brothers and four sons, with each branch controlling a key component of the original group (see Table 5-7).

Though this division of control and rumored bad blood between the uncles and nephews loosened the network, familial bonds, extensive cross-holdings, and multiple business ties held the various parts together

*Table 5-7.* 1979 division of Cai Wanchun's Cathay guanxiqiye

| Name | Relation | Group Name | Key Firms |
|---|---|---|---|
| Cai Wanlin | brother | Linden International | Cathay Life Insurance Cathay Construction |
| Cai Wancai | brother | Fu Bang | Foremost Land Development Cathay Insurance |
| Cai Zhenzhou | son | Cathay Plastics | Cathay Plastics Tenth Credit Cooperative |
| Cai Zhennan | son | Cathay Trust | Cathay Investment & Trust Lai Lai Sheraton |
| Cai Zhenxiang | son | Sunrise | Lai Lai Shopping Mall |
| Cai Zhenwei | son | | Sunrise Department Store |

Source: CCIS, 1985.

as they continued to expand through the early 1980s. By the time the scandal broke in February 1985, the Cathay business empire controlled more than U.S.$2.5 billion in assets (4.2 percent of GNP) in over 100 companies.

Over the next eight months, a series of investigations and reports revealed an economic and political scandal unprecedented in Taiwan's history that sent the financial and business communities, and even the Taiwan state, reeling. Though the scandal involved primarily the domains of half brothers Zhenzhou (Cathay Plastics) and Zhennan (Cathay Trust), it quickly enveloped other, wholly unrelated guanxiqiye, ITCs, and numerous bureaucrats and government officials. We now examine the ambitions that fueled this scandal and its consequences for Taiwan's financial system and the financing of the guanxiqiye.

## Private Ambitions

### Economic Activities

Cai Wanchun early realized the importance of accessible sources of finance to fund his business expansion. Privy to government plans to encourage savings through incentives to small savers, he gradually took over control of the Tenth Credit Association in the 1950s and, with government endorsement, launched savings incentive plans. Although credit associations could legally extend loans only to individual association members, from the outset Cai utilized Tenth Credit as a treasury for funding business group expansion. He added insurance companies (1961, 1962) and an ITC (1971) to his financial empire (in each case immediately after government bans on private participation were lifted). Unlike the credit cooperatives, insurance companies were not prohibited from investing in productive enterprises.

As Cathay expanded, it managed to maintain its favorable reputation within business circles and the public and to avoid serious government reprisals, despite growing evidence of questionable financial activities as early as 1974.[130] Also in 1974, Cathay Investment and Trust began absorb-

---

[130]In 1974, financial officials discovered evidence of illicit financial schemes involving Wan Cheng Development Corporation. A closely held member firm of the Cathay group, it purchased property valued at approximately U.S.$1 million and sold it to six individuals, all of whom were either Cai family relatives or Cathay Life Insurance employees. Two months later, these individuals resold the property for over U.S.$4.5 million. A subsequent investigation revealed that over half of the U.S.$1 million paid by the individuals came from Tenth Credit loans, with Cathay Life and Cathay Trust stocks put up as collateral. The profits made on the resale went not to the six individuals but to Wan Cheng, Tenth Credit, and members of the Cai family. In fact, the six individuals claimed they weren't aware of the transaction, their chops having been "borrowed" by a Cathay Life manager in order to conduct the deal. Despite widespread publicity, tax evasion charges against the parties involved were

ing independent firms through an aggressive policy of extending loans and then using the loans as leverage to gain control over the firms. Over a five-year period, Cathay acquired five firms in this way, several in markets where Cathay already enjoyed relative dominance. Cathay officials claimed they had no choice but to take over the companies in order to protect their investments. Although the government disapproved of the methods and potential consequences of these actions, in the absence of antitrust legislation it did not prevent this public purchase of shares.

After the elder Cai's stroke in 1979, his heirs engaged in illicit business practices with increasing impunity. Cai Wanchun's brother Wanlin first took control of Tenth Credit. But after one run-in with the MOF's Monetary Affairs Department for misappropriating funds, Wanlin turned management of Tenth Credit over to his nephew Zhenzhou. By assuming management of Cathay Life and other firms, Wanlin was able to distance himself somewhat from his nephews and the subsequent scandal (as was his brother Wancai).[131]

After assuming control of Tenth Credit, Cai Zhenzhou, with the collusion of supervisors at the state-owned Cooperative Bank (charged with overseeing the cooperatives), turned the credit association "into a private financing source for his personal enterprises."[132] By this time, his personal financial needs and those of his Cathay Plastics Group were great. His extravagant lifestyle, coupled with consistent losses at Cathay Plastics (a result of oil crisis-driven petroleum price hikes) and extensive losses in real estate investments, led Zhenzhou to seek funding from all possible sources, regardless of cost or risk. In so doing, he exploited both the high status of the Cathay name and the government's fear of taking measures that might upset Taiwan's financial stability. Dreading the potential consequences of a run on Tenth Credit or the collapse of Cathay Plastics (or the other 100-odd member firms of the related Cathay financial empire), financial authorities tolerated increasingly blatant violations of financial regulations.

Having exhausted formal sources of funds both within and outside his guanxiqiye, Cai obtained informal loans through all possible means. The most important source was Tenth Credit. Because the credit cooperative was legally restricted to lending to individual members only, Zhenzhou

---

dropped after lengthy court proceedings. Chuang notes there were "rumors that the [Cai] family spent considerable funds on bribes in this case, but there is no clear evidence so far to prove such a charge" (Chuang).

[131]In hindsight, it would seem that Cai Wanlin chose correctly. In 1991, *Excellence*, a Taiwan business magazine, ranked Cai as the richest man in Taiwan, with U.S.$3.1 billion in assets, much of it in real estate. In 1992, *Forbes* ranked him the richest of six billionaires in Taiwan, with a net personal worth of U.S.$2.5 billion.

[132]*Economic News*, 8/19/85.

enlisted at least 700 Cathay Plastics employees as members of the credit cooperative, thus qualifying them as loan applicants. He persuaded some employees to apply for loans on his behalf through incentives including promotions, raises, and bonuses. Often the amounts actually borrowed were much greater than what the employees had agreed to, and far in excess of the legal ceiling for any one borrower.

In other cases Cai used employees' chops without their consent or knowledge, taking out loans in their names.[133] Cai's trusted managers at Tenth Credit routinely approved the loans, which were typically secured by overvalued or recycled collateral provided by Cai himself. These loans were then channeled to the floundering Cathay Plastics and related enterprises under his and other Cai family members' control.

Given their piecemeal accretion, the total value of these loans is astounding. Government audits of Tenth Credit (internal audits were never conducted) revealed a total of N.T.$1.7 billion in illegal loans to Cathay Plastics affiliates as of 1979. Despite repeated inspections and warnings, the total increased to N.T.$2.3 billion in 1982, to N.T.$3.5 billion in 1983, and to over N.T.$7.7 billion (U.S.$190 million) in bad loans. Tenth Credit had virtually no reserves by February 1985, when the scandal broke.[134]

Cai Zhenzhou also solicited funds for corporate and personal use from employee and other individual deposits with Cathay Plastics. His urgent need for funds in the years preceding the collapse made Cathay Plastics particularly popular among small investors, for Cai was offering interest rates as high as 30 percent per annum. After the scandal broke, more than 3,000 creditors petitioned the government for help in recovering an estimated N.T.$4 billion (U.S.$100 million) in Cathay Plastics deposits. Cai also obtained personal loans secured by postdated checks drawn on his personal account. Although some estimates placed the value of these PDC loans to be as high as N.T.$5 billion (U.S.$125 million), Cai was ultimately convicted of issuing 539 bad checks with a total value of N.T.$100 million (U.S.$2.5 million).

Cai Zhenzhou was not alone in these irregular fund-raising activities. Tenth Credit loans also went to member firms of his brother Zhennan's

[133]A "chop" is a stamp engraved with a person's name that is legally equivalent to a personal signature in many Asian societies. After the scandal broke in 1985, many of these victims were told they owed as much as U.S.$500,000 each in loan payments. This resulted in at least three suicides, eight attempted suicides, and a dozen divorces in efforts to protect spouses' assets.

[134]This figure includes an N.T.$3.3 billion Cooperative Bank loan to Tenth Credit in the week immediately preceding the suspension of operations. It is rumored that substantial portions of this loan went to high government and party officials who had invested in Zhenzhou's operations, allowing them to get their personal funds out before the government forced Tenth Credit to close.

Cathay Trust Group, and Cathay Trust loans went to Cathay Plastics firms. Cathay Investment and Trust Company (CITC) had been involved in many questionable financial activities and had had numerous scrapes with financial authorities well before 1985. As early as 1978, CITC was charged with extending to Cathay Plastics loans valued at 50 percent of its net assets, considerably above the legal lending limit of 20 percent of the lending institution's net assets. CITC complied with MOF requests to reduce its lending to Cathay Plastics but was fined N.T.$200,000 that same year for accepting short-term deposits, a privilege reserved for banks, credit associations, and the postal savings system.

Restricted in the amount of financing his group could obtain from CITC, Cai Zhennan sought funding from other sources. He established two leasing companies in order to skirt the lending limits placed on financial institutions. These companies' primary function was to obtain loans from CITC as well as the commercial banks, then channel the loans to other group firms. Each leasing company could borrow up to 20 percent of each financial institution's net assets, which greatly expanded the group's total credit line.

Along with the other business group-controlled ITCs, CITC continued to expand its banking activities during the early 1980s, in direct violation of increasingly restrictive financial regulations, by accepting short-term demand and checking account deposits and establishing branch offices outside Taipei. At the same time, CITC continued to exploit its position as a nonbank, investing in productive enterprises (including group firms well beyond the legal limit of 20 percent ownership), taking over insolvent creditors, and speculating in Taiwan's volatile real estate market. All this was done despite stepped-up government restrictions. In 1983, the government limited the ITCs' total trust funds to no more than twenty times their net assets. That year CITC had N.T.$1.5 billion in net assets and N.T.$32 billion in trust funds, which put it over the limit. When the scandal broke in 1985, total loans exceeded N.T.$38 billion, with over N.T.$20 billion to Cathay Trust affiliated companies.

Because of these activities and the actual perceived linkages between Zhenzhou and Zhennan, the scandal and bank runs quickly spilled over to the Cathay Trust Group. These violations had persisted for over a decade—watched, scolded, but ultimately tolerated by the state. To understand why this tolerance finally ended and the scandal was exposed, we must examine Cathay's political activities.

### Political Activities

The Cai family long understood the value of political connections for achieving its economic ends. Like many of the other Taiwanese business groups, they often hired retired Mainlander government officials or military officers as nominal heads of Cathay Group companies. Though typically not involved in management of the firms, these executives had valuable government connections that could be utilized to gain privilege, acquire inside information, or smooth troubles with government officials. In addition, several Cai family members served as elected government officials. Patriarch Cai Wanchun served two terms on the Taipei City Council. Younger brother Wancai, the most educated of the brothers, served as a Legislative Yuan member from 1972 to 1983. Both were members of the Nationalist Party.

When Cai Wancai retired from the Legislative Yuan in 1983, he was replaced as political representative of Cathay's business interests by his nephew Cai Zhenzhou. Although financial authorities had already investigated and penalized Zhenzhou's Tenth Credit for serious financial irregularities, the Nationalist Party nominated him in 1983, and he was elected that December on the Nationalist Party ticket. At the time of his nomination, critics within the party attacked Zhenzhou's selection as part of the Nationalist Party's "golden ox" (*jinniu*) strategy of picking candidates on the basis of their wealth and connections rather than their qualifications. The label is apt; Cai allegedly spent an estimated U.S.$2.5 million to get elected.[135]

Once he was elected, Cai quickly set out to exert his political influence for the benefit of Cathay interests. He banded with twelve other young Nationalist Party businessmen-lawmakers in a clique that came to be known as the 13 Brothers. The union was in some sense economic: they invested together, borrowed money from each other and introduced business opportunities to each other.[136] But political interests were served as well: they pooled money and other resources for elections and voted as a bloc on legislation affecting their commercial interests. The 13 Brothers' most controversial logrolling efforts surrounded their attempts during

[135]Money in Nationalist Party politics is used in two ways. First, it is used to influence high-level party officials who are able to influence the KMT nominating committee, whose selections automatically qualify for substantial party funds. Second, money is used to buy off individual voters. For a "golden ox" with little or no name recognition or political qualifications, as was the case with Cai Zhenzhou, the necessary sums can be very substantial.

There is evidence from the Cathay scandal that Cai was indeed a "golden ox." Jiang Yanshi, then secretary-general of the Nationalist Party, abruptly resigned his position on February 6, 1985, three days before the loan suspension at Tenth Credit. Although no reason was given for his resignation, it is widely believed to be connected to his role in influencing Cai's nomination. Similarly, Guan Zhong, who was in charge of Nationalist Party nominations for the Taipei municipality in 1983 and was given credit for engineering the Nationalists' sweeping victory over the opposition, also fell from grace after Cai was implicated in the Tenth Credit scandal. He successfully contested journalistic accusations of bribery and regained his prominence in the Nationalist Party.

[136]Investigations after the scandal revealed five of these twelve other legislators accepted a total of at least N.T.$1.4 billion (U.S.$35 million) in loans from an affiliate of Tenth Credit.

1984 to legislate a revision of the banking law that would have forced the MOF to grant the ITCs greater access to short-term funds and broader investment privileges.[137]

This amendment to the banking law (*Yinghang fa xiuchengan*), they argued, was necessary to allow the ITCs to compete fairly with the banks for funds and to provide Taiwan's financially strapped private corporate sector with much-needed capital. Critics feared that these privileges would allow the trust companies to become "superbanks" attached to huge private conglomerates with no government oversight. The specter of this private concentration of financial power and the brash tactics of these lawmakers unified the senior "old guard" legislators against them and alienated even those who were more sympathetic to calls to modernize and liberalize Taiwan's seriously outdated financial system. Lawmakers "were displeased with the all-too-frequent practices of trust companies having violated government regulations in the first place, and then lobbying for legalizing their activities."[138]

The amendment efforts were defeated, and in the fall of 1984 financial authorities ordered the formation of a financial investigative committee to audit the activities of Tenth Credit. Like the earlier audits, this one discovered serious financial irregularities, huge loans, and virtually no reserves. Unlike previous investigations, however, this one led to the suspension of Tenth's lending operations in February 1985 and its takeover by the government. Moreover, the results of the investigation were made public, resulting in massive bank runs, convictions, and the virtual destruction of Cai Zhenzhou's economic (and political) power.

### Public Response

Cathay was certainly not alone in its disregard of financial regulations. However, the consequences of the deepening financial problems of Cai Zhenzhou's Cathay Plastics branch of the huge Cathay financial empire set Cathay apart from the other groups. In an effort to keep Cathay afloat and continue to fund their economic, political, and personal aspirations, Zhenzhou and his half brother Zhennan leveraged their group firms and incurred personal curb market debts far beyond their ability to repay, and pushed the government's tolerance for questionable fund-raising tactics beyond acceptable levels. It was, however, Cathay's political activities that ultimately spurred the government to take decisive action. The government was incensed with Cathay's attempts to combat stepped-up financial restrictions with purchased political power. The usual state circumspec-

---

[137]Taiwan is certainly not the only venue with these kinds of financial turf battles. Witness the savings and loan industry and bank lobbies in the United States.

[138]*Economic News*, 10/29/84.

tion in microlevel intervention and fears of the financial and political consequences of exposing the scandal were ultimately outweighed by this brazen expression of economic-cum-political power. One observer noted that it was precisely because the China Trust Group's ITC "stayed on the good side" of the Nationalist state that it avoided the government's wrath.[139]

This awareness and impatience reached the very top of Taiwan's political hierarchy. On February 4, 1985, five days before the scandal broke (and one month after the MOF completed its audit of Tenth Credit), newspapers reported on a government closed-door session on military affairs at which President Chiang Ching-kuo spoke. The reports quoted Chiang as forcefully stating that the government, for the welfare of the people, must "fight against monopoly, fight against special privilege and fight against profiteering" in Taiwan's economic affairs. Though no mention was made of Tenth Credit or Cathay, it is widely believed that he was revealing his deep displeasure with the soon-to-break Cathay affair and his dissatisfaction with the speculation and economic concentration associated with the guanxiqiye in general.

This displeasure and dissatisfaction were not unfounded. The Taiwan state did not come in and break up a thriving, beneficial business enterprise merely out of irrational financial conservatism and political jealousy. In many ways Cathay was a festering boil in need of lancing. The Cai uncles also owned branches of the Cathay empire and were certainly not untainted by financial irregularities. But because they did not use their wealth to seek state-monopolized financial and political power, they were allowed to continue to prosper.[140] Through piecemeal expansion of Cathay Trust's domain of responsibility, Cai Zhennan made financial authorities increasingly nervous. When his half brother attempted to consolidate these gains politically, the state put its foot down.

Despite initial hesitance, once the decision was made to end Cathay's abuses, the state moved swiftly and, with only a few high-level exceptions, cut quite deeply. Financial institutions suffering runs in the wake of the announced scandal—including Tenth Credit, CITC, and Overseas Trust—were taken over and reorganized by the government. The government also assumed management of six other member firms of Zhennan's Cathay Trust group, including two department stores and the Lai Lai Sheraton, and bailed out over 100 corporations shaken by investor panic. The Executive Yuan, the Control Yuan, and the Bureau of Investigation

---

[139]*Far Eastern Economic Review,* 2/1/90.

[140]Both uncles were careful to distance themselves from the scandal embroiling their nephews. When the scandal broke, Cai Wanlin dispatched 10,000 insurance salesmen to placate Cathay Life Insurance clients. He subsequently extended a U.S.$7.5 million loan to Cai Zhenzhou. Any additional support was moral, not financial.

conducted investigation and issued stinging reports criticizing not only Cathay's management but also financial authorities' collusion with Cathay and the government's handling of the entire affair for more than a decade.[141]

Despite the unprecedented candor of these reports, many criticized the government's investigations for not pushing hard enough and not properly assigning blame for the scandal. There is no question that certain government officials were spared, and punishment on the whole was quite lenient. Throughout, the government objective seemed to be to downplay the magnitude of the scandal and minimize the damage to Taiwan's financial stability and the regime's political legitimacy. Explaining the government's leniency with Cai Zhennan and his and other local bankers' rescheduling of CITC's loans, one banker-bureaucrat noted that if Cai had been arrested and jailed in March 1985, along with his brother, it would have triggered the collapse of Cathay Trust's thirty-one affiliated firms. Taiwan's economy, he argued, could not have withstood that kind of shock in the wake of the Tenth Credit failure. He concluded, "We didn't want more unemployed people, small creditors and suppliers demonstrating in the streets."[142]

Although the government's immediate response was moderate, the scandal and its aftermath provided the impetus for launching wide-ranging financial reform measures. This reform process began with the establishment of the Economic Revitalization Committee (ERC). This high-profile committee was set up in 1985 with a mandate to study and propose economic and financial policy reforms for the revitalization of Taiwan's economy in the wake of the Cathay scandal. The ERC was composed of ministerial-level officials, academics, and guanxiqiye leaders and was divided into five subcommittees charged with examining finance, taxation, trade, industry, and economic administration. Financial recommendations emerging from its meetings included expanding the business activities of the ITCs while increasing supervision over them, merging and converting the informal financial institutions while avoiding their excessive concentration, diversifying money market instruments, enhancing the role of the stock market, and chartering new private banks.[143]

---

[141]These investigations and subsequent court actions resulted in the indicting of, at last count, eighty-seven Cathay executives, including Cai Zhenzhou and his invalid father, Cai Wanchun, on fraud charges. In addition, at least four government officials were arrested and charged for giving Tenth Credit advance notice of audits. Moreover, both Xu Lide, minister of economic affairs, and Lu Runkang, minister of finance, were forced to resign, many argue, in order to protect their mentor, Premier Yu Guohua, who was not investigated. Numerous other MOF and Taipei city financial officers were reprimanded for dereliction of duty.

[142]*Asian Wall Street Journal*, 5/6/87.

[143]For a more detailed discussion of these recommendations, see K. S. Liang, 1986; *Economic News*, 9/23/85.

Although critics have charged that financial "policy change has been ponderously slow,"[144] reform is gradually taking place. Spawned by the ERC and spurred by both internal and external pressures,[145] these reforms have included broad liberalization of the foreign exchange system, further deregulation of interest rates, the enactment of a fair trade law, and the gradual privatization of the commercial banking system. These changes have the potential to significantly rationalize Taiwan's financial system and fundamentally alter the methods of guanxiqiye finance. Despite the importance of the recent chartering of private commercial banks, it is still too early to judge the full impact of this and other financial reform efforts in the wake of the Cathay scandal. The groups' fund-raising activities appear to have changed little thus far. Those business group affiliates with adequate collateral still seek the majority of their funding in the form of short-term loans from the commercial banks. Despite unprecedented liquidity in the banking system and the increasing popularity and sophistication of formal money market instruments, the informal curb market persists with continued state tolerance.[146] The stock market continues its mercurial ups and downs and still carries its casino image, attracting primarily individual speculators, not corporations seeking capital or institutional investors seeking a stable return.

Most important, as in Korea, there is still significant resistance to allowing the guanxiqiye to own and operate their own private banks. Despite the recent privatization measures, there is little doubt that the state in Taiwan, like its Korean counterpart, will retain strong control over banking operations. The Cathay debacle reconfirmed and galvanized longstanding fears of the consequences of private control of banking institutions. But also as in Korea, it will be very difficult in an environment of financial liberalization to prevent these private enterprise groups from translating their economic power into financial and political power. Since the mid-1980s, several guanxiqiye have centered their related enterprises around ITCs, insurance companies, and now banks. Writing of the bank

[144]H. S. Cheng, p. 143. Kaufman-Winn, writing in 1988, is even stronger in her judgment, claiming it is "difficult to find any examples of substantive reforms undertaken based on its findings" (p. 17).

[145]Internal pressures for financial reform included the increasingly weighty voices of younger liberal politicians and policymakers in the Nationalist Party who were pushing for reform, and the need to recycle the massive accumulation of foreign exchange and to reinvest the unprecedented liquidity in the banking sector. External pressures for financial reform have come largely from U.S. efforts to open Taiwan's financial markets to U.S. companies.

[146]However, the government effectively abolished the over 200 illegal investment houses that had sprung up during the real estate and stock market booms. These investment houses absorbed an estimated U.S.$23 billion from over 3 million depositors, offering rates as high as 10 percent per month (*Free China Journal*, 7/17/89).

privatizations, one observer predicted that "despite the caution evinced by the government officials . . . , the pace of banking liberalization will quicken now that Taiwan's conglomerates have a direct stake in the business." A newly appointed president of one of the banks likewise warned, "The Ministry of Finance will face a lot of pressure from special interests."[147]

For the short run, this dynamic of conservative public restrictions and widespread private disregard will persist. However, market and political forces compelling liberalization will gradually alter this dynamic, thereby prompting further reforms. At the same time, the pervasive influences of personal and institutional relationships within the corporate sector, and increasingly between the corporate sector and the political sector, complicate these financial networks and expand the potential for private collusive gains at public expense.[148] The guanxiqiye and the state are at the center of this evolving dynamic.

As indicated in Chapter Three, the environment in which Taiwan's business groups are embedded is extremely complex. Institutional influences—of rational economic, political, and sociocultural origin—create this environment in which the groups determine and carry out their day-to-day decisions and long-term strategies. This examination of the groups' search for capital, arguably their most essential activity, has provided a valuable perspective on this embedded situation and the utility of this comprehensive framework of institutional analysis.

[147] *Far Eastern Economic Review,* 5/7/92.
[148] Finance officials have already begun investigating the new private banks on suspicion of extending illegal preferential loans to friends and relatives of bank shareholders (*Far Eastern Economic Review,* 4/28/92).

CHAPTER SIX

# Korea's General Trading Companies

The following two chapters examine comparable efforts of industrial, or more accurately commercial, policy in Korea and Taiwan that have had direct, but virtually opposite, consequences for the business groups in these two settings. Witnessing the success of Japan's version of the so-called general trading company, Korea's and Taiwan's governments launched their own versions with great fanfare and high expectations in the latter half of the 1970s. These chapters chronicle the largely success-ful efforts of Korea's state to foster the development of large-scale trading companies and failed efforts of Taiwan's state to achieve the same objec-tive. The analysis of these two cases not only illuminates the specific incen-tives and obstacles in the two environments and their consequences for the business groups, but also sheds light on the factors influencing the fate of state-implemented industrial policies in general.

These case studies are clear examples of state-imposed institutions whose establishment entailed economic risks and challenged both social and political norms and interests. In the mid-1970s, the Park regime in Korea faced extreme economic, social, and political challenges and re-sponded by promoting general trading companies (GTCs) with the nearly singular goal of facilitating and increasing exports. The state buttressed the implementation of this policy with huge subsidies for a few favored chaebol-affiliated trading companies and ruthless disregard for the thou-sands of small trading companies forced out of business by the oligopo-lists. Though not yet rivaling the scale or scope of their Japanese models, Korea's GTCs have established themselves as the dominant channel for the nation's rapidly expanding export market, handling on average nearly half of all Korean exports. In the wake of trade liberalization and currency appreciation in the 1980s, these GTCs are striving to assume a comparable role as dominant importers as well.

In Taiwan, on the other hand, conflicts with the state apparatus concerning the concentration of private economic power led to the formulation of a large trading company (LTC) policy with ambiguous objectives and clearly inadequate compliance with mechanisms to overcome the economic, sociocultural, and political obstacles in the path of successful implementation. Taiwan's LTCs have failed to achieve the objectives of their private owners and public sponsors, handling approximately 1 percent of Taiwan's total trade.

This chapter first traces the institutional origins of these state-imposed, private trading firms by examining their Japanese predecessors. This brief analysis of the Japanese GTC demonstrates that (1) direct and discretionary government sponsorship; (2) affiliation with large-scale private business groups; and (3) access to a captive network of loyal suppliers were crucial factors in allowing these companies to become the dominant trading concerns in Japan, and increasingly in the world. Turning to the Korean case, the remainder of the chapter shows that these three factors were also necessary, if not sufficient, in assuring the establishment and survival of the Korean GTCs. In contrast, the examination of the Taiwan case in Chapter Seven reveals that both public sponsorship and private support were insufficient. While the obstacles to Taiwan's LTCs were formidable, these case studies offer evidence that they were not insurmountable. Had Taiwan's government been willing or able to formulate a policy with clear objectives and to ease its implementation with compliance mechanisms comparable to those wielded by the Japanese and Korean states, Taiwan could have overcome the LTCs' institutional constraints and successfully established large trading concerns.

The revelation that Taiwan's policymakers and entrepreneurs did not behave exactly like their Korean counterparts should not be surprising. As noted in Chapter One, comparable cases are not identical cases, nor should they be. But this juxtaposition allows us to isolate those key environmental variables that had the greatest effect on the differing outcomes. In the case of Taiwan, the failure of the LTC policy can be traced to conflicting developmental objectives and strategies among Taiwan's policy-making elite. Historical experience, educational background, and institutional affiliation shaped the perceptions of policymakers and led to fundamental conflicts among the decisionmaking elite regarding the role of private capital in Taiwan's development and the desired degree of state intervention in the economy. This, in turn, led to conflicts over the desired scope and scale of the LTCs and the extent of the government's role in determining these objectives. The result was the emergence of a vague policy with internally inconsistent objectives that provided the bureaucratic architects of the policy with no mandate by which to institute significant compliance mechanisms or even remove those policy obstacles already hampering the implementation of the policy.

## THE MODEL: JAPAN'S SOGO SHOSHA

Korea's GTCs and Taiwan's LTCs were the result of conscious government efforts to adapt to their respective settings institutional arrangements borrowed from abroad. Before examining the motives, processes, and consequences of these "grafting" efforts, it is first useful to trace the origin and nature of the transplants. The term "general trading company" comes from the Japanese *sogo shosha*, which was first used by the Japanese press in the late 1950s to describe the trading companies of the regrouped *zaibatsu*, or prewar conglomerates, such as Mitsubishi and Mitsui. As they function today, these Japanese GTCs are enterprises that "specialize in the import of raw materials for domestic industries and in the export of their manufactured goods. They also maximize cost and price margins through global intelligence networks concerning all available markets, and they perform important functions in the short-term financing of foreign trade."[1] The sogo shosha differ from other trading companies primarily in the diversity of the products they handle, and to a lesser extent in the breadth of their geographical coverage and the handling of multiple functions.[2]

Like the zaibatsu, the sogo shosha had their origin in Japan's Meiji period (1868–1925). Because of Japan's centuries of enforced insularity, most nineteenth-century Japanese wholesalers had no foreign language skills and little experience with foreign trade. Recognizing this comparative disadvantage, the government took pains to consolidate trading activities in the hands of a few specialized companies, thereby economizing on the scarce resources of language and trading skills.[3] In addition to government sponsorship, the linkage of these trading companies to the zaibatsu combines was an essential element of their success. Johannes Hirschmeier and Tsunehiko Yui conclude: "The general trading companies developed best when they were part of a *zaibatsu*. Those that were started independently of the *zaibatsu* either did not succeed or remained small. The *zaibatsu* was a system that provided them with ample capital and security as well as with room for initiative. And the name of the *zaibatsu* assured them also of qualified personnel because of the prestige and power the *zaibatsu* name involved."[4]

[1]Johnson, 1987, p. 160.
[2]Yamazawa and Kohama.
[3]Yamazawa and Kohama.
[4]Hirschmeier and Yui, p. 192.

Initially developed to function primarily as importers, these trading companies increased their share of the Japanese import market from 4.7 percent in 1887 to about 40 percent by 1900 and 90 percent by 1920. By the latter year they were handling nearly 70 percent of exports as well. As Japan's colonial empire expanded, so did the trading companies and their zaibatsu partners. By the end of the Meiji era, Mitsui, Mitsubishi, and Suzuki had developed into full-fledged GTCs, handling a wide variety of commodities and dealing with a large number of countries, even moving into offshore or triangular trade.[5] They continued to expand their economic and even political influence, vying with the militarists for control of economic policy in wartime Japan.

After Japan's defeat in World War II, the occupation forces broke up the GTCs. As soon as the occupation was over, the Japanese government set about rebuilding them. By all accounts, this government assistance was crucial to the reemergence of the GTCs. Beginning in 1953, the government implemented a series of subsidies and other incentives to facilitate their expansion. These included tax exemptions on export income, tax credits on foreign investment, accelerated depreciation on foreign branch office assets, and the prevention of overcompetition by allowing the trading companies to set up import and export cartels. The government also instituted an export-import linkage system whereby the licenses for importing scarce consumer goods such as bananas, sugar, and whiskey were given to trading companies that met government targets for the export of ships, machine tools, and other designated industrial goods.[6]

Moreover, through its licensing powers and ability to supply preferential financing, the state "rationalized" the entire trade system, assigning unaffiliated manufacturers to trading companies and forcing the smaller trading concerns to merge or eliminating them altogether. Ultimately, the government "winnowed about 2,800 trading companies that existed after the occupation down to around 20 big ones, each serving a bank keiretsu [postwar zaibatsu] or a cartel of smaller producers."[7] Today, each of the top nine sogo shosha is affiliated closely, if not exclusively, with a large business group.[8]

In summary, three factors seem to have been particularly important in determining the successful establishment and continued viability of these giant trading concerns both at the time of their creation and develop-

[5]Yamazawa and Kohama; D. S. Cho, 1987.
[6]Johnson, 1982; D. S. Cho, 1987.
[7]Johnson, 1982, p. 206.
[8]Ozawa, 1987. This is not to say that smaller trading companies do not exist. Asao notes that as of 1986 there were 17 sogo shosha and as many as 11,000 specialized trading companies, or senmon shosha, in Japan. The top nine, however, are distinguished from the others because they are so much larger in scope and scale (Asao in Ozawa, p. 77).

ment in the prewar period and again during their reemergence after World War II. The first was government sponsorship through a series of direct and often creative subsidies and other incentives given to those few traders deemed best able to succeed and compete on an international level. The second factor—institutional linkages to the business groups—gave the sogo shosha the scale and capital necessary to make them internationally competitive. Third, and closely related to the other two, was the assurance of a network of captive suppliers that guaranteed the sogo shosha a stable source of exports and a secure market for their imports. In the prewar period, the sogo shosha's monopoly of the knowledge and skills necessary to conduct foreign trade guaranteed the allegiance of the manufacturers. In the postwar period, the government forced all but a handful of the trading companies to merge or go out of business, and then assigned unaffiliated manufacturers to the remaining traders.

Spurred by these government incentives and rationalization measures, the sogo shosha became both the leaders and the beneficiaries of Japan's high-speed growth. As Japan's industrial and financial structure evolved, so did the strategies and functions of the sogo shosha. Facing challenges in the 1960s and 1970s from foreign competitors and domestic manufacturers handling their own trade, the sogo shosha have diversified their activities and are now, in every sense of the word, "general" trading companies handling numerous products, penetrating various geographical areas and performing multiple functions. In 1984, the nine largest sogo shosha handled over 40 percent of Japan's total exports and over 60 percent of total imports, with the largest of these showing an annual turnover of U.S.$60 billion or more. In 1971, these GTCs had turnover equivalents to 31 percent of Japan's GNP; two decades later they still accounted for over 25 percent.[9]

## KOREA'S CHONGHAP SANGSA

The consistent growth of the Japanese sogo shosha in the early 1970s, despite global recession, piqued the interest of policymakers in countries around the world. One of the earliest of these admirers and would-be emulators was South Korea, which in 1975 established its own version of the GTC, the *chonghap sangsa* (a direct translation of sogo shosha).[10] The Korean government sponsored the creation of these large-scale trading concerns in an effort to cope with the cumulative economic and political

[9]*Far Eastern Economic Review*, 2/11/93; D. S. Cho, 1987.

[10]In addition to South Korea and Taiwan, these would-be emulators have included Brazil, Thailand, the Philippines, Turkey, and the United States (Onis, 1992; Yamazawa and Kohama; *Far Eastern Economic Review*, 4/19/84, p. 74).

challenges facing the Park regime in the mid-1970s. A brief review of these challenges sheds light on the government's motivations for fostering these GTCs.

## Trade Situation

Economic reconstruction began in Korea in 1953 under the Rhee regime with a program of typical import-substituting industrialization (ISI). This inward-looking development strategy not only conformed to contemporary developmental wisdom, it also meshed nicely with Rhee's nationalist-inspired resolve to keep Korea separated from its colonial export markets in Japan. As explained in Chapter Two, this ISI policy allowed a coterie of favored capitalists to reap windfall profits and begin to build their chaebol empires in certain protected industries as a result of their government connections. But by the early 1960s, confronting the set of chronic problems associated with mature ISI development and the prospect of the phasing out of U.S. economic aid,[11] Korea faced a decline in economic performance and a political crisis neither the corrupt Rhee regime nor the short-lived Second Republic that replaced it could handle.

The Korean military, led by General Park Chong Hee, stepped into this political vacuum and institutionalized a number of sweeping changes, including a shift in developmental strategies from one of ISI to export-oriented industrialization. The Park regime promoted the production and export of light manufactures under the Third Republic's first Five Year Plan, beginning in 1962. From a starting point of virtually no industrial exports, foreign sales of first light and then heavy manufactures multiplied rapidly as a result of government incentives to exporters. These "carrots" included a wide variety of incentives—Y. I. Lim lists a total of thirty-eight export incentive measures implemented between 1950 and 1976—including direct export subsidies, an export-import linkage system (modeled after Japan's bananas-for-steel arrangement), manipulation of foreign exchange rates, tax exemption for export income, and concessional export financing.[12]

Although these measures rapidly expanded Korean exports, they demanded an increasingly large portion of government revenues and, by the early 1970s, spawned a number of ill side effects. First, these nondiscretionary incentives led to the proliferation of small-scale manufacturer-exporters with virtually no expertise in overseas marketing. These firms

[11] Haggard and Cheng list the following as chronic problems associated with ISI strategies: "market saturation, increased competition, low levels of manufactured exports, high levels of dependence on imports, and wide gaps in the balance of payments" (p. 90).
[12] Y. I. Lim.

competed for the same export market, a situation that led to excessive competition among domestic firms. Finally, the government realized that exporters had grown too dependent on government subsidies; they were basing business decisions solely on subsidy levels, not on international market conditions. By the mid-1970s, Korea was suffering the social and political consequences of the 1973 oil crisis: stagnating exports, global recession, and developed-country protectionism. One year prior to the oil crisis, Park had declared the right to unlimited presidential tenure, and thus by 1974 found himself trying to legitimate his increasingly unpopular political rule during a time of economic crisis. As exports for 1974 fell well below government targets and stagflation deepened, Park "became desperate to bridge the gap between political goals and economic performance."[13]

## Creation of the Korean GTCs

Under this complex of economic, social, and political exigencies, and very much cognizant of the success of Japan's sogo shosha, the Park regime in 1975 introduced its own version of the GTC.[14] These giant trading concerns "were not the natural outcome of the evolution and expansion of Korea's export-oriented trading firms—they were artificially created by government decree."[15] It was hoped these GTCs, "large enough to attain economies of scale in the world market, specialized in exportation to gain international competitiveness, and capable of overseas marketing,"[16] would be able to (1) expand Korea's exports, especially for heavy industry products, and to enter new markets; (2) provide a more rational (and local) export channel for Korea's small and medium-sized manufacturers; (3) increase the size of exporters in order to achieve economies of scale; and (4) shift some of the burden for export assistance from the government to the chaebol.[17]

With these objectives in mind, the Korean government announced in

[13]D. S. Cho, 1987, p. 50. D. C. Kim notes that the government established annual growth targets largely on political grounds based on national security considerations: "First, high speed growth was essential to meet the high defense burden in face of the constant threat from the North. Secondly, high growth rates were needed to keep the unemployment rate below six percent, with social stability being essential to the political stability that in turn was essential for economic growth" (1984, p. 248).

[14]It is obvious from the minimum requirements for GTC designation that the Korean government consciously patterned its GTC program after the Japanese sogo shosha. An executive of C. Itoh & Co., one of Japan's largest and most successful sogo shosha, was involved in the initial formulation of the South Korean system (K. H. Jung, 1983).

[15]Jo.

[16]D. S. Cho, 1987, p. 7.

[17]K. H. Jung, 1984; Westphal et al.; Yamazawa and Kohama; D. C. Kim, 1987.

April 1975 the following minimum requirements for designation as a GTC:[18]

1. Paid-in-capital of 1 billion won (approximately U.S.$2.5 million)
2. Annual exports of U.S.$50 million
3. Handling of seven products with an export value of more than U.S.$500 thousand each
4. Ten overseas branches
5. Ten export recipient countries with an export value of goods purchased of over U.S.$1 million each
6. Public offering of company stock.

These requirements reveal much about the government's motives for setting up the GTCs. Although they were called general trading companies, it is clear that policymakers were primarily concerned that they function as exporters and that their exports be large in volume and diversified in terms of both range and destination of products. Unlike the Japanese sogo shosha, Korea's GTCs were not encouraged to diversify their functions into such areas as financing (under state control), insurance, or transportation.[19] These restrictions, particularly in the area of finance, have had a significant influence on the evolution of the GTCs. Finally, it was hoped the offering of stock would provide additional capital for these large-scale operations, spread their risk, and initiate the gradual separation of ownership from management in these tightly held familial chaebol affiliates.

In order to reduce the risks to private investors associated with such an ambitious program and to facilitate the development of these GTCs once they were established, the government offered substantial subsidies and other incentives to those companies achieving GTC status.[20]

Trade
1. Priority access to government agency trade and government-initiated projects
2. Relaxed requirements for joining commodity export associations
3. Right to import major raw materials for GTC's own use and for resale to domestic manufacturers

Financing
1. Export financing
2. Inventory financing for raw materials

[18]Jo; D. S. Cho, 1987.
[19]S. S. Lee; D. S. Cho, 1987.
[20]Jo; Yamazawa and Kohama; D. S. Cho, 1987.

3. Import financing for raw materials

Foreign exchange
1. Use of revolving letters of credit
2. Relaxed requirements for management and numbers of overseas branches
3. Relaxed limits of foreign currency holdings by overseas branches

Taxation
1. Tax reductions and exemptions for GTC trade commissions.

In addition to these codified incentives, GTC designation brought with it a number of less explicit but equally valuable benefits. Among these was the GTC title itself. This government recognition (reinforced by the annual awarding of various prizes, citations, and medals to the top GTCs) enhanced the companies' credibility and prestige both in Korea and abroad. It signaled to local manufacturers, as well as foreign lenders and end buyers, that the government endorsed their activities and would support them in difficult times. This public status attracted the best and brightest of Korea's college graduates and gave the chaebol owner-managers of the GTCs a sense of accomplishment and prestige among their peers. An additional informal benefit—and perhaps one of the most valuable, given the nature of Korea's autocratic political economy and Park's "hands-on" management of economic affairs—was the regular direct access to the president afforded the GTC owner-managers.[21]

The Korean government intentionally set the minimum requirements for GTC designation high enough to limit these substantial incentives to the largest trading firms.[22] The only concerns large enough to qualify for these incentives were the diversified chaebol, which merged the trading arms of their group manufacturers into groupwide GTCs. Already much larger than their domestic competitors, and able to draw upon the financial and manufacturing support of the entire group, these newly formed trading companies grew rapidly as recipients of generous government incentives. All but one of Korea's eight current GTCs are chaebol-affiliated,[23] and as the exclusive exporters for their respective groups, they have been assured a stable source of exports from group manufacturers. Thus, although not attaining the functional diversity of their Japanese

---

[21]S. S. Lee; D. S. Cho, 1984; *Business Korea*, 11/83, 12/84.

[22]Even though there have been only a handful of firms designated as "general trading companies," these are not the only trading concerns. Korea had 816 registered trading firms in 1970, 1,842 in 1975, 2,300 in 1980, and 5,300 in 1984. This compares with 13,320 registered firms in Taiwan in 1980 and 20,597 in 1984 (K. H. Jung, 1984; Levy, 1991).

[23]The eighth and by far the smallest, Koryo, was established by the government as a means of fostering the exports of small and medium-sized manufacturers.

prototypes, the fortunes of the Korean GTCs have been tied to government sponsorship, affiliation with local business groups, and a stable source of exports. We will now examine how these Korean GTCs have fared.

### Profile of the Korean GTCs

There is little question that its GTCs have contributed to the expansion of Korea's exports and the diversification of these products and their destinations since 1975.[24] In order to understand this contribution, we will examine the performance of these GTCs, the reasons behind their relative success, and obstacles to future expansion.

In all, thirteen different firms have achieved GTC designation since 1975. Of these, as Table 6-1 indicates, only eight have maintained their status.

The disqualified GTCs failed to meet the government's rising minimum export requirement for the previous year. It was set at U.S.$50 million in 1975, doubled to U.S.$100 million in 1976, and hiked again to U.S.$150 million the next year. In 1978, the required minimum export value was set at 2 percent of total Korean GNP and has remained at that level. In an effort to meet these rising export requirements, maintain

Table 6-1. Designation date and status of Korea's general trading companies

| GTC | Designation date | Status |
| --- | --- | --- |
| Samsung | May 1975 | |
| Ssangyong | May 1975 | |
| Daewoo | May 1975 | |
| Kukje-ICC | Nov 1975 | bankrupted in 1985 |
| Hanil Synthetic | Dec 1975 | disqualified in 1980 |
| Koryo | Apr 1976 | government owned and operated |
| Hyosung | Aug 1976 | |
| Bando | Nov 1976 | name changed to Lucky-Goldstar |
| Sunkyong | Nov 1976 | |
| Samhwa | Dec 1976 | disqualified in 1980 |
| Kumho | Dec 1976 | disqualified 1984 |
| Hyundai | Feb 1978 | |
| Yulsan | Feb 1978 | bankrupted in 1979 |

SOURCES: *Business Korea*, 11/83; D. S. Cho, 1987.

[24]In fact, it was only after the creation of the GTCs that Korea's export totals began to exceed those of Taiwan. They exceeded Taiwan's for the first time in 1977 and again in 1978, the peak years of the Park regime's export drive. But Korea was able to maintain this narrow lead only for these two years before Taiwan again passed Korea, a position it has held most years through 1993.

GTC status (and privileges), and, if possible, climb in the ranks, these trading concerns did everything possible to expand their exports. Table 6-2 indicates both the rapid expansion of Korean export growth since 1975 and the GTCs' share of these exports.

As Table 6-2 indicates, Korea's total exports for 1975 were valued at U.S.$5 billion, with the newly created GTCs handling 14 percent of this total. By 1980, Korea's total exports were more than triple the 1975 figure and the GTCs had expanded their export volume by over 1,000 percent. The GTCs' share of exports peaked in 1985 at 50 percent (the year of Kukje's demise), and has hovered between 40 and 50 percent since then. Table 6-2 also indicates the widening gap between the top four GTCs and the remaining three, paralleling the trend of the chaebol in general, as discussed in Chapter Two.

The success of the GTCs in terms of diversification of products and markets is less remarkable, a reflection of the government's primary emphasis on export expansion. Among the items exported by the GTCs, the biggest shift over time has been from light industrial to heavy and chemical products, a situation both mirroring and outpacing the structural evolution of the Korean economy.[25] The Korean GTCs' dependence on

*Table 6-2.* Export performance of GTCs (U.S.$1 million)

| Year | Hyun-dai | Sam-sung | Dae-woo | L-G | Sun-kyong | Ssan-gyong | Hyo-sung | Total[a] (A) | Nation's exports (B) | A/B |
|---|---|---|---|---|---|---|---|---|---|---|
| 1975 | — | 205 | 138 | — | — | 106 | — | 711 | 5,081 | 14.0 |
| 1976 | — | 333 | 259 | 134 | 107 | 101 | 106 | 1,547 | 7,715 | 20.1 |
| 1977 | — | 445 | 480 | 212 | 232 | 166 | 192 | 2,602 | 10,047 | 25.9 |
| 1978 | 258 | 493 | 706 | 330 | 278 | 264 | 335 | 4,020 | 12,711 | 31.6 |
| 1979 | 448 | 773 | 1,120 | 470 | 320 | 421 | 584 | 5,479 | 15,056 | 36.4 |
| 1980 | 994 | 1,227 | 1,390 | 492 | 430 | 642 | 763 | 7,176 | 17,505 | 41.0 |
| 1981 | 1,721 | 1,608 | 1,895 | 611 | 578 | 754 | 784 | 9,064 | 21,254 | 42.6 |
| 1982 | 2,632 | 1,836 | 1,958 | 688 | 600 | 956 | 598 | 10,442 | 21,853 | 47.8 |
| 1983 | 3,138 | 2,199 | 2,490 | 1,059 | 653 | 1,033 | 682 | 12,376 | 24,445 | 50.6 |
| 1984 | 3,334 | 2,754 | 2,576 | 1,440 | 846 | 1,239 | 749 | 13,995 | 29,245 | 47.9 |
| 1985 | 3,969 | 3,017 | 2,990 | 1,443 | 940 | 1,262 | 897 | 15,144 | 30,283 | 50.0 |
| 1986 | 3,954 | 3,124 | 2,781 | 1,755 | 1,129 | 1,045 | 940 | 15,195 | 34,715 | 43.8 |
| 1991 | 8,680 | 7,950 | 6,300 | 3,850 | 2,100 | 2,470 | 1,950 | 33,300 | 71,900 | 46.3 |
| 1992 | 9,300 | 8,600 | 7,000 | 4,100 | 2,300 | 2,600 | 2,250 | 36,150 | 76,632 | 47.2 |

SOURCES: S. S. Lee, 1987; *Business Korea,* 4/93.

[a]These totals include exports of all existing GTCs for the years 1975–86.

[25]Jung puts the percentage of heavy and chemical goods as a share of the GTCs' total exports at 31.8 percent for 1977 and 47.3 percent for 1979 (K. H. Jung, 1984). Cho places the figure at 47.7 percent in 1977, 54.9 percent in 1980, and 66 percent of the GTCs' total exports for 1983 (D. S. Cho, 1987). These increases reflect the Korean economy's structural changes, with heavy and chemical industrial products shifting from 32 percent of total exports in 1977 to 51 percent in 1983 (KOTRA).

traditional export markets in the United States, Canada, Western Europe, Japan, and Asia has remained relatively unchanged over time. This group of countries received 79 percent of the GTCs' exports in 1977, a figure that dropped to only 75 percent by 1983. Newer markets in the Middle East, Latin America, Oceania, and Africa comprised the other 25 percent, a figure that differed little from the 23.6 percent of Korea's total exports.[26]

Another reflection of the initial export bias of the government's GTC policy has been the GTCs' relatively small role in handling imports, as shown in Table 6-3.[27]

Although the GTCs' share of total imports has grown over the years, it has not yet approached their portion of total exports, which consistently is over 80 percent of total GTC sales.[28] Similarly, the GTCs conduct little domestic business or offshore (third country) trade. In 1982, the GTCs' overall trade volume consisted of 80.9 percent exports, 13.8 percent imports, 4.7 percent local business and 0.6 percent offshore trade.[29] Although "general" trading companies in name, and despite efforts during

*Table 6-3.* Korean GTCs' imports as share of Korean total imports, 1975–86 (U.S.$1 million)

| Year | Korea's total imports | GTCs' imports | GTCs' share of total (percent) |
|------|------|------|------|
| 1975 | 7,274 | 73 | 1.0 |
| 1976 | 8,773 | 174 | 2.0 |
| 1977 | 10,811 | 289 | 2.7 |
| 1978 | 14,917 | 575 | 3.9 |
| 1979 | 20,338 | 894 | 4.4 |
| 1980 | 22,292 | 1,884 | 8.5 |
| 1981 | 26,132 | 2,690 | 10.3 |
| 1982 | 24,251 | 3,025 | 12.5 |
| 1983 | 26,192 | 4,132 | 15.8 |
| 1984 | 30,631 | 4,594 | 15.0 |
| 1985 | 31,136 | 5,364 | 17.2 |
| 1986 | 31,584 | 4,511 | 14.3 |

Sources: *Business Korea*, 12/85; S. S. Lee, 1987.

[26]D. S. Cho, 1987.

[27]The several sources from which the data for this section are derived (S. S. Lee; *Business Korea*, 12/85; D. C. Kim, 1987; D. S. Cho, 1987) vary widely in their figures for the GTCs' import totals. For example, Cho puts the 1983 total at U.S.$2,166 million, or 8.3 percent of Korea's total imports. Kim places it at U.S.$3,381 million, or 12.9 percent. *Business Korea* and Lee give figures of U.S.$4,048 and U.S.$4,132, respectively, for 15.5 and 15.8 percent, nearly twice Cho's total. Table 6-3 uses the *Business Korea* figures for 1975–81 and the Lee figures for 1982–86.

[28]S. S. Lee.

[29]*Business Korea*, 11/83.

the 1980s to promote the more profitable import and domestic sales, exporting remains the Korean GTCs' major activity.

This varies significantly from the situation of their Japanese mentors. Less than half of the sogo shosha trade volume in the 1970s involved foreign trade, with domestic business comprising 50–62 percent of the total, imports 16–26 percent, exports 14–19 percent, and offshore trade 3–8 percent.[30] Among these, domestic transactions have the highest profit margin, then imports, exports, and offshore trade. The Korean GTCs' overwhelming emphasis on exports reminds us that it was government compliance mechanisms, not market signals, that prompted the business decisions of the Korean GTCs' owner-managers. We now turn to the consequences of this compliance structure by examining the history and development of the GTCs and the GTC policy since 1975.

## Fate of Korea's GTCs

From the outset, the Korean GTCs—though member firms of the chaebol—grew and developed as quasi-governmental institutions with the nearly exclusive purpose of expanding exports in order to reap the wide variety of state-proffered incentives. Chief among these carrots was the subsidized financing of exports, which "often more than compensated for losses incurred in export transactions."[31] As shown in Table 6-4, these concessionary loan rates were first implemented in 1962, at a discount from the ordinary bank rate of just over one point. The differential between the two rates widened to as much as eighteen points and averaged over seven points' difference from the inception of the GTC program in 1975 until the concessionary rates were finally phased out in June 1982.

During the export push of the late 1970s, the differential was actually greater than the concessionary rate, meaning that the GTCs were charged less than half the ordinary bank rate for financing their exports. In addition, inflation rates during this period averaged around 30 percent, virtually offsetting any remaining real cost of the loans (see Table 2-1). In other words, because the Park regime's purposes in expanding exports were political and not economic, the GTCs could literally ignore profitability as they made every effort to increase export volume and expand their portion of the export pie. This strategy had a number of initially positive, but increasingly negative, consequences for the Korean political economy and for the trading companies themselves.

The GTCs used this inexpensive credit and their comparative advantage of scale to rapidly expand Korea's exports and at the same time aid

[30]Yamazawa and Kohama.
[31]D. S. Cho, 1987, p. 57.

Table 6-4. Korean bank and concessional loan rates for selected years, 1962–82 (percent)

| Year | Ordinary bank rate | Concessional export rate | Differential |
|---|---|---|---|
| April 1962 | 13.87 | 12.78 | 1.09 |
| End 1963 | 13.87 | 8.03 | 5.84 |
| End 1964 | 14.00 | 8.00 | 6.00 |
| End 1965 | 24.00 | 6.50 | 17.50 |
| End 1967 | 24.00 | 6.00 | 18.00 |
| End 1973 | 15.50 | 7.00 | 8.50 |
| End 1974 | 15.50 | 9.00 | 6.50 |
| End 1975 | 15.50 | 7.00 | 8.50 |
| End 1976 | 17.00 | 8.00 | 9.00 |
| End 1978 | 18.50 | 9.00 | 9.50 |
| End 1980 | 19.50 | 12.00 | 7.50 |
| End 1981 | 16.50 | 12.00 | 4.50 |
| Jan. 1982 | 15.50 | 12.00 | 3.50 |
| March 1982 | 13.50 | 11.00 | 2.50 |
| June 1982 | 10.00 | 10.00 | 0.00 |

SOURCE: *Business Korea*, 11/83.

the quick expansion of their respective chaebol hosts. Though the chaebol obviously existed and prospered before the GTCs' creation, the GTCs soon became the premier members of the groups, bringing business and prestige to their respective networks of firms at home and abroad. Meanwhile, large companies with no links to GTCs, as well as smaller trading companies, were largely unable to capitalize on the export boom of the late 1970s or take full advantage of government subsidies, lost their competitiveness, and withered away. The largest GTCs quickly moved to the top of the rankings of Korea's largest corporations, a position they have maintained.[32]

These export gains and the GTCs' enhanced position did not come without costs. The drive for new export records and larger market share in order to obtain the consequent increased sales, subsidies, and prestige, led to excessive competition among the GTCs and an attitude of expansion at all costs, with little regard for accounting accuracy or economic efficiency. One of the easiest and most widespread methods of increasing export totals was through various creative bookkeeping procedures. With tacit government approval, the GTCs inflated their export figures by including in export totals such things as domestic sales to non-Korean retailers and trading companies, exports by other companies within their own group, and exports by smaller companies that did not have trading com-

[32]Samsung, Hyundai, and Daewoo (all GTCs) are consistently the three largest Korean corporations measured in terms of sales, usually in that order. All seven of the private GTCs maintain a position in the top twenty-five (*Business Korea*, various issues).

pany licenses.[33] Some of the inclusions were even more questionable. When Samsung served as a go-between for Korean Airlines in the leasing of a Boeing 747 to Saudi Arabia in 1983, Samsung tallied the deal in its books as a U.S.$65 million export. This, however, was the value of the jet, not the value of the lease. That same year Hyundai repaired a foreign ship valued at U.S.$50 million for a cost of U.S.$1 million and added the U.S.$50 million to its export total.[34]

In addition to these bookkeeping manipulations, the GTCs and their affiliated chaebol utilized concessionary financing to rapidly expand and diversify their operations. With increased sales and exports the single goal, the GTCs invested in areas in which they had no expertise and diversified into industries more suitable for smaller, more specialized companies. They also used export loans to swallow up supplier companies and merge other companies into the group network of firms. They also speculated in real estate and other highly questionable ventures in order to quickly raise capital to fuel yet more expansionary activities.[35] Not surprisingly, these activities led to numerous business failures, worthless stocks, and more debts, which in turn led to even more competition among the GTCs to expand sales in order to reduce mounting interest payments.

By the early 1980s, the situation had come to a head. This vicious circle, exacerbated by the second oil shock, high interest rates in overseas financial markets, and the continued depreciation of the Korean currency, combined to saddle each of the GTCs with enormous cumulative debts. Although exports were up, the GTCs' equity positions had deteriorated and earlier profits had plunged. Although Korean firms are highly leveraged even during prosperous periods, the debt ratios for the GTCs by this time were perilous. In 1982, the average debt ratio for the GTCs was over 1,000 percent. Ssangyong, the most highly leveraged, had a debt ratio of nearly 1,900 percent. This compares with an average of 450 percent for the entire group of 276 companies then listed on the Korean Stock Exchange.[36] As one analyst later concluded of the GTCs at this point: "The

---

[33]K. H. Jung, 1984.

[34]*Business Korea*, 11/83. These examples not only illustrate the eagerness of the GTCs to pad their export accounts and the willingness of the Korean government to indulge them, but also indicate that the annual export figures cited do not accurately reflect the trading companies' actual contributions. Lee Jong-Cheon, general manager of Daewoo Corporation's planning department, puts the variance between Korea's stated net exports and actual export sales for 1983 at as much as 30 percent. He estimated in November 1983 that if Korea were to net U.S.$24.5 billion in exports that year (in fact, it was U.S.$25.2 billion), only around U.S.$17–18 billion would represent genuine exports, a discrepancy of up to U.S.$7.5 billion, or nearly 30 percent (*Business Korea*, 11/83). Significantly, Taiwan, with its huge black market in unreported exports—to China and elsewhere—may actually *underreport* its exports to the same extent.

[35]*Business Korea*, 7/85.

[36]*Business Korea*, 11/83. The debt ratios for the specific GTCs ranged as follows: Daewoo,

brilliant standing of the GTCs was built on sand castle foundations propped up by outside help."[37]

Assuming the presidency in June 1980, Chun inherited an annual inflation rate of 44 percent, an unemployment rate of 6 percent, and Korea's first GNP decline in sixteen years.[38] Chun moved quickly to revitalize the economy, recalling to office the economic technocrats responsible for Korea's first economic takeoff. Though they continued to stress exports as the key to economic recovery, these reform-minded technocrats began to favor value added over export volume and also began to place less emphasis on the GTCs.[39] After annual increases since 1975 in the requirements and incentives associated with GTC designation, in 1981 the government eliminated all requisites except the minimum export value and the public offering of stocks.[40] Privileges were gradually eliminated as well, with the most valued subsidy, concessionary loan rates, finally equalized with regular bank rates in 1982, for the first time in twenty years (see Table 6-4).

In 1984, the government stopped publicizing the deeds of the GTCs and removed the last incentive geared toward export volume. The prestigious Export Towers trophy would subsequently be awarded on the basis of value added and other criteria, no longer on the basis of export volume.[41] Perhaps the most striking indication of the GTCs' loss of favor in the eyes of the Chun regime was a program introduced in 1985 to promote the growth of small exporters. Under this plan, small, specialized exporters were to handle as much as 40 percent of Korea's total exports by 1988.[42]

Just as the Park regime had fostered the GTCs for purposes of political legitimacy, so the Chun regime initially distanced itself from the chaebol and their GTCs in part to enhance popular support for the newly formed government. Although they had been seen as national heroes during the early years, to many Koreans the GTCs had become predatory giants swallowing up small manufacturers that served as their suppliers, and abusing

---

448.3 percent; Samsung, 549.0 percent; Kukje, 604.6 percent; Bando, 680.6 percent; Hyundai, 783.2 percent; Sunkyong, 1,391.2 percent; Hyosung, 1,768.5 percent; and Ssangyong, 1,872.2 percent.

[37] *Business Korea*, 12/85.

[38] Suh.

[39] *Business Korea*, 7/85; Suh.

[40] D. S. Cho, 1987.

[41] *Business Korea*, 12/84.

[42] *Business Korea*, 12/85. This plan was adopted in the wake of Taiwan's continued export success despite global protectionism. Korean policymakers attributed Taiwan's success to its tens of thousands of small and medium-sized exporters. Critics of this plan in Korea argued (correctly) that only a small portion of Taiwan's exports were being handled by these small local traders, with Japan's sogo shosha and foreign retailers handling a much larger portion (see Chapter Seven).

massive government subsidies to speculate in real estate and expand their chaebol partners. While exports were booming and the economy was prospering, the government could justify these links. But in light of the GTCs' declining profitability and abuse of government subsidies during economic hard times, the government opted to distance itself from the GTCs and phase out the incentive programs.

Strapped with enormous cumulative debts, declining government sustenance, and increasing public hostility during the early 1980s, the GTCs turned to their only remaining pillar of support in an effort to reverse their financial situation. This pillar was, of course, the chaebol. Relying on the institutional supports of their affiliated enterprise networks, the GTCs took several steps during the 1980s to improve their financial standing. These steps included (1) the merging of the GTCs with other, more profitable firms (such as construction or steel) within the groups; (2) increasing current assets by selling group holdings of real estate or buildings; (3) focusing group production and sales more on profitability and less on turnover; and (4) handling all group importing and exporting exclusively through the GTCs and increasing the commission fees charged to other group firms.[43] Though long-term debt payments still consumed much of their working capital, by 1986 the GTCs' average debt ratios had been cut nearly in half (545 percent) from the 1982 figures.[44]

The mid-1980s brought another wave of rising protectionism and stagnating exports, leading manufacturers and economic policymakers to court the giant traders once again. Independent Korean manufacturers had slowly developed trade experience and expertise, and in the wake of the GTCs' financial problems, they began to handle their own exports. But as foreign markets multiplied and became more difficult to penetrate, and as the leaner GTCs of the 1980s rationalized and diversified their operations, manufacturers regained confidence in the GTCs and returned to them.[45] Similarly, just as the GTCs were seen as saviors in 1975, after the export stagnation resulting from the first oil shock, a second severe setback in exports in 1985 led the government to again attach importance to the GTCs as the most powerful engines for export promotion.

The economic success of the Korean GTCs is far from guaranteed. Critics contend that their past strengths have been in their ability to handle large volumes of raw materials and low-level, standardized industrial goods, thus achieving economies of scale. As Korea has moved up the product cycle, these commodities have declined in importance, as have,

[43] *Business Korea*, 7/85.
[44] S. S. Lee.
[45] *Business Korea*, 12/85.

they argue, the demand for these GTC skills. Similarly, as the domestic market for financing is liberalized and the global market for information is made more accessible, the GTCs' financial and information resources may become obsolete.

The evidence, however, gives less reason for pessimism. Although they were ailing financially and cut loose from direct government subsidies, the GTCs were able to draw crucial strength during the early 1980s from their chaebol partners and survive until conditions—both economic and political—improved. Still far inferior to their Japanese counterparts in terms of financial stability and the sophistication and diversification of their respective markets, products, and particularly functions, the Korean GTCs are nevertheless improving in profitability, gaining experience, and evolving in function, leading Korea's expansion into new markets (including Russia, China, Eastern Europe, and even North Korea) and taking on new functions (including offshore trade and even informal diplomacy).[46]

Japan's sogo shosha were able to avoid what many predicted as their permanent decline in the 1960s by flexibly evolving their functions and activities in response to environmental changes. They were able to do this because they could draw on crucial support from the government, related business groups, and captive suppliers. The environment in which the GTCs are embedded also is forcing them to change. Though much less firmly grounded than their Japanese counterparts, these Korean GTCs have been able, to a large extent, to rely on the same pillars of support.

## WHY KOREA'S GTCs SUCCEEDED

Success can be reckoned in numerous ways and measured against various criteria. Critics have pointed out that the Korean GTCs grew at the expense of numerous smaller firms, contributed to Korea's widening dual economy and social bifurcation, and squandered valuable foreign exchange. The GTCs' detractors further note that despite the establishment of these giant traders, Korea still lags behind much smaller Taiwan in total exports in most years and lacks the flexibility and stability of Taiwan's diffuse, broad-based trade regime.[47]

These criticisms notwithstanding, there are valid reasons for considering the GTC program a success. The GTCs have established themselves as the premier members of Korea's colossal chaebol and dominant institutions in Korea's export market. And despite their financial problems and excesses, they have used their comparative advantages of specializa-

---

[46]See, for example, *Korea Business World*, 2/91; *Far Eastern Economic Review*, 2/20/92.
[47]Levy, 1991; *Business Korea*, 8/83, 12/85.

tion, integration, and scale to maintain their dominance and increase profitability. A 1987 study by the Korean Economic Research Institute concluded that the GTCs were in fact more efficient exporters than either large manufacturers handling their own exports or the small trading companies.[48] Following the example of the sogo shosha, the GTCs are restructuring and taking on new, more lucrative tasks; handling more imports, domestic sales, and counter, or barter, trade. In 1992, the seven GTCs had combined turnover valued at 19 percent of GNP. More important, combined profits were up 25 percent in 1992 from the previous year, despite a disastrous year for the Hyundai Corporation.[49]

Most important, regardless of the degree of their economic virtue or utility, the GTCs were a policy success. The government perceived the need to expand and diversify exports and rationalize their handling, formulated a program designed to achieve the objective, created institution incentives, and transformed these embedded enterprises in accordance with its developmental objectives. Key to this transformation, as indicated previously, were government sponsorship, business group support, and exclusive access to captive suppliers. We will briefly examine each of these before turning to the obstacles that remain in the path of the GTCs' future development.

Even more than their Japanese predecessors, the fate of the Korean GTCs hinged on the sponsorship and sustenance provided by the Korean state. As discussed above, statutory incentives included priority access to government trade, relaxed limits on raw material imports, tax reductions and exemptions, and increased freedom in handling foreign branches and foreign exchange. Less formally, the government supported the GTCs by treating them as national champions: offering praise, prizes, and publicity to the top exporters and allowing the GTC owner-managers to participate in cabinet-level meetings chaired by President Park in which trade policies were established. This visible and consistent government backing gave the GTCs prestige, which, in a Confucian society that has traditionally disdained merchants and commerce, proved very valuable.[50] Most significantly, however, were the concessionary export loans that more than compensated the GTCs for any export losses and subsidized the expansion of the GTCs' second pillar of support—their affiliated chaebol.

Though these chaebol linkages were important from the very beginning, as GTC profitability declined in the early 1980s and the government phased out the concessionary loan program in 1982, the GTCs "managed

[48] D. C. Kim, 1987.
[49] *Business Korea*, 4/93.
[50] D. C. Kim, 1987.

to survive on the strength of the entire business conglomerate they belong to."[51] In the wake of the termination of the export loan subsidies, the chaebol moved quickly to prop up the ailing GTCs. Daewoo arranged for its profitable manufacturing firms to break even, shifting the rest of operating profits into its GTC's account. Samsung Electric annually surrendered 3 percent of its earnings to Samsung GTC and transferred a large office building in Seoul to the GTC's portfolio. Similarly, analysts have speculated that Ssangyong Cement, Gold Star, and Sunkyong Petroleum bankrolled their respective GTCs. Kukje GTC merged with the Kukje Group's construction firm, ICC Construction.[52]

In addition to this financial support, group membership guaranteed the GTCs a captive source of export supplies. This has been the third pillar of support. Though ties with supplier networks beyond the chaebol are weaker and less extensive than those between Japanese suppliers and the sogo shosha (or Taiwan's export regime),[53] tight control over member manufacturing firms has insured the GTCs a reliable source of exports. In addition, with the exception of Hyundai, most of the GTCs, either from the time of their designation or as a result of subsequent mergers, also have their own manufacturing facilities. Ku-hyun Jung estimated that in 1979, 16 percent of the GTCs' total exports were manufactured by the GTCs themselves, with another 35 percent coming from their respective group companies, for a total of 51 percent intragroup exports. He concludes that "the GTCs' survival may have been shaken if it were not for these affiliations with business groups."[54] Ippei Yamazawa and Hirohisa Kohama, writing in 1985, place the total at 60 percent, indicating that a dominant and growing portion of the GTCs' exports derive from within their own groups.[55]

One final aspect of this captive supply of exports must be examined. Not only were there internal constraints on member firms to export through their own chaebol, there were also external limits on alternative export channels. Unlike Taiwan, which placed few restrictions on either direct foreign investment or foreign traders in the 1950s, Syngman Rhee's policy of "deliberately sustained antagonism against Japan" led Korea to prohibit all foreign investment until the late 1950s and to exclude the sogo shosha from Korea until the 1960s.[56] In fact, only since the 1980s have non-Korean trading companies been officially allowed to

[51] *Business Korea*, 11/83.
[52] *Business Korea*, 11/83.
[53] Doner et al. For the weakness of supplier networks in Korea, see Regnier. For Japanese subcontractor networks, see Smitka. For Taiwan, see Shieh.
[54] K. H. Jung, 1983, p. 81.
[55] Yamazawa and Kohama.
[56] Ozawa, 1987; W. Y. Lee; C. S. Lee; D. C. Kim, 1987.

handle foreign transactions on their own accounts. And prior to 1992, Japanese companies were not allowed to establish wholly-owned subsidiaries in Korea.[57] This has meant the Korean branches of the Japanese *sogo shosha* were not able to perform all the trading functions of their domestic counterparts.[58] These restrictions limited foreign competitors' access to the Korean market, eased the GTCs' competition once they arrived on the scene, and limited the independent manufacturers' choices of export channels.

This guaranteed source of supplies, coupled with state and chaebol sustenance and support, has allowed the GTCs to overcome significant obstacles. Substantial obstacles remain, however, that threaten to limit the GTCs future growth.

## OBSTACLES TO FUTURE SUCCESS

These large-scale trading companies (both Korea's and Taiwan's versions) are examples of state-imposed institutions whose establishment entailed economic risks and challenged both social and political norms. In the Korean case, incentives and other institutional arrangements made it possible to partially overcome the risk and other constraints associated with the environment in which the GTCs were embedded. Nonetheless, economic, social, and policy obstacles remain.

Competition from other trade channels remains the greatest economic obstacle to the further growth and expansion of the GTCs. These competitors include the sogo shosha, foreign buyers and retailers, government agencies, local manufacturers, and small-scale trading companies. Table 6-5 indicates the export shares for the GTCs and their major competitors for the years 1976–82.

Despite the Korean state's postwar efforts to exclude the sogo shosha from the Korean market, Table 6-5 indicates that these Japanese traders were the GTCs' single largest group of competitors for handling Korea's exports in 1976. Their ability to carve out a share of the Korean export market reflects the importance businessmen on both sides attached to this complementary economic relationship in spite of political and diplomatic animosity. The sogo shosha have long been the spearheads of Japanese economic interests in Korea, with several of them setting up operations before Japan's annexation of Korea in 1910.[59] It is perhaps

[57] *Business Korea*, 4/93.
[58] K. H. Jung, 1984. However, Yamazawa and Kohama note the sogo shosha and other foreign traders were able to circumvent these legal restrictions by having employees from the foreign head offices travel to Korea to handle certain activities.
[59] K. H. Jung, 1984.

*Table 6-5.* Traders' share of Korea's total exports, 1976–82 (percent)

| Trader | 1976 | 1977 | 1978 | 1979 | 1980 | 1981 | 1982 |
|---|---|---|---|---|---|---|---|
| GTCs | 19.1 | 27.1 | 30.0 | 33.5 | 41.0 | 42.8 | 47.9 |
| Japanese sogo shosha | 15.6 | 12.7 | 10.2 | 10.4 | 9.4 | 9.1 | 7.9 |
| Foreign retailers | 11.3 | 10.4 | 9.8 | 7.0 | 9.0 | 8.6 | 10.0 |
| Other channels[a] | 54.0 | 49.8 | 50.0 | 49.1 | 40.6 | 39.5 | 34.2 |
| Total | 100.0 | 100.0 | 100.0 | 100.0 | 100.0 | 100.0 | 100.0 |

SOURCE: Adapted from K. H. Jung, 1984, p. 114.

[a]"Other channels" includes local manufacturers, local small- and medium-scale traders, and state enterprises and agencies.

not surprising that the first Japanese to be issued visas to Korea in the postwar period were representatives of the Mitsubishi Trading Company, in 1960.[60] Between this event and the normalization of the political relationship five years later, some sixty major Japanese trading and industrial companies established offices in Seoul.[61]

Once diplomatic relations were restored in 1965, massive amounts of Japanese capital, goods, and services began flowing into Korea and finished goods began flowing out, with the sogo shosha acting as the primary commercial agents. By 1970, Korea ranked first, ahead of even Taiwan, as the most popular host country for Japanese overseas investment in Asia.[62] By 1982, the Association of Foreign Trading Agents of Korea listed fifteen Japanese trading companies, including all nine of the sogo shosha.[63] The financial, technological, and informational assets of these Japanese traders, coupled with the geographical and cultural proximity and linguistic commonality between the Japanese and Koreans, have made the sogo shosha formidable obstacles to further GTC expansion in the areas of exports, imports, and offshore trade.

Despite this presence, however, Table 6-5 indicates that the sogo shosha's share of the export market declined markedly over the first seven years of the GTCs' establishment. In fact, their share of exports was cut in half during this period, even as Korea's total exports nearly tripled (see Table 6-2). This means the sogo shosha's total volume of exports increased only about 25 percent during this period, compared to an increase of over 700 percent for the GTCs.[64] The fact that the GTCs'

[60]The exact date was August 17, 1960, three weeks before the first Japanese government official was issued a visa—and, not coincidentally, one week before Chang Myon formed the first post-Rhee government.

[61]C. S. Lee.

[62]Ozawa, 1987; Ko.

[63]K. H. Jung, 1984.

[64]In fact, Table 6-5 reveals that a GTC's greatest competitors for market share are the other GTCs. The vicious competition among the GTCs to expand market share was one of

increased share came at least partially at the expense of the Japanese traders is confirmed by a 1982 poll of foreign retailers and sogo shosha in Korea. The poll found that while the foreign retailers saw the GTC operations as complementary to their own, the sogo shosha saw them as competitive.[65] Through the 1980s the sogo shosha managed to consistently handle roughly 10 percent of Korean exports.[66]

The foreign retailers' share of the Korean export market appears to have been little affected by the emergence of the GTCs and has remained relatively consistent over time. These foreign buyers include retail chain stores, department stores, and other Western agents. Most of these established buying offices in the early 1970s. They include JC Penney, Sears Roebuck, Montgomery Ward, K-Mart, Tandy Electronics, and Associated Merchandising.[67]

These foreign retailers have a minimal local presence; the resulting low overhead and no inventory have allowed them to offer very competitive prices, particularly to the small and medium-sized manufacturers with whom they conduct most of their business. In addition, these foreign buyers, as established importers into the U.S. market, have had the additional advantage over the GTCs of established U.S. market share previous to the imposition of import restrictions. These import quotas in the United States and other markets tend to favor the established traders and have limited the GTCs' opportunities to expand market inroads. In 1981, although the GTCs handled 43 percent of Korea's total exports, they handled only 27 percent of exports destined for the U.S. market.[68]

These three groups of traders—foreign retailers, sogo shosha, and the Korean GTCs—handled nearly two-thirds of Korea's total exports in 1982. The other third was shared by local small and medium-scale traders, local manufacturers, state enterprises, and other government agencies. Although these trading concerns have competed with the GTCs for exports, much of the GTCs' expansion has been at their expense. Lacking the scale economies and financial resources of the GTCs, many of the smaller traders were swallowed up or priced out of business by the subsidized GTCs, which were anxious to diversify their export lines to meet government criteria and little concerned during the early years with turning a profit. Nonetheless, some specialized traders have carved out market niches and have maintained their export share.

---

the primary reasons behind the GTCs' financial problems in the early 1980s. One trader noted that this is even more of a problem in Korea than it is in Japan: "In Japan, they [the sogo shosha] cooperate. Here, we shoot each other" (*Business Korea*, 12/84).

[65] K. H. Jung, 1984.
[66] Jo.
[67] K. H. Jung, 1984.
[68] K. H. Jung, 1984.

As local manufacturers rapidly expanded during the 1970s, many began to integrate downstream, establishing their own market operations abroad. These manufacturers' direct exports to the United States grew from a negligible amount in 1976 to more than 10 percent by 1981.[69] Despite evidence that the rise of protectionism and the multiplication of foreign markets during the 1980s lured the manufacturers back to the GTCs,[70] the highly specialized nature of many of today's markets and the need for after-sales service will likely insure that a significant portion of Korea's export market will remain in the hands of these domestic producers.

Finally, the government sector handles a small percentage of Korea's export market. This includes the exports of Korea's state enterprises as well as of Koryo Trading and Korea Trading International. Koryo is a GTC established and managed by the state for promoting the exports of small and medium-sized enterprises. Its total exports, however, have been negligible, only .02 percent of total Korean exports in 1975 and .03 percent in 1983.[71]

The public sector has proved to be a much more significant and intransigent obstacle to the GTCs' efforts to expand their share of the more profitable import market. The government's Office of Supply for the Republic of Korea (OSROK) handles the lion's share of Korean imports. Raw materials and agricultural products represent nearly 70 percent of Korea's total imports, and these markets have been virtually closed to the GTCs. Most grain and feedstuff is imported through OSROK or government-licensed industry associations that are responsible for allocating the commodities or issuing licenses for imports. Both the government and these associations have been hesitant to allocate import quotas to the GTCs, fearing they would show bias against end users not affiliated with the GTCs' own chaebol.[72] The GTCs are also barred from importing petroleum. In addition, unlike the sogo shosha in Japan, the GTCs play no part in defense procurement, a major import sector for Korea.[73]

In fact, the GTCs' share of the import market trails that of the sogo shosha's combined import arrangements for their Korean customers and end users. In 1984, the sogo shosha handled 11.9 percent of Korea's total imports, compared with 10.4 percent for the GTCs. This had climbed to 14.9 percent in 1986. Korean manufacturers' dependence on costly Japanese imports and the Japanese traders' exclusive handling of these imports guarantees the sogo shosha a substantial share of this import mar-

[69]K. H. Jung, 1984.
[70]Business Korea, 12/85.
[71]D. S. Cho, 1987.
[72]Business Korea, 12/85; Korea Times, 12/14/88.
[73]Business Korea, 12/84.

ket (Table 6-3).[74] Finally, small and medium-sized firms are given monopoly over certain imports. The presence of these various competitors, combined with the complete absence of any government incentives for importing, have limited the GTCs' access to the growing, and potentially more lucrative, import market, and thus have impeded the growth and expansion of the GTCs.

In addition to these economic obstacles, there are also social and policy obstacles constraining the further expansion of the GTCs. As with the sogo shosha in Japan during the 1970s, the Korean GTCs during the 1970s became the subject of growing public criticism because of their speculation, profiteering, and abuse of government subsidies. Although in the past Korean society had accepted these excesses as necessary for the greater good of Korean development or endured them as a people subdued by an authoritarian military regime, recent social and political trends indicate they may no longer be tolerated in the nascent pluralism of the 1990s.

Ironically, the greatest impediment to the continued expansion of the GTCs is directly linked to explicit policies enforced by the very regimes that fostered their growth. The most formidable obstacle facing the GTCs is their financial weakness. The proximate cause of this condition has been the burdensome interest payments and declining profits they have experienced as a result of their rapid, debt-based expansion of export activities. Servicing these debts, particularly since the phasing out of concessionary export loans in 1982, has become increasingly onerous. In 1985, the GTCs were paying an average of 85 percent of their earnings before interest and taxes as interest on loans to foreign and domestic lenders.[75] Although the GTCs' poor business decisions and unwise speculation contributed to this situation, the Park and Chun regimes deserve criticism for establishing unrealistic export goals, virtually giving away money to finance these exports, and then terminating the concessionary loans and restricting foreign loans during the time of the GTCs' greatest financial difficulty.

A more fundamental government policy has exacerbated this situation of financial weakness. Like Taiwan's state, the Korean government maintained pervasive influence over formal financial markets and resisted efforts by GTCs and their affiliated chaebol to take over or set up private banks.[76] Unlike their Japanese counterparts, whose institutional linkages

[74] *Business Korea*, 12/85; S. S. Lee.
[75] Kukje-ICC, the most financially strapped of the GTCs, was paying as much as 115 percent of its earnings before taxes as interest. As discussed in Chapter Four, this was one of the factors contributing to the collapse of the Kukje chaebol in early 1985 (*Business Korea*, 12/85).
[76] *Business Korea*, 12/85.

to group banks provide ready access to capital, the Korean GTCs have been constrained in their ability to use this means to obtain a sounder financial footing.

These curbs, designed to maintain the chaebol and their GTCs as junior partners in "Korea, Inc.," have hampered the GTCs. GTC executives complain that without ready access to long-term funding, the GTCs are unable to finance sophisticated trade transactions such as third-country trade or long-term projects. In 1982, Kukje was forced to scrap a U.S.$400 million railroad project in Cameroon because it lacked the funds to finance the project. Moreover, these limits on private finance have made it very difficult for the GTCs to invest in overseas trade and information-gathering networks because of the large initial investment and long payback period associated with these overseas networks. Finally, the GTCs' weak financial position has prevented them, unlike the sogo shosha, from extending liberal credit to nongroup suppliers and other customers, thus severely weakening their ties to these customers.[77]

In sum, real and formidable economic, social, and policy obstacles loom on the GTCs' horizon. But unlike the Taiwan case, situational imperatives and elite motivations gave the Korean state sufficient autonomy and capacity to implement a policy that enjoyed a high degree of sustained support from relevant policy circles. This resulted in government incentives and institutional arrangements that have been sufficient to launch the GTCs with enough momentum to assure their viability and success at least in the short run. In the following chapter, we examine how and why similar plans in Taiwan went awry.

[77]K. H. Jung, 1983; *Business Korea*, 12/84, 12/85.

CHAPTER SEVEN

# *Taiwan's Large Trading Companies*

Taiwan is smaller, more densely populated, and endowed with even fewer natural resources than Korea, so it should not be surprising that Taiwan is even more dependent than Korea on trade, and particularly exports, for its continued development. The significance of international trade to Taiwan's economy compared with Korea and Japan is illustrated in Table 7-1.

Table 7-1 demonstrates the extent to which Taiwan's economy is dependent on foreign trade in general and on exports in particular. For the period 1978–87, Taiwan's total trade represented an average of over 91 percent of GNP, whereas the comparable figures for Korea and Japan were 69 percent and 24 percent, respectively. Taiwan's export ratios also are telling, with exports accounting for an average of nearly 51 percent of GNP for that period, and an average of 47 percent for the eighteen years included in the table. Given this trade dependency and the many other similarities between Taiwan and Korea's developmental experiences, it is not surprising that Taiwan's policymakers became interested in Japan's general trading company and sought to foster their own version. But despite similar aspirations, Taiwan's policy to develop large trading companies failed. In the following section we will examine this policy, beginning with a brief look at the combination of factors that led to the original decision.

## TAIWAN'S DAMAOYISHANG

### *Trade Situation*

Like Korea, Taiwan began its postwar industrialization program inauspiciously. Most of its industry and infrastructure had been destroyed or

*Table 7-1.* Ratio of exports, imports, and total trade to GNP in Taiwan, Korea, and Japan, 1974–91 (percent)

| Year | Exports to GNP | | | Imports to GNP | | | Total trade to GNP | | |
|---|---|---|---|---|---|---|---|---|---|
| | Taiwan | Korea | Japan | Taiwan | Korea | Japan | Taiwan | Korea | Japan |
| 1974 | 39.2 | 24.4 | 12.1 | 48.7 | 37.4 | 13.5 | 87.9 | 61.8 | 25.6 |
| 1975 | 34.7 | 25.1 | 11.2 | 39.0 | 36.0 | 11.6 | 73.7 | 61.1 | 22.8 |
| 1976 | 44.5 | 28.1 | 12.0 | 41.5 | 32.0 | 11.6 | 86.0 | 60.1 | 23.6 |
| 1977 | 43.8 | 28.6 | 11.7 | 39.9 | 30.7 | 10.4 | 83.7 | 59.3 | 22.1 |
| 1978 | 48.4 | 26.8 | 10.1 | 42.2 | 31.6 | 8.3 | 90.6 | 58.4 | 18.4 |
| 1979 | 49.7 | 25.1 | 10.3 | 45.8 | 33.9 | 11.1 | 95.5 | 59.0 | 21.4 |
| 1980 | 49.4 | 31.0 | 12.5 | 49.4 | 39.5 | 13.6 | 98.8 | 70.5 | 26.1 |
| 1981 | 49.0 | 34.2 | 13.3 | 46.0 | 42.0 | 12.5 | 95.0 | 76.2 | 25.8 |
| 1982 | 47.3 | 33.0 | 13.0 | 40.3 | 36.8 | 12.4 | 87.6 | 69.8 | 25.4 |
| 1983 | 50.4 | 32.5 | 12.7 | 40.8 | 34.9 | 10.9 | 91.2 | 67.4 | 23.6 |
| 1984 | 52.8 | 36.0 | 13.8 | 38.0 | 37.7 | 11.0 | 90.8 | 73.7 | 24.8 |
| 1985 | 51.1 | 36.7 | 13.1 | 33.5 | 37.7 | 9.7 | 84.6 | 74.4 | 22.8 |
| 1986 | 54.8 | 36.5 | 11.7 | 33.3 | 33.2 | 7.1 | 88.1 | 69.7 | 18.8 |
| 1987 | 54.9 | 39.7 | 9.7 | 35.4 | 34.5 | 6.3 | 90.3 | 74.2 | 16.0 |
| 1988 | 50.6 | 35.9 | 10.7 | 41.5 | 30.6 | 7.5 | 92.1 | 66.5 | 18.2 |
| 1989 | 48.8 | 30.5 | 10.0 | 40.8 | 30.0 | 7.7 | 89.6 | 60.5 | 17.7 |
| 1990 | 41.3 | 29.7 | 7.1 | 33.6 | 29.2 | 7.4 | 74.9 | 58.9 | 14.5 |
| 1991 | .42.2 | 25.6 | 9.4 | 34.9 | 29.1 | 7.1 | 77.1 | 54.7 | 16.5 |

SOURCE: CETDC, 1992.

carried off to the Chinese mainland during and after the war. But the relocation of the Nationalist political leaders and bureaucracy to Taiwan in 1949—humbled by their defeat on the hands of the Chinese Communists and largely cleansed of corrupt elements—provided Taiwan with an insulated policy-making elite capable of leading the industrialization drive. Bolstered by massive quantities of U.S. aid and technical assistance and an industrious, educated Taiwanese work force, the Nationalist regime was able to launch a very successful program of import-substituting industrialization (ISI) several years before Korea, which was embroiled in the Korean War.

During the 1950s, this ISI program allowed Taiwan to establish its domestic industrial base, reduce unemployment, and improve its balance of payments position. But by the late 1950s, the costs of this strategy began to outweigh its benefits, and an alliance of technocratic reformers and American advisers persuaded political leaders of the need to adopt a new policy package liberalizing controls on trade and industry, stimulating investment, and promoting exports.[1] This policy package (and subsequent statutes) included a wide variety of incentives to exporters with the overall objective of easing the way for large numbers of individual firms to export efficiently.

[1]Gold, 1986.

These export-oriented policies meshed well with the situational imperatives of Taiwan's political economy. Lacking the domestic market of Japan
or even Korea, most firms in Taiwan from the outset had to think in terms
of exports in order to succeed.[2] Utilizing long-standing ties with overseas
Chinese and developing new connections with foreigners, Taiwan's entrepreneurs took good advantage of the export incentives the government
offered. These incentives, at least on this count, were very effective. By
1986, Taiwan had over 60,000 firms involved in foreign trade, and over
40,000 of these were designated as "exclusive" trading firms, not engaged in manufacturing.[3] Although this huge supply of participants
would seem to indicate a healthy trade regime, this was not necessarily
the case. A 1979 study characterized Taiwan's system of domestic traders
as one of "cutthroat competition [*exing jingzheng*] among a multitude of
trading companies" that had backward management, marketing, and financial systems, little capital, limited exports, few overseas branches and
virtually no foreign experience.[4]

Stepping into this gap resulting from the absence of internationally
experienced and competitive domestic traders, Japan's sogo shosha and
other foreign trading and retailing concerns exacerbated and further entrenched this system of domestic trade weakness as Taiwan's exports expanded in the 1960s and mushroomed in the 1970s. By the late 1970s, it
was estimated that 70 percent of Taiwan's foreign trade was being handled by these foreign concerns.[5] The dominance of these foreign traders
and buyers made it impossible for the local traders to bargain from a
position of strength, keep up with the latest trends, innovate new products, or penetrate new markets. Closely related to this reliance on foreign
traders was the heavy concentration of Taiwan's overseas markets in Asia
and North America, with Japan and the United States receiving well over
half of Taiwan's exports throughout the postwar period.[6]

## Formation of the LTCs

The dependence on both foreign traders and limited foreign markets
during a period of rising protectionism, labor costs, and oil prices
prompted Taiwan's economic policymakers to consider restructuring the
nation's trade regime. Like Korea's economic planners, Taiwan's policymakers noted the resilience of the Japanese sogo shosha during economic
downturns and were impressed with the apparent success of the Korean

[2]Pye, 1985.
[3]*Journal of Commerce*, 12/26/86; K. M. Kuo.
[4]Diyi Yinhang, p. 4.
[5]*Economic News*, 10/29/79.
[6]CETDC, 1992.

GTCs in promoting exports since their creation in 1975.[7] In 1977, Premier Chiang Ching-kuo called on the government to "encourage traders to gradually set up large trading companies and actively enlarge our trade networks all over the world" in order to strengthen Taiwan's trade vitality.[8]

Discussions concerning the establishment of these trading companies began in earnest that spring, and policymakers brought Japanese experts to Taiwan to consult with government and business leaders about the workings and potential strengths of the Japanese general trading company.[9] A formal proposal for the establishment of large trading companies (*damaoyishang*) was introduced that year, and approved and enacted by the Legislative Yuan in mid-1978. The first large trading company (LTC) was designated in September 1978.[10]

In order to receive this designation, interested parties had to meet the following minimum requirements:[11]

1. Paid-in-capital of N.T.$200 million (approximately U.S.$5.6 million)
2. Annual exports of U.S.$10 million in the year prior to LTC designation
3. Three overseas branch offices
4. Composed of the following units, with the first, and either the second or the third, as necessary shareholders
   a. A bank dealing predominantly in foreign exchange or one that has wide representation abroad (holding at least 10 percent of the outstanding shares)
   b. Standard trading company engaged predominantly in exporting
   c. Small or medium-sized enterprise or merger between such enterprises
   d. A manufacturer producing predominantly export products.

A quick comparison of these minimum criteria with those required of Korea's GTCs reveals substantial differences. While the paid-in-capital requirement was higher for Taiwan's LTCs (U.S.$5.6 million compared with U.S.$2.5 million for the GTCs), the other qualifications were all substantially higher for the Korean trading companies. Instead of three overseas branches and annual exports of U.S.$10 million, Korean GTCs, from

---

[7]*Economic News*, 10/29/79; D. S. Cho, 1987.
[8]V. J. Chang, p. 73.
[9]*Economic News*, 4/30/79; X. Chen, 1980. Koreans also were brought to Taiwan as consultants, but not until 1982, some four years after Taiwan's LTC had been established.
[10]K. M. Kuo; *Economic News*, 10/29/79.
[11]X. Chen, 1980; Diyi Yinhang; D. S. Cho, 1987.

their inception, were required to have annual exports of U.S.$50 million (raised to U.S.$250 million by 1978), ten overseas branches, and a minimum of seven products and ten recipient countries.

The other significant area of difference is that of ownership. The Korean GTCs were explicitly fostered as trading arms of the chaebol and were required to offer stock to the public as a means of generating capital as well as "deprivatizing" the family-owned business groups. Taiwan's LTCs, on the other hand, were required to include as partners small and medium-sized manufacturers or trading companies, as well as a commercial bank (those banks at the time were either owned or controlled by the state). Instead of setting the minimum requirements so high as to be out of reach of all but a few of the largest enterprises, as was done explicitly in Korea and implicitly in Japan, Taiwan's criteria required that small-scale enterprises form the core of the trading concerns. Moreover, the state made no effort to encourage the participation of the guanxiqiye and in fact took pains to ensure that the LTCs would remain "entities independent of existing enterprise groups."[12]

These differences in requirements, matched by substantial discrepancies in incentives, provide further evidence that the objectives guiding Taiwan's policymakers were more complex than simply export expansion. The following privileges were offered to those firms receiving LTC designation:[13]

Trade Administration
1. Duty-free import of raw materials to be used for manufacture of export products
2. Establishment of bonded warehouses

Financing
1. Guarantees for loans to local small and medium-sized manufacturers for the import of raw materials
2. Preferential treatment in financing based on letters of credit.

These incentives pale in comparison with those offered to the Korean GTCs. Where the GTCs were given priority access to government agency trade and relaxed entry into commodity associations, no such privileges were granted to the LTCs. In fact, Taiwan's government and quasi-government traders have virtually monopolized commodity imports and public sector trade. Similarly, although the state gave the LTCs' overseas offices special freedoms and relaxed limits on foreign currency holdings, strict controls on the amounts and uses of foreign currency held by the foreign

[12]D. S. Cho, 1987, p. 60. See also X. Chen, 1980.
[13]*Economic News*, 4/30/79, 10/20/79; D. S. Cho, 1987.

branches remained in place. In fact, the major incentives offered to the LTCs—duty-free importing of raw materials and the provision of credit guarantees—were already available to reputable manufacturers, and thus provided no added incentive.[14] In addition, manufacturers were given a 25 percent ceiling on corporate income tax and concessional bank credits. The former was not offered to the LTCs until 1982 and the latter not until 1987.[15]

These differences in requirements and incentives reflect different underlying state motives for introducing these programs. Chapter Six demonstrated that the primary objective of Korean policymakers was to expand and diversify exports; officials in Taiwan had multiple, and somewhat contradictory, objectives in mind as they fashioned the LTC policy. A review of the literature reveals the following as publicly stated goals of the LTC program:[16]

1. Establish Taiwan's own trade and information networks and name brands abroad
2. Promote the diversification of markets and products
3. Reduce dependence on foreign trading concerns and alleviate over-competition among local exporters
4. Expand the scale of trade and manufacturing activities
5. Avoid the concentration of wealth
6. Provide assistance to small and medium-sized enterprises.

These represent a puzzling range of goals. The first four are similar to the achievements of the Korean GTCs and the Japanese sogo shosha. The last two, however, were never a concern of the architects of the Japanese and Korean GTCs and in many ways are inherently contradictory to the first four goals. In a small economy such as Taiwan's, the elimination of foreign and local competition and the expansion of scale would by definition entail a degree of economic concentration. In Japan and Korea, this concentration of capital and economic power was in fact the explicit goal, and the small traders and manufacturers were its acknowledged victims. In Taiwan, this multiplicity of objectives, as well as the feeble nature of incentives and other compliance mechanisms, are symptoms of a more fundamental ambiguity among policymakers regarding the purpose and value of large-scale trading concerns. Before examining this conflict in the final section of this chapter, we will review the brief history of Taiwan's LTCs.

[14]*Economic News*, 4/30/79.
[15]*Economic News*, 12/6/82; *China News*, 2/21/87.
[16]*Economic News*, 4/30/79, 10/29/79, 6/8/81; Diyi Yinhang; K. M. Kuo; D. S. Cho, 1987; X. Chen, 1980.

## Fate of the LTCs

The actual story of the LTCs need not detain us long. In all, seven companies achieved LTC status.[17] The first LTC launched was Pan Overseas Corporation, set up in late 1978. Over the next four years, six more LTCs were formed or designated: Collins Company, Nanlien International, and Great International in 1979; E-Hsin International and Taipoly in 1980; and Peacock in 1981.[18] Because of the rising minimum export requirements necessary to receive LTC designation, and because several of the companies failed, only two LTC remained as of 1987. Table 7-2 includes minimum export requirements, the exports of each Taiwan, the aggregate exports of all the LTCs (whether or not they met the requirements that year), and their share of Taiwan's total exports for 1979–87.

It can be readily seen from Table 7-2 that the LTCs have failed to achieve significant growth in terms of exports.[19] The aggregate total peaked in 1985 at U.S.$448.7 million, then registered a 9 percent decline over the next two years. The insignificance of this total is more obvious when juxtaposed with Taiwan's total exports, which experienced a 74 percent increase over those same two years. The LTCs' record is even more

*Table 7-2.* Individual and aggregate exports of Taiwan's LTCs, 1979–87 (U.S.$1 million)

| LTC | 1979 | 1980 | 1981 | 1982 | 1983 | 1984 | 1985 | 1986 | 1987 |
|---|---|---|---|---|---|---|---|---|---|
| MER[a] | 10.0 | 10.0 | 10.0 | 10.0 | 20.0 | 30.0 | 100.0 | 100.0 | 100.0 |
| Pan | 21.3 | 37.3 | 42.2 | 42.2 | 47.4 | 41.5 | 26.6 | 20.4 | 72.7 |
| Collins | 41.5 | 57.0 | 69.1 | 73.6 | 116.0 | 150.0 | 148.8 | 193.7 | 196.1 |
| Nanlien | 1.5 | 15.7 | 32.2 | 20.2 | 18.3 | 21.6 | 10.0 | 23.3 | 14.9 |
| Great | 0.7 | 15.1 | 23.7 | 25.1 | 1.4 | — | — | — | — |
| E-Hsin | 3.2 | 35.8 | 67.4 | 104.1 | 104.9 | 108.0 | 263.3 | 117.9 | 125.2 |
| Taipoly | 7.6 | 6.7 | 13.5 | 14.0 | 28.6 | 29.3 | — | — | — |
| Peacock | 7.8 | 6.7 | 13.5 | 14.0 | 28.6 | 29.3 | — | — | — |
| Total | 83.9 | 179.7 | 260.5 | 291.5 | 289.6 | 391.8 | 448.7 | 355.3 | 408.9 |
| Taiwan exports (U.S.$1 billion) | 16.1 | 19.8 | 22.6 | 22.2 | 25.1 | 30.5 | 30.7 | 39.8 | 53.5 |
| LTC share of total (percent) | 0.52 | 0.90 | 1.15 | 1.31 | 1.15 | 1.28 | 1.46 | 0.92 | 0.76 |

SOURCES: BOFT; K. M. Kuo; D. S. Cho, 1987; *Journal of Commerce,* 12/26/86; *Economic News,* 2/8/88.

[a]MER: Minimum export requirement established by the government in order to receive LTC designation for the following year.

[17]The data derived from the major sources used for this section (K. M. Kuo; X. Chen, 1980; D. S. Cho, 1987; *Economic News*) conflict on several counts. I have attempted to reconcile these conflicts by selecting those figures on which the most sources agree.

[18]BOFT; CCIS, 1985; K. M. Kuo; D. S. Cho, 1987.

[19]LTC imports are not included in this analysis because of their insignificance. For example, total LTC imports for 1986 were U.S.$35.8 million, a mere one-tenth the volume of LTC exports and less than 0.15 percent of Taiwan's total imports (BOFT).

dismal when measured in terms of their share of this total.[20] In the peak year of 1985, the four LTCs handled only 1.46 percent of Taiwan's total exports, compared with 42 percent of Japan's total exports for the nine sogo shosha in 1983 and 51 percent of Korea's total exports for the nine Korean GTCs in 1984. For the entire nine years represented in Table 7-2, the LTCs averaged just over 1 percent of total trade. Omitting 1979, the year of inception for many of the firms, improves the average only slightly, to 1.12 percent.

In fact, only two of the original LTCs, Collins Company and E-Hsin International, have been able to maintain their LTC status and continue (albeit inconsistently) to grow. Before turning to the reasons behind this high attrition rate, a brief look at these two relatively more successful LTCs sheds light on the ultimate reasons for the failure of the LTC policy.

### Collins Company

Collins Company, founded as Collins Trading Company in 1969, had only ten employees and a total of U.S.$100,000 in exports during the first year.[21] By the time of its LTC designation in late 1978, Collins was the largest local private trading company, with a staff of 260 employees and U.S.$70 million in exports. Drawing on this experience and establishing market share, Collins led the LTCs in exports for all but two of the ten years through 1987. As of 1987, Collins had 413 employees and exports of U.S.$196 million.

Although the government required the establishment of three branch offices abroad as a criterion for LTC designation, it has not allowed the LTCs to own foreign subsidiaries. Collins, however, had a subsidiary in New York prior to its designation as an LTC. It maintained that firm and, as the only LTC with a foreign subsidiary, used it to good advantage. This subsidiary, headed by the chairman of the company, collects market information, provides sales, solicits orders, provides after-sales service, and purchases raw materials. Although Collins has branch offices in Bangkok, Hong Kong, and Manila, and Buenos Aires, over 90 percent of its largely labor-intensive exports (exports make up more than 99 percent of its total trade) go to North America and are handled through its New York company and a Los Angeles branch office.

---

[20]K. M. Kuo, in defense of the LTCs' record, argues that the LTCs' export volume and share of total national exports have grown more steadily than the comparable rates for all large firms (exporting manufacturers) with over U.S.$20 million in exports. This is not the result of any significant LTC success but can be largely attributed to the LTCs' export specialization. The majority of Taiwanese firms with exports over U.S.$20 million are manufacturers focusing most of their energies on manufacturing and placing little emphasis on exports.

[21]This section draws on *Economic News*, 6/18/79, 10/29/79, 6/8/81, 12/6/82; BOFT.

Collins's export success has been bolstered by its secure source of man-ufactures for export. Unlike most of the other LTCs, which were con-stantly searching for suppliers, Collins in 1981 had over 500 manufacturers serving as exclusive suppliers; Collins intended to ex-change stock with them in order to "cement relations." Collins also uti-lized its LTC privilege of guaranteeing loans to these small and medium-sized manufacturers and set up a leasing firm in 1981 to handle these responsibilities. In order to maintain the quality and competitiveness of its products, Collins instructs the manufacturers on new product designs and technologies. These suppliers are classified into three categories, ac-cording to the quality and punctual delivery of their products, and com-mission rates are set accordingly.

One final factor that has contributed to Collins's relative success has been its ability to train and maintain qualified personnel. As of 1982, Collins was spending 10 percent of its total revenue on personnel training and was planning to introduce an employee stock ownership program. In summary, elements leading to Collins's relative success included an exist-ing market share at time of designation, trading experience, an estab-lished subsidiary in its primary export market, a group of exclusive suppliers, and the ability to train and maintain experienced personnel.

### E-Hsin International

Like Collins, E-Hsin International began as a trading company several years before its designation as an LTC.[22] Its track record, however, has been much more mercurial. E-Hsin received much attention and govern-ment praise for its record-breaking performances as the top exporting LTC in 1982, with U.S.$104 million in exports, and as the largest ex-porter overall in 1985, with U.S.$263 million in exports. In 1986, how-ever, its exports plummeted to U.S.$118 million, and they have gained little ground since that time. But because E-Hsin has been the second most successful LTC, and because the apparent reasons for its growth differ somewhat from those we have attributed to Collins, its case is worth examining more closely.

E-Hsin International was established in 1973 as a member of the Pacific Electric Cable guanxiqiye. Its primary function was the import of com-modity feed grains to supply another group member,[23] Chia Hsin Live-

---

[22]This section draws on *Economic News*, 6/9/80, 6/8/81, 12/6/82, 7/25/83, 9/29/86, 12/22/86; BOFT; CCIS, 1985.

[23]Access to these commodity imports indicates that this Mainlander (Shanghai) business group had close ties with the government, which monopolized virtually all commodity grain imports. Government willingness to sponsor and subsidize the 1977 Hualon merger, involv-ing Hsin-hsin Fiber, another member of the Pacific Electric Cable group, is another indica-tion of these close ties.

stock Corporation, also established that year. When Weng Mingchang, the founder of the group, died in 1977, the group split into three new groups: Pacific Electric Cable, China Rebar, and E-Hsin. Weng's oldest son, Weng Daming, took over the E-Hsin group, with E-Hsin International as its flagship. Other group members include Hualon Corporation (the result of a 1977 merger of five textile manufacturers, and now one of Taiwan's leading textile firms), Kuo Hua Life Insurance, China Stock and Investment, and several others.[24]

In 1983 the E-Hsin group (now known as the Hualon group) ranked twelfth among all guanxiqiye in Taiwan in terms of sales and had climbed to sixth place by 1988, a position it still held in 1991. E-Hsin's affiliated enterprises provided significant support to E-Hsin International after its designation as an LTC in 1980. E-Hsin International registered only U.S.$3.2 million in exports in 1979 but improved this figure to U.S.$35.8 million in 1980, an increase of over 1,000 percent. Similarly, exports totaled just over U.S.$100 million for each of the recessionary years of 1982–84, then leaped to U.S.$263 million in 1985, an annual growth rate of 150 percent.

This ability to expand exports rapidly can be attributed largely to E-Hsin's access to captive suppliers. The four major manufacturers of the E-Hsin group turned much of their foreign trade over to E-Hsin International, and as of 1986, these four supplied 70 percent of its exports. Approximately one hundred contracted local manufacturers supplied the other 30 percent and were required to specialize in production (coordinated by E-Hsin to avoid excessive competition) and to obtain their raw materials and machinery from E-Hsin. E-Hsin provided credit guarantees to these smaller manufacturers and invested in many of them directly through its group investment and trust companies.

Like Collins, E-Hsin's relative success must also be attributed in part to the positive incentives it gave to its employees. In 1980, E-Hsin adopted a "sector profit system" in which each department of the LTC was made operationally independent and responsible for its own profits and losses. In the words of Weng Daming, the system "is designed to increase employee devotion to the company and all bonuses and promotions are based on it. The system also means that the employee is supposed to look out for the common interest and to share in the company's profit."[25] This program allowed E-Hsin to retain experienced personnel and gave the

[24]Other stockholders in E-Hsin International include Walsin Lihwa Electric and Wire Cable (a member of the E-Hsin group's parent group, Pacific Electric Wire and Cable), Hsin Chu Glass, All Sincere Industries, Overseas Chinese Commercial Bank, United World Chinese Commercial Bank, City Bank of Taipei, and a number of smaller companies (CCIS, 1985; *Economic News*, 6/9/80).

[25]*Economic News*, 6/9/80.

employees a vested interest in maintaining the profitability and competitiveness of their departments. E-Hsin also has been somewhat more successful than the other LTCs in diversifying its markets, with the United States accounting for 35 percent of its sales, Asia for 32 percent, the Middle East for 14 percent, and Europe for 12 percent in 1986.

From this brief profile several factors leading to E-Hsin's ability to expand exports become apparent. Though the government did not encourage the guanxiqiye to participate in the LTC program, E-Hsin International took advantage of its dual position as an established trading company and the flagship of a large business group to launch its LTC enterprise. This group support gave E-Hsin a large and, more important, captive supplier base as well as financial support and managerial and trading expertise. Also like Collins, E-Hsin was able to maintain personnel loyalty, which, as demonstrated in the following section, was a major obstacle hampering the LTCs' development. Finally, though it has not yet been a major factor, E-Hsin's success in diversifying its export market should prove to be a valuable asset in this era of rising protectionism and volatile exchange rates.

This section has demonstrated the inability of Taiwan's LTCs to achieve a stature comparable with either their rivals in Korea or their model in Japan. Although the focus has been primarily on their record in terms of export volume and market share, the failure of all but two of the LTCs and the marginal success of the two remaining made them a feeble tool by which to obtain any of the objectives assigned to them.

### Why the LTCs Failed

When a program is successful, most participants readily accept credit for the success. When plans fail, blame is not as readily acknowledged and is often difficult to trace. In the case of the LTC program, however, a near consensus seems to have emerged concerning where to lay the blame for the failure. A 1979 editorial likened the situation of the already struggling LTC program to that of a swimming instructor and a novice swimmer entering the water for the first time. The swimmer, brought into the water by the instructors' guiding hand, instinctively seeks help from the instructor when the water gets too deep. The editorial concludes: "It is up to the instructor whether he allows the beginner to flounder, in the hope he will begin a swimming motion, or goes to the rescue. In Taiwan, the recently established large trading companies are finding themselves floundering in spite of the government's enthusiastic backing at the time of their inception."[26]

[26] *Economic News*, 10/29/79.

An executive of Pan International interviewed three years later was less subtle. He complained: "We hope the government here will follow the example of the Korean government [in providing genuine incentives]; otherwise, the term 'Large Trading Company' will become a joke in Taiwan."[27] These concerns were echoed by other LTC executives, who assumed that government enthusiasm at the time of the program's inception would be reflected in the offering of substantial incentives to the participants. The vice president of Nanlien argued that under Taiwan's present conditions, the "privileges offered are of little significance."[28] Another executive, lamenting his decision to participate in the government-sponsored program, moaned: "We pulled the wool over our own eyes."[29]

These complaints were more than sour grapes. Most observers concurred that the government was not doing what was necessary for the program to succeed. One prominent economist concluded that for the government to achieve its purpose of developing the LTC, it "must not only require certain things, but must also at the same time give the LTC adequate encouragement and support."[30] A sogo shosha executive, assessing the situation of the LTCs during a visit to Taiwan in 1983, argued that the government must "take the initiative in intensifying the functions of the local trade organizations."[31] Finally, even government officials acknowledged where the burden lay. Assessing the situation one year after the inception of the LTC program, the general manager of a government trading organization admitted: "The current local situation is entirely adverse to the establishment of big trading companies. Their success will entirely depend upon government assistance."[32]

Why, then, was government assistance not forthcoming in sufficient amounts to overcome the obstacles embedded in this particular environment? In the case of Taiwan's LTCs, the magnitude of the obstacles standing in the way of a large trading company as envisioned by its architects makes these obstacles worthy of investigation. We first turn to these economic, social, and policy impediments, and then conclude with an explanation for the unwillingness of policymakers to provide the compliance mechanisms necessary to overcome them.

## OBSTACLES

The major economic factor obstructing the development of the LTCs was the formidable competition they faced in carving out a share of Tai-

[27] *Economic News*, 12/6/82.
[28] *Economic News*, 10/29/79.
[29] *Economic News*, 4/30/79.
[30] X. Chen, 1980, p. 128.
[31] *Economic News*, 6/6/83.
[32] *Economic News*, 10/29/79.

wan's export and import trade. Their competitors included the Japanese sogo shosha, American and European mass buyers, local manufacturers handling their own trade, government enterprises and monopoly traders, trade associations, and the some 40,000 local small and medium-sized trading companies. Each of these had carved out its own trade niche, and none was prepared to give up its market share to the new trading concerns.

The Japanese sogo shosha, the most formidable of these competitors, were the government's primary target for displacement. In contrast to its diplomatic ties with Korea, which were normalized in 1965, Japan concluded a peace treaty with the Nationalist regime on Taiwan in 1952. Therefore, while Japanese business was effectively banned from Korea for over fifteen years, there was little interruption in the economic relations between Taiwan and Japan. Throughout the 1950s and 1960s, as a result of positive incentives from Taiwan's government, Taiwan remained the most popular country for Japanese manufacturing investment, and the sogo shosha were the predominant link in these commercial ties.[33] It was estimated in 1982 that the nine Japanese GTC controlled over 50 percent of Taiwan's foreign trade.[34]

As in Japan, the sogo shosha have close and long-standing ties with thousands of small and medium-sized local manufacturers. Using their advantages of scale, organization, financial backing, and worldwide distribution and information networks, they have been able to offer prices and services and to take risks that the other trading concerns (including the LTCs) find unacceptable. The manager of a sewing machine company noted in 1979: "If the new big trading companies [LTCs] can help us maintain steady supplies of imported pig iron at reasonable prices, we would be more than happy to switch to them. But to my knowledge, it is going to be almost impossible for them to beat the price of our present Japanese suppliers."[35]

In addition to handling exports and imports for the local firms, the sogo shosha provide financial assistance. They extend loans to the local firms for imported raw materials and allow deferred payment for the costs of the imports. They also ask the local branches of Japanese banks to open lines of credit for the local manufacturers. These services, combined with years of managerial training, product information, and technical as-

[33]Ozawa, 1987.
[34]Accurate figures on the extent of the Japanese trading and investment presence are virtually impossible to obtain. Cho places the figure at 55 percent (D. S. Cho, 1987). Chen estimates their share at 40–50 percent (X. Chen, 1980). A 1979 account puts it at 60 percent (*Economic News*, 6/18/79). One tax officer in Taiwan estimated that the annual sales for each of the nine GTC branch offices in Taiwan averaged over U.S.$1 billion in 1985, even though the figures in their respective books showed only U.S.$1–$2 million (*Economic News*, 11/4/85).
[35]*Economic News*, 4/30/79.

sistance, have bound these local suppliers to the Japanese traders to such an extent that "a separation at this point would be unthinkable."[36]

This Japanese dominance has concerned Taiwan's government, which views the sogo shosha as the major instruments of Taiwan's chronic and increasing trade deficit with Japan. This deficit was, in fact, one of the primary motives for establishing the LTCs. The state in Taiwan has been "particularly energetic in trying to get the marketing of all exports into Taiwanese hands because both bureaucrats and businessmen alike are sensitive to the inroads in overseas marketing made by large Japanese trading companies."[37] But in the absence of early restrictions against the Japanese traders and the lack of genuine local competitors, it is not surprising that the LTCs and their state sponsors, unlike their Korean counterparts, have had difficulty supplanting the sogo shosha-supplier ties.

These long-standing commercial linkages, profitable to both the Japanese and the thousands of manufacturers they service, will not easily be severed. An executive from Nanlien International complained that efforts to attract the suppliers away were met with only token interest: "They only pay lip service to our proposals. . . . Although they also give us quotations to be offered to foreign buyers, we have discovered when checking later, that the quotations are often higher than those they give their Japanese partners."[38] In fact, if current trends continue, Japanese commercial dominance in Taiwan will likely increase. In 1981, when it was estimated that the nine sogo shosha were responsible for approximately 55 percent of Taiwan's foreign trade, Japan had only U.S.$64 million worth of officially approved direct foreign investment (DFI) in Taiwan, compared with American investments of U.S.$203 million. On the heels of a rising yen, the (official) value of Japanese DFI in Taiwan had increased to U.S.$263 million by 1986, compared with U.S.$138 million for the United States.[39] this 300 percent increase in investment, much of which is handled or facilitated by the sogo shosha, can only strengthen their already dominant position in the Taiwan market.

Although they do not rival the sogo shosha, American and European mass buyers control a significant share of Taiwan's trade. Estimates have placed this figure at approximately 10 percent of the nation's total trade.[40] Competing on the basis of low prices and extreme flexibility in changing product lines, Taiwan's multitude of small and medium-sized manufacturers have succeeded for many years in attracting large retailers

[36]*Economic News*, 4/30/79.
[37]Amsden, 1979, p. 365.
[38]*Economic News*, 10/29/79.
[39]CETDC, 1988; *Asian Wall Street Journal*, 6/8/87.
[40]Diyi Yinhang; X. Chen, 1980.

to set up purchasing offices in Taipei. These mass buyers include such American companies as K-Mart, Sears, JC Penney, and Woolworth.[41]

Like the sogo shosha, these retailers maintain a very low profile in Taiwan relative to the volume of their purchases. K-Mart, for example, estimated in 1981 to be "possibly the largest single market for Taiwan's consumer products," had a local staff of less than sixty persons that year. These staff members were primarily inspectors and merchandise specialists scouting out new products. The actual purchasing was done by K-Mart buyers who came to Taiwan twice a year.[42] In some cases, the transactions were even easier for the buyers. Gold notes the experience of a Canadian clothing buyer who found that "as soon as word spread of his arrival in Taipei, company representatives flocked to his hotel room vying for business and undercutting each other. He never had to leave the hotel to complete his assignment."[43]

During the often rancorous U.S.-Taiwan trade negotiations, Taiwan's officials accurately point out that although Taiwan consistently runs a substantial trade surplus with the United States, as much as three-fourths of its exports to the United States bear American brand names. A French trade officer in Taiwan noted the same phenomenon, arguing that "you really can't consider Taiwan an exporting nation. Taiwan is simply a collection of international subcontractors serving the American market."[44] The competitiveness of these original export market products in terms of both price and quality, and the flexibility of the producers, have made the local manufacturers very attractive to foreign buyers. Accordingly, they are not likely to surrender their 10 percent share of the market to the LTCs or any other middlemen. Moreover, while there is no love lost between Taiwan's government and the Japanese sogo shosha, Taiwan's huge surplus with the United States has made the state in Taiwan much more hesitant to assist local LTCs in displacing the American retailers as exporters.

Rather than rely on foreign traders or buyers to handle their products, many of Taiwan's manufacturers do their own exporting. This is particularly true of large-scale manufacturers who typically create trading divisions within their own operations. These producer-exporters control approximately 10 percent of Taiwan's total trade,[45] and the largest among them are consistently Taiwan's top exporters. In 1987, the top four traders (measured in terms of U.S. dollar value of total exports and imports)

[41]*Asian Wall Street Journal*, 6/8/87; *Economic News*, 1/17/83.
[42]*Economic News*, 9/14/81.
[43]Gold, 1986, p. 82.
[44]*Asian Wall Street Journal*, 6/8/87.
[45]X. Chen, 1980.

were locally owned manufacturers affiliated with guanxiqiye.[46] According to the Board of Trade, none of the top twenty traders that year was a specialized trading company or designated LTC: Collins ranked 21st, E-Hsin was 35th, Pan Overseas was 47th, Nanlien was 285th, and none of the other LTCs (or former LTCs) were in the top 500.[47]

The practice of "exporting what one produces" (zichan zixiao) is widespread among manufacturers that have accumulated the financial backing and marketing experience necessary to make it feasible to do so.[48] Although this unwillingness to specialize in production and leave the marketing to others is often attributed to cultural factors, much of it is the result of manufacturers' experience with local trading companies in the 1950s and 1960s. Exploiting the manufacturers' inexperience, these early traders often exacted commissions as high as 20 to 40 percent of the sales price.[49] This experience prompted many manufacturers to take the necessary steps to be able to handle their own exports. Given this history of abuse, and having invested much time and effort in gaining their independence, these firms understandably have been reluctant to surrender their exports to the LTCs. As the manager of a medium-sized stereo electronics company explained: "We handle almost all our exports ourselves now. It has taken us years of advertising and building up our image with foreign buyers to reach this point, and it's not likely we will hand over our export trade to any trading company—big or small."[50]

In addition to its being considered safer, there is evidence that manufacturers perceive direct exporting to be more profitable. In a 1985 survey of sixty-three electric goods manufacturers and forty-two textile manufacturers, Kung-mo Kuo determined that they deemed exporting through trading firms to be less profitable than handling the exports themselves.[51] This tendency is ingrained to the extent that even many of the manufacturers who became shareholders in the LTCs were unwilling to turn more than a fraction of their exports over to their own LTCs.

It is estimated that another 10 percent of Taiwan's total trade is shared by government trading institutions and state-sanctioned export associa-

[46]In descending order these top traders were Nan Ya Plastics, Tatung, Far Eastern Textile, and Formosa Plastics. Nan Ya Plastics and Formosa Plastics both belong to the Formosa Plastics group, Taiwan's largest (BOFT; CCIS, 1988).

[47]BOFT. In 1981, Collins ranked nineteenth, E-Hsin twentieth, Pan Overseas twenty-eighth, Nanlien forty-eighth, and Great International fiftieth (D. S. Cho, 1987).

[48]Though few Taiwan brand names are as well-known in the West as Japanese (or even several Korean) names, several Taiwan labels have made substantial inroads in the Western consumer market, including Pro-Kennex (tennis rackets), Giant (bicycles), Acer (personal computers), and Tatung and Sampo (consumer electronics) (Business Week, 7/22/85).

[49]Economic News, 4/30/79.

[50]Economic News, 4/30/79.

[51]K. M. Kuo.

tions.[52] Like the Korean state, the Nationalist Chinese government on Taiwan has only gradually loosened its near monopoly on the import of bulk commodities. As of 1980, the China Trade and Development Corporation and the trading arm of the Central Trust of China virtually monopolized the import of soybeans, and controlled three-fourths of all corn imports and one-third of all poultry feed.[53] Both institutions are largely owned by the state and have been under attack for their inefficient management and perennial losses. These trading concerns also handle virtually all of the state enterprises' imports and exports.[54] In addition, recent "Buy America" missions have involved a number of big ticket and large volume purchases that have been handled by government trading arms. Finally, several local trade associations monopolize the exports of profitable goods such as canned pineapple and asparagus, and metal products.[55]

Although estimates of the share held by each of these trading channels vary, the figures cited above are tallied in Table 7-3. If these estimates are even somewhat accurate, then less than one-fourth of Taiwan's total trade has been handled by local trading companies.[56] As of 1982, these trading companies included seven LTCs and some 30,000 small and medium-sized trading concerns.[57] By 1986, there were two LTCs and 40,000 trading companies, by one estimate twenty times the number of trading companies in Korea and four times the number in Japan.[58] Although the LTCs may have had some advantages in terms of scale and experience, the sheer volume of these smaller traders has meant that the battle for even this portion of the trade market would be one of "guerrilla warfare" (*youji zhan*).[59]

*Table 7-3.* Estimated traders' shares of Taiwan's total trade

| Trading concern | Share of trade |
| --- | --- |
| Japanese sogo shosha | 50 |
| American and European buyers | 10 |
| Local manufacturers | 10 |
| Government agencies and trade associations | 10 |
| All local trading companies | 20 |
| Total | 100 |

[52]X. Chen, 1980; Diyi Yinhang.
[53]X. Chen, 1980.
[54]*Journal of Commerce*, 12/26/86.
[55]X. Chen, 1980; D. S. Cho, 1987.
[56]Without supporting data, a 1990 *Economic News* (12/17/90) article claims that 3,000 small and medium-sized traders handled 65 percent of Taiwan's total trade in 1989.
[57]*Economic News*, 12/6/82.
[58]*Journal of Commerce*, 12/26/86.
[59]X. Chen, 1980.

A second economic obstacle concerns the unwillingness of guanxiqiye to lend genuine support to the LTCs. In his study of the LTCs, Kuo concludes that one of the three primary reasons for their failure was their inability to secure "even reasonable support" from the local business groups.[60] Although each of the LTCs was formed by a group of investors, these groups typically consisted of several small and medium-sized enterprises and trading companies, and the resultant "groups" were still severely limited in terms of scale, debt capacity, and experience when compared with their domestic and foreign rivals. With the exception of the E-Hsin group, the established guanxiqiye have shown little interest in the LTCs. The Tainan Spinning group (*Tainan bang*) sponsored the establishment of Nanlien International but turned virtually none of its manufactures over to Nanlien for export. In 1983, when the Tainan Textile group had total sales (both foreign and domestic) of nearly U.S.$9 billion, Nanlien International handled exports worth only U.S.$18.3 million.[61] In 1987, Nanlien was ranked 285th among traders, with imports and exports totaling U.S.$27.2 million. That same year, President Enterprise, a processed food manufacturer, and one of over thirty major companies associated with the Tainan group, was the forty-eighth top trader with over U.S.$100 million in combined exports and imports.[62]

The only other major guanxiqiye to participate in the establishment of an LTC was the We Sheng group, which owned a 35 percent share of Great International at the time of its designation as an LTC.[63] However, speculative investments by We Sheng led to mounting group debts and forced Great International into bankruptcy in 1983.[64] Table 7-2 indicates that Great International fared even less well than Nanlien.

There are several reasons for this absence of guanxiqiye support. First, most of the guanxiqiye's large member firms already have trading arms able, because of their size and experience, to operate with many of the same economic advantages of an LTC (though these manufacturers' trading divisions are clearly not in the league of either the Japanese or the Korean GTCs in terms of scale or diversification). This has allowed the manufacturers to eliminate the risks and expenses they have traditionally associated with commercial middlemen. Second, the strength of Taiwan's guanxiqiye has been in their manufacturing prowess, and as long as the profit margins and government incentives remain greater in manufactur-

[60]K. M. Kuo.

[61]CCIS, 1985; see also Table 7-2.

[62]CCIS, 1985; BOFT.

[63]D. S. Cho, 1987. I found two separate references to the participation of the Oemec group (*Haiwai gongye guanxi qiye*) in the formation of an LTC (X. Chen, 1980; *Economic News*) but was unable to link this group to any of the seven established LTCs.

[64]*Asian Wall Street Journal*, 3/30/83.

ing than in trade, these big manufacturers will likely continue to emphasize production. Third, and perhaps most telling in light of the Japanese and Korean cases (and for reasons as much political as economic), Taiwan's government has resisted the formation of close ties between the guanxiqiye and the LTCs. Dong-song Cho notes that the government sought to "avoid the concentration of wealth by creating the LTCs as entities independent of existing enterprise groups."[65] Xizhao Chen, in discussing the guanxiqiye's lack of participation, concurs: "Currently, those business groups with the ability to establish an LTC are already quite large. If they were to add an LTC, then some people (*bufen renshi*) fear it would lead to monopoly and thus oppose this."[66]

For these reasons—unlike their Japanese and Korean counterparts, for whom these group affiliations were crucial—the LTCs never gained the support of the guanxiqiye. Had these groups chosen (or been persuaded) to participate, evidence from the Japanese and Korean cases, as well as the experience of E-Hsin International, indicates they could have given the LTCs much-needed support in their fight for a share of the Taiwan trade market.

In addition to these economic obstacles, sociocultural influences hindered the growth of the LTCs. Chief among these has been the LTCs' inability to retain experienced personnel. To be effective, qualified trade personnel must have a certain knowledge of languages, trade procedures, and specific products and markets. These skills take years to attain, and once they have been attained, the employees possessing them have often been lured away by other trading companies or tempted by the prospects of starting their own businesses based on the clientele they cultivated while working for the LTC. In contrast, the Korean GTCs—as premier members of the chaebol—have been assured an ample supply of loyal, highly skilled managers and employees because of the greater pay, prestige, and opportunities for advancement within the GTCs and their affiliated groups. When employee defection occurs, the LTC loses both one of its most successful traders and some of its most profitable business. One trading company executive cited this as another reason why the guanxiqiye and banks have been more willing to invest in manufacturing than in trading: "Unlike trading, where the value lies in human capital, in manufacturing, technology and fixed capital are the most important inputs, and they can't defect."

This proclivity to defect from the group in order to succeed on one's own is a leitmotif of Chinese business culture. It is perhaps best expressed in the Chinese aphorism "It is better to be the beak of a chicken than the

[65]D. S. Cho, 1987, p. 60.
[66]X. Chen, 1980.

tail of an ox" (*ning wei jikou, bu wei niuhou*).[67] In a study of Chinese employees in large firms in Taiwan, Kung-mo Kuo and Shui-shen Liu concluded that employees tended to "emphasize 'self-realization' and seek power and responsibility in the business organization."[68] If this power and responsibility are not attainable within the firm, which is frequently the case if the employees are "outsiders," the employees often leave the company to start their own "spin-off" enterprises.[69]

This preference for "everyone wanting to be their own bosses" (*dajia dou yao dang laoban*) affects the organization of all sectors of Taiwan's economy but has been particularly devastating to the trading companies, which rely so heavily on the skills and experience of their personnel. It has clearly been an obstacle to the success of the LTCs and, along with the tendency of the manufacturers to want to market their own products, is another indication of the unwillingness of Chinese entrepreneurs to cooperate with or trust those not linked by well-defined familial or quasi-familial bonds.[70]

Not without some justification, this unwillingness is often attributed to a trait unique to, or at least typical of, the Chinese culture. *Business Week* notes that "unlike the Japanese, who work well in groups, Chinese prefer to be their own bosses, splitting off to form their own companies instead of building up someone else's."[71] An American attorney in Taiwan, acknowledging that Taiwan's government's efforts to push the LTC program had largely failed, concluded that "the government is recognizing that some things can be changed and some can't. There is a profound cultural difference between Taiwan and Korea." While there is obvious cultural variation between the Korean and Taiwanese cases, there is reason for caution in attributing the failure of Taiwan's LTCs simply to cultural differences. As described in Chapter Two, enterprises in Korea, including the chaebol-affiliated GTCs, also are tightly held familial concerns. In fact, the difference in defection rates may be more the result of exit options in Taiwan rather than loyalty on the part of Korean employees.[72]

---

[67]Academia Sinica's *Dictionary of the Chinese Language* (*Zhongwen da cidian*) traces the phrase back to Sima Qian's Han dynasty *Historical Record* (*Shiji*), which is dated ca. 100 B.C. The phrase is therefore at least 2,000 years old.

[68]As cited in K. M. Kuo, p. 170.

[69]Shieh.

[70]The Diyi Yinhang study cites four related cultural or "conceptual" obstacles to the development of the LTCs: (1) social values emphasizing the preference for owning one's own business; (2) rejection of the values of cooperation and the division of labor; (3) prevalence of family enterprises and the "concept of the clan" (*jiazu guannian*), which prevents the use of nonfamilial talents and the inculcation of modern management; and (4) a lack of "team spirit" (*tuandui jingshen*) (p. 13).

[71]*Business Week*, 7/22/85.

[72]Hirschman; Shieh.

The experience of the "relatively" successful LTCs, E-Hsin and Collins, also offers evidence that this desire to be one's own boss can be overcome by material incentives or creatively rechanneled in ways beneficial to the company. Both companies were able to largely overcome the problem of defecting personnel by increasing the wages and shareholdings of their employees. A former LTC employee contended that the main reason personnel left the trading companies was low wages. He argued that the company "requires too much of its workers and rewards them too little. Demands are high, while the salary was absolutely insufficient to keep qualified and experienced personnel on the job."[73] Under E-Hsin's "profit center system," wages and bonuses were tied to an individual's performance and the employees were, in the words of one observer, "practically the bosses of the company."[74]

A final set of obstacles must be included. At the same time the government was fostering the development of the LTCs, it was perpetuating or tolerating several explicit constraints on their growth. I have already discussed the government's monopolization of bulk commodity imports and access to government enterprise and agency trade, as well as the restrictions on the participation of the guanxiqiye. Three other policy restrictions have significantly influenced the fate of the LTCs.

The first concerns the establishment of foreign offices. Although the government required the establishment of three branch offices abroad as a criterion for LTC designation, the operations of these foreign branches were subject to strict statutory limits. Unlike subsidiaries set up in overseas markets (which the LTCs were not allowed to establish), these branch offices could serve only as liaison stations for contacting foreign customers. Moreover, the LTCs were allowed to have only three employees in each office and to remit only U.S.$5,000 to $7,000 per month to these offices each month. This remittance was hardly enough to cover employee wages, let alone contribute to the expansion of business.[75] Subsidiaries, on the other hand, were allowed to function independently, receive their own letters of credit, purchase raw materials, and engage in other important activities. One of the major reasons for Collins's relative success as an LTC was its ability to utilize its subsidiary in New York, established prior to its LTC designation. Although government concerns about capital flight may offer a partial explanation for these constraints on LTCs, the fact that manufacturers can establish subsidiaries abroad indicates that the government had specific concerns about the expansion of the LTCs.

---

[73] *Economic News*, 6/18/79.
[74] *Economic News*, 7/25/83.
[75] *Economic News*, 10/29/79, 12/6/82.

Government regulations regarding letters of credit and export licenses also constrained the LTCs. Although the LTCs were offered the incentive of duty-free importing of manufacturers' raw materials, regulations required them to obtain the manufacturers' letters of credit so as to guarantee that the imported materials were, in fact, destined for export. The manufacturers were generally unwilling to turn over these letters of credit because they were necessary in order for the manufacturers (1) to apply for loans from financial institutions and (2) to meet the minimum export requirement of U.S.$200,000 in order to retain their export licenses. These export licenses were necessary for the manufacturers to maintain their share of export quotas.[76] The government was unwilling to allow the LTCs to import without the letters of credit or to change the incentive structure for the manufacturers, and thus limited the value of one of the most significant concessions offered to the LTCs.

A final obstruction is the conservative nature of Taiwan's financial system, which, as discussed in Chapter Five, was until recently dominated by government-owned and government-controlled institutions. Despite the requirement that a commercial bank hold at least 10 percent of each LTC's shares, these banks have been very hesitant to offer significant support to the LTC ventures. They have become even less willing as the LTCs' fortunes have declined. Charters for fifteen new private banks were approved in 1991; Collins's application was one of four denied for either lack of diversification of ownership or "inadequate business plans."[77]

In addition, the LTCs, unlike the sogo shosha and Korean GTCs, are not allowed to reloan the money they borrow from local banks to their members or supplier manufacturers.[78] Some of the LTCs skirted this regulation by utilizing trust and leasing companies within their group of investors, but the capitalization and stability of these private institutions are much weaker than that of the banks. Finally, until 1987, the government controlled all foreign exchange, and the careful monitoring of foreign exchange's flow in and out of the country hindered the flexibility of the LTCs in their efforts to capitalize quickly on market opportunities.[79]

Although these governmental obstacles may have been as much sins of omission as of commission, and by themselves insufficient to prevent the development of viable LTCs, when they are added to the sociocultural and economic impediments noted above, the sum is formidable indeed. Moreover, because these policy obstacles originated at the state level, state policymakers were in a position to remove these impediments if they had

[76]*Economic News*, 6/8/81, 10/29/79; D. S. Cho, 1987.
[77]*Far Eastern Economic Review*, 7/11/91.
[78]*Economic News*, 12/6/86.
[79]Diyi Yinhang.

chosen to do so. The fact that they did not begs us to examine the politics behind this policymaking process.

### INCENTIVES

The preceding section outlined in some detail the significant obstacles standing in the way of the successful implementation of the government's LTC policy. The overcoming of these obstacles, it has been argued, would have required the government to provide a substantial number of compliance mechanisms. Two tasks remain. The first is to demonstrate that this supply of incentives and disincentives has in fact been low, and that a greater supply could have made a difference. The final task is to explain why the government did not institute more, or at least more effective, compliance mechanisms.

Assuming that the intention of Taiwan's state in initiating the LTC program was to establish viable LTCs that could have achieved some or all of the stated objectives, there is ample evidence that the supply of these compliance mechanisms was too low. This is true both in terms of domestic perceptions of what was needed and in comparison with what was offered to the Korean and Japanese GTCs. Virtually all observers called on the government to step up its efforts in a variety of ways. Over the years, LTC executives have requested the government to (1) allow the LTCs to set up subsidiaries in overseas markets; (2) extend duty-free import privileges to those goods imported by the LTCs but exported by the manufacturers themselves; (3) open the import business of bulk commodities to the more efficient private traders; (4) revise the export licensing system; and (5) provide a 25 percent ceiling on LTC corporate income taxes.[80]

Scholars and others have concurred that government efforts to date have been inadequate, and have called on the state to (1) limit the proliferation of the small and medium-sized traders by limiting incentives to firms with substantial minimum paid-in capital and exports; (2) give the LTCs monopoly rights to the import of bulk commodities; (3) relax restrictions on LTC applications for loans; (4) further reduce interest and tax rates for the LTCs during certain periods; (5) encourage the guanxiqiye and private financial institutions to invest and participate in the management of the LTCs; (6) encourage mergers between the well-established trading companies; (7) require the LTCs to go public; and (8) encourage the guanxiqiye to form LTCs from the export divisions of their existing operations.[81]

[80]*Economic News*, 10/29/79, 6/9/80, 6/8/81.
[81]X. Chen, 1980; *Economic News*, 4/30/79, 12/6/82, 6/6/83.

Not surprisingly, many of these suggestions are precisely the policies that were implemented in Korea and Japan and were significant factors in the success of their trading concerns. In fairness to the Taiwan policymakers, not all of these suggestions went unheeded. The 25 percent ceiling on corporate income tax enjoyed by manufacturers was extended to the LTCs in 1982, taxes on commission income were lifted, and certain stamp taxes have been reduced.[82] In addition, the import of many bulk commodities was liberalized in 1988.[83] But these adjustments fall far short of the suggestions noted above and have done little to alter the fate of the LTCs. In fact, all LTC incentives were terminated in 1991.[84]

Although it is impossible to prove that more compliance mechanisms could have made a difference, there is evidence that many of the obstacles discussed in the previous section were surmountable. The experiences of the "relatively" successful LTCs, E-Hsin and Collins, demonstrate what might have been necessary for the LTCs to succeed. E-Hsin's experience shows that links to a guanxiqiye with its captive suppliers have been a valuable asset in Taiwan, just as they are in Korea and Japan. Collins's ability to utilize an overseas subsidiary (as opposed to branch offices) offered another area in which the government could have given the LTCs a leg up, had it chosen to do so. There is also evidence from the cases of the Japanese sogo shosha and Korean GTCs that comparable government subsidies to and affiliations with large business groups could have done much to give the LTCs sufficient strength to adopt pricing, sourcing, and marketing strategies based on long-term market share instead of short-term profit. It was these kinds of subsidies and linkages for which the interested participants and observers in Taiwan called. Instead, Taiwan's government offered virtually no incentives and discouraged the participation of the guanxiqiye.

In Korea and Japan, lucrative commodity export business and government agency trade were reserved for the GTCs. In Taiwan, the LTCs were excluded from these activities. In Japan, the government openly winnowed out thousands of small and medium-sized trading companies and rationalized supplier networks. In Korea, massive subsidies in the form of concessionary loans were given to a handful of selected trading companies, allowing these oligopolists to price their competitors out of the market. In Taiwan, the incentive structure for all exporters—big or small, manufacturer or specialized trader—were virtually the same, and tax rates and concessionary loan programs actually favored manufacturers handling their own exports.

[82]*Economic News*, 2/8/82.
[83]*Economic News*, 7/9/88.
[84]*Free China Journal*, 2/4/91.

Why were the incentives not increased? To answer this question, it is necessary to examine the tensions and motivations behind the economic policy-making process in specific relation to the LTC policy. As discussed in Chapter Three, the Nationalist state has enjoyed a high degree of autonomy from Taiwanese society and has possessed the capacity to intervene in the society and restructure the economy through specific policies. This presence of a "strong" state does not, however, guarantee unified state purposes or preferences. As Dietrich Rueschmeyer and Peter Evans point out, the state is often an arena of social conflict in which policymakers, in spite of their interest in unified action, are often divided on substantive goals, may have different interests and ideologies, and may represent different social forces.[85] When divisiveness among the policy-making elite regarding a specific policy is substantial, it can hamper or even abort the effective formulation and implementation of the policy.

Despite the cloaked nature of policy-making in Taiwan, there is evidence that a high degree of conflict surrounded the formulation and implementation of the LTC policy. An executive of E-Hsin International confided: "We understand that many government officials are willing to offer more assistance to big trading companies [LTC] but that these officials are opposed by other factions within the government."[86] One of the architects of the LTC program, a high-ranking official in the Ministry of Economic Affairs (MOEA), explained that while the MOEA had tried to offer the LTCs greater incentives, these moves "did not receive broad support in government circles." In his 1985 study, Kuo similarly concludes that "sentiments towards the issues faced by the [LTCs] are mixed."[87] These statements indicate there are differences of opinion within policy-making circles regarding the role of the LTCs and the degree of state support they should receive. Although evidence is not yet available to link specific strategies and policy objectives with particular factions or individuals, it is possible to discuss some of the fundamental ideological and strategic tensions that informed this debate and the historical and institutional factors behind these tensions.

Chapter Three demonstrated how Sun Yat-sen's "Principle of People's Livelihood" has been an important norm in legitimating the autonomy and capacity of Taiwan's state. Although this vague ideology has lent flexibility to the parameters of the Nationalist state's policy responses, it also has broadened the range of opposing, yet ideologically justifiable, stances on particular issues. On no issue has this been more apparent than those concerning the scope and scale of private capital and the role of the state

[85] Rueschmeyer and Evans.
[86] *Economic News*, 6/9/80.
[87] K. M. Kuo, p. 162.

in its regulation. The policy proposing the fostering of large-scale private trading companies has been such a controversial policy. Observing the success of the GTCs in Japan and Korea, several policymakers advocated the fostering of a few large trading companies in Taiwan. They pointed out the value of scale economies and the synergies associated with vertical and horizontal integration and diversification.

Although it was difficult to deny the accomplishments of the Japanese and Korean GTCs, key political leaders and economic advisers resisted the proposal on several grounds. Perhaps the most fundamental grounds for this resistance were a historical disdain for commerce and fear of the growth of private capital. Chinese officialdom, based on Confucian social doctrine, has traditionally despised commerce and merchants as providing no benefit to society.[88] The gains of the early ride traders (*mishang*) were portrayed (often accurately) as ill-gotten and at the expense of the peasants. Victor Chang notes that these traditional values still persist in government circles: "Even now, an attitude of despising merchants is not unusual among civil servants. As a result, communication between the government officials and traders, which was once actually taboo, still remains culturally constrained." Because of this, government policies have favored manufacturers at the expense of traders. "Trading services, intangible in nature, have never been granted a status equal to manufacturing."[89]

The Nationalist Chinese experience in mainland China during the 1930s and 1940s reaffirmed this traditional perception of commercial exploitation and corruption in the minds of Nationalist leaders. Private capitalists and Nationalist bureaucrats amassed huge fortunes through collusion (*guanshang goujie*) and speculation, thereby hastening economic chaos, further undermining the legitimacy of the Nationalist regime, and contributing to its ultimate defeat by the Chinese Communists. Since its defeat on the Mainland and relocation to Taiwan, the Nationalist regime's developmental objective has been to strengthen Taiwan militarily and politically by fostering economic development under conditions of stability and relative equity. In pursuit of these goals, and bolstered both by their loss of the Mainland and by ideological justification (Confucian and Sun Yat-sen's), Nationalist political leaders in Taiwan placed restrictions on associations between government officials and pri-

[88]A former minister of economic affairs cited, as evidence that this attitude persists, the fact that prior to 1978, the government offered a multitude of incentives to manufacturers but none to specialized trading companies or leasing companies. He contrasted this attitude with that of the Japanese and Korean governments' perspective on trade and industry; international trade precedes industry in the title of their governments' ministries responsible for these activities.

[89]V. J. Chang, p. 76.

vate businessmen and have limited the growth of private capital. As a legacy of Sun Yat-sen's philosophy of economic concentration, "government policy has never been designed to favor the growth of big business. This is perhaps one of the most important reasons why it is difficult to create big enterprises such as LTCs in Taiwan."[90]

These tendencies were reinforced by the subethnic-based division of labor discussed in Chapter Three, which put virtually all political power in the hands of the minority Mainlanders and left the private sector open to the local Taiwanese majority. Fearing that Taiwanese economic power could be translated into political power, the state has relied on overt and covert means to limit the growth, and particularly the concentration, of private capital.

The Nationalist state has had other motives for resisting, or at least not facilitating, the concentration of wealth in the hands of a few large business groups and their affiliated trading companies, as was done in Korea and Japan. Learning from its defeat on the Mainland, and as an exogenous minority regime, the Nationalist state has sought legitimacy from neither a landed aristocracy nor a coterie of privileged capitalists, but from the multitude of petite bourgeoisie and smallholders its "growth with equity" policies have fostered. With small and medium-sized enterprises (firms with less than 300 employees) consistently employing more than 70 percent of the work force and producing more than 60 percent of the nation's exports, many policymakers have felt the state cannot afford, politically or economically, to use explicit discretionary compliance mechanisms that favor a few firms at the expense of the majority. The poor performance of the LTCs since their establishment has made it that much more difficult to offer remedial assistance under these conditions. As Cho points out: "Because Taiwanese LTCs have yet to contribute significantly to a quantitative expansion of exports, any special treatment for the LTCs could result in public criticism. Therefore, it is not surprising that policymakers [have chosen] not to extend new subsidies."[91]

Policymakers resisting the Japanese and Korean path received support from the increasingly influential laissez-faire-oriented bureaucrats and economic advisers trained in the West who contended that any kind of firm-level government intervention was inefficient and counterproductive.[92] Citing the instability and inflation that accompanied the fostering of the GTCs in Korea, they argued that trading companies should be allowed to develop naturally.[93] For the political leaders and policymakers

[90]V. J. Chang, p. 77.
[91]D. S. Cho, 1987, p. 63.
[92]Pang; A. Liu.
[93]X. Chen, 1980.

who had experienced the inflation and instability of the final years of Nationalist rule on the Chinese mainland, these were convincing arguments.

A final reason for policymakers' resistance to increased LTC incentives was institutional. As noted above, until very recently the import of bulk commodities and the imports and exports of state agencies had been virtually monopolized by government trading institutions. To have liberalized this substantial market (or given the private LTCs exclusive rights to it, as some suggested) would have greatly reduced the state institutions' share of the market or forced them out of business. Such a displacement of the state trading companies was likely resisted on the grounds that (1) those directly employed or otherwise affiliated with the institutions would lose their jobs; (2) the government would lose a lucrative source of income from the commodity imports; and (3) government control of these commodities and other products was vital to national security.

In order to allay these fears and overcome the significant resistance to the LTC program, the architects were forced to curtail the incentives and other compliance mechanisms, leave in place a number of obstacles inhibiting the participation of business groups, and greatly expand the anticipated objectives of the program. The incentives offered to the LTCs amounted to little more than those already given to manufacturers. Moreover, policy restrictions regarding foreign subsidiaries, export licenses, and financing actually put the LTCs at a disadvantage in relation to the manufacturers handling their own exports. As if this were not enough to doom the policy, its advocates found it necessary to enlarge the agenda of the program's potential achievements in order to garner support. In addition to expanding and diversifying exports, as Korea's GTCs were expected to do, the LTCs were supposed to displace foreign trading concerns, prevent overcompetition among local exporters, provide assistance to the small and medium-sized enterprises, avoid the concentration of wealth, and expand the scale of trade and manufacturing activities. The internally inconsistent nature of these policy goals is revealed in what Xizhao Chen refers to as the fundamental policy guiding the development of the LTCs: "developing the scale of enterprise while limiting private capital" (*jiezhi siren ziben, fazhan qiye guimo*).[94]

The result was the emergence of a vague policy with weak compliance mechanisms that was unable to achieve the lengthy list of conflicting goals, or even to overcome the significant obstacles preventing the LTCs from becoming viable exporters. Given the substantial obstacles, the fundamental conflict among policymakers, and the lack of genuine carrots and sticks, it is not surprising that the policy to develop large trading companies in Taiwan failed.

[94] X. Chen, 1980, p. 133.

It should be noted in conclusion that the primary purpose of juxtaposing Korea's success and Taiwan's failure to establish state-sponsored trading companies in these two chapters has been to understand the factors behind these different policy outcomes, not to judge their economic consequences. The policy outcomes in both Korea and Taiwan, and the distinctive environments that have shaped these outcomes, have entailed trade-offs. The Korean state's willingness to intervene in the market to foster the growth of the chaebol and establish large-scale trading companies, many contend, has come at the expense of market efficiency. Similarly, Taiwan's current industrial structure and trade regime, with their present division of labor, although unsettling to the advocates of the LTCs, continues to be remarkably successful in terms of export volume and profits.

As the embedded enterprise framework and case studies of this book have sought to establish, policy "successes," like the market's "invisible hand," do not always achieve optimal results, regardless how one chooses to measure them. Similarly, failed plans are not necessarily failures. Both, however, are valuable windows through which we can observe what has otherwise been a largely opaque policy-making process.

CHAPTER EIGHT

# *East Asia's Institutional Edge*

## THEORY: INSTITUTIONAL EMBEDDEDNESS

This book has analyzed the private business groups in the developmental states of Korea and Taiwan in terms of their organizational structure, relationship to the state, sources of finance, and trading networks. It has applied a theoretical framework of state-informed embeddedness to account for the groups' divergent developmental paths despite the strikingly similar nature and nurture of these two East Asian political economies.

In accounting for these differences, the case studies in this book demonstrate that any examination of these private business networks and their activities must give full weight to the political, cultural, and communal institutions that structure the groups' respective environments. Although the chaebol and guanxiqiye are both embedded in environments simultaneously structured by market incentives, interventionist state policies, and familial cultural norms, the historical circumstances, situational imperatives, and state ideologies shaping these forces vary substantially and account for the differences in enterprise organization.

Simply put, institutions matter. Although private entrepreneurs in Korea and Taiwan have obviously pursued profit-maximizing ventures in response to market opportunities, other motivations have modified or distorted "rational" action. All forms of human interaction—economic activity is no exception—are, by definition, enmeshed in social constructs that order them. These institutional constructs, whether formal or informal, temporary or more durable, order social life and give meaning to it. While utilitarian pursuit of self-interest (and deeply internalized cultural dictates) may propel individual human behavior, these atomistic impulses—both economic and cultural—are modified and constrained by ongoing social relations and the norms and rules governing them. In the real world, political duties and social obligations compete with and often override individual values or rational interests.

## PRACTICE: CASE STUDIES

If institutions do matter in explaining outcomes, which institutions are important in understanding the political economy of East Asian capitalist development and enterprise organization? Alice Amsden writes that "To understand variations in growth rates among late-industrializing countries, therefore, one must explore two key institutions: the reciprocity between big business and the state . . . and the internal and external behavior of the diversified business group."[1] This book has affirmed her assertion.

The chaebol and guanxiqiye are embedded in sociopolitical environments where duties and obligations to family and state (or machinations to feign compliance) exert great influence on the nature and outcome of economic activities. Market choices in these two political economies are significantly affected by social relations and cultural norms. Even more important has been the role of the state as an environmental factor in shaping, manipulating, and even creating economic institutions and organizations. Korea and Taiwan are similar to other late-developing states in that regime formation preceded industrialization, a situation giving these states unprecedented dominance over, and access to, their economies. But rather than developing as "predatory states" designed to plunder their economies, Korea and Taiwan, like their colonial mentor Japan, emerged as "developmental states" promoting economic growth. In making this distinction between predatory and developmental states, Peter Evans juxtaposes the "klepto-patrimonial" state of Zaire, characterized by "incoherent absolutist domination," with the East Asian developmental states, characterized by "embedded autonomy." This "embedded autonomy," he argues, "depends on the existence of a project shared by a highly developed bureaucratic apparatus with interventive capacity built on historical experience and a relatively organized set of private actors who can provide useful intelligence and a possibility of decentralized implementation."[2]

Chapters Two and Three document the striking degree of autonomy and capacity possessed by Korea's and Taiwan's developmental states.

[1]Amsden, 1989, pp. 150–51.
[2]Evans, 1989, p. 575.

From a position of sheer dominance and remarkable institutional capacity, the Park regime engineered Korea's export-oriented industrialization with the private chaebol as the chosen instruments to carry out this strategy. The chaebol quickly learned the virtues of complying with the state and the costs of noncompliance, and have thrived under state-proffered privileges and protection, developing as junior partners to the state. Although these mammoth combines typically bowed to government pressure when Confucian corporate culture (or rational risk assessment) clashed with regime goals, the social and political costs of this strategy, combined with an increasingly autonomous and politically powerful big business sector, has called into question the "junior" and "partner" aspects of the earlier symbiotic relationship.

Although Taiwan's Nationalist state has been at least as "strong" as the Korean state in terms of technocratic capacity and insulation from private capital, regime ideology, historical experience, and political necessity converged, thereby compelling the transplanted minority Nationalist state to adopt a developmental strategy and create political and economic institutions designed, above all, to promote economic stability and prevent the overconcentration of private capital. The combined effect of this absence of incentives and presence of constraints has been to restrict the scale, concentration, and influence of the guanxiqiye. This less aggressive policy has created an environment in which traditional sociocultural norms and institutions have exerted great influence in shaping the internal development and organization of Taiwan's groups and the guanxi networks among them. The state has not hesitated to intervene, however, when the expansion or other behavior of the groups has challenged regime goals of political control, economic stability, and relatively equitable income distribution.

Since the mid-1980s, economic liberalization and genuine democratization have taken root and begun to bloom in both countries, weakening the internal coherence and autonomy of these developmental states. Distributional coalitions are emerging alongside developmental pacts. However, powerful (and wealthy) business interests have become dominant players in these new liberal settings, creating institutional linkages to the state that undermine its capacity and will to curtail the economic expansion and political influence of the diversified groups.

Although specific market factors and historical and cultural differences have contributed to the very different natures of the chaebol and the guanxiqiye, the key factors have been the Korean state's proactive chaebol policies, and the lack of comparable promotion efforts and the presence of specific regime constraints on private capital in Taiwan. This becomes even more apparent as one examines the relationship between the state and the business groups in the financial and commercial systems.

Clearly understanding the advantages of controlling the purse strings, Korea's and Taiwan's capitalist developmental states dominated their respective financial systems with the intent of lending clout to industrial policies and influencing industrial organization in accordance with specific goals. In addition, the Confucian business cultures of Korea and Taiwan have shaped the nature and means of business group finance (often compensating for or circumventing the formal system), and hence the groups' scope, scale, and organization.

In fact, Chapters Four and Five demonstrate that formal and informal financial institutions and markets are quite similar in Korea and Taiwan. Both financial systems have been dominated by the state, even in the wake of liberalization efforts in Korea in the early 1980s and in Taiwan a decade later. Both systems depend on an extensive "curb" or informal financial market to supplement the formal one. Although group firms in Korea are much more leveraged than in Taiwan, corporate finance in both systems is debt-based, with the lion's share of business group equity tightly held by family and close associates. Banks still resemble pawnshops, and stock markets remain casinos with rapid turnovers of relatively few stocks.

Again, the key differences between these two cases lie in how the respective governments have manipulated financial institutions to achieve regime priorities and how the private owners and managers of the business groups exploit or circumvent these same institutions and policy incentive structures to achieve their private goals. Finance is the key nexus in the relationship between the business groups and the state, but the public and private objectives sought from the financial system have by no means always converged. Thus, it is necessary to move beyond the confines of atomistic rational choice and explore the specific environmental contexts that have shaped the business groups' financial activities.

In Korea, an intentional and gaping discrepancy between official interest rates and the real cost of credit (particularly during the high-growth 1970s) for the chosen chaebol created a dynamic of "public finance and private compliance" as the chaebol served as the productive means to the regime's developmental ends. Although public and private financial interests converged for much of the postwar era, these once compliant creations of the government are increasingly willing and able to express and act on their private interests, both economic and political. Financial capital is both the lifeline of the relationship and the battlefield of the struggle.

In Taiwan, the Nationalist regime's overriding motivation for creating and ruling over a repressive formal financial system has been to maintain price stability and prevent the concentration of private capital. At the same time, the state has condoned a flourishing informal market and given the private sector relatively wide latitude to pursue certain circumscribed legal financial activities and evade countless financial regulations. Under this dynamic of "public finance and private disregard," the owners and managers of the guanxiqiye have followed strategies designed to exploit this particular incentive structure within the parameters of an influential familial corporate culture. Constrained in their access to unfettered capital and eager to maintain connections with family members and close associates, the guanxiqiye have sought financing through a variety of formal, informal, and unconventional institutions.

The two chapters on the financing of the business groups conclude with the coincident collapse of Korea's sixth-largest and Taiwan's second-largest business groups during the lunar new year of 1985. Pundits at the time blamed these collapses on the poor financial structure of Asian family firms and the inability of these two highly leveraged groups to cope with the drop in inflation rates during the mid-1980s. The embedded enterprise framework of this book predicts, and the evidence from these two cases confirms, that while interest rates and cultural proclivities may have been necessary factors in the demise of these groups, they were not sufficient factors. These business groups fell because the developmental regimes in Korea and Taiwan chose that they fall. These two groups were shut down and parceled out as examples to their cohorts for political, not economic, reasons. These cases offer resounding evidence that no analysis of the environment in which the business groups of Korea and Taiwan are embedded can be complete without thorough, if not primary, analysis of the role of the state.

The final two chapters examine comparable efforts of commercial policy in Korea and Taiwan that had direct, but virtually opposite, consequences for the chaebol and the guanxiqiye. In the latter half of the 1970s, Korea's and Taiwan's governments launched their own versions of Japan's general trading companies. These chapters chronicle the largely successful efforts of Korea's state to foster the development of large-scale trading companies and the failed efforts of Taiwan's state to achieve the same objective. The analysis of these two cases not only illuminates the specific incentives and obstacles in these two environments, and their consequences for the business groups, but also reveals the factors influencing the fate of state-implemented industrial policies in general.

These case studies provide clear examples of state-imposed institutions whose establishment entailed economic risks and challenged both social and political norms and interests. In Korea, a regime politically dependent on rapid economic growth adopted a clear policy designed to foster general trading companies with the nearly singular goal of facilitating and increasing exports. The state promoted the policy by offering huge subsidies to a few favored chaebol-affiliated trading companies. These Korean trading concerns have established themselves as dominant channels in Korea's trade regime. In Taiwan, on the other hand, conflicting ideologies, goals, and strategies within policy-making circles concerning the concentration of private economic power led to the formulation of a large trading company policy with ambiguous objectives and clearly inadequate compliance mechanisms to overcome the economic, sociocultural, and political obstacles to successful implementation. Because of this, Taiwan's large trading companies have failed to achieve the anticipated profits and objectives of their private owners and public sponsors.

Markets and their organized participants do not, and cannot, exist apart from a nation's institutions and historical setting. In Korea and Taiwan, the dominant intervening influence has been the state; it has imposed institutional constraints, obligations, and incentives on the respective economies for various reasons and with a variety of both intended and unintended consequences. As this book has demonstrated, it is precisely this variety of motives and outcomes that requires the analyst of these political economies to move beyond the comparable autonomy and capacity of these "strong states." One must examine the ideologies, motivations, and politics internal to each regime from which state strategies and policies, and the rationale and will to steward their implementation, emerge.

This is a difficult and imprecise task. Policy-making and the motivation of actors within any state apparatus, particularly an authoritarian one, can only be viewed "as through a glass darkly." The nearly hermetic status of these two states and their policy-making processes has made these regimes particularly impenetrable black boxes. Although several studies have shed valuable light on the politics and personalities of policy-making in Korea and Taiwan,[3] specific evidence is sorely lacking. This lack of evidence is not, however, justifiable cause for denying or "factoring out" the overwhelming impact of state policies on these two political economies.

In addition to state intervention, sociocultural norms and practices have profoundly shaped the evolution of these East Asian business groups. Peter Evans points out that market-oriented development in East Asia has been aided not just by formal institutions such as state industrial policy but also by dense networks of informal institutional linkages. Arguing that the role of formal or statist institutions in facilitating market transactions is particularly important in the "absence of sufficient infor-

---

[3]For Korea, see E. M. Kim, 1988, 1992; Woo; Amsden, 1989; Moon and Prasad. For Taiwan, see Gold, 1986; A. Liu; Pang; Noble; Arnold; Wade, 1990.

mal embeddedness," Evans feels that East Asia in general, and Korea and Taiwan in particular, seem to have been doubly blessed.[4] As the case studies of this book have shown, informal relationships of "trust," stemming from ongoing social relations, structure (and facilitate) market transactions and have been a particular factor in the success of the East Asian variant of capitalism. This combination of formal and informal institutional aids to the market have clearly given East Asia an institutional edge over its Western competitors.

Long considered monolithic by its intellectual and ideological proponents, capitalism has in the real world taken on a variety of forms reflecting its particular institutional setting. Unencumbered by the ideological albatross of neoclassical economics, which has proscribed state intervention in the market, and possessing a culture that promotes fictive and real familial trust as a means to reduce transaction costs, East Asia has paved the way for a revolutionary new form of capitalism. The labeling of this dynamic East Asian variant has become a growth industry. Those focusing on the role of the state and the formal institutions of East Asia's embedded capitalism have chosen modifiers such as "command," "soft-authoritarian," and "developmental." Those more concerned with informal institutional influences (as well as the marketability of alliteration) adopt terms such as "Confucian," "communal," "chopstick," "collaborationist," "alliance," "guanxi" and "sweet and sour." The point of this study is that both the statist and the sociocultural approaches are needed correctives for a sterile and inaccurate neoclassical economics perspective. All point to the structural interpenetration of market and nonmarket institutions and the developmental consequences.

The complexity of embedded capitalism does not excuse us from seeking complex answers, as some elegant models would prescribe. Editorials on the pages of venerable bastions of Western thought on both sides of the Atlantic—the *New York Times* and the *Financial Times*—deride the "economic correctness" that "dominates in universities, think tanks, government bureaus and international organizations."[5] In the *New York Times*, Amsden criticizes the "tyranny of this impeccably 'objective' paradigm" that champions free trade and rejects industrial policy and in which "reality became a market imperfection." In the *Financial Times*, Michael Prowse criticizes an economics profession that "worships mathematical technique but pays little attention to the behavioral and institutional forces at play in the real world—which is too messy to model with tidy equations. It has lost relevance by trying to pretend economics is

[4]Evans, 1992.
[5]Alice Amsden, "From P.C. to E.C.," *New York Times*, January 12, 1993, p. 11; Michael Prowse, "A Wake-up Call from Laura Tyson," *Financial Times*, January 18, 1993, p. 16.

a 'hard science' totally divorced from such related subjects as politics, psychology and sociology." Nonetheless, *The Economist* continues to warn of the dangers of "neo-interventionists" running amok. Meanwhile, these East Asian political economies continue to outperform their Western laissez-faire counterparts, not to mention other late-developing nations and mired in backward economies and wrongheaded policy prescriptions of lending institutions they depend upon. The essential factor in this East Asian success has been the institutional environment in which the economies and the business groups are embedded.

Neoclassical economics provides the wrong answers to issues of development, and it asks the wrong questions. Any successor to the neoclassical paradigm must be able to identify and comprehend complex combinations of social networks, their linkages to political power and bureaucracies, and how these compare and contrast in various settings. Evans concludes that any such successor "will certainly be 'institutionalist' in the sense of focusing on the consequences of historically robust patterns of social ties and interactions, crucially reinforced by norms and culture, both in and out of formal organizations."[6] He and others have identified an emerging comparative historical-institutional approach and labeled it a "new comparative political economy."[7]

This study has aspired to be one slender strand of support for this new comprehensive paradigm. However, with the virtues of such an institutional paradigm come its vices. Any such framework will never be as elegant or parsimonious as its neoclassical predecessor. Moreover, with ongoing social relations and malleable, if sticky, institutions as its independent variables, institutional analysis is fraught with the vicissitudes of dynamic change. This project, like any institutional approach, can only be a series of snapshots with tentative peeks into the future. This book has tried to capture both the dynamic evolution of formal and informal institutions in Korea and Taiwan, and their residual "stickiness" once they are in place.

Nowhere is this clash of institutional change and inertia more evident than in the efforts of the business groups to parlay their growing economic strength into political power. These efforts come at a time when authoritarianism appears to be giving way to genuine political pluralism in both Korea and Taiwan. As the Korean chapters have demonstrated, the chaebol have shifted from a position of subordinate compliance with the state to one of symbiotic cooperation and increasingly divergent economic and political interests. Former Hyundai chairman Chung Ju-yung's unsuccessful bid for the presidency in 1992 and his outspoken criticism

---

[6]Evans, 1993, p. 519.
[7]Evans and Stephens, 1988. See also Schneider.

of the regime during the campaign are graphic evidence of these changes. As chaebol dependence on the regime lessens, so have the developmental virtues and collusive vices of this relationship.

In Taiwan, the granting of commercial bank charters to interests representing the guanxiqiye heralds an unprecedented opportunity for these private business groups to expand their financial and economic strength at the expense of the Nationalist state. In the meantime, the dual processes of "Taiwanization" and democratization have greatly broadened access to the regime, with the predominantly Taiwanese capitalist class as chief benefactors. The electoral success of both Nationalist and opposition candidates representing business interests in Taiwan's elections in the 1990s, and Formosa Plastics' tycoon Wang Yongquing's ability to pursue controversial investments in both Taiwan and the Chinese mainland despite regime resistance, attest to these changes.

Although popular sentiment in both countries fears the expanding tentacles of these industrial behemoths, there is little evidence from either of these nations or others that democracy will curb the economic or political influence of the business groups. Economic and political liberalization will continue to strengthen the hand of private, familial capital in both regimes, with conservative coalition between big business and the state the likely outcome in both countries. Each political economy will, however, retain the unique imprint of its particular history and its social, cultural, and political institutions. Short-term convergence is not in the cards.

While these predictions—as well as this book's analysis—regarding the embedded business groups and their relationships with both the state and society are tentative, they are founded upon empirical evidence of enterprise organization in these two developmental states, not on ethereal assumptions. Assumptions, like institutions, matter. Man is not, as Thorstein Veblen wrote, "an isolated definitive datum in a stable equilibrium." Nor are enterprise networks.

# References

Aguilar, Francis J., and Dong-Sung Cho. 1989. "Daewoo Group." In Dong Ki Kim and Linsu Kim, eds., *Management behind Industrialization: Readings in Korean Business.* Seoul: Korea University Press.

Akerlof, George A. 1980. "A Theory of Social Custom, of Which Unemployment May Be One Consequence." *Quarterly Journal of Economics* 94 (June):749–75.

Alam, M. Shahid. 1989. "The South Korean 'Miracle': Examining the Mix of Government and Markets." *Journal of Developing Areas* 23 (January):233–58.

Amsden, Alice H. 1992. "A Theory of Government Intervention in Late Industrialization." In Louis Putterman and Dietrich Rueschmeyer, eds., *State and Market in Development: Synergy or Rivalry?* Boulder, Colo.: Lynne Reiner.

Amsden, Alice H. 1991. "Big Business and Urban Congestion in Taiwan: The Origins of Small Enterprise and Regionally Decentralized Industry (Respectively)." *World Development* 19 (September):1121–35.

Amsden, Alice H. 1989. *Asia's Next Giant: South Korea and Late Industrialization.* New York: Oxford University Press.

Amsden, Alice H. 1979. "Taiwan's Economic History: A Case of Etatisme and a Challenge to Dependency." *Modern China* 5 (July):341–80.

Amsden, Alice H., and Yoon-Dae Euh. 1993. "South Korea's 1980s Financial Reforms: Good-bye Financial Repression (Maybe), Hello New Institutional Restraints." *World Development* 21 (March):379–90.

Applebaum, Richard P., and Jeffrey Henderson, eds. 1992. *States and Development in the Asian Pacific Rim.* Newbury Park, Calif.: Sage.

Arnold, Walter. 1989. "Bureaucratic Politics, State Capacity, and Taiwan's Automobile Industrial Policy." *Modern China* 15 (April):178–214.

Bai Kanlun. 1986. "Zhongxinweixing gongchangzhidu yu zhongxiaoqiye jingying helihua" [The center-satellite manufacturing system and the rationalization of small and medium-sized enterprise management]. *Taiwan jingji yanjiu yuekan* [Taiwan economic research monthly] 9 (September):67–71.

Balazs, Etienne. 1974. *Chinese Civilization and Bureaucracy.* New Haven: Yale University Press.

"The Banking Law." 1959. *Industry of Free China* 11 (July):35–42.

Bates, Robert. 1993. "A Reply." *World Development* 21 (June):1077–81.

Bates, Robert. 1988. "Contra Contractarianism: Some Reflections on the New Institutionalism." *Politics and Society* 16 (June–September):387–401.

247

REFERENCES

Bello, Walden, and Stephanie Rosenfeld. 1990. *Dragons in Distress: Asia's Miracle Economies in Crisis*. San Francisco: Institute for Food and Development Policy.

Ben-Porath, Yoram. 1980. "The F-Connection: Families, Friends, and Firms and the Organization of Exchange." *Population and Development Review* 6 (March):1–31.

Biggs, Tyler. 1991. "Heterogeneous Firms and Efficient Financial Intermediation in Taiwan." In Michael Roemer and Christine Jones., eds., *Markets in Countries: Parallel, Fragmented and Black*. San Francisco: ICS Press.

Biggs, Tyler S., and Brian D. Levy. 1991. "Strategic Interventions and the Political Economy of Industrial Policy in Developing Countries." In Dwight H. Perkins and Michael Roemer, eds., *Reforming Economic Systems in Developing Countries*. Cambridge: Harvard University Press.

Board of Foreign Trade (BOFT). 1988. *Manufacturers and Traders of the Republic of China with Good Export-Import Record in 1987*. Taipei: Ministry of Economic Affairs, Board of Foreign Trade.

Bunge, Frederica M. 1981. *South Korea: A Country Study*. Washington, D.C.: American University Press.

Cai, Shuzi. 1985. "Jiazu qiye di chengzhang zhi tantao" [Analysis of the growth of family enterprise]. *Zhongguo kuaiji* [Chinese accountant] (Taipei) 32 (January):17–25.

Caldwell, J. Alexander. 1976. "The Financial System in Taiwan: Structure, Functions and Issues for the Future." *Asian Survey* 16 (August):729–51.

Castells, Manuel. 1992. "Four Asian Tigers with a Dragon Head." In Richard P. Applebaum and Jeffrey Henderson, eds., *States and Development in the Asian Pacific Rim*. Newbury Park, Calif.: Sage.

Chang, C. C. 1979. "ROC Fiscal Policy and Development Financing." *Industry of Free China* 52 (December):2–8.

Chang, Chan-Sup. 1988. "Chaebol: The South Korean Conglomerates." *Business Horizons* 31 (March–April):51–57.

Chang, David W. 1965. "U.S. Aid and Economic Progress in Taiwan." *Asian Survey* 5 (March):152–60.

Chang, Felix S. Y. 1970. "China Development Corporation in Ten Years." *Industry of Free China* 33 (January):2–8.

Chang, Kia-ngau. 1958. *The Inflationary Spiral: The Experience in China, 1939–1950*. Cambridge: Technology Press of Massachusetts Institute of Technology.

Chang, Sea Jin, and Unghwan Choi. 1988. "Strategy, Structure, and Performance of Korean Business Groups: A Transactions Cost Approach." *Journal of Industrial Economics* 37 (December):141–58.

Chang, Sidney H., and Leonard H. D. Gordon. 1991. *All under Heaven: Sun Yat-sen and His Revolutionary Thought*. Stanford: Hoover Institution Press.

Chang, Victor J. 1987. "Big Trading Companies in the Republic of China." In Terutomo Ozawa, ed., *Role of General Trading Firms in Trade and Development*. Tokyo: Asian Productivity Organization.

Chen, Chinan. 1986. *Hunyin, jiazu yu shehui* [Marriage, family and society]. Taipei: Yunchen.

Chen, Claire. 1987. "A Lackluster Market Expects Rejuvenation with Far-Reaching Structural Changes" and "Financial Crises Reflect Management and Regulation Difficulties." In Kenneth Liu, ed., *Financial & Investment Yearbook*. Taipei: Central Economic News Service.

Chen Mingzhang. 1983. "Daqiye yu zhongxiaoqiye hezuojingying zhi dao" [Co-operative management of large enterprises and small- and medium-sized enterprises]. *Qiye yinhang jikan* [Enterprise bank quarterly] 7 (October):53–65.

Chen, Mu-tsai. 1990. "The Financial System and Financial Policy in the Republic of China." *Economic Review* (Taipei) 7 (July–August):1–19.

Chen, Xizhao. 1980. "Lun wo guo fazhan damaoyishangde celue" [Discussion on the strategy for the development of Taiwan's large trading companies]. *Shehui Kexue Lunye* [Essays on social science] 28 (April):95–138.

Chen, Xizhao. 1976. "Taiwan dichu jituan qiye zhi yanjiu" [Research on Taiwan's business groups]. *Taiwan yinhang jikan* [Bank of Taiwan quarterly] 27 (Fall):59–78.

Cheng, Hang-sheng. 1986. "Financial Policy and Reform in Taiwan, China." In Hang-sheng Cheng, ed., *Financial Policy and Reform in Pacific Basin Countries.* Lexington, Mass.: Lexington Books.

Cheng, Tun-jen. 1990. "Political Regimes and Developmental Strategies: South Korea and Taiwan." In Gary Gereffi and Donald Wyman, eds., *Manufacturing Miracles: Paths of Industrialization in Latin America and East Asia.* Princeton: Princeton University Press.

Cheng, Tun-jen. 1989. "Democratizing the Quasi-Leninist Regime in Taiwan." *World Politics* 16 (July):471–99.

Cheng, Tun-jen, and Eun Mee Kim. 1994. "Making Democracy: The South Korean Case." In Edward Friedman, ed., *The Politics of Democratization: Vicissitudes and Universals in the East Asian Experience.* Boulder: Westview.

China Credit Information Service (CCIS). 1983, 1985, 1988, 1991. [Zhonghua Zhengxinso], comp. *Taiwan diqu jituan qiye yanjiu* [Business groups in Taiwan]. Taipei: China Credit Information Service.

China External Trade Development Council (CETDC). 1988, 1989, 1992. *Handy Economic and Trade Indicators.* Taipei: CETDC.

Cho, Dong-song. 1992. "From Subsidizer to Regulator: The Changing Role of Korean Government." *Long Range Planning* 25 (December):48–55.

Cho, Dong-song. 1987. *The General Trading Company: Concept and Strategy.* Lexington, Mass: Lexington Books.

Cho, Dong-song. 1984. "The Anatomy of the Korean General Trading Company." *Journal of Business Research* 12 (June):241–55.

Cho, Mun-boo. 1992. "Analyzing State Structure: Japan and South Korea in Comparative Perspective." *Pacific Focus* 7 (Fall):161–74.

Cho, Yoon Je. 1989. "The Financial Policy and Financial Sector Developments in Korea and Taiwan." In Jene Kwon, ed., *Korean Economic Development.* Westport, Conn.: Greenwood.

Choi, Ho-chin. 1970. "The Strengthening of the Economic Domination by Japanese Colonialism: 1932–45." *Korea Observer* 2 (July):50–69.

Choi, Jang-jip. 1987. "The Strong State and Weak Labor Relations in South Korea: The Historical Determinants and Bureaucratic Structure." In Kyong-Dong Kim, ed., *Dependency Issues in Korean Development.* Seoul: Seoul National University Press.

Chou, Tein-chou. 1986. "Aggregate Concentration Ratios and Business Groups in Taiwan." Paper presented at the National Taiwan University Institute of Economics Seminar, October 2.

Chow, Peter C. Y. 1990. "Output Effect, Technology Change, and Labor Absorption in Taiwan, 1952–1986." *Economic Development and Cultural Change* 39 (October):77–88.

Chu, Yun-han. 1994. "The Realignment of State-Business Relations and Regime Transition in Taiwan." In Andrew MacIntyre, ed., *Business and Government in Industrializing Asia.* Ithaca: Cornell University Press.

Chu, Yun-han. 1989. "State Structure and Economic Adjustment of the East Asian Newly Industrializing Countries." *International Organization* 43 (Autumn):647–72.

Chu, Zongshao. 1982. "Wo guo guanxi qiye zhi xiankuang fenxi ji qi yingyun zongxian zhi yanjiu" [Analysis of Taiwan's related enterprises' current situation and research on their operational synergy]. *Qiye yinhang jikan* [Enterprise bank quarterly] 6 (Fall):138–58.

Chuang, Richard Y. C. 1986. "The Legal Aspect of the Relationship of Enterprise Groups in Taiwan." Ph.D. dissertation, University of California at Berkeley.

Chung, Kae H., and Hak Chong Lee. 1989. "National Differences in Managerial Practices." In Kae H. Chung and Hak Chong Lee, eds., *Korean Managerial Dynamics.* New York: Praeger.

Clark, Cal, and Steve Chan. 1990. "The East Asian Developmental Model: Looking Beyond the Stereotypes." *International Studies Notes* 15 (Winter):1–3.

Clark, Rodney. 1979. *The Japanese Company.* New Haven: Yale University Press.

Clegg, Stewart R., and S. Gordon Redding. 1990. *Capitalism in Contrasting Cultures.* New York: Walter de Gruyter.

Coase, Ronald H. 1937. "The Nature of the Firm." *Economica* 16 (June):386–405.

Coble, Parks M., Jr. 1980. *The Shanghai Capitalists and the Nationalist Government.* Cambridge: Harvard University Press.

Cole, Allan B. 1967. "Political Roles of Taiwanese Entrepreneurs." *Asian Survey* 7 (September):645–54.

Cole, David C., and Yung Chul Park. 1983. *Financial Development in Korea, 1945–78.* Harvard East Asian Monographs, 106. Cambridge: Harvard University Press.

"The Control of Security Dealers in Taiwan." 1956. *Industry of Free China* 5 (April):40–42.

Cumings, Bruce. 1987. "The Origins and Development of the Northeast Asian Political Economy: Industrial Sectors, Product Cycles and Political Consequences." In Frederic Deyo, ed., *The Political Economy of the New Asian Industrialism.* Ithaca: Cornell University Press.

Deyo, Frederic, ed. 1987. *The Political Economy of the New Asian Industrialism.* Ithaca: Cornell University Press.

DiMaggio, Paul, and Walter W. Powell. 1983. "The Iron Cage Revisited: Institutional Isomorphism and Collective Rationality in Organizational Fields." *American Sociological Journal* 48 (April):147–60.

Diyi Yinhang [First National Bank]. 1979. *Woguo damaoyishang zhi chengli yu fazhan* [Establishment and development of Taiwan's large trading companies]. Taipei: First National Bank Credit Office.

Doner, Richard F. 1992. "Limits of State Strength: Toward an Institutionalist View of Economic Development." *World Politics* 44 (April):398–431.

Doner, Richard, Frederic Deyo, and Karl Fields. 1993. "Industrial Governance in East and Southeast Asia." Paper presented at the Social Science Research Council Workshop on Industrial Governance, New York City, September.

Eacoy, Grace. 1956. "The Establishment of a Stock Exchange in Taiwan." *Industry of Free China* 5 (April):1–7.

Eckert, Carter J. 1991. *Offspring of Empire: The Koch'ang Kims and the Colonial Origins of Korean Capitalism, 1876–1945.* Seattle: University of Washington Press.

Eckert, Carter J. 1990–91. "The South Korean Bourgeoisie: A Class in Search of Hegemony." *Journal of Korean Studies* 7 (November):115–48.

Emory, Robert F. 1984. "Postwar Financial Policies in Taiwan, China." Unpublished manuscript.

Evans, Peter B. 1993. "Book Review." *American Political Science Review* 87 (June):518–19.

Evans, Peter B. 1992. "The State as Problem and Solution: Predation, Embedded Autonomy and Structural Change." In Stephan Haggard and Robert Kaufman, eds., *The Politics of Economic Adjustment.* Princeton: Princeton University Press.

Evans, Peter B. 1989. "Predatory, Developmental and Other Apparatuses: A Comparative Political Economy Perspective on the Third World State." *Sociological Forum* 4 (December):561–86.

Evans, Peter B., Dietrich Rueschmeyer, and Theda Skocpol, eds. 1985. *Bringing the State Back In.* Cambridge: Cambridge University Press.

Evans, Peter B., and John D. Stephens. 1988. "Studying Development since the Sixties: The Emergence of a New Comparative Political Economy." *Theory and Society* 17, no. 5:713–45.

Fields, Karl J. 1993. "Symbiosis without Parasitosis: The Ecology of State-Big Business Relations in Korea and Taiwan." Paper presented at the workshop "The Role of Collaboration between Business and the State in Rapid Growth on the Periphery," Princeton, October.

Fields, Karl J. 1989. "Trading Companies in South Korea and Taiwan: Two Policy Approaches." *Asian Survey* 29 (November):1073–89.

Frieden, Jeffry A. 1989. "Social Science, Institutions, and the Analysis of Third World Experience." Paper presented at the annual meetings of the American Political Science Association, Atlanta, September.

Friedman, David. 1988. *The Misunderstood Miracle.* Ithaca: Cornell University Press.

Galenson, Walter, ed. 1979. *Economic Growth and Structural Change in Taiwan.* Ithaca: Cornell University Press.

Galli, Anton. 1980. *Taiwan: Economic Facts and Trends.* Munich: Weltforum Verlag.

Geertz, Clifford. 1978. "The Bazaar Economy: Information and Search in Peasant Marketing." *Economics and Anthropology* 68 (April):28–32.

"A General Review of the Economy of Taiwan in 1960." 1961. *Industry of Free China* 15 (June):27–31.

Gereffi, Gary. 1990. "Big Business and the State." In Gary Gereffi and Donald Wyman, eds., *Manufacturing Miracles: Paths of Industrialization in Latin America and East Asia.* Princeton: Princeton University Press.

Gerlach, Michael. 1992. *Alliance Capitalism: The Social Organization of Japanese Business.* Berkeley: University of California Press.

Gerlach, Michael. 1987. "Alliances and the Social Organization of Japanese Business." Ph.D. dissertation, Yale University.

Gerschenkron, Alexander. 1962. *Economic Backwardness in Historical Perspective.* Cambridge, Mass.: Belknap Press.

Gold, Thomas B. 1988. "Colonial Origins of Taiwanese Capitalism." In Edwin

REFERENCES

Winckler and Susan Greenhalgh, eds., *Contending Approaches to the Political Economy of Taiwan*. Armonk, N.Y.: M. E. Sharpe.

Gold, Thomas B. 1986. *State and Society in the Taiwan Miracle*. Armonk, N.Y.: M. E. Sharpe.

Gold, Thomas B. 1981. "Dependent Development in Taiwan." Ph.D. dissertation, Harvard University.

Grajdanzev, Andrew J. 1942. *Formosa Today*. New York: Institute of Pacific Relations.

Granovetter, Mark. 1994. "Business Groups." In Neil Smelser and Richard Swedberg, eds., *Handbook of Economic Sociology*. Princeton: Princeton University Press.

Granovetter, Mark. 1992. "Economic Institutions as Social Constructions: A Framework for Analysis." *Acta Sociologica* 35, no. 1:3–11.

Granovetter, Mark. 1990. "The Old and the New Economic Sociology: A History and an Agenda." In Roger Friedland and A. F. Robertson, eds., *Beyond the Marketplace: Rethinking Economy and Society*. New York: Aldine de Gruyter.

Granovetter, Mark. 1985. "Economic Action and Social Structure: A Theory of Embeddedness." *American Journal of Sociology* 91 (November):481–510.

Green, Andrew. 1993. "Creating Comparative Advantage in a Changing International System: The Development of the South Korean Automobile and Electronics Industry." Ph.D. dissertation, University of California at Berkeley.

Greenhalgh, Susan. 1988. "Families and Networks in Taiwan's Economic Development." In Edwin A. Winckler and Susan Greenhalgh, eds., *Contending Approaches to the Political Economy of Taiwan*. Armonk, N.Y.: M. E. Sharpe.

Gregor, A. James. 1981. *Ideology and Development: Sun Yat-sen and the Economic History of Taiwan*. Chinese Research Monograph 21. Berkeley: Institute of East Asian Studies.

Guo Pinhung. 1986. "Zhongwei tixi yu zhongxiaoqiye jingying helihua" [Center-satellite structure and the rationalization of small and medium-sized enterprise management]. *Taiwan jingji yanjiu yuekan* [Taiwan economic research monthly] 17 (September):34–44.

Haggard, Stephan. 1994. "Business, Politics and Policy in East and Southeast Asia." In Andrew MacIntyre, ed., *Business and Government in Industrializing Asia*. Ithaca: Cornell University Press.

Haggard, Stephan. 1990. *Pathways from the Periphery: The Politics of Growth in the Newly Industrializing Countries*. Ithaca: Cornell University Press.

Haggard, Stephan, and Tun-jen Cheng. 1987. "State and Foreign Capital in the East Asian NICs." In Frederic Deyo, ed., *The Political Economy of the New Asian Industrialism*. Ithaca: Cornell University Press.

Haggard, Stephan, and Chung-In Moon. 1990. "Institutions and Economic Policy: Theory and a Korean Case Study." *World Politics* 42 (January):210–37.

Hamilton, Clive. 1986. *Capitalist Industrialization in Korea*. Boulder, Colo.: Westview Press.

Hamilton, Gary. 1991. "The Organizational Foundations of Western and Chinese Commerce: A Historical and Comparative Analysis." In Gary Hamilton, ed., *Business Networks and Economic Development in East and Southeast Asia*. Hong Kong: Centre of Asian Studies, University of Hong Kong.

Hamilton, Gary, ed. 1991. *Business Networks and Economic Development in East and Southeast Asia*. Hong Kong: Centre of Asian Studies, University of Hong Kong Press.

252

Hamilton, Gary, and Nicole Woolsey Biggart. 1991. "The Organization of Business in Taiwan: Reply to Numazaki." *American Journal of Sociology* 96 (January):999–1006.

Hamilton, Gary G., and Nicole Woolsey Biggart. 1988. "Market, Culture, and Authority: A Comparative Analysis of Management and Organization in the Far East." *American Journal of Sociology* 94 (Supplement):52–94.

Hamilton, Gary, and Kao Cheng-shu. 1987. *The Industrial Foundations of Chinese Business: The Family Firm in Taiwan.* Program in East Asian Culture and Development, Working Paper series, no. 8. University of California at Davis: Institute of Governmental Affairs.

Hamilton, Gary G., and Marco Orru. 1989. "Organizational Structures of East Asian Companies." In Kae H. Chung and Hak Chong Lee, eds., *Korean Managerial Dynamics.* New York: Praeger.

Hamilton, Gary G., Marco Orru, and Nicole Woolsey Biggart. 1987. "Enterprise Groups in East Asia: An Organizational Analysis." *Shoken Keizai* [Financial economic review] 161 (September):78–106.

Hamilton, Gary G., William Zeile, and Wan-Jin Kim. 1988. *The Network Structures of East Asian Economies.* Program in East Asian Culture and Development, Working Paper series, no. 17. University of California at Davis: Institute of Governmental Affairs.

Hamilton, Nora, and Eun Mee Kim. 1993. "Economic and Political Liberalization in South Korea and Mexico." *Third World Quarterly* 14, no. 1:109–36.

*Handbook of Korea.* 1987. Seoul: Seoul International Publishing House.

Hattori, Tamio. 1989. "Japanese *Zaibatsu* and Korean *Chaebol.*" In Kae H. Chung and Hak Chong Lee, eds. *Korean Managerial Dynamics.* New York: Praeger.

Hattori, Tamio. 1984. "The Relationship between Zaibatsu and Family Structure: The Korean Case." In Shigeaki Yasuoka and Akio Okochi, eds., *Family Business in the Era of Industrial Growth.* Tokyo: University of Tokyo Press.

Henderson, Gregory. 1968. *Korea: The Politics of the Vortex.* Cambridge: Harvard University Press.

Hirschman, A. O. 1970. *Exit, Voice and Loyalty.* Cambridge: Harvard University Press.

Hirschmeier, Johannes, and Tsunehiko Yui. 1975. *The Development of Japanese Business.* London: George Allen and Unwin.

Ho, Samuel P. S. 1987. "Economics, Economic Bureaucracy, and Taiwan's Economic Development." *Pacific Affairs* 60 (Summer):226–47.

Hofheinz, Roy, and Kent Calder. 1982. *The Eastasia Edge.* New York: Basic Books.

Hong, Sung Gul. 1992. "The State and Sectoral Development: The Semiconductor Industries of Taiwan and South Korea." Paper presented at the annual meetings of the American Political Science Association, Chicago, September.

Hsu, P. Y. 1961. "Industrial Capital and Industrial Development." *Industry of Free China* 16 (October):2–6.

Hwang, Kwang-kuo. 1987. "Face and Favor: The Chinese Power Game." *American Journal of Sociology* 92 (January):944–74.

Hwang, Sue. 1987. "Venture Capital: Starting Small, Thinking Big." In Kenneth Liu, ed., *Financial & Investment Yearbook.* Taipei: Central Economic News Service.

Industrial Development and Investment Center. 1987. *Criteria for Big Trading Companies.* Taipei: Ministry of Economic Affairs.

REFERENCES

Ing, C. K. 1957. "A Proposed Solution to Exorbitant Interest Charged to Industries." *Industry of Free China* 8 (August):2–7.

Islam, Iyanatul. 1992. "Political Economy and East Asian Economic Development." *Asian-Pacific Economic Literature* 6 (November):69–101.

Jo, Sung-Hwan. 1991. "Promotion Measures for General Trading Companies." In Lee-Jay Cho and Yoon Hyung Kim, eds., *Economic Development in Korea: A Policy Perspective.* Honolulu: East-West Center.

Johnson, Chalmers. 1992. "Capitalism: East Asian Style." 1992 Panglaykim Memorial Lecture, Jakarta, December 15.

Johnson, Chalmers. 1988. "Studies of the Japanese Political Economy: A Crisis in Theory." Unpublished manuscript.

Johnson, Chalmers. 1987. "Political Institutions and Economic Performance: The Government-Business Relationship in Japan, South Korea and Taiwan." In Frederic Deyo, ed., *The Political Economy of the New Asian Industrialism.* Ithaca: Cornell University Press.

Johnson, Chalmers, ed. 1984. *The Industrial Policy Debate.* San Francisco: ICS Press.

Johnson, Chalmers. 1982. *MITI and the Japanese Miracle.* Stanford: Stanford University Press.

Johnson, Chalmers. 1981. "Introduction—The Taiwan Model." In James C. Hsiung, ed., *The Taiwan Experience, 1950–1980.* New York: Praeger.

Jones, Howard L. 1967. "Chinese Mutual Savings and Loan Clubs." *Journal of Business* 40 (July):336–38.

Jones, Leroy P. 1980. *Jae-bul and the Concentration of Economic Power in Korean Development: Issues, Evidence and Alternatives.* Consultant Paper Series no. 12. Seoul: Korean Development Institute.

Jones, Leroy, and Il Sakong. 1980. *Government, Business, and Entrepreneurship in Economic Development: The Korean Case.* Cambridge: Harvard University Press.

Jung, Ku-hyun. 1988. "Business-Government Relations in the Growth of Korean Business Groups." *Korean Social Science Journal* 14 (April):77–82.

Jung, Ku-hyun. 1984. "Trade Channel Evolution between Korea and the United States." In Karl Moskowitz, ed., *From Patron to Partner: The Development of US-Korean Business and Trade Relations.* Lexington, Mass.: Lexington Books.

Jung, Ku-hyun. 1983. "The Sogo Shosha: Can It Be Exported (Imported)?" In Michael R. Czinkota, ed., *Export Promotion: The Public and Private Sector Interaction.* New York: Praeger.

Kaufman-Winn, Jane. 1988. "Banks, Business and the State: The Taiwan Experience." Unpublished manuscript.

Kerr, George H. 1965. *Formosa Betrayed.* Boston: Houghton Mifflin.

Kim, Bun Woong. 1986. "An Assessment of Government Intervention in Korean Economic Development." *Korea Observer* 17 (Summer):149–60.

Kim, Dong Ki. 1989. "The Impact of Traditional Korean Values on Korean Patterns of Management." In Dong Ki Kim and Linsu Kim, eds., *Management behind Industrialization: Readings in Korean Business.* Seoul: Korea University Press.

Kim, Dong Ki, and Chong W. Kim. 1989. "Korean Value Systems and Managerial Practices." In Kae H. Chung and Hak Chong Lee, eds., *Korean Managerial Dynamics.* New York: Praeger.

Kim, Duk-Choong. 1987. "The Phenomenal Growth of GTFs in the Republic of Korea." In Terutomo Ozawa, ed., *Role of General Trading Firms in Trade and Development.* Tokyo: Asian Productivity Organization.

254

Kim, Duk-Choong. 1984. "The Anatomy of the Korean General Trading Company." *Journal of Business Research* 12 (June):241–55.

Kim, E. Han. 1989. "Financing Korean Corporations: Evidence and Theory." In Jene Kwon, ed., *Korean Economic Development*. Westport, Conn.: Greenwood.

Kim, Eun Mee. Forthcoming. *Big Business, Strong State: Collusion and Conflict in South Korean Development, 1960–1990*. Berkeley: University of California Press.

Kim, Eun Mee. 1992. "Contradictions and Limits of a Developmental State: With Illustrations from the South Korean Case." Unpublished manuscript.

Kim, Eun Mee. 1991. "The Industrial Organization and Growth of the Korean Chaebol: Integrating Development and Organizational Theory." In Gary Hamilton, ed., *Business Networks and Economic Development*. Hong Kong: Centre of Asian Studies, University of Hong Kong Press.

Kim, Eun Mee. 1989–90. "Foreign Capital in Korea's Economic Development, 1960–85." *Studies in International Development* 24 (Winter):24–45.

Kim, Eun Mee. 1988. "From Dominance to Symbiosis: State and Chaebol in Korea." *Pacific Focus* 3 (Fall):105–21.

Kim, Hee-Nam. 1988. "The Insurance Industry in Korea." *Monthly Review* (Korea Exchange Bank) 22 (October):3–22.

Kim, Il-Hwan. 1990. "Stock Market in Korea." *Monthly Review* (Korea Exchange Bank) 24 (March):3–11.

Kim, Jay S., and Chan K. Hahn. 1989. "The Korean Chaebol as an Organizational Form." In Kae H. Chung and Hak Chong Lee, eds., *Korean Managerial Dynamics*. New York: Praeger.

Kim, Kyong-Dong. 1976. "Political Factors in the Formation of the Entrepreneurial Elite in South Korea." *Asian Survey* 16 (May):465–77.

Kim, Kyong-Dong, and On-Jook Lee. 1987. "Educational Background of the Korean Elite: The Influence of the United States and Japan." In Kyong-Dong Kim, ed., *Dependency Issues in Korean Development*. Seoul: Seoul National University Press.

Kim, Mahn-Kee. 1983. "Administrative Culture of Korea: A Comparison with China and Japan." *Korean Social Science Journal* 10 (April):116–33.

Kingjing. 1965. "The Economy-Controlling System of Nationalist Government." *Independent Formosa* 4 (Spring):5–18.

Ko, Seung-kyun. 1971. "Korean-Japanese Relations Since the 1965 Normalization Pacts." *Korea Observer* 3 (July):62–75.

Kohsaka, Akira. 1987. "Financial Liberalization in Asian NICs: A Comparative Study of Korea and Taiwan in the 1980s." *Developing Economies* 25 (November):325–45.

Koo, Bohn-young. 1986. "The Role of the Government in Korea's Industrial Development." In Kyu-uck Lee, ed., *Industrial Development Policies and Issues*. Seoul: Korean Development Institute.

Koo, Bon-Ho and Tae-won Kwack. 1988. "Korea's Economic Development Strategy." Paper presented at Foundation for Advanced Information and Research Conference, Tokyo, April 20–22.

Koo, Hagen, and Eun Mee Kim. 1992. "The Developmental State and Capital Accumulation in South Korea." In Richard P. Applebaum and Jeffrey Henderson, eds., *States and Development in the Asian Pacific Rim*. Newbury Park, Calif.: Sage.

REFERENCES

Korea Foreign Trade Association (KFTA). 1992. *Major Statistics of Korean Economy, 1992.* Seoul: Korea Foreign Trade Association.

Korean Traders Association (KOTRA). 1986. *Major Statistics of Korean Economy, 1986.* Seoul: Korean Traders Association.

Krasner, Stephen D. 1984. "Approaches to the State: Alternative Conceptions and Historical Dynamics." *Comparative Politics* 16 (January):223–46.

Kuo, Kung-mo. 1985. "The Role of and the Issues Faced by the Large Trading Firms in the Republic of China." In *Industrial Policies of the Republic of Korea and the Republic of China.* Papers and Discussions from the Joint Korea Development Institute/Chunghua Institute for Economic Research 1985 Conference. Conference Series 86-01. Taipei: Chunghua Institute for Economic Research.

Kuo, Kuo-shao. 1969. "A Survey of the Financial Position and Operating Results of Some Principal Private Enterprises in Taiwan." *Industry of Free China* 32 (December):27–42.

Kwack, Sung Yeung. 1986. "The Economic Development of the Republic of Korea, 1965–1981." In Lawrence J. Lau, ed., *Models of Development: A Comparative Study of Economic Growth in South Korea and Taiwan.* San Francisco: ICS Press.

Kwack, Sung Yeung, and Un Chan Chung. 1986. "The Role of Financial Policies and Institutions in Korea's Economic Development Process." In Hang-sheng Cheng, ed. *Financial Policy and Reform in Pacific Basin Countries.* Lexington, Mass.: Lexington Books.

Kwack, Tae-won. 1986. "Industrial Restructuring Experience and Policies in Korea in the 1970s." In Kyu-uck Lee, ed., *Industrial Development Policies and Issues.* Seoul: Korean Development Institute.

Kwon, Il-Min. 1990. "Bond Market in Korea." *Monthly Review* (Korea Exchange Bank) 24 (February):3–13.

Lam, Danny K. K. 1990. "Independent Economic Sectors and Economic Growth in Hong Kong and Taiwan." *International Studies Notes* 15 (Winter):28–34.

Landa, Janet T. 1981. "A Theory of the Ethnically Homogeneous Middleman Group: An Institutional Alternative to Contract Law." *Journal of Legal Studies* 10 (June):349–62.

Lau, Lawrence J., ed. 1986. *Models of Development: A Comparative Study of Economic Growth in South Korea and Taiwan.* San Francisco: Institute for Contemporary Studies Press.

Lee, Chang-Kyu. 1986. "Financial Reform Experiences in Korea." In Hang-sheng Cheng, ed., *Financial Policy and Reform in Pacific Basin Countries.* Lexington, Mass.: Lexington Books.

Lee, Chong-Sik. 1985. *Japan and Korea: The Political Dimension.* Stanford: Hoover Institution Press.

Lee, Chung H. 1992. "The Government, Financial System and Large Private Enterprises in the Economic Development of South Korea." *World Development* 20 (February):187–97.

Lee, Hak Chong. 1989. "Managerial Characteristics of Korean Firms." In Kae H. Chung and Hak Chong Lee, eds., *Korean Managerial Dynamics.* New York: Praeger.

Lee, Kyu-uck. 1986. "The Concentration of Economic Power in Korea: Causes, Consequences and Policy." In Kyu-uck Lee, ed., *Industrial Development Policies and Issues.* Seoul: Korean Development Institute.

Lee, Kyu-uck, Shujiro Urata, and Inbom Choi. 1986. *Recent Development in Indus-*

*trial Organizational Issues in Korea.* Working Paper 8609. Seoul: Korean Development Institute.

Lee, Kyung-tae. 1991. "Policy Measures to Reduce Industrial Concentration and Concentration of Economic Power." In Lee-Jay Cho and Yoon Hyung Kim, eds. *Economic Development in the Republic of Korea: A Policy Perspective.* Honolulu: East-West Center.

Lee, Sang M. 1989. "Management Styles of Korean Chaebols." In Kae H. Chung and Hak Chong Lee, eds., *Korean Managerial Dynamics.* New York: Praeger.

Lee, Sheng-Yi. 1990. *Money and Finance in the Economic Development of Taiwan.* New York: St. Martin's Press.

Lee, Sung-Soo. 1987. "Korea's General Trading Companies." *Monthly Review* (Korea Exchange Bank) 21 (July):3–19.

Lee, Tong Hun, and Sil Han. 1990. "On Measuring the Relative Size of the Unregulated Money Market over Time." *Journal of Development Economics* 33 (July):53–65.

Lee, Won-Young. 1987. *Direct Foreign Investment in Korea: Pattern, Impacts, and Government Policy.* Working Paper 8706. Seoul: Korea Development Institute.

Lee, Young-ki. 1985. "Conglomeration and Business Concentration: The Korean Case." In *Industrial Policies of the Republic of Korea and the Republic of China.* Papers and Discussion from the Joint Korea Development Institute/Chunghua Institute of Economic Research 1985 Conference. Conference Series 86-01. Taipei: Chunghua Institute for Economic Research.

Leff, Nathaniel H. 1986. "Trust, Envy and the Political Economy of Industrial Development: Economic Groups in Developing Countries." Unpublished manuscript, Columbia Business School.

Leff, Nathaniel H. 1978. "Industrial Organization and Entrepreneurship in the Developing Countries: The Economic Groups." *Economic Development and Cultural Change* 26 (July):661–76.

Leipziger, Danny M. 1988. "Industrial Restructuring in Korea." *World Development* 16 (January):121–35.

Lerman, Arthur J. 1977. "National Elite and Local Politicians in Taiwan." *American Political Science Review* 71 (December):1406–22.

Levy, Brian. 1991. "Transactions Costs, the Size of Firms and Industrial Policy: Lessons from a Comparative Case Study of the Footwear Industry in Korea and Taiwan." *Journal of Development Economics* 34 (November):151–78.

Levy, Brian. 1988. "Korean and Taiwanese Firms as International Competitors: The Challenges Ahead." *Columbia Journal of World Business* 23 (Spring):43–51.

Levy, Brian. 1987. "Causes and Consequences of the Bias Towards Large Firms in the Republic of Korea: Lessons from the Footwear Industry." Unpublished manuscript.

Levy, Brian, and Wen-Jeng Kuo. 1991. "The Strategic Orientations of Firms and the Performance of Korea and Taiwan in Frontier Industries: Lessons from Comparative Case Studies of Keyboard and Personal Computer Assembly." *World Development* 19 (March):363–74.

Levy, Brian, and Wen-Jeng Kuo. 1987. *Investment Requirements and the Participation of Korean and Taiwanese Firms in Technology-Intensive Industries.* Working Paper 8718. Seoul: Korean Development Institute.

Li, Judy. 1987. "Forex, Idle Money Prompt Overdue Changes in Taiwan Money

Market." In Kenneth Liu, ed., *Financial & Investment Yearbook.* Taipei: Central Economic News Service.

Li, K. T. 1976. *The Experience of Dynamic Economic Growth in Taiwan.* Taipei: Mei Ya.

Li, K. T. 1974. "The Role of Fiscal Policy in Economic Development." *Industry of Free China* 41 (April):8–17.

Li, K. T. 1972. "Financing Economic Development of the Republic of China." *Industry of Free China* 38 (December):2–10.

Li, K. T. 1960. "The Growth of Private Industry in Free China." *Industry of Free China* 13 (January):11–19.

Liang, Ching-ing Hou. 1966. "On the Sources of Loanable Funds in Taiwan: 1951–1961." *Industry of Free China* 25 (March):30–42.

Liang, Ching-ing Hou, and Michael T. Skully. 1982. "Financial Institutions and Markets in Taiwan." In Michael T. Skully, ed., *Financial Institutions and Markets in the Far East.* New York: St. Martin's Press.

Liang, Kuo-shu. 1986. "Financial Reforms Recommended by the Economic Reform Committee, Republic of China." *Industry of Free China* 65 (March):7–12.

Lijphart, Arend. 1971. "Comparative Politics and the Comparative Method." *American Political Science Review* 65 (September):682–93.

Lim, Ung-Ki, 1982. "Capital Structure Decisions of Korean Firms in Relation to Their Corporate Ownership Structure and Other Key Variables." *Social Science Journal* (Seoul) 9 (January):121–42.

Lim, Young-Il. 1981. *Government Policy and Private Enterprise: Korean Experience in Industrialization.* Korea Research Monograph no. 6. Berkeley: Institute of East Asian Studies.

Lin, Zhihong. 1980. "Guanxi qiye yu jingying zongxiao" [Related enterprises and business synergy]. *Xiandai guanliyuekan* [Modern management monthly] 7 (May):10–15.

Lincoln, James R. 1988. "Japanese Organization and Organization Theory." In Barry M. Staw and L. L. Cummings, eds., *Research in Organizational Behavior,* vol. 12 Greenwich, Conn.: JAI Press.

Little, Ian M. D. 1979. "An Economic Reconnaissance." In Walter Galenson, ed., *Economic Growth and Structural Change in Taiwan.* Ithaca: Cornell University Press.

Liu, Alan P. L. 1987. *Phoenix and the Lame Lion: Modernization in Taiwan and Mainland China, 1950–1980.* Stanford: Hoover Institution Press.

Liu, Shuishen, Kuo Kunmo, Huang Junying, and Situ Daxian. 1981. "Taiwan dichu guanxi qiye zhi xingcheng, yingyun yuqi yingxiang" [The formation, operations and influence of Taiwan's related enterprises]. *Qiye yinhang jikan* [Enterprise bank quarterly] 4 (Fall):5–19, and 5 (Winter):5–23.

Lorch, Klaus, and Tyler Biggs. 1989. "Growing in the Interstices: The Limits of Government Promotion of Small Industries." Paper presented at the annual meeting of the Association for Asian Studies, Washington, D.C.

Lundberg, Erik. 1979. "Fiscal and Monetary Policies." In Walter Galenson, ed., *Economic Growth and Structural Change in Taiwan.* Ithaca: Cornell University Press.

McElderry, Andrea. 1986. "Confucian Capitalism? Corporate Values in Republican Banking." *Modern China* 12 (July):401–16.

McKinnon, Ronald I. 1986. "Financial Liberalization and Economic Development." In Hang-Sheng Cheng ed., *Financial Policy and Reform in Pacific Basin Countries.* Lexington, Mass.: Lexington Books.

McNamara, Dennis L. 1990. *The Colonial Origins of Korean Enterprise, 1910–1945.* Cambridge: Cambridge University Press.

McNamara, Dennis L. 1988. "Entrepreneurship in Colonial Korea: Kim Yon-su." *Modern Asian Studies* 22 (February):165–77.

Mann, Michael. 1986. "The Autonomous Power of the State: Its Origins, Mechanisms and Results." In John A. Hall, ed., *States in History.* Oxford: Basil Blackwell.

March, James G., and Johan P. Olsen. 1984. "The New Institutionalism: Organizational Factors in Political Life." *American Political Science Review* 78 (September):734–49.

Mardon, Russell. 1989. "The Emergence of a Little Tiger: The State and Industrial Transformation in the Republic of Korea." Unpublished manuscript.

Mark, Lindy Li. 1982. "Heffalumpus Taiwanius: A Profile of 67 Taiwanese Entrepreneurs of the 1950s." Paper presented at Conference on Chinese Entrepreneurship, Cornell University, September.

Mark, Lindy Li. 1972. "Taiwanese Lineage Enterprises: A Study of Familial Entrepreneurship." Ph.D. dissertation, University of California at Berkeley.

Marshall, Byron K. 1967. *Capitalism and Nationalism in Pre-war Japan.* Stanford: Stanford University Press.

Mason, Edward, et al., eds. 1981. *Studies in the Modernization of the Republic of Korea: 1979–81.* Cambridge: Harvard University Press.

Meeng, M. M. 1967. "Some Aspects of Financing Small- and Medium-Sized Industries in Taiwan." *Industry of Free China* 27 (May):2–15.

Metzger, Tom. 1970. "The State and Commerce in Imperial China." *Asian and African Studies* 6:23–46.

Meyer, John, W. R. Scott, and T. E. Deal. 1981. "Institutional and Technical Sources of Environmental Structure." In H. D. Stein, ed., *Organization and the Human Services.* Philadelphia: Temple University Press.

Mody, Ashoka. 1990. "Institutions and Dynamic Comparative Advantage: The Electronics Industry in South Korea and Taiwan." *Cambridge Journal of Economics* 14 (September):291–314.

Mody, Ashoka. 1985. "Recent Evolution of Microelectronics in South Korea and Taiwan: An Institutional Approach to Comparative Advantage." Unpublished manuscript.

Moon, Chung-in. 1994. "Changing Patterns of Business-State Relations in South Korea." In Andrew MacIntyre, ed., *Business and Government in Industrializing Asia.* Ithaca: Cornell University Press.

Moon, Chung-in. 1990. "Beyond Statism: Rethinking the Political Economy of Growth in South Korea." *International Studies Notes* 15 (Winter):24–27.

Moon, Chung-in, and Rashemi Prasad. 1993. "Beyond the Developmental State: Institutions, Networks and Politics." Paper presented at American Political Science Association meetings, Washington, D.C., September.

Moskowitz, Karl. 1989. "Ownership and Management of Korean Firms." In Kae H. Chung and Hak Chong Lee, eds., *Korean Managerial Dynamics.* New York: Praeger.

Mutual Security Mission to China. 1956. *Economic Development on Taiwan, 1951–55.* Taipei: ICA Mutual Security Mission to China.

REFERENCES

Myers, Ramon. 1986. "Economic Development in Taiwan." In Lawrence J. Lao, ed., *Models of Development: A Comparative Study of Economic Growth in South Korea and Taiwan.* San Francisco: ICS Press.

Myhrman, Johan. 1989. "The New Institutional Economics and the Process of Development." *Journal of Institutional and Theoretical Economics* 145 (March):38–59.

Nabli, Mustapha K., and Jeffrey Nugent. 1989. "The New Institutional Economics and Its Applicability to Development." *World Development* 17 (September):1333–47.

Nam, Sang-woo, and Yung-chul Park. 1982. "Financial Institutions and Markets in South Korea." In Michael T. Skully, ed., *Financial Institutions and Markets in the Far East.* New York: St. Martin's Press.

Noble, Gregory W. 1987. "Contending Forces in Taiwan's Economic Policymaking: The Case of Hua Tung Heavy Trucks." *Asian Survey* 27 (June):683–704.

North, Douglass C. 1989. "Comments." In Joseph E. Stiglitz, *The Economic Role of the State.* Oxford: Basil Blackwell.

North, Douglass C. 1984. "Government and the Cost of Exchange in History." *Journal of Economic History* 44 (June):255–64.

North, Douglass. C. 1981. *Structure and Change in Economic History.* New York: W. W. Norton.

Numazaki, Ichiro. 1991. "The Role of Personal Networks in the Making of Taiwan's *Guanxiqiye* (Related Enterprises)." In Gary Hamilton, ed., *Business Networks and Economic Development in East and Southeast Asia.* Hong Kong: Centre of Chinese Studies, University of Hong Kong.

Numazaki, Ichiro. 1987. "Comments on 'Enterprise Groups in East Asia' by Hamilton, Orru and Biggart." *Shoken Keizai* [Financial economic review] 162 (December):15–23.

Numazaki, Ichiro. 1986. "Networks of Taiwanese Big Business." *Modern China* 12 (October):487–534.

Onis, Ziya. 1992. "Organization of Export-Oriented Industrialization: The Turkish Foreign Trade Companies in a Comparative Perspective." In Teufik Nas and Mehmet Odekon, eds., *Economics and Politics of Turkish Liberalization.* London: Associated Universities Press.

Onis, Ziya. 1991. "The Logic of the Developmental State." *Comparative Politics* 24 (October):109–21.

Orru, Marco, Nicole Woolsey Biggart, and Gary G. Hamilton. 1991. "Organizational Isomorphism in East Asia: Broadening the New Institutionalism." In Walter W. Powell and Paul DiMaggio, eds., *The New Institutionalism in Organizational Analysis.* Chicago: University of Chicago Press.

Ozawa, Terutomo. 1987. "Japan's Sogo Shosha: Current Problems and Future Prospects." In Terutomo Ozawa, ed., *Role of General Trading Firms in Trade and Development.* Tokyo: Asian Productivity Organization.

Ozawa, Terutomo. 1979. *Multinationalism, Japanese Style: The Political Economy of Outward Dependency.* Princeton: Princeton University Press.

Pang, Chien-kuo. 1988. "The State and Economic Transformation: The Taiwan Case." Ph.D. dissertation, Brown University.

Park, Chong-Hee. 1962. *Our Nation's Path: Ideology for Social Reconstruction.* Seoul: Dong-A.

Peters, Pauline. 1993. "Is 'Rational Choice' the Best Choice for Robert Bates? An

Anthropologist's Reading of Bates' Work." *World Development* 21 (June):1063–76.

Polyani, Karl. 1957. *The Great Transformation.* Boston: Beacon Press.

Powell, Walter W., and Paul J. DiMaggio. 1991. "Introduction." In Walter W. Powell and Paul DiMaggio, eds., *The New Institutionalism in Organizational Analysis.* Chicago: University of Chicago Press.

Pye, Lucian W. 1985. *Asian Power and Politics: The Cultural Dimensions of Authority.* Cambridge, Mass.: Belknap Press.

Qiu Jingbo and Ruifan Shen. 1983. "Woguo minying qiye zijin choucuo zhi fenxi" [Analysis of the capital financing of Taiwan's private enterprises]. *Taiwan yinhang qikan* [Bank of Taiwan quarterly] 17 (July):121–34.

Redding, S. G. 1990. *The Spirit of Chinese Capitalism.* Berlin: De Gruyter.

Regnier, Philippe. 1990. "Small and Medium-Sized Enterprises and Industrialization in South Korea." Paper presented at the Association for Asian Studies annual meeting, Chicago.

Republic of China, Ministry of Economic Affairs, Industrial Development Bureau. 1987. *Zhongxinweixing Gongchangzhidu Tuidongxiaozu* [Center-satellite production system promotion team]. Pamphlet. Taipei: Industrial Development Bureau.

Republic of China, Ministry of Economic Affairs, Industrial Development Bureau. 1983. "Guidelines for Establishing the Principal/Satellite Manufacturing System under Governmental Assistance." Mimeo. (internal English translation). Taipei.

Roh, Choong-Hwan. 1990. "Korean Corporate Financing." *Monthly Review* (Korea Exchange Bank) 24 (April):3–13.

Roh, Choong-Hwan. 1989. "The Money Market Development in Korea." *Monthly Review* (Korea Exchange Bank) 23 (December):3–15.

Rowley, Anthony. 1987. *Asian Stockmarkets: The Inside Story.* Hong Kong: Far Eastern Economic Review.

Roxas, Sixto K. 1965. "Institution-Building for Financing Industrial Development." *Industry of Free China* 23 (May):18–36.

Rueschmeyer, Dietrich, and Peter B. Evans. 1985. "The State and Economic Transformation: Toward an Analysis of the Conditions Underlying Effective Intervention." In Peter B. Evans, Dietrich Rueschmeyer, and Theda Skocpol, eds., *Bringing the State Back In.* Cambridge: Cambridge University Press.

Sakong, Il. 1993. *Korea in the World Economy.* Washington, D.C.: Institute for International Economics.

Samuels, Richard J. 1987. *The Business of the Japanese State.* Ithaca: Cornell University Press.

Sasamoto, Takeharu. 1968. "A Salient Feature of Capital Accumulation in Taiwan: The System of Rice Collection by the Taiwan Provincial Food Bureau." *Developing Economies* 6 (March):27–39.

Schneider, Ben Ross. 1993. "The Elusive Embrace: Synergy between Business and the State in Developing Countries." Paper presented at the workshop "Role of Collaboration between Business and the State in Rapid Growth on the Periphery," Princeton University, October.

Scitovsky, Tibor. 1986. "Economic Development in Taiwan and South Korea, 1965–1981." In Lawrence J. Lau, ed., *Models of Development: A Comparative Study of Economic Growth in South Korea and Taiwan.* San Francisco: ICS Press.

Scott, James. 1976. *The Moral Economy of the Peasant.* New Haven: Yale University Press.

Seckler, David. 1975. *Thorstein Veblen and the Institutionalists.* London: Macmillan.

Securities and Exchange Commission. 1987. *1986 SEC Statistics*, vol. 17. Taipei: Ministry of Finance.

Shen, Pe-ling. 1987. "Only a Healthy Market Can Guarantee Progress." In Kenneth Liu, ed., *Financial & Investment Yearbook.* Taipei: Central Economic News Service.

Shieh, Gwo-Shyong. 1992. *"Boss" Island: The Subcontracting Network and Micro-Entrepreneurship in Taiwan's Development.* New York: Peter Lang.

Shih, Chien-Sheng. 1968. "Recent Development in Public Finance in Taiwan." *Industry of Free China* 30 (August):227.

Shin, Eui-Hang, and Seung-Kwon Chin. 1989. "Social Affinity among Top Managerial Executives of Large Corporations in Korea." *Sociological Forum* 4 (March):3–26.

Shin, Joon-Sang. 1988. "Recent Changes of Corporate Financing in Korea." *Monthly Review* (Korea Exchange Bank) 22 (February):3–17.

Shin, Roy W. 1991. "The Role of Industrial Policy Agents: A Study of Korean Intermediate Organization as a Policy Network." *Pacific Focus* 6 (Fall):49–64.

Silin, Robert H. 1976. *Leadership and Values.* Cambridge: Harvard University Press.

Sim, Pyong-Gu. 1979. "International Comparison of Capital Formation in Korean Businesses and Improvement Measures." *Social Science Journal* (Seoul) 6 (January):121–42.

Simon, Herbert. 1961. *Administrative Behavior.* New York: Macmillan.

Skocpol, Theda. 1985. "Bringing the State Back In: Strategies of Analysis in Current Research." In Peter B. Evans, Dietrich Rueschmeyer, and Theda Skocpol, eds., *Bringing the State Back In.* Cambridge: Cambridge University Press.

Skully, Michael T., and George Viksnins. 1986. *Financing East Asia's Success* New York: St. Martin's Press.

Small Business Integrated Assistance Center. 1986. *Financial and Management Services to Small/Medium Businesses, 1986 Annual Report.* Taipei: Ministry of Economic Affairs.

Smith, Adam. 1962. *Wealth of Nations.* New York: E. P. Dutton.

Smitka, Michael. 1991. *Competitive Ties: Subcontracting in the Japanese Automotive Industry.* New York: Columbia University Press.

"The Statute for Encouragement of Investment." 1960. *Industry of Free China* 14 (September):29–42.

Steers, Richard M., Yoo Keun Shin, and Gerardo R. Ungson. 1989. *The Chaebol: Korea's New Industrial Might.* New York: Harper and Row.

Stein, Howard, and Ernest J. Wilson. 1993. "The Political Economy of Robert Bates: A Critical Reading of Rational Choice in Africa." *World Development* 21 (June):1035–53.

Stites, Richard. 1982. "Small-Scale Industry in Yingge, Taiwan." *Modern China* 8 (April):247–79.

Stokman, Frans, N. Rolf Ziegler, and John Scott, eds. 1985. *Networks of Corporate Power: A Comparative Analysis of Ten Countries.* London: Polity Press.

Su, Edgar C. H. 1958. "Financing Industrial Development in the Republic of China." *Industry of Free China* 10 (August):2–11.

Suh, Dae-Sook. 1982. "South Korea in 1981: The First Year of the Fifth Republic." *Asian Survey* 22 (January):107–15.

Taiwan Sheng Hezuo Jinku [Taiwan Provincial Cooperative]. 1985. *Guanxi qiye zhengxin fangfa zhi yanjiu* [Study of related enterprises' methods for obtaining credit information]. Taipei: Taiwan Provincial Cooperative.

Taiwan Stock Exchange. *An Introduction to the Taiwan Stock Exchange.* Taipei: Taiwan Stock Exchange.

Taiwan Stock Exchange. 1985. *Fact Book.* Taipei: Taiwan Stock Exchange.

Taiwan Stock Exchange. 1986. *Annual Report.* Taipei: Taiwan Stock Exchange.

Taniura, Takao. 1989. "Management in Taiwan: The Case of the Formosa Plastics Group." *East Asian Cultural Studies* 28 (March):63–90.

Tann Hong-num. 1970. "Chiang Regime's New Financial Overlord." *Independent Formosa* 9 (Fall):9, 16.

Tsay, C. L. 1993. "Industrial Restructuring and International Competition in Taiwan." *Environment and Planning* 25 (January):111–20.

Von Glinow, Mary Ann, and Byung Jae Chung. 1989. "Korean Chaebols and the Changing Business Environment." In Kae H. Chung and Hak Chong Lee, eds., *Korean Managerial Dynamics.* New York: Praeger.

Wade, Robert. 1992. "East Asia's Economic Success: Conflicting Perspectives, Partial Insights, Shaky Evidence." *World Politics* 44 (January):270–320.

Wade, Robert. 1990. *Governing the Market: Economic Theory and the Role of Government in East Asian Industrialization.* Princeton: Princeton University Press.

Wade, Robert. 1985. "East Asian Financial Systems as a Challenge to Economics: Lessons from Taiwan." *California Management Review* 27 (Summer):106–27.

Wade, Robert. 1984. "Dirigisme Taiwan Style." In Robert Wade and Gordon White, eds., "Developmentalist States in East Asia: Capitalist and Socialist." *Institute of Development Studies Bulletin* 15 (April):65–70.

Wang, Tso-yung. 1958. "The Role of the Banking System in Economic Development in Japan." *Industry of Free China* 10 (September):12–20.

Wang, Tso-yung. 1956. "Government Investment in Taiwan." *Industry of Free China* 6 (July):8–11.

Westphal, Larry, Yung W. Rhee, Linsu Kim, and Alice Amsden. 1982. *Exports of Capital Goods and Related Services from the Republic of Korea.* World Bank Working Staff Papers, no. 629. Washington, D.C.: World Bank.

White, Gordon, ed. 1988. *Developmental States in East Asia.* London: Macmillan.

Whitley, Richard D. 1992. *Business Systems in East Asia: Firms, Markets and Societies.* London: Sage.

Whitley, Richard D. 1991. "The Social Construction of Business Systems in East Asia." *Organization Studies* 12 (March):1–28.

Whitley, Richard D. 1990. "Eastern Asian Enterprise Structure and the Comparative Analysis of Forms of Business Organization." *Organization Studies* 11 (March):47–54.

Williamson, Oliver E. 1985. *The Economic Institutions of Capitalism: Firms, Markets, Relational Contracting.* New York: Free Press.

Williamson, Oliver E. 1975. *The Economic Institutions of Capitalism.* New York: The Free Press.

Wong Siu-lun. 1985. "The Chinese Family Firm: A Model." *British Journal of Sociology* 36 (March):58–72.

## REFERENCES

Woo, Jung-en. 1991. *Race to the Swift: State and Finance in Korean Industrialization.* New York: Columbia University Press.

World Bank. 1987. *Korea: Managing the Industrial Transaction.* 2 vols. Washington, D.C.: World Bank.

Wu, Beatrice. 1987. "Consumer Loans Register Rapid Growth." In Kenneth Liu, ed., *Financial & Investment Yearbook.* Taipei: Central Economic News Service.

Wu, Yu-shan. 1991. "Leninist State and Property Rights: Economic Reform in the People's Republic of China." Ph.D. dissertation, University of California at Berkeley.

Xu Shijun. 1974. *Guanli: Guihua yu chuangxin* [Management: Planning and innovation]. Taipei: World Publishing.

Yamazawa, Ippei, and Hirohisa Kohama. 1985. "Trading Companies and Expansion of Foreign Trade: Japan, Korea, and Thailand." In Kazushi Ohkawa and Gustav Ranis, eds., *Japan and the Developing Countries.* Tokyo: International Development Center.

Yoo, Sangjin, and Sang M. Lee. 1987. "Management Style and Practice of Korean Chaebols." *California Management Review* 29 (Summer):95–110.

Yu, Kuo-hwa. 1978. "Government Efforts to Spur Investment." *Industry of Free China* 49 (February):2–6.

Yu, Tzong-shian, and Chen Ting-an. 1982. "Fiscal Reforms and Economic Development." In K. T. Li and Tzong-shian Yu, eds., *Experiences and Lessons of Economic Development in Taiwan.* Taipei: Academia Sinica.

Zhang Huowang. 1983. "Woguo yinhang xinyung fenpei zhi tantao" [Investigation on the issue of bank credit allocation in Taiwan]. *Taiwan yinhang qikan* [Bank of Taiwan quarterly] 34 (January):175–93.

Zukin, Sharon, and Paul DiMaggio. 1990. "Introduction." In Sharon Zukin and Paul DiMaggio, eds., *Structures of Capital: The Social Organization of the Economy.* Cambridge: Cambridge University Press.

# Index

## Cornell Studies in Political Economy

### EDITED BY PETER J. KATZENSTEIN

## DATE DUE

| | | | |
|---|---|---|---|
| | | | |
| | | | |
| | | | |
| | | | |
| | | | |
| | | | |
| | | | |
| | | | |
| | | | |
| | | | |
| | | | |
| | | | |
| | | | |
| | | | |
| | | | |
| | | | |
| | | | |
| GAYLORD | | | PRINTED IN U.S.A. |